The Pressing Stones

The Pressing Stones

The Healing Journey of a Nazi's Daughter

Andrea van de Loo

Untimely Books

Untimely Books

untimelybooks.com

An imprint of Cosmos Cooperative
PO Box 3, Longmont, Colorado 80502
info@untimelybooks.com

Song of a Luscious Wench previously published in *Sisters Singing: Blessings, Prayers, Art, Songs, Poetry & Sacred Stories by Women* – Edited by Carolyn Brigit Flynn; Foreword by Deena Metzger

Back cover: The Matrimandir at dawn in Auroville, 2024. Photograph by William Sullivan
Book design by Kayla Morelli

Publisher's Cataloging-in-Publication Data
Names: van de Loo, Andrea, 1942-, author.
Title: The Pressing Stones : The Healing Journey of a Nazi's Daughter / Andrea van de Loo.
Description: Longmont, CO : Untimely Books, 2024. | Summary: Born during WWII in the Netherlands, Andrea van de Loo experienced a traumatic childhood, with her father's past as a member of the Nazi SS casting a long shadow over her life. Despite these challenges, she embarked on an inspirational journey toward healing and self-discovery. Her search for self took her across the globe, where she found solace, purpose, and community. Encompassing eighty years of the author's life, *The Pressing Stones* guides readers through a deeply intimate and emotional journey, exploring family, relationships, sexuality, spirituality, motherhood, psychedelic therapy, addiction recovery, and the generational impacts of war. It also presents a personal portrait of life in Auroville, the "City of Dawn," dedicated to the spiritual visions of Sri Aurobindo and The Mother. This poignant portrayal of one woman's courage and determination to follow her inner guidance, and overcome her childhood trauma, is a testament to the power of consciousness and the human spirit, inspiring readers to find their own paths toward healing and fulfillment. Andrea's story illustrates how freedom, joy, peace of mind, and happiness are possible, as we face our deepest truths and emerge from our darkest tribulations.
Identifiers: LCCN 2023947864 | ISBN 978-1-961334-11-3 (hb) 978-1-961334-07-6 (pb)
Subjects: LCSH: Van de Loo, Andrea, 1942- | Women – Biography. | Children of Nazis – Biography. | Spirituality. | LCGFT: Autobiographies. | BISAC: BIOGRAPHY & AUTOBIOGRAPHY / Personal Memoirs. | BIOGRAPHY & AUTOBIOGRAPHY / Women | BODY, MIND & SPIRIT / Inspiration & personal growth.
Classification: DDC 305.4092
LC record available at http://lccn.loc.gov/2023947864

To the Mother

"Like a rose I wish to stand in the wind.
No resistance."

—Rainer Maria Rilke

"You will know very little until you get there.
You will journey blind, but the way leads towards
possession of what you have sought for."

—T.S. Eliot

"I felt down in my soul the clear and unmistakable
conviction to disobey all, and pursue my own way."

—Walt Whitman

"Not everything that can be faced can be changed,
but nothing can be changed until it is faced."

—James Baldwin

Contents

Part IV: California 261

Part V: Psychedelics 331

Poems

Dear Reader

I offer my life to you.
May you be inspired to find and follow
your own truth and pursue your healing
one step at the time, in your own unique way,
as you feel yourself to be guided.

Preface

Invariably, when I make a new friend and we develop trust between us, there comes a time when I feel compelled to tell them the truth about my father. Always, I am afraid of the horrified reaction that might come my way. I might begin with sharing the fact that I was born in the Netherlands during WWII. When the listener quickly comes up with tales of their American father's heroic participation in the liberation of Europe, I tend to drop the subject and may not even pursue the friendship.

My father was Dutch, my mother German. Both were born and raised in Germany. Both were swept up by the ideological propaganda in pre-war Nazi Germany. My father became part of the German occupying forces in the Netherlands. In the post-war international court in The Hague, he was sentenced to death for war crimes but was later released. The war and its aftermath destroyed my childhood.

Denial is one of the most effective coping mechanisms for trauma, especially for those of us who are dealing with childhood trauma. As a child, I had a profound—unconscious—need not to be aware of what I could not cope with. Since I can only share what I am aware of, I do not even have language to describe my feelings. All I can do is describe my experiences and trust that they will convey my difficulties.

Healing from the impact of war, and clearing my being from the massive shadow cast over my psyche by my father's past, has been a major focus of my life.

In my experience, relationships are the fast track to healing and liberation, if we are willing to do the work. My trauma has been repeatedly triggered through my relationships, making them ideal opportunities to increase my awareness and the ability to heal. The willingness to be vulnerable and honest has been essential for my journey; so has spirituality. I started in Catholicism, then chose to be agnostic until I met The Mother, Sri Aurobindo's spiritual companion, in Pondicherry, India. Looking into her eyes turned my life around. Since then, their Integral Yoga has been my path. Eventually, I became the proverbial wounded healer.

Only when I got together with a shaman in my fifties, and with the help of psychedelic therapy, was I able to break through my dissociation. Then, after I became inadvertently addicted to marijuana, I learned basic life skills and spiritual principles in Twelve Step recovery programs.

I love my father and I am profoundly concerned about offending those whom he harmed and their surviving families. I also do not wish to offend any one of the millions of people whose loved ones were ruthlessly exterminated in the death camps of WWII. Nevertheless, I hope to invoke at least some understanding of, and perhaps even compassion for, the perpetrators. We naturally feel mercy for the victims, but the perpetrators have no place to turn. They carry their unspeakable shame, guilt and horror to their graves.

How often have I heard people in the United States say that they cannot understand how the German people as a whole could have been seduced into WWII. Except for Pearl Harbor and 9/11, the United States has not experienced warfare on its own soil since the Civil War ended in 1865. All wars this country has since so freely participated in have been on foreign soil, far removed from our visceral reality. I feel that there is an innocence in this country that casts a long shadow, indeed.

In 2003, when a dubiously elected president and his partners in crime perpetrated shameless lies about weapons of mass destruction in Iraq, nearly the entire Congress voted for the country to go to war. I watched in dismay how millions of people waived their flags to proclaim America's glorious superiority. I knew I had to tell my story.

Andrea
Winter Solstice, 2022

Part I

War

My Father's Shadow

It is 1948. I am six years old. My older brother Reinier and I stand in front of the Catholic boarding school in Acht, a hamlet near Eindhoven in the south of Holland, saying goodbye to our mother, who was visiting. She always looks so beautiful with her big brown eyes and her dark brown hair softly waving around her face. This day she is wearing a light blue wool coat trimmed with white fur. She turns to us with a troubled look, then cups her hand under my chin and tilts my little face up to her, her dark eyes looking very seriously into mine. Reinier is standing close behind me. Her voice drops as she says, "I have to tell you something very difficult… Your father has been sentenced to death… I believe he is innocent. The only thing you can do for him is pray." She pauses, then adds, "You can never talk to anyone about this."

The moment my mother said that, I realized, young as I was, that the Dutch people, *my* people, *my* country, had decided to kill my father. I stood there, shattered. I understood that I had to keep this terrible knowledge a secret. If I had been lonely before, my isolation was now sealed like a tomb. I watched my mother, looking quite forlorn, walk back to the bus stop. My brother and I turned to climb the stairs into the gaping darkness of the school entrance.

I turned to God with a vengeance. He could not let this happen! I realized I had a job to do and began to storm the heavens,

7

where in some vast distance there was this vague all-powerful Being who loved us, whom no one had ever seen. Day and night, in bed, in the classroom, at the table, on the playground or in the chapel, I prayed desperately to God, with all the passion in my little heart, to save my father's life. I prayed and begged, never sure if He would hear me. I became a deeply religious child with a dark secret.

I could not then imagine how the shadow of my father's past would hang over me for the rest of my life.

My Father

Willem Rudolf Clemens Maria van de Loo, my father, was born on March 6, 1909, the sixth of seven children in a well-to-do family of Dutch colonials, who had lived all over the world. The family was Catholic. At the time of his birth, they happened to be living in Germany. My father's father had grown up in Suriname, one of the Dutch colonies along the North coast of South America. Jo, his mother, was the strikingly beautiful, headstrong and vivacious daughter of the director of the Bank of the Netherlands in Suriname. There they met and married.

Later they moved to Cameroon, a German colony in West Africa, where my grandfather became a plantation owner. My father's older siblings were born there. After Cameroon regained independence, they moved to Germany where my grandfather became the director of the first Unilever Margarine and Oil Factory in Munster. He was an imposing figure.

Grandfather Willem van de Loo

The story about my grandmother's irresistible beauty and my grandfather's jealousy was told again and again in my family. When they lived in Cameroon, every few months an English ship would come into the harbor, unloading numbers of dashing officers. These would quickly find their way to the family's estate where my grandmother threw lavish parties and the officers vied for her graces. Once, when my grandfather was out in the bush for a few days of hunting elephants, he heard the sound of blow horns in the distance, announcing the arrival of a ship. He turned his horse around and, riding back at breakneck speed, galloped straight into their foyer where the party was in full swing. He undoubtedly established his dominion!

After they settled in Munster, my father, their sixth child, was born. Although the new infant was the third son, he was given his father's name, Willem. He seemed to be the one designated to follow in his successful father's footsteps. However, Willy turned out to be a highly sensitive, dreamy child. His mother sometimes amused herself by ridiculing him in front of the large high-society companies gathered around her dinner table. He was raised by nannies who doted on him. His mother mostly ignored her children while she was entertaining the rich and sewing for the poor. I have a startling picture of my father as a six-year-old boy. His tender little face is dead serious with such a dark look in his eyes that I can't help but see how he must have been affected by his mother's ridicule and neglect, or maybe, sensitive child that he was, he sensed the dark future that lay ahead of him.

It was also at the age of six that his baby sister, Annelies, was born. He became her most avid and adoring babysitter, entertaining her with endless stories he invented on the spot. As she grew into a toddler, he would lie with her in the garden and ask her, "What would you like me to tell you a story about?" She might point at a butterfly and he'd spin her fascinating tales about the adventures of the butterfly. The story could continue for days.

My father with his mother

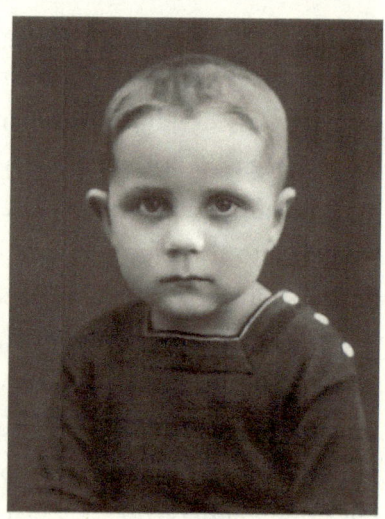

My father, age 6

When he was twelve, he ran away from home. Romantic dreamer that he was, he went to announce himself at the Foreign Legion, imagining fighting heroic wars in North Africa. As soon as the commander laid eyes on the boy, he called his mother, who arrived huffing with indignity. The boy's action was considered a serious offense against the honor of the family.

His father felt it necessary to take him into the basement and ordered him to strip down. His older brother Henri, an eighteen-year-old arrogant medical student, was to be present to ensure the boy's genitals wouldn't get injured. He received a thorough beating with a whip made of rhinoceros hide, which his father must have brought with him from Africa.

Possibly as a way to cope with his shame, my dad became the joker in the family. He taught himself sleight of hand and magic skills. He loved to play tricks on people, including his imposing father. Willem knew that his father made a last round through the house every night, turning off all the lights and making sure the doors were locked. One evening, my dad had fastened a frog to the handle of the back door. When his father grabbed the mushy creature in the dark, he thought he had grabbed a turd and shouted, "*Stront! Stront!*" (Dutch for shit). He woke up the entire household. My dad gleefully remembered seeing his mother standing in the bedroom door, doubled over with laughter.

During his adolescence, Willem delved into the writings of the great German and Indian authors and philosophers, immersing himself in the romantic and spiritual movements of his day. Goethe introduced him to Germanic mythology. With *Siddhartha* and *The Glass Bead Game*, Herman Hesse opened a window in his mind to spiritual and occult powers. Rabindranath Tagore offered him mystic poetry. Nietzsche effectively exposed him to the flaws of established religion.

In his early twenties, my father was initiated into some occult sect by a mysterious figure, named Stekete. I believe it was this man who gave him his spiritual name, Ludar (from *ludare*, Latin for 'to play'), the Game Player.

Under these influences, my father developed into a deeply spiritual, big-hearted, open-minded, poly-sexual, larger-than-life charismatic man.

My Mother

My mother, Eleonora Henriette Wilhelmina Henoumont, was the fifth of six daughters born in Saarlouis, Germany on the 11th of March 1911, to a family of old Prussian military nobility. They called her Ellen. Her parents were Mimi Surmann and Carl Henoumont. Their love story was a great romance. When they met at a ball, it had been love at first sight. Mimi's strict parents required that she work to put together her dowry. They also demanded that Carl promote himself in the military and acquire a fine horse before considering him worthy. The young lovers were forbidden to see each other for two years. I have a photograph of my grandfather as a young officer in full uniform with a white plumed headdress, posing proudly on a gleaming black horse. He had succeeded in winning my grandmother's hand.

Grandfather Carl became a lieutenant at the court of Kaiser Wilhelm. During WWI he engineered an adjustable under-carriage for military trains heading East to allow a change-over to

Grandfather Carl Henoumont   Grandmother Mimi Henoumont

the different width of Russian rails. He ended up being the only surviving male heir of his family since two of his brothers died in the war and one brother was born with a severe mental handicap. Carl was a vivacious, intelligent man with a great sense of humor. My mother definitely took after him, developing a quick sense of humor and a *joie de vivre* like his. My mother's childhood was a happy one with much music and singing. For special occasions, my grandmother and her six daughters performed home concerts and plays. My mother became an outstanding classical pianist.

Like my father, my mother remained the youngest in the family for six years. She remembered fondly being her daddy's favorite. He often chased her through the house as she ran squealing for sheer delight. Her abundant energy could not be contained, encouraged as she was by her father's adoring playfulness. When I asked her once, how she became so proper and controlled, she recalled her baby sister's birth when she was six years old and her four older sisters teasing her, "Now, you're no longer the baby and you'll have to learn to behave just like us!" Likely, theirs was a collective effort to bring her in line and become, like them, a proper, well-behaved, respectable little lady. They were painfully successful. Throughout her life, my mother was always a "proper" lady who craved her sisters' approval.

When my mom was only four years old, her mother had taken her along to the river to do laundry. Her mother was carrying a large bundle of clothes and a washboard. Little Ellen wanted to help and asked her mom if she could carry the washboard for her. Her mother said, "No, sweetheart, the washboard is much too heavy for you." But, the little one wouldn't give up and kept insisting. Finally, her mom let her carry the board. As they trudged along, the little chatterbox became very quiet, until finally, she said in a small voice, "Mommie, if you were as little as I, the washboard would hurt you just a tiny bit under your arm!" This story was affectionately retold many times.

In 1922, when Ellen was eleven, a great tragedy befell the family. After Germany's dismal failure in WWI, the army was dismantled. My grandfather had to find his way into the normal world. The military was all he had ever known. The story goes that he could not cope and fell grievously ill. My mother was always moved to tears when she described the scene of all her sisters and their mother surrounding their father's deathbed, singing one of Bach's immortal cantatas, "O Lord, take me by the hand and guide me to my very end into the Light." That night, my grandmother Mimi was left a widow with six young girls and a very small pension.

My mother would sometimes take my brother and me to visit her mother in Saarbrücken, Germany. My grandma Mimi lived in a large old apartment with high ceilings. The walls of their large living room were covered with books from floor to ceiling. She lived there with her older sister Elsa as well as with one of her daughters, my mother's oldest sister, Erika, and with Tante Gertrud, Tante Erika's best friend, who had lost her husband and three of her sons in WWII. Her tears had created permanent grooves on her face. All these women were ladies in the true sense of the word, generous, soft-spoken, kind, educated, gracious and elegantly dressed. My great-aunt Elsa had been the respected principal of one of the first high schools for girls at the beginning

Reinier and me with Grandmother in Saarbrücken

of the century in Germany. I loved my grandma Mimi. She was kind and gentle and sweet to me.

Curiously, after having lived through two world wars in an area that had been off and on French and German for centuries, the family's favorite pastime was to play a large board game with little French and German uniformed soldiers engaged in battle.

My mother grew up into a quick-witted, genteel, beautiful woman with large brown eyes and flowing hair, always a 'proper' lady. Fortunately, her passionate nature continued to have an outlet at the piano. She played all the great Romantics with a wonderful depth of feeling. Chopin was her favorite. My fondest memories from my high school years, when we finally had a home again, were the afternoons or evenings when I curled up in our living room with a book and listened to her playing the piano.

Later in life, she successfully tackled twentieth-century composers like Poulenc, Fauré and Willem Andriessen. At age

My mother celebrated after a concert

eighty, as the oldest contestant in a Dutch national competition for amateur pianists, she won first prize and experienced her moment of glory performing at the Amsterdam Concertgebouw. At age ninety, in 2001, during her last visit to me in Santa Cruz, she gave a concert in a local church, attacking Brahms' Rhapsody like a lioness! What a temperament she had, so well concealed by her demure and always ladylike appearance.

Their Secret Engagement

Both my grandmothers met because their daughters attended the same school in Munster. They quickly became best friends. It was an unusual combination. Jo, my father's mother, the generous but intimidating powerhouse, living in wealth, must have enjoyed being protective of Mimi, my mom's gentle, soft-spoken, well-educated but impoverished mother. Between them, they had thirteen children, ten of them daughters. They spent many afternoons together, drinking tea and sewing for their children and for the poor. Perhaps they figured that some of Jo's three sons might make a good match for some of Mimi's daughters. In fact, two marriages did result. My father married Ellen and his older brother, Henri, married Ellen's older sister Gretel.

When my father was eighteen and my mother sixteen, he spent a few days with her family. My father was enthralled by this beautiful girl with her big brown eyes who played the piano so soulfully. By that time, he had become quite a dashing young man. Both had a wonderfully funny sense of humor. They fell in love and after their first kiss decided to get engaged, in secrecy of course, both knowing full well that neither of their parents would approve of this bold move at such young an age.

When somehow the secret was leaked, it caused great upset. They were not allowed to see each other or have any contact for a couple of years. History repeats itself! My father was sent off to the Colonial College of Agriculture in Deventer, Holland. And, if my mother was serious about marrying Willem, she must give up her dream of studying at the Music Conservatory to become a concert pianist and had to attend a Household School instead, to prepare herself to become a proper housewife. This she did, much to her regret.

My father had a change of heart by the time he graduated from the Colonial College. He intended to join a Benedictine monastery. With his spiritual inclination, he was never particularly interested in ordinary life. The introspective life of prayer, meditation and study resonated strongly within him.

Just before his departure to the Benedictines, he received a letter from my mother:

My dearest Willem, I hear that you have come home from college and that you want to become a monk. What a big decision that must be for you. I was so shocked when I heard about it. I haven't stopped crying since. I have waited so long to see you again. I dream of you every night. I love you so much. Please, Willem, I beg you to reconsider your decision and come back to me. I long to be in your arms. I am forever yours, Ellen

My father took her plea as a sign from God and decided to resume his engagement with her instead. He had fallen for her beauty and charm, her quick wit and her sense of humor. Her passionate and lyrical interpretations of Chopin, Schubert, Brahms and Beethoven seemed to promise a depth of soul he could not resist. He paid no heed to early warnings that she showed little interest in exploring the philosophical and spiritual dimensions of life. He told me once how he had been impressed by a profound insight she had jotted down in the margin of her high school copy of Goethe's Faust. When he remarked on it, she said, "Oh, that's not mine. My teacher said that." I'm sure he was convinced that, given some time under his loving influence, he would succeed in seducing her into the fascinating realms of his multi-dimensional universe. He was sorely mistaken.

Meanwhile, my mother believed that her love and common sense would heal his wounded soul and that her faithful love and stability would lead him onto the narrow path of propriety and responsibility. As he was a kind and loving man, he would make

Ellen swooning in Willem's arms

a fine father for her children. She imagined that, by her side, he would surely turn out to become the respectable, successful gentleman and husband she desired. Each thought the other could be molded to their wishes and fulfill their dreams. How vastly different these dreams were. Naturally, neither was able to change the other.

To become a responsible *pater familias*, my father started his training at the Unilever Oil and Margarine Factory in Munster, to eventually step into his father's position as the director. There he began to familiarize himself with all the many aspects of the business and manufacturing processes. Among the workers, he found ease and a down-to-earth atmosphere, which was sorely lacking in the arrogant, upper class to which he belonged. He was drawn to workers, farmers, handymen—to "ordinary" people for the rest of his life.

Rebellious Idealists

My parents married in Saarbrücken in 1933. In those first years, they loved and enjoyed each other. I have old photographs of their early happiness: my mother leaning in sweet abandon against my smiling father; or out in the woods, both of them in funny Charlie Chaplin poses; another one of a picnic with friends out in the fields. I always felt that they were a part of the first generation in the twentieth century to break with the stifling patterns of their parents' world. Together with other like-minded, idealistic friends, they left the church, became vegetarians, drank, smoked, danced the Charleston and swam naked in the rivers. My father used to paint vivid pictures to me of their life of love and freedom before the war. Cutting loose from the pernicious control of the church, they defied the old morality with abandon, celebrated their sexual freedom with each other and with other men and women, exploring all kinds of erotic game playing, fetishism, bisexuality and even sadomasochism.

I am quite sure that the sexual explorations between my parents originated mostly in my father's unbridled and adventurous mind. My mother, trained to be a good German girl, believed that her husband's wishes were her commands and, surely intrigued by these forbidden adventures, went along.

Many decades later, I heard a story from a friend who had become close to my father. My father had described ecstatic sexual experiences with my mother, after which she would play the piano ever so passionately and he would jump on his horse to go for a wild ride. Upon returning home, he would find her behaving as if nothing had happened.

I believe my mother must have been emotionally and psychologically under the influence of my father's seductive personality, since her socially appropriate persona as an impeccable lady was her true identity. She was stretched so far beyond her own beliefs and sense of propriety that she never spoke of these adventures to me, as if they didn't exist. It was only when I was well into my fifties that she once confided that "it was kind of fun to be a little slave girl."

In addition to seeking sexual liberation, their generation also experienced the first large-scale wave of spiritual teachings from India entering Western culture. My father was deeply influenced. One of his favorite quotes he would share with me came from Rabindranath Tagore, translated into German, *Der,* *der die Knopfe öffnet zur Blüte tut es so einfach.* (He who opens the bud into blossom does it so simply.)

However, the inherently racist attitudes and belief systems of the patriarchy and colonialism went unquestioned. This, combined with the deeply romantic tendencies in the German soul, and the pernicious German pedagogy where the father was the unquestioned authority, became fertile ground for the adoration and adulation of ideals, both personal and national. These belief systems were in fact still fully operational in all levels of society as the unquestioned natural order of things.

When, after the profound humiliation of the Treaty of Versailles and the subsequent crash of the German economy, Hitler stepped up as the Father of das Reich, he was seen as the great savior who would not only restore Germany back to glory but establish its racial and cultural superiority over the rest of the world.

The Great Seduction

Like many other bright-eyed young idealists, both my parents were swept up by the great seduction of minds that began to pollute the German people. The grave danger of the exclusive identification with an idealization of one's own country had not yet been detected on any significant scale. The potential pitfalls of national pride were largely unexamined and the willingness to go to war for some real or imagined threat was still active, as it continues to be in this country and around the world.

It was only after the horrors of the Second World War and the reality of the atom bomb that the sixties' generation began to question government authority. The notion of Question Authority, one of the central slogans of my generation, had not yet entered the minds of the young dreamers of the thirties. As they explored new philosophical and moral ideals, they wanted to break the shackles of the stifling past and create a new future of freedom and happiness for themselves and their children. In the Germany of the thirties, when their leader agreed with them and confirmed that they were indeed the young and shining future of the race, they rallied behind him. They were not able to detect the fatal flaw in the massive and clever propaganda of the great vision for Germany. They did not have the necessary awareness to see that a great future for one nation cannot be won at the expense of another. It was still quite acceptable to see the "other" as the problem, as we continue to see happen today.

How many Americans realize that Hitler was elected democratically and that the Nazis learned from the United States how to effectively use the media as a propaganda machine to manipulate the minds of the people? Fascism, the belief that one group is innately superior to another and therefore has the right to impose its will by whatever means it sees fit, still runs rampant in our world today. The power-hungry elite manipulate the people into going to war by fueling fear of the "other." Just as the Germans were able to scapegoat the Jews, the United States used the 9/11 tragedy to fashion and fuel a collective dread of Muslims, then conveniently added the "invasion" from refugees South of our border, and now from the many people seeking security from wars, famine and climate disasters.

Baring the shame of being the daughter of a Nazi war criminal, and knowing my parents as loving and caring people, I am motivated to clarify what many do not seem to realize: The evil of any belief in superiority fostered on a collective scale can seduce otherwise perfectly harmless people into warfare. In war, under the threat of death everywhere, both soldiers and their superiors commit horrifying criminal acts on the perceived enemy, many of them turning temporarily into evil monsters, damaging themselves and others for life.

Our Family Moves to Holland

In 1939, my father's Dutch parents were still living in Münster in the northwestern part of Germany. One day, when my grandmother was being driven into town by her chauffeur to go shopping, they came to a barricaded street where she witnessed the cruel rounding up of Jews. Horrified, she ordered the chauffeur to turn around and started packing up their household. She refused to stay in that country any longer. My grandparents moved to Holland, where they had never lived before, and bought a small villa in Driebergen, a unique village in one of the most beautiful forested areas of Holland, just south of Utrecht. The name is derived from *de Drie Herbergen*, the Three Inns, where, in previous centuries, royalty and noblemen came to hunt, rest and have their horses restored.

The village consisted of two distinct parts. One was a sprawled-out area of gorgeous estates for the well-to-do, a mixture of the old nobility and the *nouveau riche*. The other was a small compact village of a few streets with a Catholic church, shops for the butcher, the baker, the milkman and the shoemaker, where the servants and tradesmen who catered to the wealthy lived.

My parents were still living in Delmenhorst, Germany, at the time. After five years of not conceiving, they turned to a famous mesmerist. When he ran his hands along my mother's body, he suggested they spend a week in a health resort to take healing mud baths. My brother was conceived soon after. He was born in September of 1938 in Delmenhorst. In naming him, they followed the old Catholic tradition of adding Maria to his middle names. His full name became Reinier Henri Carl Maria van de Loo. He was my mother's sunshine!

In 1940 my mother took her little boy to visit her parents-in-law in Holland. There she got a conflicting earful from my grandmother, who despised the German ideology and what was happening in that country. While she was staying with them, Germany invaded Holland. Of course, the Dutch were incensed as was my grandmother. My mother could not help but share their upset. The borders closed and she could not return.

In the meantime, my father joined the German forces. Since he was Dutch and his family was already in Holland, his superiors dispatched him there and he became a part of the German occupation of his own country. My mother told me how confusing it was for her when she saw him again. He would enthusiastically wax on about the great German Ideal for a superior future. With her loyalty to him at stake, she let herself be swept along by him again.

He became the Commander of a workers' camp, where young Dutchmen were put to work for the war machine. My father loved them and was passionate about training them in discipline and obedience, intending to turn them into "real and useful men" to serve the Reich. When I was born in May of 1942, these men spontaneously carried my father on their shoulders around the camp in celebration of the birth of his daughter. Despite their dire situation, they apparently appreciated him as a person. He was after all a big-hearted, generous and charismatic man, who at that time, fully believed in the righteousness of the German Ideal.

My grandmother was horrified and deeply embarrassed about my father's unholy alliance. She forbade him to show himself at her home in uniform during the day. He was entirely too proud to take it off and therefore visited only under the cover of night, resulting in him not being present when I was born.

My First Two Years

The fact that my baby book survived the war seems like a miracle. My mother only showed it to me when I was well into my fifties. She had kept it hidden because in it she had recorded some of the many painful events that she had tried to forget. She wrote in Dutch. I translate:

On Sunday, May 17 at 7:05 a.m., a sweet little girl was born to us. She immediately started screaming with a mighty little voice. She weighed 6 pounds and 330 grams and was 51 cm long. When she was allowed to try to drink after eight hours, she seemed to know exactly what to do. Within twenty minutes the little lady has had her share and looks content or sleeps deliciously satiated in my arms. Often an adorable smile plays around her little mouth. After four weeks she started to lift

*her head and also to look around. She consciously directs her eyes at
the person who is speaking with her.*

She did not write about it at the time, but later told me how
stressful the circumstances were for her. For many hours during
her labor my grandmother and her old friend, Jeanette, sat by
my mother's side complaining bitterly about the war. They must
have been quite upset with her too since she was emotionally
completely allied again with my father and with her own German
identity. She told me how uncomfortable she had been to give
birth to her baby amidst all this antagonism.

Not yet knowing of my birth, my father woke up on that
sunny Sunday morning of May 17, 1942. The calendar on his wall
showed the sweet face of a radiant little girl and he "knew" I had
been born. The picture is pasted in my Baby Book. They named me
Angela. My full name became Angela Joanna Hubertine Maria
van de Loo. Referring to the calendar picture, my mother writes:

*May our little angel become that cheerful! She is already ten weeks old
by now and smiles a lot to anyone who speaks nicely to her. For two
weeks, fortunately, she sleeps through the night. I'm very glad about
that. But towards evening she still gives quite a concert. I wonder if
she'll mend her ways about that, too?*

*Angela has big eyes blue as the night with long lashes, her little
head full of dark blond hair, which is falling out now, a small turned-up
nose that still has to find its shape, a sweet little mouth that can smile
so adorably and scream so ferociously. Her whole body is round and
cuddly and her little hands are very beautiful and fine. I already have a
feeling that someday these hands might play the piano quite beautifully.*

Reinier is very proud of his little sister. Anyone who teases him that they'll take his little sister away with them makes him very angry. It also scares him a little, it might really be done. He loves to come into the baby room, when I am busy with her, and helps me with pouring out the water and other things. He is especially interested in watching her nurse and likes to stand close to me to push a little on my breast, as he has watched me do.

What wonderful treasures these are, two such sweet children you must take by the hand during their first steps into life.

Eventually, my father found us a home with a garden in Apeldoorn. Even with the war in full swing, our little family experienced a relatively peaceful time. My mom must have been greatly relieved to be away from her dominating mother-in-law and finally settling in a home of her own. She loved to garden. Friends came to visit. Happy pictures indicate a sweet time of family life.

After much trouble, we came to live here in Apeldoorn in a nice home, where the little girl shares a large sunny children's room with her brother. In the beginning, we were quite worried about her because her weight stagnated for three months. I could nurse her till the seventh month and only towards the end had to add other milk. But still, she wouldn't grow. The doctor wasn't worried, since the little lady looked so radiantly healthy. Barely had I begun to give her solid foods and she started to gain weight, and especially when I changed to giving her four meals a day, she quickly crossed the median.

Together with her assertion that she only nursed me when it was time, no matter how hard I cried, this little passage makes

Me with my Papa

me wonder how hungry and neglected I may have felt from the beginning. Apparently, she didn't even know that babies need to be fed more than three times a day!

Angela has radiant, large, dark gray-blue eyes with beautiful long lashes. She reminds Willem of his sister Hansi. Since a few weeks, she is sitting in Reinier's high chair, often does her pee and other business in the potty, like every morning after the bottle. It works beautifully. She is very late with teething. At eight months the lower teeth began to show, now she's working on the upper ones. Also, she still can't pull herself up, let alone stand on her little legs. For a few weeks she's getting a phosphor supplement and vitamins, which should help her. But I'm not worried about her any longer because she looks like "Dutch Prosperity" with fat, little red cheeks and such a bright and cheerful way of being that you can only be grateful and happy with her!

Her little stories are so cute, tai-tai and ya-ya and so on. Then
she plays with her finger over her lower lip and pushes out noises that
sound like blah-blah. She does the same with others and enjoys herself
immensely. Her little hands make the sweetest little movements, it is
just a pleasure to watch her play with blocks, a rattle, a rubber duckie
or her doll.

Angela, our little sweetheart, is now spending a bit of time each
day in the playpen. Sometimes she rolls over like a teddy bear and just
keeps lying there, that's how lazy she still is. I hope that she'll now
learn quickly how to get herself upright and to stand. When I hold
her, she stands quite solidly on her chubby little legs. Today she had
a visitor in her playpen, the little white bear which belonged to Reinier
before. Their acquaintance should have been filmed! We all sat around
her and enjoyed it. She was a little frightened of it and yet she tried
again and again to touch it, then quickly pulled back her hand all the
while chatting excitedly. Tomorrow the little white guest shall return and
strengthen her courage.

Besides the charm of these passages, I am struck by how
motivated my mother was that I learn to become diligent and courageous. She already calls me lazy when I am only ten months old!

The first two years in Apeldoorn turned out to be the only
happy years of our early family life together. My parents were
intimate friends with a woman named Kitty and her husband,
both Germans. With their little son Bubi, they lived with us for
some time.

Until September 5, 1944, both of our children grew up peacefully in
Apeldoorn. Reinier became quite independent, went for some time to
a German kindergarten, whose teachers often came and visited us. On

September 1st, he entered grade school. Vati [daddy] and I took him there.

Angela found a playmate in Kitty's Bubi. She became a delightful child. Everyone adored her. Little blond curls graced her head and gigantic dark eyes dominated her sweet doll's face. Her little figure was always nice and chubby and one might well call her sexy. She spent the entire winter in the playpen in our crowded room. Her toys interested her less than small buttons and the like. She preferred to stand close to the sewing machine where Mrs. Spitter mended our clothes once a week.

I was put in the playpen regularly so my mother could go about her housework. I hated it. After she put all my toys in it to keep me happy and occupied, I would immediately throw them all overboard and clamor loudly to be let out. I have some internal sense of my anger to be locked up while my brother was free to move about. My cries and screams were to no avail since my mother firmly believed in the Germanic pedagogy of never spoiling the baby. Learning obedience was one of the central

Hugging Bubi

tenets in child-rearing practices those days and my mother was determined to do the right thing.

I remember during my teens after my father had come home when this seemingly open-minded and sophisticated man seriously expounded to me the values of learning obedience. "You cannot become a leader," he would admonish me, "if you haven't learned to obey."

Obeying the father was a central principle in the child-rearing practices of Germany. It undoubtedly contributed to the massive success of the Third Reich. "I was following orders," was the common defense of most who were tried after the war. They had no sense of personal responsibility because they had handed that power over to the Reich's authorities, just as they had been trained to obey their fathers, no questions asked. Parents were encouraged not to "spare the rod and spoil the child." Fathers regularly beat their children. Thankfully, my father never did. The explicit goal of this discipline was to break the will of the child and force them into obedience.

Thanks to the invaluable contributions of psychology, we now realize that such parental behaviors amount to child abuse. Abused children often have an unconscious rage and need for revenge. They grow up believing it is acceptable to exert their will over those in their charge. In warfare, people find themselves in situations of having unbridled power over the life and death of others and the most heinous crimes are thus committed. In this vein, psychotherapist Alice Miller describes in *For Your Own Good* the child abuse Hitler experienced at the hands of his father. She posits that he thereby suffered serious injury to his self-esteem, which was then compensated for by illusions of grandeur and cruelty to all he considered inferior to him.

Going back to those early years in my family, here's one of my favorite stories about myself as a feisty, independence-loving little one. One afternoon, when I was barely two years old and my brother five, my mother sent us out into the garden to play. Of course, the gate to the street was safely closed. Hours later, an upset neighbor knocked on our front door with me in tow. She had spotted me happily trotting along the streets across the canal. I had somehow found my way out of the garden and taken off to explore the big, wide world. My brother had either been too absorbed in his own games to notice my absence or kept real quiet, being a little frightened of my mother's wrath at his failure to keep me in. My adventure caused quite a consternation. After all, crossing the bridge was dangerous and I was only two. Surely, the women had scary visions of this little one falling into the canal without anyone noticing.

With my father in uniform

Me and Reinier

My mother retold this story many times during my life, always recalling both her fright and her admiration for my bold sense of adventure. Nothing could hold me back. From the beginning, I was the more willful and adventurous one.

The Nightmare Begins

Early in 1944, my father received an order to get his men ready to go to the Eastern Front. They were to take all the ammunition they had in stock, which was only a few rounds each. My father, aware that logistics to the front were seriously lacking, understood that these young men were being sent as cannon fodder. He would be taking them into certain death. He loved them. He could not do it.

He was well aware that disobeying orders would result in his immediate execution. To save his life, he offered himself to the service of the SS, since their members were invulnerable. He once told me how he had presented himself to the SS, whilst being commander of a work camp and having the rank of Oberstfeldmeister, "Take me and I'll do whatever you want. I will be your gopher."

He was accepted and the secret insignia of the SS was placed under his lapel. He presented himself to his superior and stated that he refused to take his men to the East. Just as the order was being given to take him into the courtyard to be shot, he turned his lapel revealing the SS insignia. He was free to go. Little did he know that this choice would lead him straight to hell.

Fleeing into Germany

In June of 1944, my baby sister was born. They named her Almuth, a name from Nordic mythology, which had become popular in Nazi Germany.

In September, my father came home with frightening news. The German Intelligence had discovered that the Dutch were planning a violent uprising against the hated collaborators, the many Dutch people who were siding with the Germans during the invasion. My father, being Dutch and part of the occupation, clearly would have been a target, including his family.

We had to flee the country the next day. My mother packed as much as she could carry in a suitcase and in Almuth's pram, warm clothes and food for her three children. Overnight, we had to leave everything behind. Together with thousands of others, we fled by train into Germany.

The day of the uprising became known in Holland as *Dolle Dinsdag* (Mad Tuesday). Terrifying medieval scenes took place. The angered Dutch, sensing that the Germans were losing the war, were taking revenge. Women who had slept with German soldiers were tarred, feathered and dragged nude in carts along the streets. It would be another eight months before Holland was liberated by the Allies. My mother writes:

Willem suddenly arrived on September 1st. I went to get him from the station. He looked like a real soldier, heavily armed. He had to make a service trip for five days. When he returned from his trip he announced that we had to flee within one day. On September 5th Holland was in total uproar. We left carrying the most needed luggage, the pram, etc. In the last moment, I picked our little Almuth from her cradle, dressed her in triple layers of wool and carried the little bundle sadly out of our sweet little home, looking back one last time in farewell. Flowers greeted me from all the windows and from the garden. It was bitter to leave everything, with the uncertain prospect of a return. It is good I didn't know then, all that was going to happen to me and the three little ones. Our train trip into Germany lasted twenty-six hours.

To avoid being a target for overflying bombers, the train drove without lights through the dark of night. When I asked my mother about the experience, she remembered nothing of that journey. Since I was only two, I am left with vague disturbing cellular glimpses of fear, discomfort, nowhere to go to the bathroom, not enough food and great uncertainty.

My father took us to Berlin to present himself to SS headquarters. Since he was with that all-powerful organization, he was able to command some farmers near the town of Userin to provide a room for my mother and the three children. The secret animosity of the farmers made it a difficult situation for my mother. She writes:

Willem found us a small room in Userin at the home of simple cobblers in the village. There we lived, the four of us, as well as possible. I felt healthy and in the full strength of my life. Our children who slept together in a large bed at night enjoyed themselves in the autumn with the small animals that were running around in the village, and everyone knew the little twosome, walking hand in hand on the dirty village roads. Little Almuth lay outside with every ray of sun. There wasn't really a good place for her. First, I put her pram outside among the ducks, the geese and the chickens, right next to the manure pile. That's where she got a bad rash around her little mouth, which bothered her for fourteen days. Reinier and Angela were infected by it some, too. After that, I put the pram simply out front in the street. It was a bit dangerous since there were quite a number of horse-drawn carts rattling by. I nursed Almuth completely for five months. When she needed solid food, it was always difficult to get vegetables for her. After that, it was always one meal less a day but I was able to nurse her every morning till the morning of her last day.

The Insanity

Just a couple of months before the end of the war, the SS sent my father together with six others back into Holland on a secret mission. Our little family traveled with him. We found temporary refuge in an old monastery in a village near the border. We stayed there for several weeks while my father was trying to delay our departure. The monastery was deserted but for a family of a kind customs official who welcomed us and offered my mother and the children a safe haven until the war would be over. She wrote:

On my birthday, March 11, 1945, we left for Frenswegen—near the border with Holland. The trip took four days! Changing and feeding Almuth was not a small matter in the train stations and yet she survived all that confusion. We got a room in a very old monastery with the sweet family of customs inspector Ivers. It was wonderfully light and sunny, unheard of for us since we had looked out on a wall in Userin and the room had been facing north. It was especially good for me to *be treated with great consideration, politeness and compassion after the rudeness with which the farmer family had treated us. They even put a little stove in my room so I could cook for us in peace. Almuth got an ugly bronchitis with high fever. A local nurse came to look at her. I feared pneumonia.*

The political situation developed so quickly that, in one night from Easter Sunday to Monday, I suddenly had to make the decision to travel to Holland. It was a bitter and difficult decision to make. None of the children were well, and besides: whereto? The future lay entirely bleak before me. We packed in the night and I kept thinking, I should not go, better not. But early in the morning, the decision was made and I took leave with a bleeding heart. Herr Ivers was so kind and sweet. I saw him standing there watching us leave until we were out of sight.

Such tremendous suffering resulted from that decision. What mother takes her three little children from safety back into a war zone just to follow her husband? For a long time, I judged my mother harshly for her weakness. It has taken me a very long time to forgive her and understand the horrendous choice she felt she had to make. As I am writing this and taking a deeper look into what might have driven her, I realize how desperately she must have needed the safety of my father by her side and my heart opens to her in compassion.

Many years later, she told me that it was the most difficult choice she ever had to make.

Germany was already on the verge of losing. I've always had images of our little family traveling upstream against a tide of bedraggled German soldiers fleeing back over the border from the impending defeat. I found that later confirmed in my father's testimony.

I have vague memories of all of us riding in a truck through the pitch black of night, without headlights. Suddenly, there is danger and we have to get out and hide in the bushes. I feel my mother's terror, trying to keep her three little ones from making any noise.

My father took us to Groningen, in the north of Holland, to a family who had supposedly agreed to house my mother and the children. He hoped that he was delivering us into safety, however precarious. He left the next morning to join his comrades and face his destiny. I would not see him again for many years.

When we arrived "there was no room at the inn." In my mother's words:

I sensed immediately that we were not welcome. Everything was too much for the lady of the house, and there really wasn't any room for us. The material situation was also pretty bad in Holland. No light, no coal, no gas and little food. We needed to leave urgently since the man who had rented the room was returning.

All on her own now with her three little children, she reached out into a haphazard network of Nazi collaborators who were all frantically scrambling for safety. The end of the war was near. No one knew what would happen to them. They were like rats on a sinking ship. I am grateful to have this nightmare in my mother's own words:

Our little Almuth was lying in her pram almost all of the time, mostly alone. She did not develop any further at all. She had survived the journey but remained small and delicate. The next day, Monday, April 9th, I got the terrible news that I had to go. After a lot of effort to find housing, I was told to go to a school building. I begged for transportation! We had to be there at 11 a.m.. It was a dreadful walk with the heavy bundle in my arms and a crying Angela by my side. She had weakened a lot and could hardly walk that far. Someone helped carry our remaining luggage. Most of our possessions had been in a large trunk which was lost in Germany. What we have left is not much. Will we be able to keep it?

At 4 p.m. we were taken in a large cart to Grotegast near Groningen. Fortunately, the weather was good. There were low-flying planes, but no attack. The children slept mostly and were very sweet. In Grotegast, we stayed overnight, my first time sleeping on straw! Almuth cried during the night, I'm sure she was hungry. All next day, we had to stand and wait, the baby in my arms, since the pram had been packed full. Once in a while, we received a delicious cheese sandwich that tasted so good, and for the children I got porridge, which was cooked from my own supplies. Then the group got divided and I hoped I would end up with a good farmer. We had to get back on the cart to Opende. I will never forget what happened next.

We were dropped off and there we were on the street. No one was there to take us where we had to go! An error had been made and we were sent off to an old hag's hovel outside of the village. The locals called her the Village Devil. At first, she was stone cold. When she saw who we were, she softened a little, but we had to sleep in an old shed with dirty straw. It was full of farming implements, junk and cobwebs. I emptied the pram, cleaned potatoes off a shelf and spread out a canvas on the floor to put everything on so Almuth could lie in her pram again. The sun was shining outside. I was so happy that she had a quiet place to be.

At the Camp

My mother found her way to a large mansion near Groningen where entire families of collaborators were hoping to find refuge in numbers. She wrote:

I called the same evening to ask if we could go to the Hoeve. I had heard that it was a big old mansion that could house some 300 people. The situation here was so terrible that I thought it was the worst thing that could ever happen to me. I had to hold on tight to keep my courage up. The thought of Willem always gave me strength and the fact that I had to take care of the children also kept me going, but I felt terribly alone.

So, the next morning we got onto a cart that brought the last people to the Hoeve. The building is nicely furnished but the hygienic provisions are of no use since there is no water. Water is fetched from rain barrels and from the pond. The large garden is wonderful with lawns and beautiful trees, shrubs and flowers. Nature is the source of life force that I can dip into anytime.

Within a month, on May 5, 1945, the war ended. Farmers and farmhands from the surrounding villages, who had just survived the desperate hunger winter in Holland, irate at anyone who had anything to do with the much-hated Germans, stormed the mansion and took everyone captive. Their first action was to separate the men from the women and children. The men were taken elsewhere. Then they stole everything the women still had with them.

My mother never talked much about what happened there, but it was clear how deeply insulted she was by the rudeness with which they were being treated by these "insolent clod-hoppers," as she called them, a dark angry fire in her eyes. The women were made to work in the fields. Because she had a sick baby she was allowed to stay indoors. Food and medical help were extremely scarce.

Bathroom facilities consisted of large holes dug in the garden, with planks laid over them. I have a bodily memory of having to walk with my little two-year-old legs up onto those planks above that big smelly pit, and as my mother held onto my hands from the edge, having to squat with my naked bum over that disgusting mess, terrified that I might fall into it. I can still smell it.

My Baby Sister

I have never been able to share this part of my story without bursting into tears.

Together with the other women in the camp, my mother celebrated my third birthday to the best of her ability. She writes:

There was much illness, especially diarrhea. Angela suffered from that for a long time. On May 17, her birthday, she had recovered nicely, she even had a real birthday spread. One cube of sugar, which I still happened to have in my purse, little crusts of cheese from the kitchen and some raisins from a woman's pocket, those were her fantastic birthday gifts. She ate everything immediately on an empty stomach, for which she had to pay dearly. She must have vomited at least ten times and the diarrhea returned in full force. That morning, I had braided a little wreath of daisies which graced her blonde curls until she became ill.

Only six days later, my little sister died. Here's my mother's sad account:

And now, Almuth—sweet angel—I have to write down how you left us. During the last weeks, she had been lying and sitting outdoors in the sunshine and even gotten a healthy little tan, which made me very happy until her diapers were full of black diarrhea. The doctor ordered that she shouldn't eat anything at all, just to give her the little bit of breast milk I had left and some weak tea. Her small fragile body diminished day by day, and every time I looked into the pram, her little eyes were filled more strongly with a frightened hungry expression. Soon she didn't even have the strength to nurse, her little mouth being so dried out. I would squeeze the few drops I still had into her mouth. She would drink that eagerly. The doctor knew it was hard for me but he insisted on not giving her any food. When I nursed her, I tried to give her all of my life force, but to no avail. On Wednesday, May 23, when I looked into the pram in the afternoon, I was shocked to see her pale little face covered with sweat and her little legs were ice cold. The nurse carried her with pram and all into the sick bay. She had a 40-degree [104° F] fever. I sat by her side for another twenty minutes, a hot water bottle was warming her feet. I held her sweet little hands in mine. Her breath became shorter and shorter and suddenly her eyes turned outwards and upwards and after a few weak small breaths, her little mouth was silent and my Almuth was no longer alive.

Willem, how I called for you then, wishing we could have taken leave of our beloved little child together.

As she told me later, well-meaning women advised her, "Don't let your children see her body. They're too young to understand. They'll be too shocked. Since they are so young, after a little while they will simply forget her." The other children at the camp were allowed to lay flowers around her little body. So, my brother and I were denied our grief. The unacknowledged and unprocessed loss of my sweet baby sister got buried deep inside my poor belly—under the terrifying memory of what happened the morning after.

My First Memory

The women are standing very still in a dusty courtyard. I am barely three and am standing next to my older brother, who is standing next to my mom. We are not touching one another. Everyone is facing toward a loud disembodied angry male voice shouting something from somewhere way in front of the crowd. All I see are the dingy skirts and brown stockinged legs of the women in front of me. After every shout, one of the women responds. Fear is thick in the air.

Something is terribly wrong and I know in my gut that it has to do with us. I freeze in terror. Any moment now, they'll find out... unspeakable horror looms large, coming closer with each call. My terror mounts to unbearable intensity. Then, it's our turn. He calls... silence. For an instant, the world is suspended and life seems to hang in the balance. Then a woman in the crowd says something, I don't know what, and inexplicably the moment passes. Nothing happens. We all go back inside and my memory fades into the dark. No one ever knew how terrified I was.

I believe this moment froze itself into my psyche. Some unspeakable terror is waiting to happen. I am at the mercy of it and do not have any recourse. Then, strange oblivion. My mother and everyone around me goes about their business as if nothing had happened.

Sometime in my fifties, during one of my infrequent visits back to Holland, I finally shared this memory with my brother, which had played itself out in my mind so many countless times during my life, always equally terrifying, never understanding it.

"Oh yes," he knew right away, "that was the morning after Almuth died. It was roll call. They hadn't yet removed her number from the list. Mom was grief-stricken and could not speak when Almuth's number was called. After a moment of silence, one of the women spoke up and explained."

What strikes me now is how long it took for me to even talk about it to my brother. I never asked my mother. Our past was cloaked in her silence. Much later, I realized that I internalized the idea that she did not know what was going on with me and that maybe she did not care. I know today that I was wrong.

At My Grandmother's House

In the meantime, my father had been taken captive. I do not know when my mother found out. After some time the authorities contacted my grandmother. When she agreed to take us, my brother and I were released into the care of the Salvation Army, who would oversee our transition. At the Salvation Army, we slept on thin mattresses on low wooden platforms set out in long rows on the floor. After a few days, they put us on the train to Driebergen with the conductor in charge of getting us off the train in the right place.

I will never know how long we had stayed in the camp, I must have been three or four and Reinier seven or eight. I feel safe being with my big brother. I love him. He has a soft sweet face with friendly brown eyes and floppy ears. Once on the train, we are guided to a compartment and sit by the window. I feel the warmth of his body close to me and the rough texture of the cheap clothes he is wearing.

With a sudden push, the engine lets out its first loud blast of steam, horns blaring. The train shakes and creaks and slowly starts pulling up and gaining speed. The sounds of the locomotion create an ever-increasing multi-toned cadence, *tsjoeketsjoek*, *tsjoeketsjoek*, *tsjoeketsjoek*, interspersed with the regular clicks of the wheels when they cross the gaps in the rails. All those rhythmic noises feel soothing to my little body and make me drowsy, but it's way too fascinating to look out of the window to fall asleep now. As far as my eyes can see and flying by the window with ever-increasing speed are endless rows of green meadows intersected with narrow ditches in straight lines. This creates a rapidly fanning succession of waterlines gathering at the horizon. Sometimes, the water widens, reflecting white clouds and sky. Swans float regally in the peaceful scenery. Here and there I spot a mysterious blue heron. Everywhere lazy cows graze quietly, standing knee-deep in the grass.

On the train to visit family

When the conductor calls out 'Driebergen,' the name rings familiar. I was born there. It is a place where I belong and I sense that a new and better part of life is about to begin. Two old ladies meet us at the train station. My great-aunt, Tante Pempi (God only knows how she ever got that name) is dressed in a long black dress, her disorderly gray hair gathered in a doodle on her head, a pair of thick glasses sit on her knobbly nose. I am repulsed by her. She doesn't smell so nice, either. The other one, Tante Jeanette, one of my grandmother's old friends, is a little, wrinkled old lady looking dry and prissy. They both feel completely foreign to me. They're sent to bring us safely to my grandmother's house. Tante Pempi takes me brusquely by the hand and off we go.

It must have been autumn. I am enjoying kicking through layers of sodden leaves in various shades of red, brown and yellow. The air smells rich with decay. The moistness is penetrating. As we are tromping along, the old women talk steadily over our heads. Suddenly, Tante Pempi exclaims, "Oh look, the poor child is wearing house slippers. She doesn't even have shoes!" It is the very first moment in my little life that I become aware of myself as a separate entity. I look down and notice the beige and brown checkered soggy terry-cloth house slippers I am wearing and I realize my feet are getting quite wet. It is strange to be called a poor child as if there is something wrong with me. We walk past old stately mansions, one more impressive than the other, surrounded by vast manicured lawns, shrubs, and trees dotting the large estates.

Finally, we arrive at number eighty-two, my grandmother's house. Brick pillars flank the gate to the driveway. A small square pond sits in the center of the garden in front of the house surrounded by ferns and reeds. A weeping willow gracefully curves over the pond, trailing its leaves in the dark water. Later, I will hear my grandmother complain that the frogs keep her awake at night. The small red brick villa seems like a fairytale house, completely overgrown as it is with ivy, with mysterious-looking windows and a chimney on the roof.

The heavy front door opens into a small hallway which is separated from the dark interior of the house by stained glass windows and a door. A friendly, plain-looking woman opens the door. She is the maid. My brother and I step into the small front hall. Then a door opens somewhere inside and an old woman appears, smiling, out of the dark. She's not very tall but rather big around. From the way she welcomes us so warmly, I understand she is my grandmother, but she is a total stranger to me. She greets me with a sweet little nickname, *Poppedijntje*, Little Doll. I am somewhat taken aback by her familiarity. She doesn't even know me. I pertly correct her and introduce myself, "I am Angela!"

When my grandmother laughs, all her fat jiggles. Later, I pick up from conversations that she had contracted elephantiasis in Africa. From under her long dresses, I sometimes glimpse how her legs go straight down like elephant legs, no ankles. But, she always smells nice. Lily of the valley, I imagine. Her skin is soft and wrinkled. A fat little pouch quivers under her chin and when I have become more familiar with her, I reach up to pet it, which she good-naturedly allows. She also lets me stroke her smooth fat arms which are always dressed in soft velvet. I am like a baby monkey starved to feel something soft and luxurious.

The house is dark and mysterious. I remember the suspense that first night when we were being brought upstairs to our very own bedroom in the attic. From then on, every night, my brother and I are on our little knees praying fervently to God for our mother's return and for our father to be freed from prison.

Cooking and baking were my grandmother's favorite passion. She usually did not want us around and sent us off to play outside. I remember once when she called me into the kitchen handing me a spatula covered with sweet batter and encouraged me to lick it clean. I thought I had gone to heaven. Even though I was already forgetting the past, it was not that long ago that I had been hungry. I certainly hadn't ever tasted anything so delicious.

My brother and I played in the garden behind the house. It was blooming heavily in a riot of color with gladiolas, foxglove and dahlias. In the far back was a small orchard, which always felt a bit dark and foreboding to me. I never went there. About halfway down the garden a sand box had little forms for baking cookies with the sand where I often played by myself. Reinier soon found his way through the hedge to the neighbors to play with other boys his age.

One time, Tante Pempi called me in for dinner. I was fully absorbed with my play in the sand box. I remember looking up and seeing this unpleasant looking old aunt hollering at me. It did not occur to me to respond. Then I watched her heading for me, an angry scowl on her face. I froze. She grabbed me roughly by the arm, dragging me out of the sandbox and back to the house, scolding and complaining all the way.

How happy I would be when my brother was around and he would deign to play with me. I have a sweet picture of him and me by the rain barrel behind my grandmother's house. I loved him showing me the little treasures he always seemed to have in his pockets. A small race car or some marbles he had won. His favorite game was counting cars. He would help me climb up onto one of the pillars at the end of the driveway, then he would

Me with Reinier behind our grandmother's house

climb on top of the other one and count the cars driving by. In 1946–47, not many cars were on the road, so there was always a slight element of surprise when another car drove by.

Reunited with My Mother

There is a picture of me taken very shortly after we had come to live in my grandmother's house. I look quite frail, pale and skinny, with the frizzy curls of an undernourished child and a rather stunned look on my little face. About half a year later, my mother was released from post-war internment and came home to my grandmother's. How happy we were to be reunited with her. I belonged with her. To celebrate our reunion, my mother took us to a photographer in the village. Looking at those pictures, no one would guess what we had just been through. My mother had dressed me in a rich, dark brown velvet dress with an ivory lace collar fastened in front with a little button. She had curled my hair with a hot curling iron. My brother is wearing a shirt and a polka-dot tie. My mother looks like a countess, her hair carefully coiffed, wearing her antique long gold earrings. She has a kind, peaceful smile. I always thought I had the most beautiful mother in the whole wide world.

Looking more deeply into our faces, I notice the close resemblance between my mother and my brother. They clearly belong to each other. I belong too, but I am different. Later I will realize that I am much more like my father. My eyes seem to express a more intriguing complexity. My body remembers the sweet shyness I felt, posing for the photographer, absorbing at the same

Undernourished just after camp · Reunited with our mother

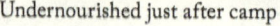

time the warmth and safety of my mother's body behind me. We all felt the same deep happiness of being reunited. The great absence in this picture, of course, is my father, still imprisoned in Scheveningen for his involvement in the war. We continue to pray every night for his release. I remember my little body in sweet imploration to God, to bring my daddy safely back home.

For Christmas, Reinier and I were both surprised with gifts. We gathered in my grandmother's dark and exotic living room, filled with art, fine batiks, racks of deer horns and elephant tusks from my grandfather's hunting days. The room was full of women, my mother, grandmother, aunts and great-aunts. My brother received a real leather soccer ball. All the women oohed and ahhed over the quality of that fine ball. It was clear that it was a very expensive ball for such a young boy to have. My brother's eyes gleam with pride over the exceptional possession.

Then it is my turn. I am given a red baby carriage for my doll. I am told that my father made it himself in prison from a small barrel he had sawed in half. One half was nailed at a right angle to the other half, so it made a hood. It had clunky wooden wheels and a wooden handlebar. It was painted red and decorated with small blue flowers along the edges. It seemed a completely magical gift to me. This was not supposed to happen. How could he have made such a lovely thing, all for me, in the ugly place where he was held captive? In my four-year-old heart, I understood the love and care he must have felt to create this gift for me with his own hands out of nothing. I remember how puzzled I was to hear one of my aunt's comments to my mother: "What a sweet child she is. Her brother is getting such a special gift and she is not jealous at all!" Even though I liked hearing the compliment, I knew it was undeserved. I had absolutely no desire for a soccer ball and I had just received the loveliest gift from my own papa!

I put my doll into the carriage. My mother walked me across the street so I could take the carriage for a stroll. She went back into the house and left me there all by myself. I felt like a proud and grown-up little mommy, walking my baby up and down the sidewalk. The street was lined with trees and it was just slightly hilly right there. The wooden wheels were rickety. I had trouble keeping it from going sideways, especially when pushing it up and down the gentle slopes, but it didn't diminish my pleasure.

Catholic Boarding School

My mother needed to find work. She chose to become a doula, a midwife's assistant at home births. She would stay on for ten days to take care of the mother, the baby and the entire household. It was hard work. In the winter she would be called out to some farm without running water. Before dawn, she would have to go out in the bitter cold to haul water, light the fire, feed the family, and prepare stacks of sandwiches for lunch for the father, sons and farmhands. In between assignments she would come home to my grandmother's.

A big change came when it was decided that my brother and I should go and live in a boarding school. Later, I understood that my grandmother who had raised seven children, was not really prepared to be looking after two more children for an unforeseeable length of time. A Catholic boarding school was found in Acht, a tiny hamlet near Eindhoven in the south of Holland. The school housed both boys and girls. I am sure my mother was imagining we would at least have each other. From then on, my mother divided whatever free time she had between her heavy workloads, alternating between taking the train to Scheveningen to visit my father and traveling south by train and bus to visit us.

When she brought us to the school the first time, she bade us farewell and admonished my brother to take good care of me. Apparently, she did not know that boys and girls were kept completely segregated.

I entered a cold and regulated world, where the Sisters of Love and Mercy ruled with iron hands. The only sweet nun, Sister Veronica, worked on the boys' side. She had one blue and one brown eye. My brother soon became her favorite altar boy. The only time I would see my brother, besides during my mother's brief and sporadic visits, was during Mass, way in front of the altar. I was only five and felt quite forlorn.

One morning, our kindergarten class met in the hallway rather than in a classroom. There were many doors and a dark stairwell. The floor was of a black and white speckled granite. Suddenly, the nun yelled at me. God knows what I had done. Probably talked to another child. I must have irked her considerably because she ordered me angrily into a dusty broom closet. Closing the door on me, she shouted, "Don't let me hear you again!" It was pitch dark in there. When she had opened the door, I had glimpsed brooms and mops and stuff. It smelled musty. There was just enough room for me to stand. Then I noticed three small holes drilled in the top of the door. To this day I wonder if they were made with the specific purpose to keep a punished child from suffocating.

I am standing there very quietly for a long time. I hear the children's noises and the nun's voice ordering them about. Suddenly, a bell rings for lunch and I hear the commotion of all the kids moving their chairs, getting up and leaving. Then I hear the nun leave. Then silence.

I realize I have been forgotten. I have been so intimidated that I do not dare make a noise. After some time, a door opens and to my great relief, I hear Sister Veronica chatting with my brother as they cross the hallway. I cry out to them. I hear the quick rushing sounds of her long habit as she runs toward the closet and opens the door. She is shocked to find me there. "Oh, how terrible. Who did this to you?" Blinded by the sudden light,

I feel her friendly care. She comforted me with a gentle, "Go on upstairs now and have your lunch." I still see the startled look on Reinier's sweet face. How lucky he was to have the one kind nun in the entire place as his protectress.

What miserable women they must have been, these Sisters of Love and Mercy. They were supposedly the chosen ones who thought themselves to be the brides of Christ. I would sit quietly amidst the playing children and observe the nuns in charge. Everything about them seemed wrong. They were completely covered in black. All you could see were their hands and faces. Not a strand of hair would escape the strange-looking white contraption holding back their black veils. They always looked stern and were often angry. I felt that they particularly hated me. I believe I must have made them uncomfortable sitting there with my serious dark brown eyes observing them, but mostly, they all knew that I was there because of my father's situation. These were women who had just come through the hunger winter, who hated the Germans and especially despised Dutch collaborators, the traitors. I was the daughter of scum.

My Father's Death Sentence

Every second or third Sunday, my mother came to visit my brother and me. Not only was I happy to be with my mommy, but it was also wonderful to be with my brother, for the three of us to be together. The nuns maintained a near-hermetic separation between boys and girls. We did not even attend the same school. The girls went to school in-house and the boys attended the elementary school in the village. We ate and played in separate quarters. As I mentioned before I would only catch a glimpse of my brother during Mass because he was an altar boy.

One moment got engraved in my memory when the bottom fell out of my life. At the end of one of my mother's visits, we were standing in front of the school to say goodbye. My mother was wearing a light blue wool coat trimmed with white fur. She turned to us with a troubled look. She cupped her hand under my chin and tilted my little face up to her, her dark eyes looking seriously into mine. My brother was standing close behind me. "I have to tell you something very difficult… Your father has been sentenced to death… I believe he is innocent. The only thing you can do for him is pray." Then, undoubtedly for our protection, my mother added, "You can never talk to anyone about this."

With a sinking feeling in the pit of my stomach, I realized that the Dutch, my people, my country had officially decided to kill my father. I intuitively understood our need for secrecy. Surely if anyone found out, they would hate us. If I had been lonely before, my isolation was now sealed like a tomb. I watched my mother, looking quite forlorn, walking back to the bus stop. My brother and I climbed up the stairs into the gaping darkness of the school entrance.

Of course, those nuns knew what was happening with my father. I'm sure it was in all the newspapers in post-war Holland. They knew why we were there. They had accepted us out of charity to begin with.

My six-year-old self turned to God with a vengeance. He could not let this happen. I began to storm the heavens, where in some vast distance beyond the clouds, there was this great, all-powerful grandfather type of Being, whom no one had ever seen. My little mind became very loud, shouting desperately at Him to save my father. I prayed and begged day and night, in bed, at the table, on the playground and in the chapel, never sure if He would hear me. I became a deeply religious child with a dark secret.

Boarding School Continues

That night I woke up vomiting. I cried. The nun who was sleeping in a cell next to the dormitory came out, cleaned me up, changed the sheets and said, "Go back to sleep now." Before long, I vomited again. She goes through the same routine of cleaning me up and changing the sheets, muttering. After the third time, I am standing beside my bed, she is furious and slaps me hard around my face. I am shocked to my core. I knew that was very wrong of her! Sometimes, I still feel the cruel imprint of her hand on my face.

Every Sunday morning, Mother Superior made her rounds with a can of sweets that were gathered from parents' gifts for their children. It was the one small pleasant highlight of the week. Each child got to pick one. I always wanted the red slightly tart ones that looked like raspberries, they seemed the most exciting and made my mouth tingle in anticipation. When it was my turn, I would stand on my toes and peer eagerly into the can to spot the brightest red one. All through my life, red has been my happy color and I have been happy with one small treat.

One Sunday, I happened to be in the bathroom when I heard her making her rounds. I became anxious I might miss her. As I was trying to rush, it seemed to take forever to complete what I had to. When I finally ran out of the stall, I spotted her at the end of the corridor just as she was heading down the stairs. I ran to her breathlessly in my excitement to catch her just in time, "Sister, sister, I almost missed you. I haven't had a sweet yet."

As soon as she saw it was me, she rose ominously and, towering over me, closed the lid on the can even more tightly. "You don't get a sweet today," she barked, "because you have been bad!" Coming completely out of the blue, her reprimand was crushing. What had I done? I had not the faintest idea. She never told me. It seemed I was just supposed to know that, naturally, I was bad.

When I was only in second grade, I had to learn the Catechism by heart, that horrid little Catholic book of rules. I couldn't do it. I hated it. I would be so full of resistance and revulsion that I could barely read it, let alone memorize it. When I was called on in class to recite, I invariably failed. Every time I got bombarded with angry tirades and was ordered to stand in the corner for the duration of the class. It didn't help. I just couldn't learn the damn little book. At some point the exasperated nun sent me to the head of the school, a pale, severe nun who was teaching sixth grade. She made me stand in front of her classroom facing all those older children and mercilessly put me to shame. I felt so embarrassed, I wanted to sink into the ground. I was also very angry at the unfairness of it all but knew I was completely helpless in the situation.

My brother was turning twelve at the time. To everyone's amazement, from his prison cell, my father had been able to organize for Reinier to participate in a pilgrimage to Rome. He joined a large contingent of pilgrims traveling by train all the way through France and the Alps for an audition with Pope Pius XII. One of the accompanying priests was to look after my brother, who was by far the youngest one on board. There he was overwhelmed by the pomp of the Vatican and the extraordinary privilege of seeing the Holy Father in person. Pius XII had great charisma, able to invoke powerful devotion in all who came into his presence.

Shortly after this amazing adventure, my parents had to find a high school for Reinier. My father organized another surprise for him, this one rather unwelcome. One day, a priest came to visit Reinier and talked with him about joining a seminary, as if that had already been planned. My brother knew nothing about this. Terrified, he panicked and ran screaming out of the room. Here was a painful example of my father's fantasy life and his

Reinier shares his treasures with me during a visit from our mother

unexamined projections on the ones he loved. Apparently, he believed that my brother was deeply religious and had the desire to become a priest. He himself had cherished the dream of entering a monastery in his younger years. In the end, my parents sent him to a Catholic high school in Eindhoven, run by the highly educated and respected Augustinian priests.

When my mother explained to me during one of her visits that my brother was going to change schools, I finally found the courage to tell her how unhappy I was at that boarding school. I could feel and see her kindness and concern as she listened to me and drew me into her arms. I had never mentioned to her how nasty the nuns were to me. Since I always felt that the difficulties she was dealing with were so much bigger than mine, I had not wanted to add my little complaints to her burdens. Miraculously, during our summer vacation, my mother told me she had found another boarding school for me. I had never thought that sharing any of my difficulties with her could possibly make a difference, that she would be able to take any action. I must have thought she was as powerless as I was.

A Second Boarding School

When I was ready for third grade, I went to a new boarding school, which appeared much friendlier. It was an all-girls school called the Maria Stichting located in Nieuw Wehl, a tiny hamlet in Gelderland, a province in the east of Holland. The building looked rather majestic to me, with a large circular lawn in front, and trees all around. Besides the elementary school, which I was there to attend, there was a household school for older girls. The front section of the building was a senior rest home. The nuns lived in their own hidden quarters. Behind the school were "the little woods" as we called it, where we were free to roam and play during our breaks from school. Behind the little woods, the institution maintained a farm with cows, pigs and chickens to provide for all of us. The complex was surrounded by farm fields as far as the eye could see.

Even though this school had a much friendlier appearance, I soon found out that nuns will be nuns. Again, what seemed to matter to them most is that we followed the rules, sat still and remained quiet. They demanded perfect and immediate obedience. Kindness was scarce.

I loved being in the chapel, where I felt safe and was able to savor my connection with the Divine, which at that time was embodied by Jesus and Mary. I also loved the woods where I had my private conversations with them, quietly walking in circles under the fragrant trees. There was one particular tree I loved to climb. When perched up there very quietly, I enjoyed the view over the neighboring fields and the fact that nobody knew my whereabouts. Children ran around below me, but I was in my secret place, invisible.

During the first few years there, I did not really relate to any of the girls. Most of the children were placed in the school for a year or less due to family circumstances, like the illness of a mother. When the difficulties had passed, they would not come back. Nobody stayed on as indefinitely as I did. When I would tell them that I had already been in boarding school for five years, they looked at me in disbelief, thinking I was lying.

We slept in dorm rooms, one for the elementary school girls and one for the older household school girls. Ours was a long space under the attic. About thirty of us slept in a single row of beds, separated by a sink on top of a bedside cabinet. Every morning we had to make our beds perfectly. The beige bedspreads were decorated with a stripe of blue floral fabric, which had to be perfectly aligned across the row of beds. When we were ready to leave the dorm for breakfast, a nun would come and inspect the place, and if any of these stripes were crooked, they first had to be straightened out.

Opposite that long row, four alcoves were set under the slanted roof, each with one bed and a small vanity. In between the alcoves were large cabinets storing our clothes and linens, each item marked with our personal numbers so they could be identified in the laundry. In a corner of the room was a private cell with a bed for a nun, who would quietly come in after we

Boarding school group photo; I am in the front row to the right

were asleep. That area was only separated from us by a set of floor-length white curtains. The secrecy was quite intriguing to me. A few times I was awake when she came into her cell. I would hear the rustling of her clothes as she prepared for bed. Curious, I would hang my head down from my bed to see if I could catch a glimpse of her from under the curtains. I never saw anything.

At some point, I was able to volunteer for a bed in one of the alcoves. I enjoyed feeling more private. I especially loved to secretly climb up to sit in the window and look out over the farmlands under the night sky. Great thunderstorms were my favorite. Most of the kids were scared, but I loved to open the window and feel the excitement and wildness of the elements. Finally, something was actually happening!

One year, a new girl arrived. She looked quite different from us. She seemed small for her age. Her skin was pale and freckled. She had long black curls. She was terribly homesick. Every night at bedtime she would burst out in hysterical sobbing. The nun in charge did not know what to do with her, since she was inconsolable. I was quite annoyed with the racket she made. What was she crying about? Couldn't she just shut up? What was the big deal? Much later in my life I realized that I was angry with her because I could not afford to cry about missing my own parents. I did not even have a home. I did not have the luxury to display my emotions or even have them. My survival depended entirely on my being strong and stoic. More embarrassing was the realization, much later, that deep in my subconscious, I despised people who were acting like victims.

Every so often, we suddenly heard the squealing of a pig as it was being chased from the farm through the woods toward slaughter. Evert, the farmer, performed the slaughter in a small cement room adjacent to the kitchen. Besides the priest, Evert was the only man on the compound, a strong, silent type, who also served as janitor, stoking the big furnaces in the cellar. Once the pig had been forced into the slaughter room, we would crowd by the door to watch the gruesome spectacle. With an axe, Evert would hack repeatedly with all his force in the middle of the poor pig's head while she screamed for her life until she was dead. Then she would be hoisted onto a ladder by her hind feet and leaned upside down against the wall, split from head to toe through the middle. The slippery intestines were caught in a large metal basin and buckets placed below her head to catch the blood. As horrifying as it was, I could not tear myself away from the scene. Then the nuns were up to their elbows in the blubbery intestines, cleaning them out, so the membranes could be used to make sausage.

The next day we would have to eat the results. Yikes… I abhorred the squishy fat on the meat. Head cheese was the worst. I always hoped to sit by one of the girls who loved fat, so I could sneak it to her. Eating had become an ongoing problem for me. Breakfast was mostly ok, but lunch and dinner usually consisted of greasy meat and overcooked vegetables. We *had* to finish our plates. No excuse. Long after the other children had gone outside to run and play, I would often still be at the table staring at my plate of cold food in the deserted dining room. I could not escape the ominous supervision of whatever nun was on duty. I would then secretly keep the last bite in my mouth and run to the bathroom to spit it out.

One day, when I was sitting alone in front of my cold food, feeling quite lonely and dejected, a nun came in and announced that I had a visitor. Visitors would only come on Sundays and were never expected during the week. She took me outside to meet a rather rotund, friendly priest who had been sent by my family to look in on me. He asked the nun to take our picture with his camera. That picture turned out to show the reality which was always so neatly washed and combed away at more official occasions. My hair was unkempt and I looked quite bedraggled, like a neglected orphan. Later, when my mother and I were looking at the picture, my mother grumbled that they could at least have combed my hair! Never would I hear: "Oh sweet Angela, you look so miserable. Was it that bad?"

That was my mother's unmistakable message. No matter what is going on, make sure you look perfectly fine. Do not embarrass me.

Visiting My Father in Prison

I must have been about eight when my mother picked me up from boarding school with the unexpected announcement that she would take me to Scheveningen to visit my dad in prison. Ever since I learned to read and write, my father and I did send each other letters. Sometimes, I would receive a thick envelope with many pages of a handwritten fairy tale he had written for me, with lovely illustrations in the margins. It made my little heart leap for joy. I always felt connected with him, even though

I had not seen him since our lives had been so rudely disrupted when I was only two years old.

We arrived by train in The Hague and from there took the tram to Scheveningen. When I spotted a big brick building with many small barred windows, my young voice rang out, "Mommie, is that the prison where Pappie is?" Shocked by my public revelation, my mother hissed at me, "Shh, don't say that out loud!"

Somewhere in the innards of the building, having passed through a number of heavy doors, we entered a large, dark, mostly empty space. At the far end, a long table stretched from one wall to the other. Behind it a number of prisoners were seated, all looking equally drab. At the far end of the table under a high barred window sat a guard.

I watch my mother walking over to the one man who must be my father. I don't really recognize him. He smiles at me. There's a little back and forth between my parents and the guard. I am encouraged to walk all the way around that long table, past the guard, to sit on my father's lap. I feel shy, happy and confused all at the same time. I don't know this man and he is slightly repelling. He looks kind of grubby with unshaven stubbles. He's wearing shabby, brown clothes. He lifts me on his lap. He is too warm and he doesn't smell fresh. He is my father and he is a stranger. How strange, after all my longing and praying for him, to suddenly be sitting uneasily on his lap.

My mother has brought *The Great Story Book* for me to read to my dad so that he will be proud of me. I start to read my favorite story to him. It's called *Angelijntje*. Her name is the diminutive of my name Angela and when my mother first read it to me, I knew secretly that it was about me. She is very small and wears a red dress and is floating down a canal on a cabbage leaf. She is so tiny that from the shore she looks like a bright little ruby. When the leaf floats under a bridge, the toll master spots her and hauls her in. Thankfully, the great giant is rather good-natured and puts her for safekeeping in a glass jar. When he leaves to get the town's people to see the little miracle, a curious mouse comes to check her out. He takes pity on her and drops his long tail in the jar for her to climb out. He then carries her on his back to safety.

I only read for a few minutes when I notice my parents quietly talking to each other as if I were not there. Then my dad starts leafing through the book. I am confused and feel ignored. When I look up at him, I see him close the one eye that was away from the guard and talk with my mother in their private B-language. Something they had both practiced for fun when they were young. You repeat every syllable with a "b" in front of it and it becomes completely unintelligible to the unsuspecting listener. Much later, after our family had miraculously been reunited again, we would enjoy talking in our secret language with each other in public and watch the puzzled look on bystanders' faces.

On our way home, my mom explained that she had smuggled all kinds of useful things, like flint stones and razor blades, for my dad in the book. And whenever he had a special message or instruction for her, he would close one eye without moving a single muscle in the rest of his face, so she would know to pay attention and the guard would not suspect anything. My mother was very clever and my father was an experienced magician. I had been used as a decoy for their smuggling.

I had been made to believe how happy my dad would be to see me and he probably was. But I did not seem nearly as important to him as the razor blades and matches my mother brought to him. I returned to my boarding school feeling uneasy, disappointed and more invisible than ever.

The Miracle Happens

During my last year in boarding school, when I was almost twelve, my mother was staying with a friend of hers, a social worker, in a large apartment in Rotterdam, the second biggest city in the Netherlands. When the Germans invaded the country at the beginning of WWII, they bombarded and burnt down the entire heart of the city to force Holland to surrender. It worked. Holland did not have any means to defend itself.

Each from our respective boarding schools, my brother from the south, in Eindhoven, and me from Gelderland in the east of the country, traveled by train to Rotterdam. After so many years, we had a home to come to for Easter vacation. It was a wonderful experience. The apartment was on the third floor, large and beautifully furnished. One day, my mother told us that our uncle Hubert, my father's older brother who lived in Hamburg and who looked very much like him, was coming to visit us. When the bell rang we all ran to the door of the apartment. My mother pressed the button that unlocked the front door two stories down. As I looked down the long flight of stairs, I saw my father looking up at us with a big smile on his face.

Great excitement and confusion ensued. What bizarre ideas grown-ups have sometimes that it should be fun to spring such a momentous event as a complete surprise upon their children.

My insides were all a-jumble. I didn't know what to do with myself. How could my father suddenly be free and walking up those stairs?

I understood later that certain high ranking members of our family, one was a bishop, had worked behind the scenes to arrange a psychiatric review of my father's condition during those last three weeks of the war. He was considered not having been accountable for his actions and was released on the condition that he would spend a year in a mental hospital under psychiatric supervision. He would be free to come and go to attempt his re-entry into society. A seeming miracle had occurred.

When he arrived at the top of the stairs, we fell all over each other in a confused happy tumble of hugs and smiles and exclamations. When we came up for air, my mother ushered us into the living room. Chairs were set around in a small circle. My father got the easy chair. Just as I was about to sit down, both my father and mother suggested that I may go sit on my daddy's lap. Except for when I was too young to remember and during that one awkward time when visiting him in prison, I had never done that before. When I sat stiffly and uneasily on his bony knees, apparently, he didn't know what to do with me there either. I felt his hands on my sides, gently pushing me off his knees, saying kindly to me, "Why don't you just go sit on that chair."

When I was fifteen, my father spoke about his experience when he had moved me off his lap during that first visit. Since he hadn't been close to a woman for so long, when I sat on his lap, being almost twelve and budding, he had gotten an erection and had to gently push me away from him. He had spoken with his psychiatrist about his concern that this experience might have a negative effect on me. He told me that the psychiatrist had thought I might possibly become a lesbian. That suggestion was rather confusing to me since I had as yet no clear idea about my own sexuality.

Later, I realized the sad irony of having been denied the sweetness of physical closeness with my father as a child, and that when he finally came home, it was too late. I had grown too old to sit on my daddy's lap.

Part II

Growing Up

My Budding Femininity

Almost twelve and still in Catholic boarding school, I was completely unaware of my body, let alone of my femininity. My mother, who worked as a doula, had told me how the baby "rests under the heart of the mother." I tried to figure out how the baby would come out. Looking at my own body, I had a belly button and breasts. I didn't even know about having a vagina. The closest parts to the heart were the breasts. I was the laughing stock in the dormitory when girls would ask me from across the room, "Angela, where do babies come from?" and I would answer, "From the breast!" They'd all burst out laughing hysterically. I wondered how dumb they were that they didn't know. After all, my mother was a doula and who should know better! They would tell me that babies were born from 'down there.' I had horrifying images of women giving birth on the toilet and frantically trying to prevent the baby from falling in. That couldn't possibly be right.

One day, a new, young and handsome chaplain arrived, Chaplain Roelinck. I was vaguely aware that he aroused an unusual kind of interest in the older girls. He had curly dark brown hair, big brown eyes, a gentle face and a friendly demeanor.

Right after my return from Easter vacation, I came down with a high fever. Little red spots appeared around my waist. I was placed in isolation in a small sick room across from the dormitory. The girls were forbidden to enter my room. I wasn't allowed to leave the room and was given a chamber pot for my bathroom needs. Three times a day, a nun came to bring me food, take my temperature and sometimes empty the pot. I remember the long peaceful hours drifting and waking, looking at the little square of blue sky through the window at the foot of my bed, hearing children's voices in the distance.

One Sunday morning a nun came to ask me if I would like to receive Holy Communion. Yes, I would. She gave me a sponge bath, combed my hair and prepared my bed nicely, laying a white starched cloth across the bed right up to my chin, and left. I felt very peaceful. The big school was quiet. Everyone was attending Mass in the chapel. Then, from a distance, I heard the sound of a little tinkling bell slowly coming closer and soft footsteps approaching. When the door opened, the young chaplain entered. Dressed in priestly robes, he was carrying a small golden plate with the host, softly murmuring prayers in Latin, approaching my bed. I looked at him transfixed. Very slowly he bent over me, his kind brown eyes gazing into mine, closer and closer. As he placed the host on my tongue, a warm tingling wave rushed through my belly. Ever so slowly he moved away from me. The nun who had brought him to my room had been standing in the doorway, immobile, watching. After they left, the host on my tongue slowly dissolving into me together with the lingering blush that stirred in my body, I simmered in blissful confusion.

After some time, the same nun returned and as she bustled around folding the white cloth, scolded me mildly for having kept my eyes open during communion.

The next morning, when all the children were in class, a doctor came and diagnosed scarlet fever. I had to go to the hospital. Clearly, the fear of contamination was great. I was wrapped in a bed sheet and walked through the empty halls to a taxi waiting by the front gate. I was driven to a Catholic hospital in Zevenaar, the nearest town. A nun explained to me that my bed was made over the top of a bathtub since they did not have an isolation room. I was their first scarlet fever patient to be treated with penicillin and, I was told, I would be better in ten to twelve days instead of the usual five to six weeks the disease would have lasted. I couldn't believe the luxury of having a bell I could ring whenever I needed anything. Sooner or later a nun would appear and bring me whatever I wanted. She would also knock on my door before entering. Such novel respect and catering to my needs.

A doctor entered with a nurse in tow. He asked me how I was doing. He gently removed my bed covers and lifted up my pajama top to look at my body. He listened with his cold stethoscope. Then he asked me to lower my pants to have a look at my belly. I lowered my pants. Confusion everywhere. The doctor turned scarlet. I heard the nun catch her breath. Apparently, I had lowered my pants lower than expected. I must have been showing some budding femininity. In my embarrassment I just lay there paralyzed, understanding that I was too naked for this man's eyes.

A few days later, a nun knocked at my door and announced my father! I could hardly believe my eyes. There he was, warm, smiling, laughing, joking with me. He was not allowed to touch me and had to sit in the far corner of the room. It was my first glimmer of seeing who my father actually was and of feeling his abundant love for me.

I stayed in the hospital for a couple of weeks. When I returned to school, the chaplain was gone. I was never to see him again.

For several Sundays in a row, Mother Superior called us twelve-year-olds in, one at a time, for a private conversation. She talked mysteriously about a rose that blooms once a month, revealing some unfathomable secret to me about growing into a woman. I had no idea what she was talking about.

My First Outing with My Father

In May of that year, 1954, my father came to visit me for my twelfth birthday. From his parents' inheritance he had been able to buy a cute little car, a Morris Minor. We were both so excited to see each other. He took me to the movies in the nearby town of Arnhem. *Roman Holiday* was playing. It was my first time to the movies and my very first time out with my father, just him and me, this man I had prayed to be with for as long as I remembered.

He was so very happy he could do this with me, he was smiling broadly as he bought the tickets. We entered the semi-darkness of a large Art Deco theater with rows and rows of red plush seats. Way in front, a man played on an organ. When at last the lights dimmed and while he was still playing, man and organ slowly sank beneath the floor. The heavy red curtains slid open. Newsreels came first.

Without warning, we were bombarded with horrifying images of the concentration camps. Large pits filled with white, naked, emaciated corpses; piles of shoes and glasses, ovens in which people had been burnt alive. My mind and my insides plunged into chaos, unable to comprehend the unimaginable cruelty, my father sitting next to me, both of us silent, paralyzed.

Roman Holiday came on with all its witty, sweet charm and we laughed and laughed. When we left the theater, my eyes blinked in the sunlight. My mind was filled with pictures of the lovely Audrey Hepburn. Having big brown eyes myself, I happily identified with her. The horror of the newsreels seemed forgotten. It was never mentioned. After a happy day together, my father dropped me off at boarding school for my last quarter there.

Deep in my psyche the images of the holocaust became engraved. My family's big secret turned out to be much more ominous than I could have imagined. I knew that my father had been sentenced to death for his participation in WWII, but had no idea what horrors had been perpetrated by the regime he had idealized and believed in. I did know that he had not been directly involved in the death camps. Nevertheless, unspeakable shame and guilt by association settled in my gut. Because I loved my father more than anybody in the whole wide world and knew that I belonged with him, I too must be guilty of this horror. Much later, of course, I realized it was the unavoidable conclusion of a child's mind.

Living in a Basement

A few months later, when school was over, I was at last able to come home. For seven long years, I had lived in boarding schools. A whole new world opened up. My mother had rented half of a basement in Rotterdam from an unmarried friend of hers who lived upstairs with her bachelor brother, their aging mother and a cat. It was small, but she and I were happy to have a home.

My brother continued his high school years in the Augustinian boarding school and my father could come and visit from his stay at the psychiatric hospital in Heiloo, in the North.

The modest living room was packed with the furniture my mother had somehow managed to salvage through the war and the post-war years. How and where she managed to pull that off, I have no idea. My parents must have had friends to do this for them, since we fled our home in Apeldoorn in such a rush on that fateful night in September of '44, never to return to it again. An elegantly curved small couch with matching chairs and a coffee table on an oriental carpet, a chaise lounge which would be my temporary bed when my dad and my brother came home, my mother's maple desk with hutch and the dining table and chairs were all crammed into that one small space. The windowsill in our living room was level with the pavement outside. It was a bit strange to watch people's legs and dogs walk by.

Curtains separated the living room from an alcove which fit my mother's bed on one side and my narrow bed on the other. At the end of the space between our beds was a table with a large washbasin and a water pitcher for us to wash up. The bathroom in the dark hallway was so small that you sat with your knees against the door. In the back of the hallway was a dreary kitchen which the bachelor brother used for his ablutions.

One day, when I went to the bathroom, there was all this blood! Oh my god, there's something terribly wrong with me. I ran to my mother, "I am bleeding!" She smiled and reassured me that I had begun menstruating. "But it is from the front!" I shouted, horrified. "Of course," she laughed and explained that I was now becoming a woman.

We were quite poor. I remember once my mother turning over her wallet in front of me, showing that there was nothing in it. Even though she was quite serious when she showed me, she didn't seem ruffled. The neighborhood baker, butcher, milkman and grocer, a friendly and helpful lot, were all willing to add our small purchases to a running tab, trusting that my mother, always the lady, would surely pay the bills when she could. Within a week we received a letter with a fifty Deutsch Mark banknote from Tante Erika, my mother's oldest sister, who still lived in Germany. It felt like an answer to her prayer. My mother had a deep, abiding faith in God and seemed to trust that everything always works out somehow. This was one of the many fine gifts my mother bestowed on me which has served me well over my lifetime.

Occasionally my father spent a few days with us. He would always be there when my brother came home for his vacations. Then my parents slept in the alcove. I would sleep on the chaise lounge and my brother on an air mattress on the floor. Even though it was tight, we were thrilled to be together. In the morning, we bustled around to put the living room back together again.

When the four of us would be together, we loved playing games. Our favorites were a card game called Canasta and endless rounds of Mah Jong. We laughed a lot, so happy to be family together at last.

A Home of Our Own

After he had completed his court-ordered year at the psychiatric clinic, my father came home permanently. His youngest sister, Tante Annelies, who lived with her husband and seven children in one of the finest neighborhoods of Rotterdam, managed through her social network to find us proper living quarters. I'll never forget when we first went to see the empty apartment. Entering the front door, we had to climb a long flight of narrow stairs to the third floor. The living room in front with large windows opened to a dining room in the middle which had sliding glass doors to the back room. This was to become my father's study. Doors from the living room and from the room in back came out on a long narrow hallway with the kitchen at one end, a small bathroom next to it and my little bedroom at the other end. A narrow curving stair led up to another half of a floor with my parents' bedroom with balcony, a shower stall with a sink which had to serve the whole family and a tiny little room for my brother when he would be home from school. Small stairs wound up to a flat roof where we could hang our laundry to dry. On rainy days, clotheslines were strung above these stairs.

Ever since the war ended, we dreamed about having a home together. We were so happy, we ran through the house laughing at the luxury of so much space which was all ours. My father and I played peek-a-boo, dashing back and forth through the doors at each end of the hallway, our laughter ringing through the empty space. Our dreams were coming true.

My dad had a friend who came with his grown son to help us wallpaper and paint the house just the way we liked it. We all chose patterns and colors together. We chose an elegant vertically striped damask, and a sunny yellow for the woodwork.

My bedroom had its own little balcony facing the street. I was thirteen years old and had never had a room of my own. I got to choose my own wallpaper. I picked a cheerful light blue with pretty little bouquets of flowers. The room was so tiny that it barely fit a folding bed. In the daytime, I folded it up under a broad bookshelf and closed a curtain in front of it. Only then would I have room to move my chair away enough from a narrow table so I could actually sit and do my homework. A cubby for clothes was mounted above my desk. I could hang some clothes on hooks on the wall next to it. A small trunk for treasures stood between the desk and the door to the balcony. I hung a mirror with a little shelf above the trunk to serve as my vanity.

I have precious memories of long hours, my father reading or writing at his desk, me curled up on the couch with a good book and my mother playing her favorite Chopin. We were home, we loved each other, all was peaceful.

We were always looking forward to vacations when my brother would be home from his boarding school when we played endless games of Mah Jong, which we continued throughout the year. Reinier would always take care of the complicated calculations, just as he had loved counting cars when he was a little boy. He loved numbers and statistics as much as he loved soccer. He kept endless records of all the scores of Holland's soccer clubs. Feyenoord, the Rotterdam soccer team, remained his favorite throughout his life. Many years later, as an editor of a regional paper, he created contests for readers about which clubs played where and when and what the scores were, all based on his decades of seamless record-keeping.

Sunday morning breakfast was my favorite meal of the week, especially when Reinier was home. After returning from Sunday mass, we set the breakfast table as only the Dutch can. A big pot of tea was kept warm in a tea cozy on a small side table next to my mom. A basket with soft-boiled eggs had a little knit blanket to keep them warm, a bread basket with slices of brown and white bread, pumpernickel, spice bread (ontbijtkoek) and crackers, a platter with sliced cheese and ham or prosciutto, then a plethora of jams and jellies, chocolate sprinkles, peanut butter and marmite, and most importantly, real butter because it was Sunday. On weekdays we had only margarine to put on our bread with a smaller assortment of cheese and other toppings. Next to each plate sat a fine china teacup with a dainty little teaspoon and a small egg cup. The last item to be brought to the table was a hot bun for each of us. We felt rich like kings and cherished this happiest of family time together.

Eating a soft-boiled egg involves a small ritual of tapping the back of your knife in a circle around the top of the egg, then inserting the tip of the knife under it to lift off the top carefully so the soft yolk won't spill over the edge. Now you set the egg back in its cup, sprinkle a little salt on it, dip a thin strip of buttered bread into the soft yolk, and quickly bring it to your mouth so you catch it before it dribbles down. I swear it is the most delicious way to eat an egg!

A Sunday morning breakfast wouldn't go by without my father playing a silly little game with me. He would have finished his egg and surreptitiously put it upside down back into the egg cup so it would look like a new egg again. He would then sweetly offer it to me, "Would you like another egg, Angela?" I would happily accept the unexpected pleasure of getting an extra egg from him, feigning great surprise. "Oh, yumm! Thank you, Dad!" Then I'd carefully cut off the top of the egg, discover it was empty and play out my fury at having been fooled by him, much to everyone's delight.

One Sunday morning, we had all just sat down, the tea was poured, and I got up to fetch something from the kitchen. When I came back, I sensed a faint air of suspense. I sat down, started eating and when I took a sip of my tea, it was very salty. Inwardly, I chuckled at the prank. I wouldn't give them the satisfaction. Without moving a muscle in my face, I set the cup back down and continued with my breakfast as if nothing out of the ordinary had happened. Soon my brother couldn't stand the suspense any longer. Puzzled by my lack of reaction, he decided to check if maybe it wasn't so bad. He scooped a spoonful of salt into his own tea and took a swallow. "Aaarggh," he yelled, spitting it back into his cup. "It's disgusting!" We all laughed so hard. Everyone was quite impressed with my impeccable self-control. I know my dad was particularly delighted and proud of me. He had been the merry prankster in his family from early on.

Bonding with My Father

When my father finally had come home for good, I was thirteen. Suddenly, his love filled my world. His body is warm, his skin is golden, his heart so generous and his mind vaster than the sky.

He looks into my eyes with deep love and twinkling smiles. He showers me with compliments like I am the most beautiful girl he has ever seen. All of a sudden, from having felt like being nothing much at all, I feel adored. He makes it abundantly clear how much he delights in me. I am soaking it up.

He speaks the language of mystics and saints, of poets and philosophers and of wild, passionate, lovers. He readily expresses his disdain for the ordinary lives and small-mindedness of most people. His imagination knows no bounds. He breaks open the world I have known, a world of loneliness and predictability, so stiflingly proper, everything moving like orderly clockwork, so very boring.

All those years, I silently observed the unhappy demeanor of the sisters who called themselves the Brides of Christ. Poor Christ, I thought. With all their talk of a loving Jesus and his sweet Mother Mary, no love shone in their eyes, so severe and controlled, their hearts and bodies completely covered, only the bare necessity of faces and hands exposed. I would peek into the deep folds of their black habits, looking for something that might betray the presence of a real live body. A large silver cross always hung heavily over their well-hidden flattened breasts. White stiffness encased their unfriendly faces.

In one of his letters to me when I was still in boarding school, my father had referred to "the good sisters." I understood then, with a disturbing pang, that he had no idea what they were really like and what kind of world I lived in. I vaguely comprehended that he might be trying to get on their good side since they always read the mail.

Now I am home. I love it when my father is comfortably seated in his armchair, a cup of coffee by his side, cigarette between his fingers, reading the paper or a book, the ashtray filling steadily. Especially during the hours after dinner, when my mother is still in the kitchen, he turns to me and starts talking. She never joins us. When she comes back in, she sits down to play the piano, as if not wanting to disturb us.

Much later, I wondered what went on in my mother. I imagine she had little or no patience with her husband's long monologues and his unbridled fantasies. After all, it was his enthusiasm that had drawn her back into the idealism of Nazi Germany and which had caused all of us such horrendous distress. Also, she and I had only been reunited for about one year before he came home. We had enjoyed such a sweet, affectionate time being together after seven long years of separation. Now, she found herself in the shadow of his overwhelming personality, and lost me, too. Everything had changed. I was drawn to him like a bee to honey.

My father speaks of worlds beyond worlds in fascinating flights of mind. I fill myself with him, I need his love so much. He opens vistas to me deep into the universe of his soul. His words are a blend of Eastern and Christian mysticism. Spirituality and sexuality are his two favorite topics, inextricably intertwined. I find myself quite naturally resonating with him spiritually as if he were revealing truths that were somehow already known to me in the deeper recesses of my being. I often would nod in agreement or find myself whispering, "I know, I know."

Sometimes he seems at a loss for words and drops into deep, long silences, pregnant with meaning. It was a lot to absorb as

I scrambled to keep up with him. I loved these special times with my father. Here I was at last with the one and only human being who had ever bothered to sit down and talk with me as if I actually mattered.

One conversation made an indelible imprint on me. With a soft thoughtful voice, almost as if conspiring with me, he leaned over, "You know, you're not really like all the other girls in your school. You have experienced so much in your young life. You're really much wiser than they are." Puzzled, I remember looking inside of myself and seeing only white, like a blank slate. Was he talking about me? I who barely existed and had no sense of self or value? He seemed to be creating me out of nothing.

But his tales of sexual adventures, however fascinating, were at times disturbing. Sometimes, I would feel overwhelmed with too much information. After all, I was only thirteen and completely innocent. I knew nothing. Even though my mother had been a doula, I didn't even know how babies came out of a mother's body. By the time I was fourteen, in one year's time, my father had thoroughly educated me about every imaginable sexual fetish and deviation under the sun, his favorites being the need for submission and domination. He told me later that he was motivated to make sure I would become a wise woman who would fully understand her eventual husband and know how to meet his needs; that I would not turn out like the Dutch housewife who walks around in slippers with curlers in her hair, making sure her front porch is scrubbed clean, whose husband has to turn to prostitutes to get his sexual needs met.

Any fostering of awareness and respect for my own needs and preferences was completely missing in the countless hours he talked with me, or should I say, talked *at* me. Not a word was ever said that I had the right to refuse a man's advances or even the freedom to consider whether his proposals were appealing to me. Later, looking back, I thought he wanted me to become the most compassionate and understanding great mother-whore that ever lived. My mother never interfered or contradicted. She remained silent in the background.

Having been so neglected in my past, I soaked up his affection and attention like a sponge. However, my father definitely violated my boundaries! Not only because of the sexual content but also by the unspoken demand to keep listening without a break to what seemed like unending hours of monologue of great intensity directed at me. I was his captive audience! I now call it *psychic incest*.

It took me until I was forty years old to learn that I had a right to say No! and quite a bit longer to even know, let alone speak, my own needs and desires. So, I became a helpless victim of overwhelming men who not only loved to indulge in their own stories and wouldn't give me any space but also felt free to impose their sexual needs on me, whilst I had no idea how to assert myself.

Somewhere inside of me, I must have felt like I was living a lie. No matter how much praise and admiration my father lavished upon me, even as I was happy to receive it, all dissipated in the quicksand of my confused internal self, laced with the insecurity anchored in some forgotten depth of shame and fear and empty nothingness. The shadow of my father's unspeakable past loomed dark and unseen. I had no way of reconciling this loving man, full of life, with the shame he had inflicted upon our family. Nor could I bridge the gaping hole between my forgotten childhood and the competent, bright, cheerful, sweet and juicy young woman I was becoming. Nevertheless, I appreciate deeply how his love and praise boosted my self-esteem and allowed me to face the world with my head held high.

Much later, I realized, how out of nothing, he had put me on a very high horse indeed. That, combined with belonging to a class which considered itself elite by birthright, provided a ready breeding ground in my subconscious mind for a high degree of righteous arrogance and superiority. Having been at the mercy of righteous nuns in my formative years only compounded the complex.

And so my father's unbridled adulation of me solidified the isolation I had already internalized from my younger days. If you are that unique, you don't belong with the rest of humankind. The only belonging I knew was with God and with my larger-than-life father, which was undoubtedly the source of my lifelong restless search for an *extraordinary man* who might match my father's enormous imprint.

My Father Talks with Me about the War

Off and on during my high school years, my father told me fragments of what had happened during the war. I already described the enthusiasm of the men in his work camp when they carried him around on their shoulders to celebrate my birth. Sometime, during the middle of the war, when he was still commander of the camp, he had received an order to take his men to the Eastern Front with whatever ammunition they had in store. He knew that the supply lines to the front were poor and that his men would simply serve as cannon fodder. He could not, in good conscience, accept that responsibility. To save his own hide, he joined the SS as his only way out.

When he came in front of his superior and told him of his refusal, just as the order was given to execute him for disobedience, he turned his lapel and showed his SS insignia. The SS were untouchable and he was let go.

Later, after we fled from Holland, he had presented himself at SS headquarters in Berlin. Just weeks before the end of the war, he and a group of others were sent back into Holland to undermine the Dutch resistance. They were under Otto Scorzeny's command and referred to as the Zeppelin Commando. My father told me how they were set up to mistrust one another completely.

After he brought our little family into what he had believed to be relative safety in Groningen, in the north of Holland, he went to rejoin his comrades. The group confiscated an estate near a lake in Loosdrecht in the heart of Holland. They imprisoned the inhabitants in the basement, together with other captives they suspected to be part of the Dutch resistance. The group began planning the prisoners' torture. My father knew that the rogues in his company would only be too happy to get their vengeful hands on them. He volunteered to do the torturing.

My father told me that he intended to protect the prisoners from his mean-spirited cohorts and that, privately, his heart went out to the captives. In the process of torturing them, he said he hoped that his love for them would make their suffering more tolerable. When he spoke to me about it, I sensed that his attitude around sadomasochism may have led him to believe that he could bring them secretly to ecstasy. At the same time, he had to be convincing for his comrades. His toughness had to impress them, or they would surely snatch that responsibility from him.

It seems that captives are tortured in all wartime situations when people wield absolute power over others. We see it constantly in the news today, wherever there is armed conflict. Something must happen to the human spirit in the circumstances of war, where values that seem essential to human nature, such as not to harm one another, give way to unimaginable cruelty. Perhaps the combination of living in acute fear for one's own life, together with the need to appear fierce and powerful, causes us to project the shame of our own weakness onto the helpless captive, violently unleashing the intensity of the internal stress.

When my father's group realized the war was ending, they wanted to be rid of the prisoners. They did not want any witnesses to their cruelty. In the rush of those last days, according to my father, the plan was to put them all in a leaking boat and send them off into the middle of the lake to drown. This plan always puzzled me since it seemed like a rather unreliable way to kill people. I wonder if the plan was not to kill them first and then drown the bodies in the lake.

My father told me that he had to agree with the mad scheme at the risk of his own safety, but could not accept participating in murder. He secretly went to the Sicherheits-Dienst to report his group's intent, begging them to dismantle the group. After doing so, he managed to sneak back in and avoided raising his companions' suspicion. In the dark of night, Dutch armed troops surrounded the property and charged in. They were all taken captive.

It soon became clear to his comrades that my father had betrayed them. Now he was an enemy to all, a traitor to the Dutch and a traitor to his own men. From all sides, he was hated with a vengeance. Because of this, I suspect that some of the charges may be questionable. However, there is no doubt in my mind that he did commit heinous crimes for which he was sentenced to death at the post-war court in The Hague. The British prosecutor punched his teeth out inside the courtroom.

I remember when I was maybe sixteen years old, my father took me for a nasty surprise. I was sitting in the living room, reading quietly. Suddenly, the door opened and he came in, hiding his face. "You want to see how terrible I can look?" He revealed his face. I gasped, horrified. He had pulled his thin dark hair in strands over his face. A tooth stuck out of the corner of his mouth. His grimace was so frighteningly evil, he looked like a monster. When he saw my shock, he quickly rearranged his face and tried to laugh it all away.

It seemed he took pride in his skill of making himself look so terrifying. This skill might have been considered an art form if he did not have such a sinister history. I shudder to imagine what he must have looked like to his prisoners. Later, I wondered if, unconsciously, he wanted me to know what he had been like then.

My father was incarcerated on death row in Scheveningen. He told me about the sounds. "Every time I would hear a guard approach, his keys clanging loudly, I thought, this is it. He is coming for me. These may be my last few minutes." At times, those around him were taken out into the prison's courtyard and shot. Pieters, who was the head of their group, was the last one to be executed. In 1948, the death penalty was abolished. All death sentences were converted to life in prison.

While in prison, my father returned to Catholicism and renewed his previous interest in the world's great mystics and philosophers. I am sure his choice of books from the prison library marked him as an unusual prisoner, as did his inclination to initiate profound conversations with the librarian and the prison clergy.

My father spent ten years in prison amidst the worst of criminals. Some of that time in isolation. He was marked for life.

Naturally, when my father spoke to me, his teenage daughter whom he loved, he presented himself as not quite so evil as one might suspect from an ex-SS man who had been sentenced to death. It seemed that he particularly wanted me to realize that there was often an underlying noble cause for the decisions he made which inadvertently led him down such an ominous path. He certainly did not include any of the gory details.

My Adolescence

Transitioning from a backward boarding school in the Dutch countryside to a Catholic all-girls lyceum in the big city of Rotterdam was not easy. After I took the entrance exam, my mother was called in. They told her that, officially, I had failed. I was behind in all subjects, but apparently, my language skills and comprehension were above average. They were willing to give me a chance, and I was accepted. It turned out that Sister

Louise, one of their nuns, was a distant relative of our family. She had been quite excited to discover her family name on the list of applicants, which probably earned me some special consideration.

Socially, I was completely inexperienced. While I no longer felt like an outcast, I could not relate to my seemingly sophisticated peers—lively, uncomplicated girls who had friends, played tennis, knew how to swim and generally had grown up in "good" families. I didn't even know how to ride a bicycle, which is unheard of when you're twelve years old in Holland.

I failed my first year with D's and F's in almost all subjects. This was not surprising, since I'd just emerged from the boondocks into the big city without any preparation. Both the teachers and my parents were kind and understanding and I was heartily encouraged to try again.

A strange thing happened during my second time around of that first year in high school. Suddenly, I had status. Everything had changed. I was the one who knew her way around the school and was familiar with the teachers and the curriculum. I was immediately chosen to be the class representative.

That's when I met Yvonne, a beautiful Indonesian girl, who was a bit older than the rest of us because she'd spent a few years in a sanatorium with tuberculosis. Since I was now a year older than the other girls in our class, we naturally gravitated toward each other. I was thirteen. She was sixteen. My first friend. Her velvet brown eyes, the gorgeous, warm color of her skin and her Indonesian culture drew me to the depth and the mystery of her. She quickly became my first crush.

Yvonne lived with her mother and a couple of her older brothers. The father, who may have been a Dutchman, was nowhere

With my Indonesian friend Yvonne at the Expo in Brussels

in sight. I often went to visit her. She had her own room, quite a large one. She would play the guitar and I would gaze at her, mesmerized. I longed to get close to her and touch her cheeks. She looked so warm and appealing. I never dared. It turned out to be a pretty one-sided friendship. She rarely came to my house. In spite of her warm appearance, she was rather cold and standoffish.

My classmates elected me as class representative again and again during all my years at the lyceum. Every year, their confidence in me would catch me by surprise. I found a new self-respect there and my shame and insecurity went underground, where it continued crawling under my skin, out of sight, even below my own awareness. Nobody at school knew anything about my father's past or mine. My identity solidified around belonging to a respectable upper-class family, attending one of the best schools, being intelligent and feeling respected and, last but not least, becoming quite a sexy young woman. I strutted around on high heels, dressed in fine quality hand-me-downs from one of my wealthier cousins, with my long hair often coiffed into an elegant chignon. I grew accustomed to compliments on my beautiful, big brown eyes and my lovely appearance. One of my younger cousins, who attended the same school, once told me I had the nicest legs in the entire school.

When I was fifteen my parents enrolled me in ballroom dancing classes, a skill every self-respecting teenager needed in those days. None of us Catholic boys and girls, all attending gender-segregated high schools, had ever been thrown into such proximity with one another. I found myself looking around for the one boy who would be right for me. I loved dancing.

A Christmas ball for boys and girls from all the Catholic high schools in Rotterdam was announced. At the large venue, a bundle of mistletoe hung in the center of the floor. The couple who got to dance right under it was supposed to kiss! I was sixteen and had never been kissed. I felt excited and apprehensive at the same time. I tried to imagine what it would be like. Some fairytale dream would surely come true. I was going to be kissed by a prince!

The place was packed. At first, the boys and girls were directed to opposite sides of the dance floor and guided to walk in counter-clockwise circles, passing each other. Then the boys were told to pick a girl. I wasn't picked during the first round. I felt quite worried and confused, wondering if I wasn't all that attractive after all. We were also told that anyone was free to tap a dancer on the shoulder, who would then have to change partners and dance with us.

I frantically looked around for an attractive young man. As masses of moving bodies twirled passed, I finally spotted a handsome, dark-haired Adonis. I tapped him on the back and we began to dance together. When we approached the mistletoe, I was full of anticipation. At last, we were directly under it. I kissed him eagerly. As we moved away, pushed around by the crowd, he said, "It would be much more appealing if you were a little bashful!" leaving me quite mortified. When we twirled back under the mistletoe, I was appropriately shy and he approved. Then a boy from my dance class, who I found particularly unappealing, got a hold of me. He slobbered all over and into my mouth with a vengeance. It was disgusting.

However, dancing lessons opened a new world for me. I loved to dance and was good at it, from the quick-step and the slow-fox, the English waltz, but especially the tango. That's where my temperament found an outlet. Then came the South American dances, the rumba, the mambo, the calypso and the cha cha cha. I loved the sexy moves. I quickly moved up through the classes and soon was eligible to participate in dancing contests. I didn't

Ballroom dancing contest

notice that my high school peers never got that far, and I found myself among blue-collar boys and girls only. I was paired with a compatible dancer and we began to train to compete.

One day, my dancing instructor invited my father over for a private conversation. He said to my dad, "On cruise ships, you'll have the high-class dancing on the upper deck. They're all pretty stiff. On the middle deck the dancing gets better. But on the lower deck, where the common folk are, that's where you see the really fantastic dancing. Your daughter is unusual. She dances like the people on the lower deck, which is obviously not where she belongs. I just thought you should know."

My father happily shared this story with me, chuckling. He was so proud of me. He loved that I was a juicy dancer and didn't seem to worry at all that I was surrounded by "common" boys with the supposed risk that I might fall in love with a man below my standing.

What no one expected was that I should have been protected from my own family, not from those common boys! One weekend, my family went to a large gathering at a castle in the country-side, which brought together members from various branches of the van de Loo family tree, many of whom had never met. A distant uncle, named Broer (brother in Dutch) showed particular interest in me. I was seventeen. He was thirty-five, short and somewhat overweight. Not particularly appealing. I was too young to realize how my childhood deprivation set me up to find any interest shown toward me, especially by men, completely irresistible. When he promised to come and visit me and take me out to dinner, I felt special and wanted.

So he did. My parents agreed. Broer wined and dined me and lavished me with attention. I was flattered, which quite overshadowed the fact that I did not particularly like him. He started to call on me regularly and flirted with me unabashedly, and soon we started petting in his car. He would get his hand into my panties, open his fly and encourage me to pleasure him. Even though it wasn't all that pleasant, I figured this is what you are supposed to do. I had never gone that far before.

Looking back, my parents must have been well aware of the potential problem posed by this uncle getting close to me. They did not seem to have the courage to address the issue with me or, better yet, to tell him to go packing and leave me alone. Not that I would have accepted that without a fight, strong-willed as I was. This went on for a while.

In an attempt to offer me guidance, my father drove me to The Hague to visit a Jesuit priest, who was his confessor. My father went in first and I sat in a small waiting area. After some time, they came out and in the semi-dark doorway to a large colonial-style conference room, my father introduced me to the short, rotund, balding priest in black robes. With his pudgy hand, he shook mine and broke out in a big smile, exclaiming, "My, what beautiful brown eyes you have!" I can't help but be reminded of Little Red Riding Hood.

The priest invited me to take a seat at the large mahogany table. In a soft, caring voice he asked me questions about my "friend." "Does he touch you?" he asked. "Does he make you touch him?" Slightly blushing, I admitted that he did. The priest gently took my hands in his and said, "Look at these lovely hands of yours. Keep your innocence, Angela. Don't let them get soiled."

Afterward, my father took me to the beach. We had coffee on one of the many terraces that line the beaches in Schevenigen. Soon after we sat down, a young man started eyeing me from across the terrace. When I returned from a trip to the restroom, he was sitting at our table, apparently invited by my father to join us. When we were ready to go back to Rotterdam, the young man mentioned that he incidentally had some business to attend to in Rotterdam. My father generously offered him a ride and suggested he sit in the back seat with me so we could get to know each other. My father's unique way of helping me solve my problem.

However, my relationship with Broer continued. During one of our dinners together, Broer said that he would love to take me for a picnic someday, to a very special place—a beautiful spot alongside one of our big rivers where we could go for a swim. That sounded like fun to me. I made it quite clear to him that my virginity was very important to me and I did not want to lose it before getting married. I was still a good Catholic girl. I made him promise to respect my wish.

On a sunny afternoon, he picked me up with a picnic basket packed with goodies in the back seat and we headed into the countryside. We drove for a while. The special spot was a grassy clearing amidst the reeds on the banks of the river Waal. In the distance, I could see the large double bridge in Dordrecht, one for traffic and one for the railroad. We spread our blanket and had our picnic. I enjoyed the quiet, sitting amongst the tall reeds, the light on the water, the clucking of waterfowl. It's a rare treat to be alone in nature in the Netherlands as overpopulated as our country is. Like most girls in Holland who have practiced on our always crowded beaches, I was quite skilled at getting into my bathing suit without revealing any essential body parts, so when it was time to swim, I changed using this technique. Of course, there was the critical moment of slipping off my underwear from under my skirt before stepping into my bathing suit. No sooner were my panties at my feet when he jumped upon me, throwing me to the ground and shoving himself between my legs. He was strong like an ape.

"No!" I shouted. I fought and screamed with all my might, until in the split second when I felt my strength give out and I had to take a breath, he forced himself through my hymen. The moment I felt my body give, I pushed him off me in one powerful burst of rage. He landed several feet down the incline of the river bank. I brought my hand between my legs. It was covered with blood.

I howled from the very core of me. I believed I had lost God. I had lost my virginity. I couldn't stop wailing and Broer became concerned. He stammered an apology and tried to comfort me. After I calmed down a bit, he told me that he had a Chinese friend who was a gynecologist. He would take me there to see if my hymen could be restored. We drove all the way back to my home in silence.

I was terribly upset and ashamed and couldn't talk about the experience, not even with my father. Later, Broer did take me to visit his friend, a courteous Chinese man who had an examination table with stirrups (in his living room!). He was very friendly and understanding and examined me. He told me the hymen was only partially torn and no, unfortunately there wasn't anything he could do about it. My relationship with Broer was already finished.

I always hated wearing napkins during my periods and after a few months I realized that since my virginity was lost, I should be able to use tampons. My mother always gave me money to buy my monthly supplies. Tampons were more expensive than napkins, so I had to ask her for more money. When I hesitantly told her that I wanted to get tampons, she broke out in a bizarre tirade, saying, "The pope recently gave an audience to a large group of midwives from all over the world. He told them that the use of tampons was forbidden because women would have to touch themselves!" I was shocked. I had worried that she might ask me about losing my virginity, but instead, I was confronted with this sickening piece of Catholic ideology. Grumbling, she consented to give me the little bit of extra money.

As the months passed, I felt more and more estranged from my mother and disenchanted with the Catholic church. My father was particularly kind to me. I felt that he sensed that I was having a difficult time, but we never spoke about what had led me to separate from Broer. The shock of the rape slowly slid out of sight into the underground reservoir of my shame.

Gregarious as he was, my father often picked up hitchhikers on his many business trips around the country. One day he brought home a charming young man named Simon, who lived in Eindhoven in the south of Holland. We quickly became friends and enjoyed each other's company. It didn't take long for us to fall in love. He was very sweet and good-looking with a friendly, slightly crooked face which only enhanced his charm. My parents allowed me to go and visit him for the weekend. He lived with his parents in a nice home with a large garden in the suburb, within walking distance of woods and heather, where we could find quiet spots for some sweet necking.

I slept in the guest room upstairs, across from his parents' bedroom. Simon slept downstairs. After everyone was sound asleep, he would quietly climb up the rain pipe and crawl through my bedroom window. We would snuggle up and have a sweet time. Because we were both Catholic and innocent, we remained modest even though we were quite attracted to one another. In the daytime, Simon would serenade me on his guitar and sing sweet songs to me. I wrote a poem about the adorable soft curly fur on his chest and arms. We were happily in love. I must have felt somewhat redeemed after my nasty beginnings in the realm of love and physical closeness.

In the meantime, school continued as if nothing particular had happened to me. Social events were beginning to get organized between the different Catholic high schools in Rotterdam. A few young men started a magazine called the *Interscholaire*, to cover anything that interested us. I wrote a scathing article about a dance evening with a live band. The music had been quite terrible and the band leader had treated us like immature children.

Me at 17 (in love)

I had felt insulted and enjoyed spewing my righteous indignity. The editors were impressed and happily welcomed me in their midst. I had a voice!

Ton, a skinny, dark-haired, intense young man, and his best friend, Frans, were the editors of this publication. I became one of their regular contributors. During a party they had organized—the Beatles had just come on the scene and we all loved their lively romantic songs—Ton asked me to dance. He was rather clumsy on the dance floor, but with my dancing skills and my intuitive kindness, I managed to guide him into a fairly decent dancing experience. He kept wanting to dance with me.

A few days later he invited me to take a walk. He confessed that he had fallen madly in love with me. He had never had such a wonderful experience dancing with a girl and he knew I was the one for him. "I'm so sorry to disappoint you," I said, taken aback. "I am not available. I have a boyfriend in Eindhoven." He kept pursuing me. He begged and cajoled and argued that he deserved to have a chance. This went on for weeks or months, even though I kept denying him. But, apparently, I was unable to set my boundaries clearly enough. He kept wiggling his way into my heart and mind. There certainly was a sweetness about him. He would surprise me by picking me up from high school and produce a frumpled little bouquet of anemones from under his jacket when I got near him.

Since Simon lived in another town, Ton had much greater access to me. Like a lawyer defending his case, insisting that it was my duty to be fair, he finally wore me down and I agreed to give him three months. When I reluctantly explained my situation to Simon, he ended our relationship there and then. I was heartbroken and resentful of Ton. Still, I could not boot him out of my life and, defeated, agreed to be in a romantic relationship with him. I broke the relationship off a number of times, each time only for Ton to return with renewed determination. It was his apparent suffering at my hands which made me cave in again and again. I couldn't stand the guilt.

Since my rape, I had become quite promiscuous, feeling I had nothing left to lose, and I sure liked getting close to boys. Enjoying freely kissing and necking on Friday night and then having to go to confession on Saturday morning quickly became too contradictory for me. Also, I was deeply repulsed when, in religion class, I learned about the Catholic dogmas surrounding matters of life and death pertaining to women in childbirth. When a doctor has to choose between the life of the mother and that of the baby, even if she has a whole brood of children already, he has to choose the life of the child and let the mother die, never mind all the orphans she would leave behind. I could barely tolerate this religion anymore which had once been so very dear to me. Mass lost its mysticism, all I saw was tomfoolery and manipulation. I was truly done with it. I needed to leave the church. I talked with Ton, who was two years older than I and

At the beach

had already left the Catholic Church. He supported me in my decision. I said to God, "I will never again believe what I am told by others. If you exist, you'll have to show me directly. I will only believe my own experience and if you do exist that must surely be alright with you." I did not doubt for one minute that if God existed, my absolute honesty would certainly be valued. So began my secular phase.

Uncle René

As I mentioned before, my father took a strong interest in my spiritual and sexual education. He seemed to be particularly committed to making sure that I understood the spiritual depth and significance of sadomasochism. He explained to me that it was out of profound love that the dominator would gently inflict ever-increasing intensity of sensation to the recipient in order to induce in her a state of complete surrender, a giving up of all resistance and a profound acceptance of love in all its intensity, ultimately causing her to dissolve in ecstatic abandon. Guiding the beloved into a total dissolution of the self was the singular and highest purpose of sadomasochism. Even then I understood it to be a powerful, if unusual, path to accomplish the release of the ego's surrender.

I don't know about the network through which my parents came in contact with those who shared these views and practices. My mother continued to pretend that the men and women who came to visit us were merely friends.

One day, my parents shared their excitement with me about having come into contact with an artist in Sweden. He was creating a painting my father had commissioned from him, and he was planning to come visit. The anticipation of his arrival was palpable. When I finally met him, he did not seem all that interesting to me. He looked kind of bland, a bit puffy and slightly disheveled. He brought a few of his oil paintings. The one he made for my father was of a joker sitting on a mountain ledge overlooking a river valley far below, blowing bubbles from a long curved meerschaum pipe. Later in life, I came to understand that he had painted The Fool from the Tarot. It seemed a perfect fit for my father's free-spiritedness and his desire to be unbound from all ordinary constraints.

Since I left the house for school around 8:30 in the morning and did not return till after 3:00, they had plenty of time to go about their business. Never was there a trace left of their adventures by the time I came home, and we all enjoyed tea and cookies and polite conversation in a perfectly proper fashion. Everyone present was silently in cahoots with my mother to pretend that nothing out of the ordinary ever happened in our home. I quietly played along. Those were the unspoken rules.

Sometime after my misadventure with Broer, I came home from school to the sound of music. A distinguished-looking older gentleman was playing the violin accompanied by my mother at the piano. He was introduced to me as 'Uncle René.' He was visiting us incognito because of his high social standing. I never knew his real name. He came from an old aristocratic family and had spent several years as a young artist in Paris, painting and making music. Against his artistic inclinations, he eventually succumbed to his family's demand to pursue a respectable career. Eventually, he became the director of one of Holland's big national banks. Wearing an expensive tailor-made suit, a vest buttoned up over his generous girth and a monocle on a gold chain tucked in a little breast pocket, he would lean back in the easy chair, close his eyes and thoughtfully puff on his aromatic pipe. His was a remarkable face with piercing eyes and a sharp angular nose above a bristly moustache. Thin strands of shoulder-length gray hair neatly combed and parted suggested his bohemian streak. His voice, too, was distinguished; he spoke in clipped phrases, slightly wheezing in between puffs on his pipe. He was quite brilliant and endowed with a unique sense of humor. I had never met such a fine man.

Afterwards, my father confided in me. Not only was 'Uncle René' a grand master of the Freemasons, but he was also a great adept in the art of sadomasochism. He owned one of the finest collections of leather whips and other related artifacts and pornographic literature in the country. We were in the fifties and pornography was still illegal and completely underground.

Uncle René became a regular visitor, officially because my mother and he loved to make music together. I enjoyed coming home to their little house concerts. As the two played, my father would be moving about, happily beaming in the background. Then we would visit over tea and cookies. These were delightful times in our home. Everybody was happy and there was always a sense of festivity in the air. Uncle René was utterly charming to both me and my mother.

One afternoon my mother announced that Uncle René, who had clearly become rather fond of me, wanted to visit with me alone. She and my dad were going to the movies, she said. That had never happened before. I felt a little flustered, but also honored and curious. When my parents left after dinner, I made some coffee and poured him a small glass of cognac. I may have had some, too. I was barely eighteen.

He was quite skilled at making me feel very special. My clothes did not come off that evening, but there was plenty of playful teasing. He drew me onto his lap planting affectionate kisses on my cheeks and joking about the special thrill of his tickling moustache on my skin. He spanked me lightly on my butt but did nothing too serious. I felt giggly and warm and aroused by our little cat-and mouse games. Of course, by the time my parents came home, we made sure to look absolutely proper. My parents' collusion was seamless.

A month or so later, my mother announced that Uncle René wanted to take me to dinner at a fine restaurant in Amsterdam. I could barely believe my good fortune. Since our family was quite poor, we rarely dined out. For special occasions we might go to one of the affordable Indonesian restaurants, which, due to Dutch colonialism, were quite common in Holland.

Uncle René picked me up in his sleek silver Studebaker. We drove through the beautiful Dutch countryside for a while and then to the restaurant Het Zwarte Schaap (The Black Sheep) in the heart of Amsterdam. It is one of the most exclusive restaurants in Holland. I was treated like royalty. The environment was intimate and super chic, the food was incredible and the wine was warm. René confided that he had a special attic in one of the old mansions along the canals, which contained his entire collection of the finest whips and state-of-the-art S&M tools.

Would I be interested to go there with him and see it? We could play some poker and have a liqueur for dessert, he said. That sounded exciting to me, so off we went.

We arrive at one of the old colonial houses on the Herengracht, a lawyer's office. He has a key to the building. Everything is dark. Up we climb several steep narrow flights of stairs. The last set of even narrower wooden steps brings us to the attic. When he turns on the light, I feel like I am entering a medieval world. The warm light casts a glow on the wooden paneled walls and bounces off countless, fascinating implements, most of them made of leather. A great variety of whips decorate the walls. Some are solid, some thin, with all kinds of strands, some knotted, others braided. He explains how each one is designed for a very particular sensation and how important it is always to start gently, and slowly increase the arousal until the recipient eventually begs for more intensity.

In the center of the space stands a large leather horse. All kinds of grips and ropes hang from the ceiling. A bed is half hidden in a small alcove with a dark brocade curtain as I had seen in paintings from the old Dutch masters.

We sit at a little table. He pours us each a small glass of Cointreau and produces the poker dice. He suggests, "Whenever you win, I will put ten guilders on the table, and when I win," his eyes twinkle at me, "you will take off a piece of clothing. What do you think of that?" I laugh a bit nervously, realizing somewhere in the back of my mind that I am skirting rather close to the edge of prostitution, but, since this is a game, and I actually feel very safe and respected with him, the clever little ruse works with my full cooperation. I do like the money!

When the game is over and I am not wearing much of anything, the real playtime begins. By now, I do understand that none of this is about hurting me but rather about giving me pleasure and him too, of course. "Feel how soft this is," he lets me touch a fine multi-stringed whip. It feels silky soft. It couldn't possibly hurt. He suggests that I bend over the leather horse and pull down my panties a bit. Ever so gently, he strokes my bottom with the silky strings and lets them slide all over me. Then he begins with soft but well-aimed strokes alternating with firm but gentle slaps of his hand. It all feels very nice. In between the spanking, he gently caresses my buttocks. He then picks a new whip, shows it to me and explains its specific purpose. With that one, the intensity slowly increases and my butt is getting pretty hot. I'm laughing a lot because it is such an unusual experience. I find it all quite amusing.

When I feel like my bum is burning, he fills a hot water bottle and guides me to lay face down on the bed in the alcove. Then he lovingly places the hot bottle on my burning cheeks. "Here, this will make it feel better." It does.

I never felt like begging for more. In fact, when I got quite aroused, I only wanted to get close to him, kiss and make love. He did recline with me and hold me, but his interest waned and we just rested in each others' arms. Much later, my father told me that he and René had discussed the experience and concluded that S&M wasn't my thing. I figured that he set me up with René to find out if I shared their inclination. I did not.

When I got home and my mother found out that I had been to the attic, she was rather upset and acted as if René had betrayed her trust. What did she think he would do? I was astonished by her naïveté. At that moment, I began to realize more fully the depth of her hypocrisy.

Years later, after my first marriage had broken up, I was studying psychology and living on my own in Amsterdam. René came to visit me a few times. He would bring a bottle of fine wine and I'd provide the brie and crackers. We enjoyed our conversations. Once, he gifted me with a record of Brahms' Clarinet Quintet, Opus 115. Silently, we lay together on my bed, fully clothed, listening to the heavenly music. It was a most exquisite experience. The quintet became one of my all-time favorites. I still have the record he gave me. This gift made me feel like he knew my soul.

During his last visit to me, I was then in my mid-twenties, he admitted to feeling quite guilty about seducing me when I was barely eighteen years old. He said he had been very wrong and offered me his deeply felt apologies. I assured him I had never felt harmed by him and that I had very much enjoyed his attentions and our little adventure. It was obvious he could not really accept my view. He was full of remorse.

Paris

When high school came to an end, I was ready to spread my wings. I loved French, so I made plans to go to Paris for a year and work as an au pair. I would be housed and fed by a family and would receive a small stipend in exchange for taking care of the children in the morning. In the afternoon I would go and study French at the Alliance Française at the Sorbonne. The evenings were free. I contacted the agency that connects French families with foreign girls seeking these positions. When I received an address, I wrote the family a letter in the perfect French I had learned in school. They accepted.

After a six-hour train ride, I arrived in Paris and found my way to an imposing apartment building. I took an antique elevator to their floor and knocked on the door. When the lady of the house appeared, I greeted her with a "Bonjour Madame." She looked surprised and asked if I really had never been in France before. "Non, Madame, c'est la premiere fois que je sois ici." Apparently, the German girls she had employed before never spoke well and always had a heavy accent. Later, it appeared, this had made her distrustful of me from the beginning.

I loved Paris. I enjoyed figuring out the metro system. There, in the underground tiled hallways, I was surprised to see old women, their lips painted wiggly in bright red, wearing flowery dresses, clearly wanting to still look young and sexy. I would take the metro to the Sorbonne in the afternoon. I loved the classes. The French was rather advanced and I was pleased that I was good at doing the exercises. I met another Dutch girl and together we would be off afterwards to the Quartier Latin to hang out in cafes on the Boul'Mich, drink large cups of hot chocolate and go dance in the cellars. Sometimes, we climbed the stairs to the Sacré-Coeur, strolling among artists in Montparnasse, where we happily accepted an invitation to have our portraits painted. We also visited what became my favorite impressionist gallery, le Jeu de Paume.

Much to my chagrin, Ton, who had been conscripted into the Dutch army, had managed to get placed at the NATO base in Fontainebleau, just south of Paris. He was again pursuing me. He continued to insist that I was the only one for him and relentlessly turned on his charm. I couldn't help but respond to his efforts and finally simply could not resist. I agreed to get engaged. He gave me a ring. Wanting to respect my commitment, and aware of the intensity of his jealousy, I made a valiant effort to be faithful. Once, he brought me to his quarters so he could show me off to his compatriots at Fontainebleau.

One night, I was sitting by myself at a bar in one of the underground cellars. I met the bartender, Mack, a tall pock-faced American who was also stationed at Fontainebleau. We chatted in English until a German fellow sat next to me and I spoke with him in fluent German. I had already been speaking French to others. Mack turned to me in disbelief. "Where are you from?" he asked. "I'm from Holland!" "No! Speak some Dutch to me." I did. He was genuinely flabbergasted and of course, I was highly flattered. He begged for the next dance. Ducking low through a carved stone opening, we descended onto the dance floor. He was good and he was hot and he wanted me. I told him I was engaged. "Oh no! Please, please, I want to fuck you so bad," he pleaded in my ear, pressing me close. He never let up, although I kept resisting. Tighter and tighter he held me as we moved to the music, pleading all the while until my body was ablaze. "Come with me," he urged, "I'll take you to an American bar."

We jumped into a taxi and went to a dance hall favored by American GIs. We managed one dance, our bodies consumed by fire and quite drunk. "Let's go to a hotel," came his raw whisper in my ear. I was putty in his hands. I could barely walk. We stumbled into another taxi, got a hotel room and made love in wild abandon. That's when I experienced an overwhelming explosion like I never had before. I burst into tears from the sheer magnificence of it. I had just experienced my first orgasm!

Mack and I heard sirens and, unbelievable as it seemed, I sensed that the cops were looking for me. The next evening, Ton appeared on my doorstep, fuming. GIs coming home to their barracks the night before had told Ton that they had seen me with Mack. When he had not been able to reach me, he had actually called the police. During the confrontation that followed, I made the final break. I knew I did not really want him and I certainly was not ready for any kind of commitment. I threw his ring in the Seine and was done for good—or so I thought.

At some point, I felt it was time to look for another family since the distrust of the one I was with was getting to me. The *au pair* agency gave me a new address of a family with five boys who were urgently looking for an *au pair* girl to help. I was warned that they didn't have a spare room and I would have to sleep on a couch in the dining room.

When I arrived on the ninth floor of the high-rise, which was still under construction, I saw that the doorbell had not yet been installed. Two wires were sticking out of the wall. I touched one to the other and the bell rang. A thin, olive-skinned woman with a fascinating, birdlike face opened the door and exclaimed, "You are the first one to ring our bell! Even the workers bang on the door." She was happy to invite me in.

She told me she was a graphologist and asked for some of my writing. She had barely glanced at it, when she exclaimed, "Ah, que vous êtes intelligente!" I felt happy to be so warmly welcomed and appreciated by this strange but kind woman. We made an instant heartfelt connection. I agreed to sleep on the couch in the dining room. After I moved in, I was introduced to the boys. Thierry was the oldest at twelve, then Olivier. The youngest was an adorable little two-year-old, Benjamin. Their father, a short stocky man, was in the insurance business.

Everything went fine, until one morning when I was startled awake feeling a hand searching between my legs. "Shhh," he commanded. His wife was sleeping in the room to my left and his boys just down the hall to my right. There was not even a door to the dining room. I kept quiet as a mouse, not wanting to expose this man's shocking behavior to his family. Furiously, I pushed him from me.

Later he accused me of tempting him. He said, when I was in the shower one morning, I had failed to lock the door. When he had come in, he said that I had not covered myself completely and he had seen my breast, suggesting I had done that on purpose. I did remember that he had once rather violently crashed through the bathroom door, which I thought I had locked. I had quickly covered myself.

A few weeks later, he invited me to lunch. I thought that he wanted to make things right with me and, as usual, I felt flattered to be invited. He met me downtown and presented me with a beautiful mossy green silk shawl. Then, he drove us quite a ways to a rather expensive inn on the outskirts of Paris. We enjoyed a fancy lunch. When the waitress came at the end, he said to her, "We'll take our coffee upstairs." He turned to me and explained we would take our coffee on the terrace. I believed him.

The waitress guides us upstairs and pretty soon we are walking down a hall with many doors. No terrace in sight. Inwardly,

I groan. So well trained to be polite at all costs, I can't make a scene in front of the waitress. I feel ushered into a bedroom like a sheep being taken to the slaughter. I am also completely dependent on this man since I have no idea where I am. Just like Broer who took my virginity by force, this man is short, stocky and strong as an ape. At first, he argues and pushes me against the wall, trying to kiss me. Furious, I make it clear that I do not want him. He hurls me onto the bed and flings himself on top of me. I keep trying to fight him off but eventually don't have the strength and I am raped, again. While he was at it, he growled, "See, this is what you really want!" I felt completely defeated. This particular rape lodges itself into my body in a gnarly mix of shame, weakness and helplessness.

Shortly before that event, I had become involved with Constantin, a Russian artist, one of the many loners I would attract in my life. He had grown up as an orphan and spent most of his childhood roaming the woods around Besançon. I liked his pottery and to this day I still own one of the pieces he gifted me with. He also made a fine vodka from berries he had picked in the woods. He was short, with a broad face and a fine goatee. He hadn't been with a woman in many years. We grew quite fond of each other and I was glad that I had someone to talk to about what had happened to me. He was furious and threatened to go and confront the man. I pleaded with him not to do that, since I felt very protective of the wife.

A few weeks later, however, after I got home from the Sorbonne, monsieur and madame called me into their room. They were both looking very serious. He is standing behind her and she questions me about this Russian man I am seeing, who had come and accused her husband of giving me gonorrhea. How could I have possibly said such a thing about her husband, she asks. I am struck dumb. Behind her back, her husband is frantically signaling not to say anything or he will kill me. There is nothing I can do. I don't know what to say. I mumble that I don't know anything about gonorrhea. She looks at me puzzled. She can't understand because she knows this is not like me and I have no words to defend myself without betraying her husband.

When I saw Constantin again, he said he had gone to the hospital to get himself checked out, since he had experienced some discharge. He had already taken antibiotics though, so nothing could be found. The doctor told him that he could have had some discharge just because he had been sexually inactive for such a long time. I felt I needed to get myself checked out, too, so I went to the Hopital Salpêtrière. I was led to lie on a table in a semi-curtained-off cubicle in the enormous hospital hall, like a train station. I still recall how forlorn and embarrassed I felt, lying there with my legs spread wide for all to see. Nothing was found, but when I was told that the condition is easy to miss in women, I continued to feel insecure.

Sometime later, I met a handsome, medical student who lavishly complemented me on my excellent French. He was quite charming. After we had met a few times, he invited me to come and visit him in the hospital where he interned. He showed me into a little room and immediately began coming on to me. Figuring he wanted to have sex, I told him how I couldn't be sure that I didn't have gonorrhea. He didn't seem to mind and asked me to undress and undo my hair which I wore in a Grace Kelly chignon. When my hair fell down around my shoulders, he groaned, "Ah, la vâche!" I felt deeply insulted. I was not familiar with the expression and thought he had called me a cow. He then proceeded to rudely turn me over and penetrated me wildly from behind without any lubrication. It was excruciatingly painful. I screamed. He just hushed me up until he came. I left without a word and felt like a piece of dirt. I never saw him again.

Well into my sixties, I told this story to a friend of mine who grew up in France. When I mentioned how offended I had been with his expression "Ah, la vâche!" she said, "Oh no! He was expressing being in total awe of you." I felt just a bit redeemed.

Even though I was deeply disenchanted with Paris, especially with the men, I continued to work for the same family. They planned their spring vacation to go to Holland. They were all excited to see the country I came from and grateful to have me with them to guide and translate for them. We would also go and visit my parents in Rotterdam. I knew that as soon as I was back home, I would have to leave them right there. I could not imagine continuing on, let alone returning with them to Paris. Still, I was unable to speak to the woman. After our visit with my parents ended and she and I were walking down the stairs, all I could mumble was, "Je suis désolée, Madame. I can't go back with you. I am so sorry, I'm so very sorry, I can't. I just can't." It was excruciating. I felt devastated. I couldn't tell her the truth and she was completely baffled and hurt. "How can you abandon us like this?" she said.

I Miscarry

I felt relieved to be home again. My parents were happy to have me back. We agreed that I could live with them and that I would look for a job and pay rent. Since I was now fluent in four languages, I got a summer job at the Tourist Information Center (VVV) in the heart of Rotterdam. Tourists from all over Europe and the U.S. would flock in and ask questions about sites to see and about lodging. We toured the hotels in town, so we could advise people according to their preferences. I immensely enjoyed being able to switch from one language to another at the drop of a hat and notice people's surprise at my fluency.

Since I desired financial independence, I taught myself shorthand so I would be well-equipped to get a decent job as a secretary. In the fall of that year, 1962, I placed an ad, looking for a small international firm that could use my skills. The employers who invited me for interviews expressed their admiration for my proactive approach. It was now my choice who I would accept, rather than being at their mercy.

Of course, driven as I was to find love and affection, with the ever-present motivation to find the "right man" to give me that elusive security that would surely come with marriage, again and again, I would hook up with another young man. My parents always accepted my boyfriends staying overnight with me. It gave them the opportunity to get to know these young men, and I had a safe place to be with them.

I don't remember how I met Hedi, a tall, gorgeous North African young man from Tunis. He worked in a dairy factory in Rotterdam as a so-called "guest worker." I loved his brown skin,

Getting engaged with Hedi   Me at 20

his tight black curls and his soft thick upper eyelids. He looked like a brown Buddha. We spoke mostly French and enjoyed each other's company tremendously. He introduced me to Arab music and poetry and told me stories about his life in Tunis, which had a culture so very different from mine. As a twelve-year-old boy, he had been seduced by one of his mother's best friends. Then his mother chuckled at him and invited him to crawl into bed with her, too. This sexual intimacy seemed to be very normal to him.

He very much wanted me to come with him to Tunisia to meet his family. He spoke very highly of his father. His siblings, all from the same set of parents, apparently were all different shades from white to black. When I got pregnant, I was delighted. We fantasized about getting married and moving there. He explained that I would become his "first wife." Having longed for intimacy with a woman ever since my early teens, imagining being the first wife in his harem and having free erotic access to his other, undoubtedly beautiful wives, was particularly appealing.

I began having fantasies of spawning a large family with him. I imagined having six boys.

Ever since I started smoking when I was fifteen, sore throats and bronchitis were regular occurrences. Less than a month into my pregnancy, I came down with bronchitis and a high fever. When I was in my third month, I noticed a pinkish blob of mucus in the toilet bowl after I had peed. I mentioned it to my mother who thought it must have been the cervical plug. She called our house doctor to come and see me. I explained to him how much I wanted the baby and told him that I was willing to do anything to keep it. He suggested bed rest. It was awkward to be on sick leave of indefinite duration, without being able to explain to my employer what was the matter with me.

I stayed in bed for three weeks until I began to have cramps, which wouldn't let up. My mother, being experienced in these matters, was fully prepared to help me through this and had me stay in my parent's bedroom with her. My father slept in my little room downstairs. That night the cramping developed into full-blown labor. My water broke and I felt a sudden down-rushing in my body. In a desperate attempt to prevent losing my baby, I clamped my hands in front of my vagina and screamed, "No! No!" However, there was no holding back the force of nature. My mother caught the water and membranes in a bucket. No fetus was found. It had likely died and disintegrated during my fever in the beginning of the pregnancy. I must have kept it going through my sheer desire to have this baby.

I rested for several days from the ordeal. I felt profoundly at peace and reviewed my situation. It was a few days before my twenty-first birthday and it felt like I had just been initiated into adulthood. I saw clearly that I had hoped to escape from my life as it was and that my whole relationship with Hedi had been a fantasy. Feeling strangely at peace and grounded, I decided to disengage from Hedi. I wrote him a letter, expressing my regret but explaining that I needed to terminate our relationship. I never saw him again.

I went back to work, feeling shy and not knowing how to explain my absence. No one asked for an explanation. The bookkeeper, a married man, was particularly kind to me. During lunch hour, he quietly mentioned that eating apricots would help me recover. I smiled at him gratefully.

Cees

I need to backtrack here to write about Cees. My parents had befriended Cees during the early years of the war when we lived in Apeldoorn. He had held me on his knees when I was a baby. Like thousands of Dutch people before and during the war, he had been sympathetic to the great German Ideal. After my brother and I had been returned to our grandmother, my mother was transferred to an official post-war camp in Amersfoort. Here she saw Cees again, who had also been interned there. These facts were briefly mentioned by my parents.

During my high school years, Cees was a regular visitor in our home. He was a music critic for a prestigious national newspaper in Holland. He was close friends with both of my parents and, of course, he shared his love of music with my mother. Sometimes, he would invite me to attend organ concerts with him in the old,

Gothic stone church in Delft. We quickly became affectionate. He was fifty-six and married with grown children. I was eighteen.

I loved his broad solid head. Deep furrows plowed around his moon face. Even his lips were round, often slightly parted in expectancy of my favors. His thick glasses made his eyes seem very big and round too. These were usually stained and fogged over. I would gently take them from his broad head and wipe them clean. With a sheepish little grin, he would appreciate my gesture and realize the world was a bit brighter when he put them back on. His compact body seemed to house an enormous strength that I never saw him use.

Sometimes we would go to a movie. It quickly became clear that he wasn't so much interested in the movie as he was in sitting in the back of the theater in the dark to fumble and smooch with me. Taking the train back from Delft after a concert late in the evening, alone in the compartment, we would sit across from each other. He would lovingly pick up one of my feet at a time, take my shoes off and press my feet against his body, stammering adoringly, "*Mijn goddelijk kind!*" "My divine child!" His eyes and lips exuded love and gratitude.

Those were the days when I found myself off and on in relationship with Ton. When he discovered some frilly underwear in my room, he asked where they came from. Since I was never good at lying, I told him they were a gift from Cees. Not only was he exceedingly upset, but not long after that, my mother reproached me with dark hurt in her eyes, "Ton told me that Cees is giving you sexy underwear. I am shocked. How can you?" Instinctively, I realized that Cees had been her lover and maybe still was, and how betrayed she felt by his intimacy with me. I felt very sorry for her, but of course, none of this could be spoken.

After my return from Paris and not long after recovering from my miscarriage, Cees and I picked up our friendship again. This time, our affection quickly accelerated into a true love affair. We had intimate conversations and went to concerts, but mostly we wanted to be close to each other. He never undressed, nor did we ever have intercourse. We kissed and held each other while he adored pleasuring me.

I began to imagine us getting married and living a bohemian life. What a delicious scandal it would make! He was still Catholic and married. His daughters were older than I was. He couldn't believe his good fortune that I loved him that much, yet he assured me over and over again, "If ever a young man comes along with whom you would like to build a future, just leave me," he said. "Don't even look back. I have no right to claim you. You are so young." It was an honorable position for him to take and I knew he meant it.

When I did meet Ton again, and this time decided to marry him, I did exactly what Cees had urged me to do. I left him without looking back, so afraid to trigger my prospective husband's jealousy. I did send Cees a wedding invitation. He did not come.

Ton and I got married and moved to Amsterdam. Some time into our married life, my mother told me on the phone that Cees had fallen in the street from a dizzy spell. Then it happened again, and again. He seemed to be going downhill fast. I appreciated my mother's generosity to keep me informed. She must have realized how much Cees and I had meant to each other. She talked with me as one woman talks with another in the realization that they both love the same man.

All along, I had felt terribly guilty at having left Cees so suddenly. It felt cruel. I knew in my heart that he had lost his joy of living. When my mother told me that he was in the hospital with lung cancer—he had been an avid smoker his whole life—I wanted to go and see him so badly, to hold him and kiss him and apologize and show him that I loved him still.

Terrified as I was of Ton's jealousy and also genuinely not wanting to hurt him, I would have had to leave town secretly. Since I was also working full-time, I didn't see how I could make it happen. So I waited and postponed, lacking the courage to run the risk. I told my mother how much I wanted to see Cees. "Oh, don't," she said. "You would hardly recognize him. He looks terrible, like a skeleton. He wouldn't want you to see him like that. I've told him that you have asked about him. He smiled." A few weeks later, Cees died. I was devastated.

Remorse at my lack of courage, at having failed him, followed me for years. How could I ever be forgiven? Always I felt my love for him so strongly. When I became aware of life after death, my feelings of guilt eased a little. I began to trust that he knew of my love and of my remorse.

Years later, when I was living in India and my father came to visit, I confided in him about the harm I had done to Cees, and about my love for him and my feelings of guilt. He had been a close friend of Cees and knew him very well. "Cees has never blamed you," my father said. "You did exactly what he wanted you to do. He was immensely grateful for the sweetness of your gifts. He is free now. He would not want you to blame yourself in any way. Let it go, Angela. You are free, too." I knew that my father spoke the truth. Something shifted in me that day and I felt relieved of my burden. I was free to just love Cees again, wherever he was.

Ton

About a year or so after my return from Paris, when I was living at home with my parents and working as a secretary in Rotterdam, I was riding home after work on the tram. At the first stop on our street, I saw Ton step down from the same tram. Startled, we caught each other's eyes and could not disengage. Everything seemed to come to a halt; even the tram did not move. It was as if the whole universe was waiting to see what would come next until some unknown force made me get up and off the tram and face him.

Tentatively, we gave each other an update of our lives. He spoke of his political involvement in the Pacifist Socialist Party. That did peak my interest. His descriptions of left-wing ideals resonated deeply with me even though I had never had any political inclination. I experienced an opening to new avenues of thought. He was actually on his way to a meeting and invited me to come along if I was interested. I was.

On the way, he asked me why I had refused to speak to him when he had seen me in front of a store window on Boulevard St. Michel. Since I had left Paris not long after our break-up, I wasn't even there at the time he referred to. It seemed he must have met my double. He said he had talked to me over and over, in

Dutch of course, trying to coax me to respond. I can only imagine what the girl must have thought of him, this intense-looking young man speaking a strange language to her and being rather insistent. Well, it hadn't been me and no matter how hard I tried to convince him, he wouldn't believe me. Later, I wondered why I didn't walk away from him then and there.

However, as before, I easily responded to his sweet charms. Driven by my pressing need to find the right husband and so to secure my future, I half agreed to resume our relationship. He had always been clear that he wanted to marry me and kept pressuring me in that direction. In an attempt to get clarity, I decided to spend my vacation by checking on a few of the men I had left behind in Paris. I wanted to see Mack again, but also felt the need to verify the quality of my connection with Constantin, the Russian artist. Constantin had moved to Normandy in the meantime, so I made a trip on my own, first to Paris and then to the coast of France.

My stay in Paris was not particularly memorable nor was seeing Mack again. Clearly, he was no match for me. I enjoyed the train ride along the Seine into the countryside of Normandy. Constantin picked me up from the station. Even though I felt affection and friendship for him, I wasn't moved. When we took a bus ride along the coast in the pouring rain, I contemplated my situation. It was becoming clear to me that sexual attraction was not a basis for marriage. I realized that Ton was making me think. I valued that his social and philosophical passions made me question my rather unconscious assumptions about many things. It seemed that such a man was a far better and more intriguing choice for a husband. I decided I would marry Ton.

I began my return travels to Holland immediately. Arriving in Paris, I checked out the train schedule and sent a telegram to Ton that I had decided to marry him and to please pick me up at the station in Rotterdam at such and such a time. The express train had a stop-over in Brussels where one part of the train would get uncoupled and stay there and the other section would go on into Holland. I thought I was sitting in the right section and the conductor had checked my ticket without comment. In Brussels, the train seemed to have stopped for a very long time when suddenly all the lights went out. The section I thought I was on had long since left the station without me.

Frantically, I found local trains that would take me on a long, arduous journey with a number of stopovers and having to change trains on the way. There was no way to contact Ton. After many long hours, I arrived in Rotterdam in the middle of the night and called him. He did come to the station. He was livid.

"You sent me a telegram to come and pick you up! I came to the station all excited to see you again and then you weren't there," he fumed. It didn't seem that my explanations about the helplessness of my situation in Brussels and how terrible I had felt, had any effect. I had wired him my promise and he had come to the station full of happy expectations and then I wasn't there. I saw that he felt so utterly betrayed that he actually no longer wanted me. Since I had just reached the big conclusion that he was surely the right man for me, it became my turn to do the convincing. Probably against his better knowing, we did continue our relationship.

He had moved to Amsterdam to start his studies in psychology and soon I found a job there. Under his mild protestations,

I moved into the small room with a single bed he was renting from a family in one of those narrow homes on the Prinsengracht, an old canal in the center of town. Somehow, it seemed quite romantic. I loved Amsterdam, this ancient, lively, artistic city where people readily chat with you on the street and in the tram, so very different from the modern, business-oriented Rotterdam, where everyone moves about in stoic silence. It was a completely different culture. Later I would compare the two cities' different atmospheres to those of San Francisco and Los Angeles.

We decided to get married and had to tell our families that we were not going to have our wedding in the church but preferred a civil ceremony at the town hall. I found a long, white damask body-fitting wedding dress that made me feel and look rather elegant. Both of our families were invited. When signing our documents in front of the officiator, I distinctly remember my heartfelt intent and dedication to the marriage which was going to be our life together till the day we died. It was a holy moment.

Marrying Ton

In the photograph I have, I look so very serious and innocent. I was all of twenty-one years old.

It was 1963. The first birth control clinic had opened in Amsterdam. I felt much relieved that I could now take the pill and not worry about getting pregnant. Ton was very fond of children and wished to have them, but when I examined my own motives, I could only see having children as a self-centered proposition. I hadn't asked to be born. I had to deal with the life I was given and I was clearly not on earth for my parents' sake. Life as I knew it was not a happy one. Overshadowing every-thing was the ominous reality of the atomic bomb. The threat of nuclear annihilation did not make the earth a safe place for anyone, let alone innocent newborns. Also, Ton and I were both quite aware of the problem of over-population and I didn't feel the need to contribute to that, either. I continued to take the pill throughout our marriage.

Through my father's friends, we found a beautiful room in a stately patrician home on the Apollolaan in the South of Amsterdam. The straight couple who were the landlords, lived downstairs. They had a policy to only rent rooms to gay men, because "women were trouble." They made a big exception for us because of my father's connection with some of the men who lived there. In our spacious room with large windows overlooking the gardens, we felt quite romantic and were off and on quite happy. I enjoyed cooking scrumptious multi-course meals in the communal kitchen for us and our friends, as I had learned during my stay in Paris.

One evening the doorbell rang. We heard some voices down-stairs. Then the landlady shouted up to us that there was a French gentleman to see me. When I came to the top of the stairs I was shocked to see my rapist from the last family I had worked for in Paris. I couldn't believe my eyes. *"Q'est-ce que vous faites ici? Je n'ai aucun intérêt de vous voir. Foutez-moi le camp!"* (What are you doing here? I have no interest in seeing you. Get the hell away from me!) I hollered at him and without waiting for any response, went back into our room. I was furious. How dare he come to see me, as if I could possibly want that.

During my married years with Ton in Amsterdam, I had several secretary jobs, one at the Dutch office of Radio Luxemburg, the only commercial radio station in the region at that time, where I became very much attracted to my assistant, a young woman with whom I had quite the personal conversations. But, I was way too fearful to approach the unsuspecting girl with my interest.

The only friends we had were the psychology students in Ton's circle since I didn't have the space or time to make friends of my own. I felt strongly that it was not a healthy situation for Ton to have never had another girl but me. I kept encouraging him to get it on with one of these not unattractive women students, to widen his horizons and open his mind to a more inclusive lifestyle. Somewhere, I knew full well that, on some fatal day, the marriage would get on the rocks, because I just could not seem to adapt myself to the monogamous life, however hard I tried.

I found a fancy job at the headquarters of an international European car rental business, a conglomerate of all the biggest national car rental companies in Europe, which intended to band together to compete with Hertz and Avis. They had attracted a business lawyer as their top manager and I became his secretary. The office was located on the ground floor of one of those fabulous mansions in the chic quarter near the Rijksmuseum. My boss's office was facing the street and my spacious office had French doors opening out to a beautiful garden. I could make full use of all my language skills. I had an electric typewriter and a fax machine which was still quite a novelty at the time. I felt at the top of my game in my profession.

One of their international meetings was held in Paris and my boss decided I could come along to take notes. I loved being back in Paris. That's where I got close to Herr von Lehmann, the dignified director of the German company. He was missing a hand due to the war and wore a leather prosthesis. I was pleased when he invited me to go out with him in the evening. We went to one of the caves on the left bank where we ate well and drank expensive wine while a Middle Eastern belly dancer performed in front of us. Quite loosened up already, we went off to his hotel room. I enjoyed being with this man. While making love, his hair, which was usually so neatly combed back, sprung up in little curls all around his head. He reminded me of those sweet drawings of de Saint-Exupéry's *Little Prince*. I was so charmed by the vulnerability of this powerful man that I couldn't help laughing for joy. He was surprised and delighted with my happiness. I found him quite adorable.

On another occasion, I met his wife, a mature, full-bosomed, warm-hearted, elegant woman with expressive brown eyes, her hair softly flowing around her beautiful face. We took an immediate liking to each other. I was quite attracted to her and began to have secret fantasies of being with the two of them. When the team gathered again the next year in Amsterdam, he invited me for a stroll through the red quarters where we spent a few sweet hours in a cheap hotel room. There, for fun, he challenged me to tell him something that would shock him. I knew right away what would do the trick. Eyes twinkling, I told him, "I would like to make love to your wife!" Well, that got him alright. He *was* shocked but also immensely intrigued and actually began considering the possibilities.

All this time, I was working a job, running the household, shopping, cooking and cleaning, and trying to keep Ton emotionally together. He turned out to be quite depressed, and paranoid to boot. At the university, he was not doing very well. He believed his teachers had something against him. Scatterbrain that he was, I frequently had to help him find his keys and his wallet to get him out the door on time. At night he invariably pressed me for intercourse, no matter if I was already sound asleep. Since he was also overly well-endowed, I ended up with chronic cervicitis. It was not until my early forties before I learned that I had the right to say *No*.

Eventually, Ton succeeded in getting his bachelor's degree. We threw a party and invited our friends who had also just graduated to celebrate the occasion. In the midst of the party, I suddenly realized that these young women were not any smarter than I was and a light went off. If they could graduate from college, so could I. It had already begun to gnaw at me that I was at the peak of my career as a secretary at twenty-five, and had nothing to look forward to. I was bored.

I had always known that if I were to ever go to the university, I would study psychology. Witnessing the success of our young women friends clinched the deal for me. My decision was made. I discovered that to obtain a student loan at my age, I was required to plead my case. I wrote a convincing letter to the Ministry of Education applying for a student loan. I described my vision of a future with both my husband and me having careers in psychology. I received a full student loan and registered at the University of Amsterdam. Ton was happy for me.

After years of having been cooped up, an amazing new life of freedom and exploration opened up to me. I absolutely loved making friends, walking the old cobblestone streets, crossing the little bridges over the canals in the morning sun, stopping in for a tosti and an espresso, then entering the old stone halls of wisdom of the university and milling around with the other students. I did much better than Ton and our friends ever had. I got straight A's on all my exams. As a reward, I received a free grant for the next year. I felt gloriously happy. A new world had opened.

My First Woman Lover and Her Jewish Husband

The longing to be intimate with a woman had haunted me since I was thirteen. It seemed unavoidable that this desire would come to fruition with the new freedom I found when I went to the University of Amsterdam to study psychology. At twenty-six and married, I was quite a bit older than most students who came straight out of high school. I was quickly drawn to a woman who was also married and had a two-year-old son. Maya was smart, vivacious, full of stories—and Jewish. She drove around in a little red Deux Chevaux and we soon became fast friends. Her husband was a psychiatrist. He drove a Saab, she told me. They lived with their little son and a maid in a large home in Amsterdam-Noord, which at the time, was only accessed by ferry. So it was that I never actually went to her house. One time she brought her little redhead boy to class. He was adorable.

I had never had the courage to approach a woman—not for lack of desire or infatuation, but for the sheer terror of provoking a horrified reaction. One afternoon, Maya and I were sitting together on the couch in my living room, yakking away. I told her how Ton and I had gone on vacation to Denmark, the first country in Europe to legalize pornography, and I had bought some titillating lesbian porn.

"Would you like to see it?" I asked.

"Yeah, sure," she smiled.

"Have you ever been with a woman?"

"No, I haven't," she admitted.

"I haven't either."

Giggling like school girls, our temperatures rising, we looked at the picture story of two well-endowed women playing doctor and patient, slowly removing each other's clothing, revealing their voluptuous breasts until their gorgeous bodies were fully exposed and the doctor mounted the patient. It didn't take much to admit to each other that we had become quite interested.

"Shall we give it a try?" I blurted.

"Oh yeah!" she laughed.

We practically ran to the bedroom, laughing in excited antic-ipation, both of us virgins in the territory of loving women.

I fell head over heels in love with Maya. We spent quite a lot of time together, and in between classes and lunches, we feasted on each other's bodies and souls. I did everything to keep our relationship secret from my jealous husband. I hadn't forgotten that a few years before, when distressed by my unrequited love for the young woman I worked with, I had been silently crying myself to sleep, hoping Ton wouldn't notice. When I couldn't suppress one of my sobs, he had come to me, concerned. "What's the matter, Angela? Why are you crying?" Of course, I couldn't say. He put his arms around me. "Please tell me. You can tell me anything!" It was clear that he wasn't going to accept my silence. With great trepidation, I confessed between sobs.

"I don't know what to do, Ton. I am so attracted to Katie. I long so much to be close to her, but I am too afraid to approach her. And, I'm also afraid that you'll be upset with me."

For a moment his comforting arms stayed around me and then he chilled. Within minutes, he worked himself into a fury. "How can you do this to me? You're so selfish, you never think about me," he ranted. "I knew you would betray me." Suddenly the whole thing had become *his* problem. So, this time, I knew better than to tell him anything.

It just so happened that Ton would be in an exam for several hours on Maya's birthday, so she and I were planning to celebrate appropriately. In one of Amsterdam's little stores, I spotted an exotic Moroccan blue-beaded leather belt. I imagined placing it around her bare waist and so I did. An hour into our tryst, both of us flushed with excitement and stark naked, with the sheets on the floor, we hear my husband's footsteps on the stairs. As his key enters the lock, we look around in a panic at the scene. There is absolutely nothing we can do to hide what's happening. We are just a few feet away from the front door and there he is.

All three of us are stunned by the unexpected exposure, scrambling to deal with the shock. Maya and I quickly throw on our clothes, and the three of us gather in the living room. I'm in a bizarre mix of emotions, still silly from my happiness with my newfound love and reeling with the shock of Ton finding out. I'm also acutely aware that I need to save my marriage at all costs. I go into overdrive trying to convince him that, even though I am very much in love with Maya, my love for him is not at all diminished, which is true. I beg him to accept the situation and make things work for all three of us.

Suddenly, Ton jumps to his feet and barks at Maya, "If all this is supposed to be okay, why don't you and I go to the bedroom right now and we'll see!" It's not an invitation. It's an order. I watch Ton and Maya disappear into the bedroom, a bit worried for her but with a ray of hope in my heart that everything may work out after all. I go to the kitchen to wash the considerable pile of dishes that had gotten stacked up.

Ton is overly well-endowed and from what I can hear, he's obviously banging away at her full force. I hear her moaning loudly, and assuming that they are having a great time, I am so relieved that I spontaneously break out in one of my favorite arias from *Carmen Jones*, "Love's a baby that grows up wild, and he won't do what you want him to. Love ain't nobody's angel child..." I did identify with Carmen. I knew all the lyrics and was happily singing away at the top of my voice, naively believing, against all odds, that we were in the process of creating the life I really wanted: freedom—heaven on earth!

When they reappeared, Ton was irate. He *hated* my happy singing. He hollered at me to shut up. It then dawned on me that his purpose had been to take revenge by fucking my girlfriend as hard as he could and giving me a piece of my own medicine. I felt like a bomb had dropped into my life. In that instant, I knew my world was falling apart. I had nothing left to bring him around. Maya went home and I was now completely at the mercy of his rage. I got so frightened, I withdrew into myself and plunged into a dark hole of despair.

His rage never let off. All my hopes for resolution were shot to hell. I felt trapped. Inside of myself, I was frantically looking for a solution and finding none. I imploded into a nightmare of distorted terror. Quite late that night, we finally had some dinner. The moment I sat down at the table, my eyes were drawn to the knife next to my plate. I quickly shoved it out of sight under the placemat, for sheer terror that I might attack him with it. I realized I was going insane. Then I heard loud steps stomping up the stairs to our front door. I yelled at Ton that someone was coming. He hadn't heard anything. I panicked. He went to open the door. No one was there. I had been hallucinating. I was losing my mind.

All through the next morning, my executioner never let up on his efforts to demolish my character. I sat in the rocking chair, like a trapped animal, still feebly trying to defend myself, when he hit upon his final insult. "What is really despicable is that you are using Maya for your own selfish ends!" Everything in me came to a screeching halt. My eyes closed shut. I turned into stone. All sounds became muffled as if I was underwater. Incapable of responding in any way, I vaguely realized that I had become catatonic.

In the distance, I heard him getting fearful. He tried to coax me out of my stupor. I couldn't move. After a while, he became afraid. He called Maya to ask for help from her husband since he was a psychiatrist. He wasn't able to come, but she did. After Maya arrived, some sense of safety began to return to me and my hearing became more acute. As Maya and Ton talked with each other, she mentioned the possibility of my needing medication. Feeling their genuine concern, the ice began to melt and my rigidity relaxed. I slowly re-emerged.

After I had fully returned, we had tea together and were able to have a serious and fairly civil conversation. The marriage was on the rocks. I knew I couldn't be in the same space with Ton as long as he was so upset with me. "I believe you need to have time by yourself to sort things out and to see if you want to continue our marriage," I said to him. "It would seem only fair that I should be the one to leave our home since I caused all this trouble." Knowing that Maya lived with her husband and child in a large home with a maid to boot, it seemed only natural to ask her if I could stay with her for a while. She said she would have to talk with her husband. Ton accepted the idea, and things calmed down.

The next day, Maya returned. I was alone at home. She sat next to me and seemed to be quite uncomfortable. I asked her how things had gone with her husband. She hesitated. "I have to tell you something," she said.

"Yes?"

She couldn't get the words out. She hemmed and hawed and squirmed. When I couldn't seem to reassure her enough, I finally said, "Whatever it is, love, you can tell me," and I added, I don't know why, "Even if some things weren't true, you can tell me. Whatever it is, I won't mind. I love you."

In bits and pieces, one lie after another was revealed. Instead of going home the day before, she had run in a panic straight to her psychiatrist who had encouraged her to tell me the truth. Her husband, Nol, was not a psychiatrist. He was a journalist. They didn't have a large home but lived in a small flat in Amsterdam-Noord. He did not own a Saab, in fact he did not drive at all. She was not Jewish, but her husband was. Then came the most difficult one for her. After more hesitation, she confessed, "A few years ago I had a miscarriage. I was devastated. Then it turned out that I can't have children at all. The little boy I brought to class is the son of our German neighbors. He is exactly the age my son would have been." She wept. I felt so sad for her and forgave her for everything. I just wanted to comfort her and make her feel safe. Later, I learned that the miscarriage was also a spun part of the story since she was trying to earn my sympathy.

She told me that Nol was quite a bit older than she was. He was a film critic for a national newspaper. They had met at a psychiatric clinic. Nol knew all about her compulsive lying problem. He had understood her dilemma and agreed that I could come and stay with them for a few days in their small guest room. I packed a few belongings and we took off in her little red Deux Chevaux to what would become a new chapter in my life. I knew it was right to leave Ton for a while so he could figure things out for himself.

On the way there, Maya admitted she hadn't told Nol that we were lovers. I looked at her and said, "I am so in love with you, I can't imagine being able to hide that from him when we live in the same place. Why don't we invite him into a threesome?" However outrageous it seemed to her, she liked the idea. "Just let me do the talking," I said, so sure I was that any man worth his mettle would jump at the occasion to have two women in his bed.

Nol was a short, somewhat balding and potbellied, very kind man, a bit shy. He jumped to his feet and introduced himself, shaking hands with me. As we sat down rather formally, he offered me a glass of sherry. It didn't take long before I laid things out for him. "Maya hasn't had the courage to tell you but she and I are very much in love with each other. We decided to be honest with you because, frankly, I am so enamored, I can't keep my hands off her," I smiled. The ice was broken. We all laughed and toasted and drank some more.

Not to beat around the bush, I boldly went on. "So, Nol, what would you think of the three of us having some sweet times together? That way you wouldn't need to feel left out and we could all be happy together?" He squirmed and blushed and then he stammered, "Really? Are you sure?" He looked very happy indeed, if a bit incredulous.

"Yeah, of course. Wouldn't that be the best for all of us?"

"I can't quite believe how I got this lucky!" he exclaimed and jumped out of his chair to plant an eager kiss on my lips.

Neither of them were at all experienced in the art of lovemaking, so my addition to their bed was quite a revelation to them. It gave me the pleasure of feeling that I was with two virtual virgins and could help to liberate them both. Usually, Nol and I would both focus on pleasuring Maya, our primary object of desire and when she was properly spent and went to the bathroom to clean up, he and I would go for a final quick romp and finish each other off.

We spent many hours at the dinner table, talking and drinking late into the evenings. Nol was quite a drinker, so beer, wine, cognac and *jenever* (Dutch gin) flowed freely. A few times I got quite drunk. They shared their stories. Maya and Nol had met in a mental hospital. He had suffered a serious mental breakdown after his first marriage fell apart. Maya's parents had been so painfully ordinary and boring to her that, even as a child, she had begun to spin fantasies to make life and herself more interesting. She had been in and out of mental hospitals since her adolescence. When Nol had noticed Maya wearing a necklace with both the Star of David and a little cross, he had been intrigued.

Nol shared stories of his childhood in WWII. When his parents knew that their deportation was imminent, they managed to find a farmer's family who were willing to hide him and his little sister in an attic. They spent years in hiding. He never saw his parents again. After the war, it turned out that, except for one aunt, their entire family had been wiped out. He described poignant scenes of himself as a young adolescent after the war, having heard stories of people contacting the dead, spending hours upon hours searching through the static on the radio, desperately hoping to receive messages from his dead parents. He became quite embittered and started to believe that his parents must not really have cared about him. He turned into a cynical atheist.

I am distressed by his stories, and the secret about my father's past keeps disturbing me. One evening, the three of us are sitting down for dinner and I feel the pressure mounting. I must tell him the truth. I am frightened but I can't keep silent any longer.

"There's something really difficult I need to tell you, Nol, and I am scared to." He turns to me ever so kindly, "What is it, Angela?" Shaking, I confess. "My father was a Nazi. After the war, he was sentenced to death for war crimes." Stumbling over my words, I tell him what I know and also, thank God, that my father was never directly involved with the persecution of the Jews. "I'm so ashamed and I'm afraid that you'll hate me."

I will never forget the serious but compassionate look in his brown eyes as he stroked my face, "Ah, sweet little Angela. Don't you worry. You had nothing to do with this. You were just a babe. You are not guilty." The healing waters of our tears co-mingled. I felt immensely relieved and so blessed to be forgiven by a Jew. The moment marked a turning point for me. Healing had begun. A deep caring friendship blossomed between Nol and me, a friendship that would last a lifetime.

It was a bit odd to have Maya witness all this since she had merely pretended to be a Jewess and really had no part at all in this painful history her husband and I shared. It struck me that I hadn't experienced any uncomfortable feelings with her before. Her Jewishness had been presented as one more glistening bead on her shiny string of pearls, the chimera I had swallowed hook, line and sinker.

After a few months in paradise, Maya began to act a bit strange. She started to accuse Nol and me of trying to get her out of the way so we could be with each other. Nothing was further from the truth. Once this thought took hold of her, it grew like a cancer. Nothing we could say or do would convince her of our love for her and a shadow began to creep over our little threesome.

In the meantime, Ton and I met a number of times. Each time, I hoped that our marriage could be salvaged. Each time, he battered me with unending streams of bitter accusations and assaults on my personhood. When he accused me of never having loved him, I felt he was destroying five years of my life and my love for him. After he left, I walked along the dikes for hours sobbing and wailing. Afterwards, when I was sitting rather forlorn on the couch, Nol returned. He took one look at me and came right over and stroked my head ever so gently as if soothing a child. I soaked up the gentle, comforting gesture as if I had been starving for it since I was a little girl. In fact, in my memory, it seemed to be the first time that someone actually noticed my feelings and paid attention to me.

Our life together continued rather peaceably until one day after Maya had gone for an appointment with her psychiatrist, we got a call from him. She had attempted suicide in his waiting room. I was deeply shocked. When she came back home we were careful to be even kinder to her than we had been before. A few weeks later, the three of us had gone out for dinner close to her psychiatrist's office. She had a session scheduled right after dinner and the plan was that Nol and I would hang out there with coffee and cognac until she returned. Not long thereafter we heard the siren of an ambulance. We looked at each other. We knew it was her. We raced to the ER where we met her psychiatrist. He talked with us while Maya was getting her stomach pumped.

I got quite resentful of her drama. After a third suicide attempt, my mind was made up. I had to leave and started to look for student housing.

A Psychiatric Evaluation

It was not clear at all that Ton and I would resume our marriage, so I turned to Student Housing to find a place for myself. They had obtained some of the old *beguinages* in Amsterdam. These were three-story blocks of small one-room apartments, each with a kitchenette and a closet-like toilet, arranged around an inner courtyard with gardens and benches. They had been home to the Beguines, a Roman Catholic lay sisterhood from the Middle Ages, and had later become senior housing. Now they were made available for students. Everything had been fixed up and freshly painted. A dark, brick archway led into the inner courtyard and to the front doors, sheltering the entire complex from the street. A public bath house around the corner provided showers.

The apartment was on the Westerstraat in the Jordaan, the charming Jewish quarters of Amsterdam. Narrow streets and canals with tiny stores for daily necessities brought everything within easy walking distance. Next to the baker and the butcher, a small store sold only cheese and milk, another, only vegetables. Quaint dark bars, cafes and liquor stores were just around the corner.

It was the first time I lived on my own and was able to create and decorate my own space. Because I was in search of my true sexuality and was deeply conflicted about my relationships with men, I hung a large dramatic poster above my bed of Oedipus making love to his masked mother. It reflected to me the feelings of being used and not being seen.

During all the emotional upheaval around Ton and my anger with Maya, I had developed serious stomach pains. I decided to go to the student doctor. He checked me out and sent me off with a prescription. As I walked out the door, I looked at it and discovered I had been prescribed Valium. I turned on my heels and indignantly said to him, "I'm not taking any Valium! Obviously, I need to see a psychologist." Being a psychology student, I couldn't believe that he hadn't bothered to tell me that I wasn't suffering from a physical problem.

Now, I wasn't about to put my mind in the hands of just anyone. I had heard of a psychiatric research institute where one could get extensive testing to be diagnosed and receive a recommendation for the most appropriate therapy. First, I spent hours completing quite a battery of tests, like the Rorschach, the MMPI and a variety of others. These tests were then given to an expert (who had not seen me) to be interpreted. Next, I received six one-hour intake sessions from an experienced psychiatrist, after which all the results would be presented to a panel of six psychiatrists, including the person who had given me the tests and the one who had interpreted them. After discussing the case, they would come up with a well-founded diagnosis and a recommendation for treatment.

I was assigned to a female Jungian psychiatrist. On the appointed day, I rang the brass bell at the door of a stately home in one of the old patrician neighborhoods near the opera. A rather distinguished-looking, elderly woman met me at the door. She seemed pleased to see me and welcomed me into a classic, warmly lit room with books covering the walls from floor to ceiling. She invited me to sit across from her at her desk. She looked like she was eighty years old. Kind eyes peered at me through her wrinkled face. Besides eliciting my instant respect, she made me feel very much at home. She encouraged me to tell her everything about my life, right from the beginning.

And so began a six-week-long journey through my life. She really did want to know every detail. She listened with genuine interest, asking questions if she wanted to know more. She didn't flinch about my father's past nor about my interest in women. Everything was welcome. When I had just described my seven lonely years in boarding schools, from kindergarten through elementary school, how I didn't make any friends with the other children because I felt so very different and had to guard my dark secret, how the harsh, accusing and punitive nuns were only after our complete obedience and that no one ever paid any friendly attention to me, she stopped me. Looking deeply into my eyes, she exclaimed, "No one? There was no one paying any positive attention to you for all those years?" "No. No one. Never." She seemed to be genuinely astonished that I was doing as well as I was.

Coming to see her was like entering a sanctuary. I felt honored to be in her presence and looked forward to each of my visits. Imperceptibly, the opportunity to share my story and her listening with such kind and total attention must have brought me relief. My stomach pains disappeared. By the end of our sessions, I was feeling much better and excited about starting my new life. It would take about three months for the institute to process all my information. I would then be called in again to see her and she would share the results of their investigation with me and give me a recommendation for therapy.

My own most pressing issue was to get clarity about my sexual orientation. I figured the surest way would be for me to find another woman. Since I knew well how terrified I was to approach a woman in person, I was intrigued by the possibility to advertise. A progressive newspaper in Holland, the NRC Handelsblad, had begun publishing a personals section. It was quite a novelty and everybody was excited to discover a whole new way to find partners. It soon expanded into a full-length page. It seemed to be a perfectly safe way to go about it. This is what I wrote:

> Psychology student looking for a sweet woman with a smart mind and a yummie body.

I received several letters. One of them intrigued me. It was written in a tiny scribble by someone who seemed to be at odds with herself about responding to me. She was a medical student at the Catholic University of Nijmegen in the last year of her studies. She had never been with a woman and seemed both terrified and compelled to write to me. She talked about Eros and wrote the word in Greek letters. Since I had no classical training, I was a bit intimidated. Feeling that she would be intellectually superior to me and the bristling tone of her approach made me hesitant to reach out to her. I met a few of the other women first, but none of them clicked for me. Finally, I wrote her back.

Beth and I corresponded for a few weeks until we agreed it was time for us to meet. With some trepidation, I called her from the public phone booth around the corner. I was surprised to hear a hesitant, slightly hoarse voice with a thick accent from the southern parts of the country. It instantly invoked my tenderness. We made a date for her to come and visit me. She would take the train and the tram to my little abode in Amsterdam.

I opened the door that Sunday morning to a short, shy tomboy, who tried very hard to look tough. Above a heavy overcoat, her soft broad face was framed by short, curly dark blonde hair. She was nervous and excited and scared all at the same time. Over coffee, we sat and talked. I did my best to make her feel at ease. We laughed about her letter and her mixed feelings. When Beth smiled, her soft gray eyes twinkled and the cutest dimples would appear in her chubby cheeks. She told me how she had always played rough and tumble with the boys in her village. When she got to be twelve, they suddenly wanted to get under her skirt. She was abhorred. In high school, she had fallen deeply in love with one of the nuns, who she was still friends with. Over the years she had a number of crushes on women but had always been too frightened to take any action.

By the afternoon, since we both knew what I had asked for and why she had come, and she was so adorable and shy, I couldn't help but move closer and be sweet to her. Even though she squirmed, she didn't protest. We tentatively kissed and necked ever so lightly until I carefully unbuttoned the top of her blouse to expose tender little breasts that had never been touched. I was deeply moved.

We fell head over heels in love with each other. Beth had a fascinating personality and a probing mind. She did not confine her interest to medicine but was an avid reader and student of philosophy. Thoughts about my marriage to Ton were disappearing. After a few magical weekends in Amsterdam, where we happily walked hand in hand through the city, showing our love to the world, she gathered the considerable courage to invite me to a party being held by her sorority in Nijmegen. She wanted to introduce me to the friends she had known at the University for the last six or seven years. She had not dared to say anything to prepare them for her revelation. She bravely introduced me to her unsuspecting sisterhood. They were a tough bunch of gals, drinking and smoking like there was no tomorrow. Totally in love with each other, we danced and flirted and laughed all night. Even Beth didn't seem to have a care in the world what anybody thought.

In the following weeks, it appeared that we had dropped a bomb in the middle of their collective denial. One after the other came out and admitted that they too were interested in women. They were impressed that their little Beth had been so bold! Everyone was relieved and grateful that they could finally be honest with themselves and with one another.

When I talked to my mother on the phone, I told her about my newfound relationship with Beth. I loved hearing her response. "I know how beautiful it is to love a woman. I am very happy for you." I knew she would tell my father too.

Soon, my father had to be in Amsterdam for business. I invited him to come over and meet Beth. He adored her at first sight. He showered her with all his big open-hearted warmth and appreciation. When she stepped out of the room for a moment, he looked at me, obviously quite moved by her and whispered, "Oh, those little feet...!" I knew exactly what he meant. No matter how intelligent and educated she was, her body exuded a childlike innocence that was quite irresistible, especially as it was combined with her tough masculine outfits. Even though she was about to graduate to become a physician, she looked like an adorable twelve-year-old boy.

Beth's own father was the house doctor in the village where she had grown up. He was a severe, opinionated Catholic man and she had not felt very safe with him as a child. She was terrified that he would find out that she was a lesbian. My father's instant warmth and friendly interest in her was a whole new experience for my Beth.

During those days, I also met Doortje at one of the workshops for us psychology students. Invariably, she would arrive late, striding in like a queen, flaunting flamboyant hats, a shawl flung around her shoulders. All heads turned to her. We became fast friends. She was married to Paul, tall, slender, intriguing and equally good-looking, who had already graduated as a psychologist and who was involved with a brand new Institute for Gestalt Therapy based on the methods of Esalen's Fritz Perls. They lived in a wealthy neighborhood of a nearby small town with two darling children. I particularly loved sweet Nellieke, their little girl, who surely reminded me of my own child self.

Having been separated from my loving father since I was so very young, bittersweet feelings stir in my heart whenever I see happy little girls with brown eyes and round faces like I had, who blossom in the safety of their family and have a daddy who cherishes and protects them. I loved being welcomed into Doortje's family.

Paul told me that his Institute was just about to start a year-long training for people who were interested in becoming group facilitators. I jumped at the opportunity. Suddenly, my life was taking off in new and exciting directions.

Then came the call to go and see the psychiatrist to receive the results of my evaluation. Some three months had passed.

She and I were glad to see each other again. After we settled down at the familiar desk, she asked me how I was doing. "Oh, I'm doing great," I happily announced.

"I've fallen in love with a fine woman and I've started training at the Institute for Gestalt Therapy to become a group facilitator." She actually sat with her mouth open for a moment.

"I can't believe it," she exclaimed. "You are doing so well! You are proving exactly what we found. You must have come in with some remarkable gifts. We would expect anyone with your history to be severely depressed and possibly even be hospitalized by now." Then she explained how I do have a problem of moving very quickly. "You make radical decisions before thinking things over. Then you have to scramble to catch up with yourself. So the waves can get pretty high at times, but you always come out better on the other side." She told me that they were actually not recommending therapy for me. "Just know that when things get difficult, you are always welcome to come and see me." I was very happy to hear that. I also knew she was right.

Not long after that, Ton and I had a final conversation. It was clear to both of us that our marriage was over and we agreed to get divorced. Since he continued to live in the apartment we had shared together and I was moving on, I left him everything, including the car we had bought the year before. It was a clean break and I had no desire to look back. I certainly didn't want anything from him.

Expanding Horizons

No matter how much I loved Beth, I found myself unable to stay away from men. Since we lived in different cities and were unable to be together every weekend, I continued to participate in student life in Amsterdam, make friends and party. Even though I was sick and tired of men seeming to be after sex all the time, and felt used and abused, I couldn't resist them. Since I have never been able to live with lies, each time I fessed up to Beth. It was painful for both of us. I couldn't understand why I kept doing it. The notion of sex and love addiction was still unknown in the culture.

I particularly remember meeting a young man at a party. He looked like a gentle angel with long blond curls. We were drawn to each other like magnets. Against all my better judgment, I just had to take him home. We made love under the poster of

Pensive Angela

Oedipus. During our lovemaking, I was torn up inside to the point of making myself sick, so upset at not wanting to have sex with men and finding myself unable to resist. At the same time, I liked this young man, who did not deserve my aversion, but I was too confused to be able to address the situation. Much to his consternation, I suddenly convulsed and had to run to the bathroom to vomit.

Later, I realized that it never occurred to me that I could have seen my psychiatrist again. Asking for help was not part of my internal makeup. There had been no one for me to turn to when I was little. Being alone with my problems, never speaking of them, and dealing with them all by myself was deeply ingrained. Beth and I rode the waves as best we could. I never stopped loving her, but sadly, I gave her a lot of grief.

As part of my psychology curriculum, I participated in study groups. Sitting around a large table, we were asked to reflect and share our insights with one another. Rudi hardly ever spoke. He seemed shy, somewhat hidden behind small, wire-rimmed glasses and a great halo of frizzy brown curls, the first afro I had ever seen on a white man. When he did speak, everyone would fall silent. In a soft voice, he would utter something mystical, something which seemed infinitely more meaningful than whatever the rest of us were sharing. He stirred my soul. Naturally, I was irresistibly drawn to him.

Rudi was quite handsome and beautifully built. His tall, slender body was supple and harmonious. He had grown up in a small village near Amsterdam, played in a band, rode a motorbike and practiced Hatha Yoga. He was six years younger than me. When we spent time together, I felt my heart open to his kindness, shyness and depth of soul. I felt safe around him. He didn't try to get in bed with me. But since that was really all I knew, it didn't take me long to seduce him.

One day, in somebody's living room where friends had gathered, we sat in a quiet corner on the floor and Rudi introduced me to the *I Ching, the Book of Changes*, an ancient Chinese text of divination. I was still in my materialistic phase, having sworn off all religion, vowing to believe nothing unless it became real to me. He explained to me how everything is connected, the flow of Yin and Yang and the law of karma. It was a new language for me and a foreign set of concepts, which I found surprisingly appealing. I felt as though I was being initiated into some ancient wisdom of which our culture had no knowledge. He showed me how to use the sticks to throw the hexagram and suggested that I become quiet and focus on a question I might have. Concentrating on the ritual opened a space inside of me I had never entered. Even though I do not remember the question or the answer anymore, I do distinctly remember how startling the accuracy and depth of the answers were. My view of reality cracked wide open.

Around the same time, marijuana became available. I had been offered a toke at a few parties, but it hadn't done much for me. Then a friend gifted me with a bud. I will never forget the first time I smoked marijuana by myself. It was evening. I was sitting in my grandmother's rocking chair in my cozy little student flat. When it came on, I deepened into silence as if the universe had come to a standstill. I noticed my posture. I was leaning forward slightly and my hands were folded. I recognized the gesture from the many years of praying as a child. I understood the true nature of prayer, one hand holding on to the other with this small empty space in between them. I was getting in touch with myself, with some inner part of me. It was the inner space of union that I had experienced so vividly as a Catholic child when I felt at one with Jesus inside of me during those most intimate moments after receiving Holy Communion.

Rudi became the instrument to reconnect with my inner life. He gave me the *Autobiography of a Yogi* by Yogananda. I devoured it as if my soul had been starving. Being presented with the idea of reincarnation seemed to immediately bring all of life into its right perspective. I felt a visceral memory of having been on earth "since we crawled out of the mud." Reading about Babaji, the immortal yogi who lived in the Himalayas since ancient times, moved me into spontaneous prayer to him. I don't believe I was praying *for* anything but entered in communion with him and with that eternal something that surpasses all understanding. Little could I have imagined that within a year I would be in India.

When that famous article on LSD came out in Playboy, with its drawings of colorful swirling water in a glass, I couldn't imagine anyone wanting to take the risk of becoming insane. I had put the idea of ever using acid firmly outside my realm of interest. Now, getting to know Rudi, who had already journeyed on LSD and Mescaline and who spoke with reverence about the amazing mind-opening experiences which had brought him into the presence of God, I became cautiously interested. We talked about it at length, and when he assured me that I would be safe and that he would watch over me, we set a date to journey together.

Surprisingly, when the effect came on, I found myself empowered and expanded into what seemed the realm of the immortals. Everything came alive and I within it. Looking into Rudi's blue-gray eyes, it seemed I was beholding the Madonna herself. The altered state was not at all frightening. In fact, it was a relief to see with different eyes, beyond ordinary reality.

Sometime later, on one of those sun-drenched summer days in Holland, Rudi and I together with his previous girlfriend Patricia, an American woman in her late twenties like I was, took the train to the coast and dropped Mescaline. I can still see the three of us walking off into the sand dunes, leaving all the people behind who were heading for the beach. We morphed into seven-foot-tall angels, striding with holy purpose into the sacredness of nature. We each veered off in our own direction and I got lost to the world on the warm sand, fully immersed into a miraculous tiny universe of fat bumblebees dancing and buzzing in small flowering shrubs. I was in heaven.

I became more and more focused on Rudi, both spiritually and sexually. I was still very much in love with Beth, but the situation had become intolerable for her. She felt so deeply hurt and betrayed that she had to break off our relationship. I remember her standing there, my beloved little Beth, on the far side of her room, raging in tears at my betrayal and at having to cast me out of her life. She had never before let anyone so deeply into her tender heart and I had stomped all over it. I, too, was heartbroken. I felt terrible. My remorse and my love for her stayed with me for decades.

Rudi and I both got our bachelor's in psychology in the spring of '71. To continue our studies, we each applied for clinical psychology. As it turned out, clinical psychology had become so popular that both of us ended up on a one-year waiting list. Rudi had the desire to go to India. We talked about going together.

159

I was squarely presented with a unique and enormous adventure that I couldn't just dismiss. Whenever I heard of people traveling the world, I always felt they were different from me. I never thought I would do such a thing. A true homebody, I was happy just traveling around Europe on vacations. However, I was facing the undeniable truth of an open road before me. I would receive my student loan for the next year and could work all summer. I had the freedom, the time and the money to go with him, but I was reluctant. One day, I took a good look at why I didn't want to go and I realized I was afraid. Declining such a big adventure out of fear was not acceptable to me. I had myself a good cry and said, "You're going!"

Part III

India

Hitchhiking the Hippy Trail to India

Earlier that year, before Rudi ever mentioned the idea of traveling to India, I had read an article in a Dutch magazine about Auroville, the "City of the Future," founded by a woman called "The Mother" in South India in 1968. She was the spiritual companion of Sri Aurobindo, a great Indian sage and seer. I had been struck by one small quote from Sri Aurobindo: *All Life is Yoga.*

These simple words rang like bells in my mind. I didn't know what it meant—I wondered if one was to do asanas in the kitchen—but it felt like a window into an all-encompassing spiritual way of life. I had left the Catholic Church when I was eighteen because it had been all too narrow-minded and dogmatic for me. I cut the picture of the spiral nebula design of the city out of the magazine and put it on my wall. It looked like a promise for a better future.

Rudi already knew of the Mother. Somebody at the university had a photograph of this woman in her office. He took me to see it. As I was looking at her ancient face, he told me that when she saw you, she would know everything about you and, as if that was not mysterious enough, she herself apparently was working on the transformation of her cells, whatever that meant!

Since we had a whole year in front of us, we decided to travel around the world, with only one place as a specific destination: Auroville in South India. My mother came to visit me and expressed her premonition, "I'm afraid that you will never come back." When I looked at that possibility, my mind's eye scanning across the globe, I said to her, "If there is any place on earth where life is good, I will stay there. Maybe that is Auroville. But I don't really believe it exists." I didn't even know what a good life would be. In the years after the war, with the terrifying reality and ongoing threat of the atomic bomb, the world in my experience was a rather ominous place.

We planned to hitchhike all the way to India and then possibly around the world. I considered carefully what to bring. As a two-year-old refugee, tired, cold, hungry and afraid, I had to keep walking while carrying a tiny suitcase. Then during my early school years, I had to carry my suitcase, walking all by myself from the train station to the boarding school through farmland with frightening watchdogs. I was determined to travel light. I put a year's worth of birth control pills and tampons at the bottom of a very small backpack, then some underwear, an extra pair of jeans and a few shirts. I strapped a bedroll underneath. My passport and traveler's checks got tucked in a pouch under my shirt. I was ready to go.

My father was elated with my plans. He seemed to know how auspicious this adventure would be for me. On September 29, 1971, he drove us to the border with Germany to send us off with his blessings. We walked across the border to catch our first ride. I turned around and waved goodbye to my beaming father. I felt as if we were leaving on a ray of light.

We picked up our first ride at the border. To our great surprise, he drove us all the way to Munich. We spent the night there and decided to take a train through the Swiss Alps to Yugoslavia where we spent our second night in Ljubljana. The next morning we made a little cardboard sign for Belgrade, the next major city. A young man from Germany, driving a beat-up Volkswagen Beetle, picked us up. His name was Volkert. He proudly smiled at us and announced that *he* was driving to Istanbul. Bursting out laughing, we said, *"We* are going to *India!"*

We drove all day and camped somewhere along the road in Greece. The next day we took the ferry across the Bosporus Strait from where I beheld the fairytale skyline of Istanbul, my first impression of the non-Western world. We had hitch-hiked to Istanbul in four days!

We left Volkert to his business. He was planning to buy a large quantity of hashish in Turkey and hide it behind the door panels in his beetle. He was convinced that he would cross the borders into Greece and then into Yugoslavia without any problems and make a lot of money in Germany. We heard later that he had bragged at the border about having hashish hidden in his car, so sure that it wouldn't be found. He was jailed in Greece for years and only with his father's money for lawyers and the discovery that his 'hashish' actually consisted of compressed dung, was he eventually released.

We stayed in a funky hotel. I vividly remember the dank and filthy bathroom, which proved to be the first of many, eventually progressing to the total absence of any facilities at all. We strolled through the colorful Grand Bazaar where I bought a small oriental rug and had it shipped back home. We were in awe of the exquisite beauty of the Hagia Sofia, its walls and ceilings entirely inlaid in blue mosaics.

It was our first experience in a Muslim country and we quickly learned from fellow travelers to beware of the men.

Apparently, Western women are by definition considered whores. As a woman, you're not even supposed to make eye contact with a man, which is rather difficult when you're dealing with hotel clerks, shopkeepers, waiters and other public figures. Having to become a second-rate citizen overnight and needing to turn all negotiations over to Rudi changed our dynamics, making me dependent on him. It undermined my self-confidence. Neither of us liked it one bit.

Other travelers strongly advised me against hitchhiking, even though I had a man with me. We decided to travel the nearly 3,000 miles by bus throughout the width of Turkey, to Iran and from there to Afghanistan. For days we rode through endless desert, the bus always packed to the gills with a constantly shifting population of men, women, children, goats and chickens. The view consisted of endless sands sprinkled sparsely with bits of thorny shrubbery from one horizon to the next. The bus would stop in the middle of nowhere. People boarded and got off, with not a dwelling in sight. I wondered where and how they lived.

Looking out the window at one of these desert stops, I saw a girl. She must have been about thirteen or fourteen. Hers were the greenest eyes I had ever seen. We locked eyes and couldn't stop gazing at each other, a deep wondering in my heart about what her life was like and what it would be for her as she grew into a woman.

When we finally arrived at the border of Iran, we got off the bus. I badly needed to use the bathroom. I asked one of the customs officers where the bathroom was. He made a generous sweep of his arm around the back of the building, where there was nothing but desert. Men were traipsing off a ways and squatted in the sand. No women seemed to ever need to pee. I was dressed in jeans and had no way to cover myself. I couldn't do it and had to hold it till we got to Tehran.

I am sorry to say that I have only unpleasant memories of Tehran. Endless crowds of small, dark men as far as the eyes could see. Not a woman in sight. I did not feel safe. We took the bus out of there the next morning.

Then came Afghanistan. How I came to love that country with the straightforward ruggedness of true mountain people, their fierce eyes, not afraid of anybody, their weathered brown skin stained in shades of indigo from their hand-dyed clothing; push carts piled high with pomegranates; the tantalizing fragrance of broiling lamb kebab on every street corner and the inscrutable gaze of men sitting on porches and verandas smoking their enormous hookas. It must have been at a bus stop in Kandahar. I saw a large bundle of laundry lying on the sidewalk. When the bus arrived, the bundle stood up. It was a woman covered from head to toe in a white burka, with a small grid of fabric as a window for her to see through.

After arriving in Kabul, Rudi got sick for a bit, which gave me the luxury of hanging out on my own for a couple of weeks, enjoying some very fine Afghan hashish. After Rudi recovered, we heard frightening stories from other travelers about train robberies along the Kyber Pass, but it seemed the only way to proceed. With some apprehension and together with some other travel companions we took the train and drove all night through the pass and straight through Pakistan to Lahore's border with India.

We heard rumors about a much-feared female customs officer at the border who could detect hashish no matter how well hidden. I had a small metal container with cough drops in my pack in which I had stored some nuggets during our stay in Afghanistan but which was now empty. We entered a barren room with benches, travelers milling around everywhere and got in line to face her at the customs counter. As soon as I handed her my small pack, she got a glint in her eyes. "I will find it!" she smiled triumphantly. I smiled right back at her. When she got to the little box and opened it, the smell was still there but no contraband. I acknowledged her skill and her disappointment. We both laughed.

I will never forget her surprise when she discovered my stash of birth control pills and tampons at the bottom of my pack. She looked at me with sheer admiration and maybe some envy and sent me on my way. Moving to the exit, one of our traveling friends, who was still in line, handed me his coat and asked if I would take that with me. "Sure," I said and walked outside with it. We waited for our little group to be gathered again outside.

Due to the threat of war between Pakistan and India in 1971, there was about a mile of no man's land between the countries where no traffic was allowed. We found ourselves walking on a wide straight dirt road lined on both sides with big trees creating an enormous cathedral as far as the eye could see. In the cool, deep shade, with parakeets and other brightly colored tropical birds flitting and screeching through the foliage, a gentle breeze caressed my cheeks. I felt kissed by God and found myself transported into the sacred. I knew in that instant that I was intimately and completely loved. It was my first, spontaneous and authentic experience of the living presence of the Divine.

Our traveling companion reached into his coat, the one I had carried for him across the border, and pulled out a kilo of hash. "We don't need this anymore," he said and flung the dark brown block into the bushes. Apparently, he had a spiritual experience at the same time I did.

After boarding the waiting train and riding through the north of India to New Delhi, seeing the teeming masses of people in all their abundant colors, outrageous variety and extreme poverty as only India can display, my view on life changed so radically that I decided to stop taking my birth control pills. Looking back, I am slightly aghast at the bewildering levity and speed with which I made such a momentous decision. As many have reported before me and I am sure since and without quite realizing it, I had a life-changing spiritual experience the moment I set foot in India.

From then on Rudi and I happily tried to conceive. Fortunately, and dare I say, by the grace of God, we did not succeed.

Traveling through India

When Rudi and I got off the train in New Delhi, we gingerly navigated the throngs of porters and beggars to arrive at a vast town square with scooters, taxis, colorful trucks and overloaded buses, all of them honking and driving at breakneck speed. Rickshaws and people everywhere and in the midst of the onslaught of noisy commotion, the large, bony, white Brahmin bulls with their huge horns lumbering along or lying down chewing their cud unperturbed.

Standing around, waiting for a bus, it didn't take long before we were surrounded by poor, skinny children staring at us boldly with unflinching big brown eyes, all urgently begging for paisa. It made me quite uncomfortable. I quickly found out that giving them anything while you still had to stand there was a big mistake. The crowd of children would instantly triple and the whole situation would become most unpleasant.

In the midst of the crowds, Western hippies easily spotted one another and would exchange helpful travel tips. A blond, young man from California hooked up with us and invited us to take a bus with him to a suburb on the outskirts of Old Delhi, Mehrauli. After crossing a market square and passing through fields, he took us to an abandoned monastery. It had become a crash pad for hippies from all over the world. Only one old monk was left on the premises. The building sported stone rooms with cement bunk slabs. We appropriated a couple of slabs and decided to stay put for a month to absorb the taste and feel of India.

Strolling through the narrow cobblestone streets of Mehrauli, we marveled at the open storefronts, merchants sitting cross-legged in the midst of their colorful wares, some of them equipped with large stainless-steel vats full of milk from which, through constant stirring, a great variety of delicious milk-sweets were produced. I particularly loved the fresh lassis.

We had brought a minimum amount of clothes and, to be more in tune with the culture in which we found ourselves, we bought light cotton fabrics and had tailors sew kurtas and pajama pants for Rudi. I enjoyed buying burgundy-colored cotton with paisley patterns for long wrap-around skirts and had some thin cotton shirts made for me.

All of us hippies were regularly invited to the home of a local merchant, who would sit cross-legged in his white dhoti and speak of India's ancient wisdom to all who would hear, while his wife would treat us to endless cups of sweet milk tea and Indian delicacies. The market square was surrounded by rickety cafés and tea shops. One of the owners had figured out just how to please these newfangled, long-haired western visitors with fresh chapatis and scrambled eggs. We quickly became his loyal customers.

Once a week, the old monk would open the valve for the irrigation system, located in the center of the compound. A powerful stream of water would pour into a large cement basin and we all enjoyed taking turns refreshing ourselves under the pounding cool water.

All kinds of substances were making the rounds among us. There were a few junkies who were injecting themselves with heroin. I knew to stay away from that. One evening we tried some opium. I did not find it very interesting. However, I did love getting stoned on ganja out in the fields immersing myself in the spirit of this sacred land.

I noticed one young man who would often sit quietly and meditate. A light shone in his eyes. I was intrigued. He told us about an ashram in Haridwar, near Rishikesh, where he had been initiated into a secret meditation technique. We decided it was worth the trek and we took the train up North into the Himalayan foothills. I had heard of Rishikesh and it sounded incredibly romantic and intriguing to me.

Indeed, Rishikesh was a small, picturesque town along the Ganges. Chanting filled the air from a number of low-roofed stone-built ashrams along its banks. I was impressed to see an old man in a white loincloth perched like a grasshopper on the stone riverbank, his knees sticking out and up behind his bony shoulders. He was bending deeply forward to wash his clothes in the river. I couldn't imagine being able to do that myself and certainly, old people in the West, having sat on chairs their whole life, would never accomplish such a feat of flexibility.

In Haridwar, we found the ashram the young man had recommended and were admitted. It was crawling with young people from all over the world. The guru was a fat teenage Indian boy whose family, especially his mother, was running the show. We were initiated by some of the guru's assistants in a few secret meditation techniques, which we were only allowed to practice under cover of a cloth over our heads. One of these was supposed to produce the nectar of the gods. The essence of the teachings was about the illusion of existence, Maya, and focused on the Light.

I enjoyed sitting by the bank of the very fast-flowing Ganges, its waters a curious pale green as it came hurtling down the mountains. If you got in the water you would immediately be carried downstream and had to make sure to clamber out pretty quickly not to end up too far from the ashram grounds. On the banks of this sacred river, inspired by the teachings we had received about Maya, I did have a luminous moment of awareness of the illusion of existence.

One day, darshan was announced, a chance to see the guru. A long line of young people wound its way around the building. The pudgy young man stood in a doorway, his family around him. He looked perfectly ordinary to me, in fact rather boring. One by one, everyone prostrated in front of him. I was greatly perturbed. I felt contempt for the whole situation. I didn't want to do something phony that was supposed to be a profound gesture of worship. However, when my turn came I didn't have the courage to just stand there, look at him and walk on. I went through the motions with a sickening feeling. Internally, I apologized to whatever God there was for my cowardice.

After about a week, we decided we had enough. This one wasn't for us. We boarded the train and headed back to New Dehli for another short stay at our old stomping grounds in Mehrauli. We figured we would travel towards the west coast and down to the far south, then come back up along the east coast to Pondicherry to explore Auroville.

Getting on trains was always a struggle, first to obtain tickets, then to navigate jostling crowds and trying to find a seat. The cacophony of noise was quite overwhelming, as well as the many pungent smells, the shrill whistles of the conductors, the deafening blasts when the steam engines started up, and vendors, lifting large trays of sweets above their heads, shouting to sell their wares. The bathroom situation, or lack thereof, continued to be most unpleasant.

We took the train to Bombay (now called Mumbai) passing through Agra. Because of the war with Pakistan, the entire Taj Mahal had been covered, because it would make a perfect target at night, gleaming like a jewel in the light of the moon. I still regret having missed seeing this timeless work of beauty and devotion.

Bombay was a nightmare. One horrific experience can still haunt me. We were being moved forward in the midst of a dense crowd of packed bodies on a sidewalk. You couldn't change course if you wanted to. Suddenly, I almost stepped on a woman on the ground with a burned stump of a head. There was no face. No eyes.

Just some holes for nose, mouth and ears in the midst of scar tissue. She was lying there, reaching up a hand begging, being trampled by the crowd. I couldn't even stop, and nearly stumbled over her, trying not to fall. It obliterated any desire in me to explore the city. Rudy agreed. We practically fled from Bombay.

From there we traveled to the Ajanta Caves, surely one of the finest treasures of India. My soul was deeply moved as I gazed onto the serene, intimate and tender expressions on the faces of the Buddha, Bodhisattvas and Devas, all painted in rich earth tones, faded and chipped, but still hauntingly present after thousands of years.

All along, traveling hippies had been praising Goa on India's west coast, which had been a Portuguese colony, as a small paradise where you could swim naked at the beach. Being nude in nature had always been quite alluring to me. It seemed such a lovely promise of being completely natural, to experience one's original innocence. So, we chugged along to Goa.

We arrived at one of Goa's picturesque fishermen's villages situated directly on the beach, with boys and men hauling in the large nets and women and girls running along the beach, carrying heavy baskets full of fish on their heads, the wet drippings from the freshly caught fish covering them from head to toe in glistening goop.

A unique phenomenon in Goa are the little wild pigs that run around, freely eating whatever they can find. We discovered small outhouses perched on ledges, where after dropping my load in the field below, I was startled by a grunting little pig rushing over to scarf up the delicacy.

We were enjoying tea in one of the huts on the beach when I saw a young boy running at full speed along one of the open sides of the tea hut and suddenly disappearing from sight. I looked around. He was nowhere to be seen. Then I discovered him high up in the palm tree. Without stopping and faster than I could see, he had run straight up the tall tree trunk to harvest a coconut.

We joined a small band of Westerners who were lounging in the dunes a little further up and following their example, even though I felt quite awkward, we stripped and ran naked to the water. Indian men on motorcycles came roaring up the beach to watch the spectacle. I ran back as fast as I could to cover myself up. That had been no fun at all. Over time, as I got to know traditions in India more deeply, I was mortified at having so gravely violated their moral codes. If women go into the ocean at all, they go in their saris, fully dressed! Later, when I came to live in a village myself, I learned that most men in rural India never even see their own wives nude, making love in the dark in their little huts with their sleeping children beside them.

Continuing south, we came to Kerala. The landscape reminded me of pictures I had seen of Indonesia, water everywhere and effervescent green rice paddies surrounded by palm trees. Long ago, the capital of Kerala, Cochin, had been a Dutch colony. In an old graveyard behind a church, I discovered Dutch names on headstones. I wondered if I had once lived there and could have been buried there. Kerala was then known as the state with the highest level of education among its people. It did not make for a particularly pleasant experience. The general pace of life was faster, much less relaxed than we had grown accustomed to. We were frequently insulted in English by aggressive young men.

An interesting shift had taken place in the food scene. As soon as we hit the Southern parts of India, the restaurants would consist of long wooden tables with benches. A banana leaf was laid open on the table in front of us. Waiters walked around with buckets of rice, sambar (a spicy broth), a variety of vegetable curries and dhal, each of them ladling portions onto our banana leaf. They would continue to walk around and keep adding on to our food, always urging us to accept more as if wanting to prevent at all costs that we might not have enough to eat. And, of course, we happily ate with our hands. There's nothing quite like it.

All through southern India, we found comfortable lodging in bungalows, remnants from colonial times, with cool verandas, lovely gardens and old-time courteous service. English teatime is observed religiously. I felt transported to those times of undeserved luxury, when the Indian keeper of the inn wearing white gloves bowed to us, serving us tea as if we were royalty.

When we came to the Mudumalai Tiger Reserve, we rode an elephant. She carried a platform on her back, carpeted and laid out with pillows for tourists to sit on. The mahout, her care-taker, gingerly climbed up to sit right behind her ears and guided her through the jungle. I was amazed how silently this gigantic animal moved, slowly rocking us sideways as she walked. Not a twig broke under her feet. In fact, we spotted a whole family of deer nibbling away within very close range and none of them seemed to even be aware of our presence. The only sound she produced was a deep low rumbling right under our bodies when she defecated.

We traveled as far south as Tirunelveli, then turned to the northeast. We stopped and stayed for a few days in Madurai, which I always remember as a most pleasant city. Our last stop before heading toward Pondicherry was in Tiruchirapalli. The Sri Ranganathaswamy Temple is truly a mountain temple, in fact, it seems like the temple and the mountain are completely merged. We joined many devotees, climbing steep worn stairs, weaving in and out of dark temple halls and corridors all the way to the top. Poojas were performed everywhere. Priests were droning endless chants. Incense wafted in front of the statues of gods opulently draped with garlands of marigolds and jasmine.

From there we took the train north. Little did I know how radically my life was about to change.

A True Coming Home

On the train from Tiruchirappalli to Madras, we debated whether we still wanted to bother going to Pondicherry. No matter how amazing India was and how many fascinating sites and marvelous temples we had seen, after having traveled throughout that enormous country for several months, we were frankly quite sick of it. Of course, as travelers, we had spent a lot of time at dismal bus and train stations, with disgusting sanitation, throngs of poor people and hassles everywhere. We were eager to head for Nepal and then farther east from there. I was thinking Indonesia. As we approached Villapuram where we would have to change trains to head towards Pondy, it seemed a shame to pass it by. I bargained with Rudi, "Hey, we've been wanting to see Auroville all this time. Let's just go for three days and then head up to Nepal."

We arrived in Pondicherry on February 12, 1972. When we asked the rickshaw driver to take us to the ashram, he gave us a little sideways shaking of the head, a unique Indian gesture of agreement and took us to a hotel in town instead. We were led to a room on the third floor via stairwells on the outside of the building, where, overlooking the city, my body was suddenly hit by the force of the Mother coming over the rooftops from the direction of the ashram. Shaken and somewhat frightened by the unexpected impact, my first thought was, "She's a witch!" Because I knew that she was good, I quickly reassured myself, "Well, she must be a white witch."

Pondicherry had been a French enclave during the British rule of India. The French Quarter situated directly on the coast of the Bay of Bengal, consisted of many old colonial-style buildings with large shady trees and parks. As the Sri Aurobindo Ashram expanded over the decades, they had acquired many of these buildings. The ashram itself was a large three-story building

With Rudi in India

around an inner courtyard. Mother's room was on the third floor above the courtyard with a balcony facing one of the side streets.

It turned out that we had arrived just days before Mother's ninety-fourth birthday. 1972 was also Sri Aurobindo's centenary year. There was a huge celebration, and Pondicherry was buzzing with thousands of visitors. On Mother's birthday, February 21st, she would appear on her balcony to give darshan to the crowd. Naturally, we decided to stay until then. To be able to participate in the Ashram activities, you were supposed to stay in one of the many Ashram guest houses. You would then be given a pass which allowed access to the inner courtyard with Sri Aurobindo's white marble tomb, referred to as the Samadhi, the ashram dining room, the library and so on. We entered the main gate and crossed a small courtyard filled with large tropical plants and knocked on the heavy doors of a building overgrown with bougainvilleas to ask for help. We were told to sit on the steps and wait for one of Mother's secretaries to come and assist us.

We sat on the ashram steps for three days. Since the steps were directly across from the main gate, we just relaxed and watched people coming and going all day long. We couldn't see the main courtyard from where we were sitting. On the second day, I suddenly noticed how the stream of people coming in to meditate by Sri Aurobindo's tomb were not the same people as the ones leaving the compound. The people coming in were ordinary people, preoccupied by their daily affairs, immersed in their thoughts. The people coming out were completely silent and seemed to be emanating white light. It was eerie, as if they were a different species altogether, not really from this planet. Some mysterious transformation had taken place during the time they had spent in the courtyard. I realized that something significant was happening there.

Finally, on the third day, an Indian gentleman greeted us. He invited us into a large dark room, furnished in old colonial style, and indicated for us to sit down. I was expecting some kind of interview, but Madhav Pandit sat with us in total silence. I became silent, too. Suddenly, he seemed to approve of us and after a few perfunctory questions, he smiled and said, "You can stay. Because of the centenary, all of our guest houses are completely booked, but just yesterday a Dutch woman broke her leg. She is in the hospital now. You can have her room."

We were given a room in the Parc à Charbon guest house situated directly on the coast. Later I would discover that many Westerners started their adventure with Mother and Sri Aurobindo in the Parc Guesthouse.

The inner courtyard of the ashram was a very special place. Droves of people quietly moved around and meditated sitting under the shade of a large peepal tree spreading its branches over Sri Aurobindo's white marble tomb. A profound peace permeated the area. Every morning, devotees covered the Samadhi with colorful, fragrant mandalas of fresh blossoms. As I saw others do, I would often sit close to the Samadhi and put my forehead on the cool marble, immersed in the intoxicating fragrance of thousands of blossoms and incense, the all-pervasive silence accentuated only by bees buzzing over the blossoms and punctuated by loud, startling caws of the occasional crow overhead.

We befriended Ron, an American, who kindly took me under his wings. He seemed to sense that I was meant to be there. When he heard that we were only going to stay until after

Ron Jorgensen in the 2000s, photograph by Bill Leon

Mother's birthday, he told us that we could write to Mother and ask to see her in person. Mother would always try to see visitors, knowing that they might never have the opportunity to meet with her again. So I did. I took my letter to Madhav, and the next day, he told us we could see her the following Sunday. This added another week to our stay, but we weren't going to miss this unique opportunity. Ron impressed upon me to make sure to look into her eyes. Many Indian devotees, he explained, would simply prostrate before her and never look at her. He really didn't want me to miss out on that most important opportunity of looking into her eyes. He also told us that people usually bring Mother flowers. My no-nonsense attitude immediately rebelled. "I'm not bringing her flowers," I objected. "I don't even know her."

On her birthday, February 21st, we experienced her public darshan. Thousands of visitors thronged in the street below Mother's balcony. When she slowly appeared, a hush fell over the crowd. As she gazed down at us, a vast silence descended as if the world came momentarily to a standstill. We all seemed to

Mother's darshan, printed with permission of the Sri Aurobindo Ashram

hold our breath in the sheer awe of her. Later, I heard that everyone felt as if she gazed at them personally.

On Sunday morning, February 27, 1972, Rudi and I put on our best clothes and headed for the Ashram. Just as we were leaving the guest house, the manager came out. Seeing us all dressed up, he smiled and greeted us in his wonderful Indian accent. "Good morning! Where are you going?" "We're going to see Mother!" "Oh, wait, wait," he ran to the overgrown wall of the building and picked us each a large, single, orange hibiscus blossom with a deep crimson heart.

"Here, take these to Mother!" We accepted his gracious gesture and started off on our walk along the oceanside, each of us carrying our magnificent flower. I discovered later that the orange hibiscus was the symbol for Auroville.

We joined a long line of people who were slowly winding their way through the courtyard, up the stairs, on landings, and up the stairs again, all the way to Mother's room on the third floor. By the time we entered her room, it was close to noon. It being the end of February in South India, the heat was already intense, and my flower was sadly wilting.

Due to her considerable age, Mother sat slightly bent, so to be able to look into her eyes you really had to get down on your knees. When my turn came, I knelt in front of her and presented my poor hibiscus. In that instant, the hibiscus opened itself to her in its full radiance. I stared in disbelief at this transmutation, as if I was on an acid trip. Suddenly, I remembered to look at her. I handed the flower to her assistant and looked into her eyes. She was so absolutely still, it seemed to me as if she were dwelling on the other side of the galaxy. Nothing happened. But I kept looking, until I heard my own voice inside of me command, "Open up!"

In that instant, we recognized each other. "It's you!" my whole being shouted. She seemed to feel exactly the same. We were both equally ecstatic, beaming at one another for the sheer joy of recognition. In that moment, even as we were two, we were the same. Actually, the notion in the back of my mind was "six thousand." Only afterwards I figured it related to years. We couldn't let go of gazing into one another's eyes. When I felt a nudge that it was time to move along, I slowly got up. Our eyes remained locked, our heads turning until the distance forced us to disengage.

In a daze, I walked out of the room. Tears began to stream down my cheeks. I wept for three days. Wherever I went, bitter-sweet tears kept streaming down my face. Tears of unimaginable joy at having been seen, at finally being known to her and to myself, mixed with the grief that it had taken so very, very long for this to happen. It was as if I had been waiting since the beginning of my countless lifetimes of searching for God. In front of her, in one fell swoop, all my veils were torn and my soul stood revealed. I had come home to myself.

My First Months in the Ashram

Three days later, I woke up and felt I was back on the ground. Rudi felt it too and said, "So, are you ready to go?"

"I'm not going anywhere," I replied. That's when I found out that Rudi had a very different experience upon seeing Mother. He had been directly behind me and, overwhelmed as I had been with my own experience, I had not been aware of what was happening with him. Apparently, he had been acutely confronted with his attachments. He wasn't ready to give up on going back to Holland, studying psychology, playing the guitar, riding motorcycles and, in his own words, "fucking little fat-assed virgins." After all, he

After seeing Mother

was only twenty-three and just beginning his life, whereas I, at twenty-nine, had already been married, worked and studied and felt as though I had a complete lifetime behind me. There was no question in my mind that I was ready to give it all up, now that I had found what had been my longing for lifetimes.

Suddenly our paths were diverging. Late that morning, I accompanied him to the train station. He would continue on to Nepal on his own. Our farewell was very sad.

I continued to live in the Parc à Charbon guest house and participated in the Ashram routines of daily meals in the dining hall, sitting in silence by Sri Aurobindo's white marble tomb. I attended the weekly meditations in the courtyard of the International Center of Education, where Mother's dramatic voice was played over the loudspeakers, reading Sri Aurobindo or playing the organ, followed by an ever-deepening silence.

I was grateful to have Ron's friendship and support. He introduced me to Satprem's *Sri Aurobindo, or the Adventure of Consciousness*. Discovering the essence of Integral Yoga, to establish the Divine Consciousness, transforming life itself here on Earth, I experienced an immense relief to have found a spiritual path which was not focused on the hereafter, on getting out of here, but rather on transforming life itself. My whole being said YES to that.

I met Roger Anger, the French architect (and Mother's grandson) who had designed the spiral nebula model of Auroville. He had also designed the first model of the Matrimandir, the Mother's Temple, a large sphere rising up out of the earth, which would be the geographical and spiritual center of Auroville. When Roger discovered that I was multi-lingual, he asked if I would

The Matrimandir at dawn in Auroville, 2024. Photograph by B William Sullivan

make myself available as a secretary to Professor Newcombe, a Delegate of UNESCO (the United Nations Educational, Scientific and Cultural Organization), which seeks to build peace through international cooperation. He was on an assignment to study the principles of Auroville's charter, their application, and the progress made in the community. I felt honored to be asked and glad to accept his offer, which provided me with many interesting trips to Auroville. I helped to record and translate his interviews. A typewriter was available for me in Roger's office.

Since it was Mother's vision for the collective realization of human unity that drew me most of all, I asked her for permission to live in Auroville. Mother herself determined if a person was ready to participate in that experiment. When I received her acceptance, she asked if I would please first complete my service to Professor Newcombe for the three months of his stay.

In the meantime, I had begun to miss my sweet Rudi sorely and, regardless of the immensity of having met the Mother, in my new daily life, I felt quite lonely. I felt so far removed from anything or anyone familiar—walking the streets of Pondicherry, riding in rickety rickshaws, every single smell and color unfamiliar to me. To make things worse, the 'gatekeepers' of the ashram made me feel like I had entered another boarding school with its rules and regulations. One evening I went to the courtyard for the meditation. I had forgotten my little Ashram pass. They wouldn't let me in. Quite offended, I said, "Mother knows who I am!" It didn't work. I was furious.

That event triggered my childhood trauma of feeling like an outcast, and added to my ever-increasing sense of loneliness and not belonging. I descended into a dark depression. I felt completely stymied. I couldn't leave and I couldn't stay. I felt so stuck, I started to consider walking out into the sea. The Bay of Bengal at my doorstep was wild and treacherous, and I am not a good swimmer.

In my despair, I finally wrote a letter to Mother. I had my photograph taken to send along with my letter. I wanted to make sure that she knew who I was. My plea for help felt like a matter of life and death to me. I described my torment to her. I couldn't leave because in my soul I wanted to stay but staying had become intolerable.

The next morning, I went to the Ashram to give the letter to Madhav to take to Mother, knowing that he always went to see her in the morning. He told me to come back after 10 a.m.

I went to Ron's apartment to bide the time. A Tai Chi teacher, Ron demonstrated some of the elegant moves to me when, suddenly, I caught Mother's eye in the photograph on his desk. Time stood still. It was as if she looked right through me, as if my brain were a translucent crystal. She must have been looking at my picture at that very moment.

A little while later, I made my way back to Madhav's small office. When he saw me come in, he silently got up from behind his desk. He came very close to me with a look on his face indicating that something important had transpired. "Mother said, 'Stay!' and also, 'These are merely vital movements.'" I felt a bit indignant that my black depression was so easily dismissed as "merely vital movements." (In the language of Integral Yoga, the "vital" is the term used for the emotional body/mind consciousness.) I was confused. Madhav continued, "Mostly when people ask Mother this question, she will tell them to go because they have unfinished business in the outside world. But she said 'Stay!' When I first saw you, I knew you had come through many lifetimes and that you were ready." He returned my photograph and reassured me that Mother had "done something."

Slightly dazed, I walked out of the Ashram compound. As I walked onto the street, I suddenly realized I was filled with light. Startled, I actually turned around to see where that dark cloud had gone. It had vanished. Mother had "done something."

Not long after that remarkable experience with Mother, I happened to come upon a book on animal communication. One evening, reading by the lamp on my table, I noticed a little spider in a small web between the lamp and the wall, right in front of my face. Inspired by my reading, I smiled and said hello to it.

To my surprise she started to bounce her web up and down and then suddenly jumped into my hair. I couldn't help swatting her out of my hair, feeling a bit foolish and sorry for the little creature.

Later that week I went to the meditation in the ashram playground where hundreds of people were sitting on the ground, listening to Mother's powerful voice reading some of Sri Aurobindo's writing, then dropping into silence. Suddenly, the clouds opened and a torrential rain came down. Everyone jumped up and ran for cover. Having not experienced any rain since leaving Holland, I happily stayed seated and let myself get blissfully drenched. Then I spotted a cockroach having sought shelter under my leg. When it was time to leave, I was worried that if I got up, the little one would get trampled by the many people rushing to the gate. I gingerly picked it up and carried it with me to my room in the guesthouse. It stayed with me during the night and in the morning I put it on my shoulder and carried it around with me. I felt I had made a little friend, if a rather unlikely one. When I met Patricia near the Samadhi, she was startled and wanted to slap the cockroach from my shoulder. "No, no, don't," I laughed, "He's my friend!"

My Father's Spiritual Fulfillment

During my travels from Holland to India, I had written letters back home for my parents to circulate among family and friends. After seeing the Mother, I instinctively knew that my experience might not be comprehensible to most people and began to write just to my father. I knew in my bones that he had the spiritual depth to understand what was happening to me.

A few months into my stay in Pondicherry, in my ever-growing faith in the Mother's spiritual powers, I wrote her a letter asking her to help my parents. I explained that they had become ever more estranged from each other and that it pained me to know that by staying together they were causing each other a great deal of unnecessary suffering. Couldn't she do something for them?

Within three weeks, the usual length of time for letters to arrive, I got an ecstatic letter from my father. He had known nothing of my request. He had been away from home for a three-week job in Nijmegen. He so much enjoyed staying in this university town. There he had ample contact with students, eager to delve into deep philosophical discourse with him. They loved his radical spirit, and some of them found a true mentor in him. Upon his return, my mother had admitted to him how much happier she had been living by herself, and since he obviously loved being around the young people in Nijmegen, she suggested that they separate. Since he had never ceased to love and respect my mother and knew how important social propriety was to her, he would not have suggested this himself. Relieved and grateful, he accepted her offer. At the time of his writing, he had already moved back to Nijmegen and had found himself a little farmhouse at the edge of town where he was discovering a new freedom and a new happiness, living life among an ever-widening circle of friends.

Shortly after that, I found out that Satprem's *Sri Aurobindo, or the Adventure of Consciousness* had been translated into Dutch and was being published in the Netherlands. Right away, I wrote

Ludar

my dad to tell him to look for it. Soon, I received the following letter from him:

> The other morning, as I went for a little stroll in the neighborhood, I passed by the bookstore around the corner and there in the window was a Dutch translation of *Sri Aurobindo, or the Adventure of Consciousness*. I bought it on the spot. I received your letter later that same day! I couldn't stop reading and stayed up all night.

He had obviously found the same inspiration I had and began to devour Sri Aurobindo's writing. The comprehensive spiritual synthesis Sri Aurobindo offers allowed all of my father's lifelong insights and spiritual intuitions to coalesce into one great coherent worldview. He never ceased studying and meditating on both the Mother's and Sri Aurobindo's writings. In fact, I inherited his copy in the original French of all thirteen volumes of *L'Agenda de Mère* (*Mother's Agenda*). Every volume is densely underlined and annotated by him.

Soon, another letter came from him with the two golden rings he had worn all of his life, his wedding ring and the ring with his family's coat of arms. He asked me if I would please translate the following words into English and give it, together with his rings, to Mother:

> My being turns to you. My inner lamps are lit. As a symbol of my surrender, I offer you these rings. I wish to belong to the Divine only. I beg you to choose a mantra for me, possibly from Sri Aurobindo's *Savitri*.

Madhav told me that Mother had been "very pleased" with my father's request and accepted his rings. She had concentrated and gave him the following mantra from *Savitri*:

> Enter my life, Thy chamber, Thy shrine.

I immediately recognized how deeply this mantra would resonate with him, the chamber referring to the most private, humble place and the shrine to the most exalted aspects of his psyche. I was delighted to mail him Mother's response.

Seeing Mother for My Birthday

Once you were accepted to live in the Ashram or in Auroville, you were allowed one private darshan with Mother per year, on your birthday. According to Mother, the psyche is more open on your birthday and therefore, on that day you would be most open and receptive to her force. Barely three months after my first experience of seeing her, my 30th birthday was approaching. Rumors had it that Mother was not feeling well and was not seeing people at the time. There was nothing I wanted more than to see her again. I *had* to ask. I wrote to Mother and brought my letter to Madhav Pandit.

> Sweet Mother, I am so sorry to hear that you are not feeling well and are not seeing people. Even as I respect your need, the truth is that I really long to see you on my birthday. Forgive me for asking. Angela.

Anxiously, I awaited Madhav's return from his morning visit with Mother. Again, he came quietly close to me and with a small affirmative wobble of his head, he said, "Yes, Mother wants to see you. You can come with me on the morning of the seventeenth and I will take you to her."

Now, I definitely wanted to bring her flowers. Wanting to express my humility and my desire to surrender to the Divine, I consulted *Flowers and Their Messages*, a beautiful book of pictures and drawings of all the flowers to which Mother had given their spiritual significance. I created a small bouquet to bring to her, with basil, *Joy of Union with the Divine* and a few small lavender roses, *Humility in the Love for the Divine*. I followed Madhav upstairs to Mother's room. He indicated for me to sit on the balcony and wait for him to call me in. There I sat, all by myself on Mother's balcony with my little bouquet, and wondered how I could possibly make sure to be open and receptive to her. I didn't have the slightest idea how to go about that. My anxiety increased and I was quite a bundle of nerves when Madhav called me in. He indicated that I kneel in front of her, so I could look into her eyes. He took his place by her side. She turned to Madhav and asked, "This is Angela?"

"Yes, Mother." She took one look at me and threw her head back in laughter. I was utterly confused. What could be so funny? When she turned back to me, she motioned to put my head in her lap. She then stroked my head ever so softly, exquisitely, for a long time, all over. Then I was quietly guided back out of the room. Her touch had been soft like rose petals or the feel of a newborn. I didn't know what to think or feel about the whole experience. Since I was still so dissociated from my childhood trauma, it took me decades to understand what she had given me, after chuckling affectionately at seeing me so utterly helpless and confused. She had reassured my anxious child self. It was as if her gesture had conveyed to my body, "It's ok, it's ok, be calm my child."

Later in life, in my healing practice, I would have clients on my table, relax their necks and shoulders, and then softly lay my hands on their heads for a while and tune in. In those moments, I would often feel Mother's love pouring through my hands. Some of my clients would share with me afterwards that they had seen "that woman in the picture." I always kept a photograph of Mother in my healing room. So, it seemed I was able to pass some of her gift to me along to others.

Auroville

I had become friends with Patricia, an American woman, who had arrived in Pondicherry around the same time I did. She was expecting her husband to follow her. She and I had been equally inspired by our first encounter with the Mother and were opening our minds to the vision and the promise of life in Auroville. We threw ourselves wholeheartedly into offering our beings to the Divine for its conscious manifestation upon the earth. We felt like soul sisters.

Soon, we were approached by Sadhana, another American woman, who was running the kitchen in Auroville's Matrimandir Workers' Camp, referred to as the Center. Sadhana told us the Mother had put her in charge of creating order in the Center kitchen which had been haphazardly run by whoever felt inspired to cook for the community. The place was in chaos. She told us in no uncertain terms that we were the perfect women to help her with this somewhat daunting project. We were both excited about the invitation.

Towards the end of my stay in the Ashram, I had completed my task of assisting Professor Newcomb, and my friend Patricia announced that her husband Roger, also an American, had arrived. Before too long, the three of us moved to Auroville.

Mother had been inspired to create Auroville based on a dream. She said,

> Earth needs a place where men can live away from all national rivalries, social conventions, self-contradictory moralities and contending religions; a place where human beings, freed from all slavery to the past, can devote themselves wholly to the discovery and practice of the Divine Consciousness that is seeking to manifest. Auroville wants to be this place and offers itself to all who aspire to live the Truth of tomorrow.

She named Auroville after Sri Aurobindo. Auro indicates the dawn, and *ville* is French for city. Auroville, the "City of Dawn," the dawn of a new consciousness. Underwritten by the government of India, as well as by UNESCO, this is Mother's charter for Auroville:

1. Auroville belongs to nobody in particular. Auroville belongs to humanity as a whole. But to live in Auroville one must be a willing servitor of the Divine Consciousness.

2. Auroville will be the place of an unending education, of constant progress and a youth that never ages.

3. Auroville wants to be the bridge between the past and the future. Taking advantage of all discoveries from without and from within, Auroville will boldly spring towards future realisations.

4. Auroville will be a site of material and spiritual researches for a living embodiment of an actual human unity.

Auroville's official inauguration took place on February 28, 1968, with a remarkable ceremony where young people from 124 nations placed a handful of soil from their native land into a centrally located urn. Dignitaries from the Ashram, the Indian government and UNESCO attended. Young people from India and from all over the world became the pioneers who offered themselves, body and soul, to realize Mother's dream. By the time I arrived in 1972, small settlements and individual huts were spread far and wide over the few square miles of barren land.

Auroville is situated several miles inland from the Bay of Bengal and about eight miles north of Pondicherry. Some eighty years before, this land had been a lush jungle, but the trees had been cut for firewood, and together with the many voracious goats, wind and water had stripped the earth bare. Torrential monsoon rains washed away the topsoil until the entire plateau turned into a desert, dotted by a few remaining stands of trees. Deeply eroded gullies scarred the barren, red earth, baking under a glowering sun. The heat was incessant and overwhelming.

After the first Aurovilians constructed simple bamboo huts with braided palm fronds (keet) for roofs, the primary work consisted of planting trees, reclaiming the land, creating bunds around the fields to prevent water run-off, and building small earthen dams to collect the massive amounts of rain-water that poured down yearly during the monsoons.

Patricia, Roger and I were invited to move into the Matrimandir Workers' Camp. It was an extensive cement floored bamboo and keet construction, consisting of a large thatched dining area with a kitchen in back, central showers and bath-rooms, and quite a number of rooms around a small courtyard. Gardens surrounded the entire complex.

The Workers' Camp housed the Aurovilians who were building the Matrimandir, the Temple of the Mother. Roger Anger created the original design according to Mother's precise instructions. She had stated there should be a large golden sphere, symbolizing the dawn of a new consciousness, rising up out of the earth like the rising sun. It should rest on four pillars, each representing one of the four main aspects of the Divine Mother: Maheshwari—Wisdom, Mahakali—Strength, Mahalakshmi—Harmony, and Mahasaraswati—Perfection. A large meditation hall would be created high up in the center of the sphere.

Mother said that the Matrimandir would be the soul of Auroville and that the sooner it was built the better it would be for Auroville and for the world. The city would be built around the Matrimandir in much the same way as the individual would

Digging and building the foundation of Matrimandir

aspire to be entirely under the influence of the center of their own being. Mother and Sri Aurobindo called that aspect of our soul which evolves over lifetimes: the *psychic being*.

When we arrived, the construction of the Matrimandir was in its first phase. Many villagers were hired to help excavate a gigantic hole in the ground out of which the four pillars would reach up to support the enormous sphere rising high up into the sky. Inside the sphere, ramps were to lead up to the Inner Chamber which was going to be built according to Mother's specific vision. It would be laid out in white marble with twelve columns. At the center of the high ceiling, an opening would allow the rays of the sun and moon to shine a beam of light onto a large crystal sphere.

In this sacred space of great beauty, Mother envisioned Aurovilians opening themselves in complete silence to the Presence of the Divine, receiving Her Force. There were to be no images, flowers or objects, only silence around the light.

Hundreds of villagers were hired to help with the excavation. Each heavy scoop of red earth was loaded onto a metal dish. The dishes were lifted onto the workers' heads and carried in endless rows of dark bodies up the earthen stairways, which were hewn into the sides of the crater. It was an extraordinary scene, making me think of what it must have been like in ancient Egypt when workers were constructing the pyramids.

Patricia and I each got a room adjacent to one another and Roger moved into a bamboo hut in the garden in back. Both of them were deeply committed to the yoga and had vowed to be celibate to offer themselves solely to the Divine.

In the course of those first few months in Auroville, I came to the same conclusion. All I wanted was to be close to the Beloved,

Serving Tea to Matrimandir Workers. Copyright Dominique
Darr / Fonds de Dotation Art et Recherche Paris

to belong only to the Divine. So, I, too, made the choice to remain celibate. Since I had just turned thirty, I knew full well that I was also giving up on the idea of having children. I threw myself with complete abandon into the yoga.

Patricia and I got to work organizing the primitive kitchen. We started cooking three meals a day for the Aurovilians living in and around the workers' camp. We also looked after the general maintenance of the living quarters, sweeping hallways and scrubbing the bathrooms and showers.

Gabriel was our French-speaking cook from Pondicherry. I particularly remember the perfect way he quick-fried okra in generous amounts of garlic and mustard seeds, to keep them crisp. Turmeric would give the "lady's fingers," as they were called, a bright green color. We made large amounts of yogurt. We had help from Sagundala, a graceful lady from the Harijan colony, where the untouchables lived. Mornings and afternoons, we carried big pots of tea to the workers at the construction site.

With great joy, I gave myself wholeheartedly to the inner and outer work of transformation. Helping to create a living harmony on planet Earth was surely the highest ideal I could imagine living for.

Facing My Sex and Love Addiction

Once a week we would send a bullock cart with a village driver to the market in Pondicherry and often I would take the rickety village bus to meet them there. I shopped for vegetables, fruits, grains and spices at the colorful stalls. I haggled with the vendors for the best prices, then helped load up the bullock cart with provisions for the coming week. Being in Pondy always gave me the wonderful opportunity to spend some precious time at the ashram in the silence around the Samadhi. I would top off my little outing with a meal in one of the local restaurants. I loved the mutton biryani and was grateful for some extra protein.

One day, after finishing my errands, I ran into a small group of Aurovilians in a jeep who were about to drive back to Auroville. They offered me a ride even though the jeep was already full. Roger was sitting in the passenger seat in front and invited me to climb onto his lap. With some hesitation, I did, keeping myself carefully upright so as not to lean into his body. The jeep was open on the sides, so he held one arm around my right side to keep me safe.

It was a bumpy ride, especially on the dirt roads leading into Auroville. All was well, until suddenly, where his hand was on my leg, I felt his thumb ever so softly stroking my skin. I held my breath. Oh no... I froze. When we finally arrived, I fled to my room. But the damage had been done. It felt as if a little burr had entered my body and crept deeper and deeper into me until I was in flames. I couldn't stop from obsessing about him. I felt that I couldn't talk with Patricia, my best friend there because I was too embarrassed and he was her husband. In the evenings, I knew that he was in his hut just feet away from my room. It was pure torture.

Acting on the attraction was out of the question since I had made such a deep commitment in my soul to live for the Divine alone. On other levels it was all wrong, too, since I knew that he and Patricia had made the same commitment. I did not know

Soul-searching at the Matrimandir Nursery

which way to turn. I was burning up with desire. Both my body and my mind were on fire. I was in desperate need of help. At last, I thought, maybe Roger would help me. After all, *he* started it. I was certain he would support me in my desire for abstinence. Perhaps, if he told me in no uncertain terms that intimacy between us was out of the question, I could let go of my crazy-making obsession and calm down.

So, one evening I gathered my courage and, with trembling heart, I knocked on his door. Surprised, he invited me to sit down. I blurted out what was troubling me, begging for his help. Instead of assuring me that his boundaries were clear and inviolable, he lit up and smiled, "Let's go to my loft!" Deeply confused, I followed him like a sheep, up the bamboo ladder to his loft and into his bed. Our lovemaking was as powerful as it was desperate. I did not want it and yet I could not help myself. It didn't help that he had a gorgeous body—tall, strong, and lean with smooth, golden, sun-burnt skin. On top of that, his name, Roger, became Raju in Tamil, the King. I have always loved powerful men. He was definitely the alpha male in our camp.

The affair lasted for some time. I felt deeply torn, but couldn't stay away from him. My stomach began hurting until it got so intense that on a Sunday morning, while I was cleaning the showers, I doubled over and broke into convulsive vomiting. I wondered if I had an ulcer. I was taken by jeep to the small French hospital Cluny in Pondicherry, run by Catholic nuns. Because it was Sunday, the doctor was not available. I was given a spacious room and laid down to rest. I was exhausted. The room was peaceful. Relieved, I rested throughout the day and the night. In the morning I felt much better. The nun doctor came to see me. As she examined me, we talked and I told her of my upset. She agreed that all I needed was several weeks of rest and I should be fine.

I made arrangements to stay in Golconde for two weeks. Golconde was an astonishingly beautiful guesthouse close to the ashram. It had been designed on Mother's request by Antonin Raymond, a Czech architect, together with the American-Japanese artist woodworker George Nakashima. Mother had been directly involved with the supervision of all details. Everything was of exquisite beauty and simplicity, from the shining black marble floors to the fine sheen of ground shell with which the walls were whitewashed. Every handle and hinge was of the finest craftsmanship. Large horizontal cement shutters provided a constant breeze of fresh air and the necessary shade to keep the place cool. Mother's presence was tangible and I gratefully let myself recover in the peace and nearness of Her.

It was clear to me that I could not return to the Center and had to give Roger a wide berth. I realized my helplessness. Larry came to visit me and offered the possibility of living in Kottakarai, a small community of Aurovilians dedicated primarily to reforestation, agriculture, and village relations. A small hut was available for me. I gratefully accepted it. And so, a new life awaited me again.

Decades later, I discovered there was a name for my affliction: sex and love addiction. I had forgotten how compulsive my behavior had been during my year-long relationship with Beth. Like any true addict, I was in complete denial and always thought that my active sex life was an expression of my freedom. Not anymore.

Barefoot Village Doctor

I felt warmly welcomed by the small community of Kottakarai. A simple octagonal bamboo hut out in the fields was available for me. It had a dirt floor just like a village hut would. With a few mats on the floor, a little dresser and a simple cot with mosquito netting, it provided me with a peaceful space and I was happy to make myself at home.

I was told that when a small group of them, early Aurovilians, had asked Mother if they could settle near Kottakarai village, she had encouraged them to be humble. She said that villagers were innately more spiritual than us and that we, as Westerners, shouldn't think we knew more than them, and we shouldn't be egotistical in our thoughts and activities, feeling proud that we were doing so much to "help" the villagers.

The community was situated just across a canyon from Kottakarai. It was an extremely poor village. The houses were made of mud walls and palm-leaf roofs. Floors and walls were regularly plastered with a fresh sludge of cow dung, which smelled quite pleasant and clean and was actually disinfectant. These homes were haphazardly placed around a village square, where the grandfather of Radhakrishna, one of our friends in the village, had planted a tree many years ago, which now offered a huge canopy of shade for all to enjoy. There was a temple but the village was so poor, they did not have a Brahmin to tend to it. The Auroville community employed quite a number of the villagers, the men for labor, the girls and women for housework, child care and handicrafts.

In those early days, when you came to live in Auroville, you let yourself be guided by what was true within you, by how you were moved. Nobody told you what to do or where to go. You

Drawing water

In Kottakarai storeroom

found work by expressing your natural inclinations and gifts and allowing yourself to be led to wherever you happened to be drawn. In that surrendered state, things just seemed to flow. Little miracles became everyday fare.

I started by going out into the fields to weed around the base of the newly planted trees. I worked in blissful solitude, enjoying the quiet, the heat, the insects, careful of the occasional scorpion. I also helped with the food distribution for our community from a small storage room, where we received the provisions which came once a week by bullock cart from Pour Tous, the distribution center in Auroville. I divided everything into baskets for each individual and family.

A rather primitive community kitchen had been constructed in the palmeira grove, where we took turns cooking communal meals. One time, a boy from the village came limping in, crying. His knee was bleeding. Using a small first aid kit, I cleaned and bandaged his wound. I got a big smile in return and off he went. The next day he came back with a few of his friends, some of them with infected sores, others with scabies. I treated them all from my little box. Pretty soon a daily stream of children showed up in our kitchen, asking for help. When I made a trip into Pondy, I would pick up some bandaging material and Calamine lotion which supposedly helped heal scabies. My little box began to feel like the miracle of the loaves and fishes.

One day, I happened to be in the kitchen when a visitor from New York showed up. Since our community was situated on the outskirts of Auroville, we rarely had visitors. As we were sipping tea and chatting, a sad-looking young boy came in. His whole head was infected with scabies, oozing pus. I cleaned him up as well as I could and covered his head with the pink medicine. After the boy had gone, my visitor burst out in admiration, "Oh my god, you are the Albert Schweitzer of South India and you are doing all of that out of this little box? What do you need? Make me a list of everything you think you might need and I will go and get it for you." Two days later he came walking up the path with a suitcase full of supplies!

We became concerned about having all these children bring their infections into our kitchen. We got together to discuss the matter. One of our members had previously lived in a small two-story house that he owned in the village. It had a cement floor, and he had even installed an Indian squatting toilet, the only one in the village. He no longer lived there, so the community suggested I use the house to bring the first aid directly into the village.

We heard through the grapevine that an Indian doctor had just been moving her practice from Pondicherry into Auroville

My clinic in Kottakarai village

and had some medical furnishings to spare. She offered them to me for use in my little impromptu clinic, so off we went with a bullock cart to the other side of Auroville. We brought back a table with a glass top for medications, some shelves, a desk and various supplies. I moved everything into the small house and simply opened the doors. Of course, my every move had been keenly observed by the villagers. The children came crowding in. After a few weeks of seeing them, the mothers followed. Then old folks started to arrive and after several months even the men showed up.

I definitely needed a Tamil-speaking helper. Radhakrishna, a bright young man from the village who spoke English quite well, was happy to interpret for me and to help with the treatments. Everything was free.

There was no medical help of any kind for miles around. The nearest facility was Jipmer, a university hospital on Madras Road on the way to Pondy. It was about six or seven miles away. People were frightened of it. They were convinced that if you

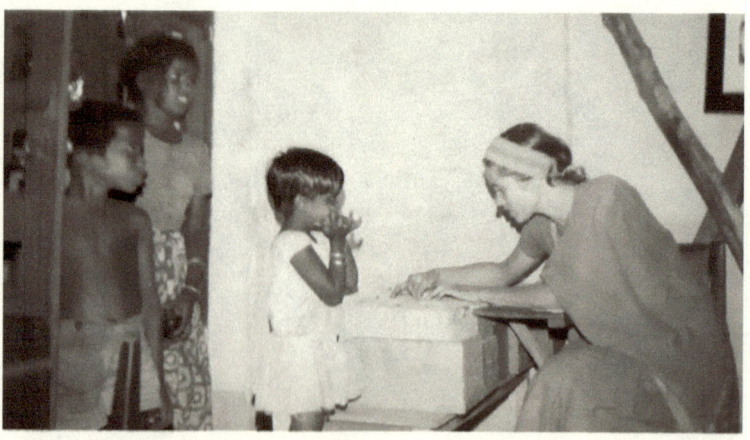

With children in the clinic

went there, you'd probably die. Over time I saw this to be quite the self-fulfilling prophecy. Since they were so afraid, people would often wait to go to the hospital until it was too late. Most would not go at all.

Several months into my experiment, I began to feel dissatisfied giving the villagers Western medicine. It was all I had. It just didn't feel right. I spoke with my community, and everyone agreed. I decided to go to the homeopath in Pondicherry and to the old Ayurvedic doctor in the Ashram to see if either one of these would be willing to help. The homeopath was incensed at my proposal. So, off I went to see the Ayurvedic doctor. In his spacious marble-floored clinic, he welcomed me most graciously and motioned for me to sit in front of him on the floor. The doctor, wearing a white dhoti loosely wrapped around him, was quite old. His white hair hung in thin strands around his shoulders. "What can I do for you?" he asked with a sweet smile.

"I have opened a little first aid clinic in the village of Kottakarai and I am not comfortable giving them Western medicine. There is no medical care for miles around. Everyone is being treated for free. I wonder if you might be able to help and provide some of your medicine?" With his broken English, our conversation was a bit confusing, though I could see that he tried his best to comprehend what I was after. I told him that this week most of the children had diarrhea. At other times, they all had eye infections and so on. Could he by any chance give some medicines for the conditions that might be prevalent at any given time? Although he shook his head agreeably, he clearly was still puzzled. He asked me to come back the next week.

For several weeks, I returned to him and described whatever health problems were current that week. He would give me some pills or powders and instructions for how much and when to take them. Then one beautiful day when I walked in, there was a sparkle in the air. The moment he saw me, he beamed, "I give! I give! I give!" He must have received some inner guidance and decided from then on to be completely generous towards my project.

Later, when more and more people were coming to my clinic, some with serious problems, he agreed that he would drive out one Sunday morning every month. I could ask those patients to come and see him at that time. It was always a beautiful scene. His ashram car would drive into the village and the old white-haired doctor, together with an assistant, would stoop into my simple little clinic. People had come from far and wide and were lined up to see him.

His generosity was extraordinary. Ayurveda is an ancient traditional medicine and it takes years of training to study. Students normally start grinding powders and turning pills for the first few years, before they get any closer to the actual study. Ayurvedic doctors are particularly skilled in reading many different pulses, looking at the tongue and at the entire demeanor, skin color, etc. of the patient to come to a conclusion. Knowing full well that I could not learn the advanced skills of his practice, he educated me about symptoms that could be readily observed so I could provide the best possible care with a combination of Ayurvedic medicines and local resources, some of which were a little startling. He simply skipped over all tradition and instructed me, "Look at his skin. You see how shiny it is? That means he has kidney problems. The best treatment is for him to drink morning cow urine." The recommended treatment for scabies was to rub the infected area with fresh cow dung. The villagers never cringed at any of these suggestions. They actually followed them and got better.

Over time, I did learn to speak some village Tamil. I was told that Tamil is the most ancient living language on the planet. It is quite complex and sophisticated. It sounds like water bouncing over pebbles. Even though I have a gift for languages and was fluent in four, I never managed to utter one completely correct sentence in Tamil. But I did learn how to ask about belly aches and knew how to instruct people to take 'rende matirei sapita-pirage,' two pills before meals.

One memorable experience taught me the true nature of healing. I had walked to the clinic that morning feeling very close to Mother, my heart full of blissful love and surrender. For months, a miserable little old man had been coming to the clinic several times a week, always complaining and kvetching about this pain or that. Nothing I gave him made any difference. That morning, he was the first to arrive. "Oh, there you are," I said, smiling. Right then, I couldn't help but just love the poor old man. I beamed at him, my heart overflowing with Mother's love. I gave him the same pills I had before with some encouraging words and great kindness and sent him on his way. A few days later, he came in, radiant, falling to his knees in front of me, making pranayams, "I'm all better. I'm all better. Thank you, thank you!" I realized then that love is the true healer. And who knows what Mother had to do with it?

One day, June, an American friend, came and visited us at our hut. She was suffering, as many Aurovilians did, from an ugly infection on her leg. These were especially common during mango season. When the mangoes were ripe, they were so incredibly delicious that people over-indulged in them. The mango's acidity seemed to affect the body's capacity to heal. Since we all walked barefoot or in sandals or flip-flops and did a lot of physical labor, cuts and scratches were easy to come by. These would quickly become infected.

With the first aid supplies I had available in my hut, I cleaned her wound and applied a healing oil which I concocted for the clinic, using sesame oil, marigold flowers and neem leaves—plant materials widely known in India as having fabulously antiseptic and healing properties. As I was bandaging her up, she relaxed deeply and sighed, "Oh, your hands feel so good. I feel like I am healing already!" I looked at my hands and wondered, puzzled. In my childhood, I had heard about magnetic healers in the old days in Germany. I had never heard of energy healing and, besides massage, had no familiarity with bodywork.

One time, as I was walking home from the clinic, I realized that I was living my childhood dream. Growing up in Catholic schools, most of our reading consisted of stories of saints, martyrs and hermits. Even as a child, I knew that above anything, I wanted to be close to God. I imagined living like a hermit in the desert, eating grasshoppers and healing the lepers. Except for the grasshoppers, my present reality was quite remarkably close to that dream.

I certainly felt that the desire to help and heal was a part of my true nature. After all, my work in the clinic had evolved from my spontaneously helping a little boy with a bleeding knee. Over the years, people were coming from the surrounding villages, some of them walking for miles. I kept records of over 4,000 patients. Without any training, I had become a barefoot doctor.

The Kali Temple

The vast plains of eroded red earth between Kottakarai and the Matrimandir were dotted by two small jungle groves which had been saved from the general deforestation because they were temple lands. The Kali temple was located along the dusty little path by the grove closest to the Matrimandir.

The temple was a low-ceiling, rectangular, brick and cement structure, with a black metal gate in front. The dark, dingy cave-like building had no windows. In the far back, stood a black statue of Kali, gleaming with ceremonial oils and wrapped in old saris. Because Kali, as the Goddess of Death, is often depicted with a trident, three tall, black iron tridents were placed in the dirt in front of the temple. People used to cover the prongs of the tridents with marigolds, oils, and colored pastes as part of their devotion, surely hoping to pacify her wrath. The marigolds would slowly wilt and decompose until the next pooja (ceremony).

The grove closer to Kottakarai was considered Kali's house. It was an impenetrable jungle, dominated by two large cottonwood trees, one with a male bulge near the bottom of its massive trunk and the other with a deep cleft, like the yoni of the goddess herself. Much to the villagers' dismay, Daniel, one of Kottakarai's Aurovilians, had built himself a hut directly under the shade of these trees. Since the villagers were terrified of Kali's powers, they couldn't imagine anyone choosing to live that close to her. They surely feared Daniel's intrusion would incur her wrath.

When I was still living at the Matrimandir workers' camp in Auroville's Center, I had heard stories about a dark entity inhabiting the Kali temple along the path to Kottakarai. Then, when I moved to Kottakarai myself, the stories seemed even more ominous. Peter, a tall, gruff Dutch sailor, and member of our community told me that he had decided that all this talk about a dark being in the Kali temple had to be a bunch of hogwash and he meant to debunk those stories himself. He set out for the Kali temple and had boldly walked up to the gate when suddenly a great dark ominous force rushed at him. He ran for his life.

I had read of Mother's own dealings with dark entities, or Asuras. She said that when confronted with the Light, these entities had two choices: to convert or to flee. I knew in my warrior soul that the presence of such a being of darkness on Auroville soil was entirely unacceptable. I was determined that it should leave or convert if it could. Implied in that assertion was my readiness to be instrumental in that process. Little did I know what I was getting myself into.

Daniel

About nine months into my celibacy, Daniel, the man who lived under the trees of Kali's house, started to catch my attention. He was a soft-spoken American from California with dark blond, shoulder-length hair often tied in a ponytail, a full, curly, dark brown beard and kind, hazel eyes. After getting degrees in both linguistics and architecture in the mid-sixties, he had dropped out of American society completely. His parents were from old aristocratic New England stock and his father was a wealthy, renowned heart and lung surgeon in Los Angeles. In the late sixties, Daniel left America together with his wife Iris. They lived in Holland for a year and then traveled through Europe, the Middle East and India. In a hut in Goa, they had given birth to a son, Mitra. Eventually, they made their way to Auroville. The little family settled in Kottakarai. Both Iris and Daniel became best friends with Constance. After some time, Iris chose to be with Constance and moved in with him, taking Mitra with her, who was now about four years old. Daniel seemed perpetually sad, but he never spoke about his feelings.

I admired Daniel for his natural and gracious relations with the villagers. He spoke Tamil with surprising fluency, to the point that he could even joke with them. Like many of the young Westerners in Auroville, he had adopted the villagers' casual clothing style. Most of the time, he wore a lungi, a straight piece of cotton men wrap around their waist and tuck in. When left at full length, it's like a long skirt. But for practical purposes, the lungi often gets picked up at the lower end and folded back up over the hips and loosely tucked in front to make a short skirt. Men usually left their upper body bare. Kurtas were worn in the evening when it cooled off or to go into town. A thin cotton towel would be wrapped like a turban around the head to prevent sweat from dripping into their eyes, and handy for all purposes.

Besides being involved with planting trees and care of the land, Daniel had become the local cobbler. He was making

Daniel

handsome leather sandals for any and all who needed them, including the villagers who were quite amazed that this velakare (white man) would stoop to do work that was normally only done by Harijans, the outcasts. Small wonder that the villagers adored Daniel. We couldn't have had a better ambassador for Auroville.

When it was my turn to need new sandals, Daniel humbly sat on the floor in front of me and had me place my foot on a piece of cardboard to draw its circumference. I loved feeling the warm gentle touch of his hands on my feet. Clearly, he loved feet. He made me a nice new pair of sandals, which he put on my feet to make sure the fit was correct. The moment may have marked the awakening of my attraction to him, even though I wasn't aware of it, yet.

One full moon night, the villagers were going to perform the Mahabharata, one of the two epic poems of ancient India. Our whole community had been invited. The performance would go on all night. A few of us strolled over to the village square where mats had been laid out in front of a makeshift stage.

All the villagers with their children and babies were sitting, squatting and running around, nibbling on jalebi, little greasy sweet cakes which they generously shared with us. We enjoyed the scene for hours.

While I was sitting close to Daniel in the crowd, inside the warmth of his aura, my feelings slowly grew more and more intense to the point of no return. By two in the morning, when the rest of our group had already left, Daniel and I decided to call it a night. We walked back through the canyon and the palmeira grove past our kitchen, my heart beating faster and faster. What was I going to do? We arrived at the crossroads. He would be turning right to his hut under the cotton trees, and my hut lay straight ahead. I couldn't let him go. With a gutsy leap of faith, I blurted out, "May I come with you?" He stopped in his tracks. Then, quietly, he said, "Sure."

We walked the rest of the path in awkward silence. Arriving in his simple bamboo hut, I sat down on his bed on the floor. There was no other place to sit. He picked up his flute, sat down on the floor on the other side of the room and started playing. I became quite anxious. I desperately needed to be close to him and realized that he was not going to take any initiative. Finally, I managed to ask, "Would you mind lying down with me? I would just like to be close to you. I'm not asking for sex. I'm just wanting some closeness."

He did. We lay down together for a while, holding each other. As we were gazing into each other's eyes, we began to smile and eventually shared a light kiss. It felt awfully nice. After lingering in this closeness for a while, we happily said good night to each other and as if in a dream, I floated back through the moonlit fields to my hut to sleep.

The next evening, he invited me over. This time it didn't take too long for us to get intimate. Our clothes came off and a delightful lovemaking began. Afterwards, we stepped outside in the moonlight, nude, like Adam and Eve. I turned slightly away from him when I heard his quiet voice, "Botticelli."

The next day, the floor in my hut was scheduled to be refinished with fresh cow dung and we decided that I would stay with him for a few days. It felt so good and so right to be there with him that I asked him, at the end of those days, if I could continue to stay with him. He agreed. Within a month, I was pregnant! I felt truly showered by grace. Not only was I now loving this very fine man, but I was also blessed with a baby growing inside of me. What sudden abundance.

During those first months, I noticed Daniel never initiated intimacy with me but whenever I approached him, he would be immediately and happily available for closeness. Our sexuality was affectionate and delicious. For years, I was grateful to be with a man who was not pursuing me for sex but happy to have it when I felt the desire. It was a healing experience for me. I always loved looking into his kind hazel eyes.

And so, in October of 1973, I had come to live in the hut Daniel had built in the shade of Kali's house, just one field away from the temple with the much-feared entity of darkness.

Mother Leaves Her Body

When my thirty-first birthday was approaching, I knew I wouldn't be able to see Mother. Over the previous year, she had more and more withdrawn from all public contact, and since April she had stopped seeing people altogether. As my birthday arrived, I became acutely aware of my ongoing internal unrest. I had never learned how to deal with my problems or my feelings, nor how to communicate with others when there were disagreements or my feelings were hurt. I did not know how to express myself or how to seek a solution, and I didn't know that I could ask for help. All I knew how to do was shut down, be strong, and act as if everything was fine. As a result, I found myself struggling and endlessly mulling things over in my mind. On the morning of my birthday, knowing I wouldn't be able to see Mother, I walked out into the fields to tend to the young trees, my soul crying out to her for peace of mind.

I moved through the day in a state of quiet prayer. In the late afternoon, I was approached by an Aurovilian whom I barely knew who had just returned by village bus from Pondicherry. He handed me a yellow Peace rose and said, "Here, I am supposed to bring you this rose from Mother for your birthday." Mother's name for yellow roses is "Mental Love for the Divine." To this day, I do not know how that came about. It seemed like a miracle. She had heard me!

Little did I know at the time that it would take me decades more of struggling and healing before a genuine peace of mind became my reality.

In the meantime, rumors of Mother's ill health continued to abound. From her conversations with Satprem, her French confidant, which were later published in thirteen volumes as *L'Agenda de Mère* (*Mother's Agenda*), one can see her daily battle and ever-deepening surrender to divinize the very cells of her body. These would alternately open into indescribable peace, extraordinary plasticity, then protest with episodes of painful upheaval. The doctors around her could only attest to her physical difficulties, so her condition was being described as "gravely ill." In the *Agenda*, she tells how she was waging a foundational battle of transformation for the world.

Both Mother and Sri Aurobindo saw death as the ultimate falsehood which had to be overcome. They had both dedicated themselves to that final battle between the Divine Consciousness and the Ignorance. I felt that we all had the unspoken expectation that she would succeed and thought that she might not die.

Shortly after I realized I was pregnant, in the early morning of November 17, 1973, Daniel and I awakened early and stepped outside to see a bicyclist driving down the path to Kottakarai. He stopped and turned. He seemed to hesitate for a moment, and then announced, "Mère a quitté son corps!" (Mother has left her body). It seemed like the fabric of the worlds tore open. We stood in silence. Our messenger appreciated that we were able to receive the news so quietly since he had just delivered the message to someone who had broken into hysterical sobbing. As he went on his way, Daniel and I looked at one another as never before: soul to soul, pure, wide open, even ecstatic. I felt her presence in my heart. She was with us now, within us, closer than ever. No more distance to travel, no more letters to write. The word that arose in me was "transcorporation." I mentioned it to Daniel. He nodded. It best described what we were both experiencing.

We were aware that it had been Mother's explicit request that her body not be moved for three days if she seemed to have left it, since she did not know how the ultimate transformation of her cells would be realized. She also had described a nightmare to Satprem, in which she woke up in a coffin under the ground and no one could hear her. So, we were quite dismayed when we heard that Mother's body was laid out in the Ashram's front hall for all to come and receive her final darshan. Daniel and I felt that it wasn't right to participate in that scene. But when all of Auroville streamed empty, we caved in and got on the bus to Pondy.

Thousands of stunned devotees and Aurovilians were slowly winding their way through the Ashram courtyard and into the hall to pass by her body. There she was, against her specific wishes, laid out in public with candles, incense, flowers and a crowd all around her. I was shocked by her appearance. With her head propped up, her face was dreadfully serious, her long thin nose pointing like a sword into the abyss. None of the infinite sweetness I had experienced from her was now visible, as if she was waging a cosmic battle.

Aurelia, the Golden Child

Now my attention turned to the growing child within me. Never had I experienced such inner contentment as during my pregnancy. A deep peace settled over me. The baby's aura seemed larger than our hut. Even though it was growing inside of me, I felt as if I was living inside of it. I would softly sing my favorite mantra to my baby, *Aum Namo Bhagavate Sri Aurobindo.*

When I told one of our community members of my pregnancy, he spontaneously bowed in reverence to "The Golden Child," an expression in Sri Aurobindo's writings, symbolizing the Divine manifestation upon earth. It made me feel like Mother Mary.

I lived in complete trust. I never went to a doctor for a check-up and naturally did not know the gender of the child. One quiet evening, sitting in contemplation of the being inside of me, I made a pencil drawing of its sweet face. It reminded me of the magical drawings of those children with large, mysterious angel eyes by Sulamith Wülfing. Even from the drawing, I couldn't tell if it was a boy or a girl.

Someone handed me a wonderful book, *Naissance sans Violence* (*Birth without Violence*) by Frédérick Leboyer. He makes a powerful case against the birthing practices which were common in Western culture at the time, having the birth take place under bright lights, holding the baby upside down and spanking it to clear its lungs (which had been done to me) and separating the baby from the mother. He talked of soft lights, underwater births and laying the baby on the mother's body as soon as it came out. I was struck by the serendipity of this book coming to me during my pregnancy and felt so blessed. I wrote to Frédérick Leboyer to thank him.

When I was seven months pregnant, I woke early one morning with a name ringing like bells throughout my universe, *Aurelia, Aurelia.* My heart bounced in my chest. No doubt this was to be

Pregnant with Aurelia

the baby's name. I found a passage in *Savitri*'s Book XI, Canto I, "The Soul's Choice and the Supreme Consummation."

> ...The world creates itself invincibly;
> For its body is the body of the Lord
> And in its heart stands Virat, King of Kings.
> In him shadows his form the Golden Child
> Who in the Sun-capped Vast cradles his birth...

When our community had gathered for a picnic, some pictures were taken. There is a shot of me sitting in the field with my ample belly, a simple sarong wrapped around me, my long hair hanging loose. I seem to be surrounded by an aura of shimmering light. On closer examination, I saw that there had been a cart behind me in the camera's field of vision and its wheel had caught the light to produce the mysterious effect.

Shortly afterwards, I was still in my seventh month, it was a quiet afternoon, and I was sipping tea when Judith came running across the fields towards me. She was obviously in distress. As soon as she came near, she shouted for me to come, asking if I knew CPR. Aurolouis, Dyane's little two-year-old boy, had drowned in the well. I had only a vague idea of CPR, but of course ran with her to the well, only to find the little boy very dead on the ground. I looked at his mother, whose eyes were broken in grief. Even though I knew it was too late, I had to try and resuscitate him. As I compressed his chest, I had someone else breathe into his nose. Nothing. We went at it for a long time. Then, someone had the desperate idea to swing him around really fast hoping the centrifugal force would clear his lungs. All to no avail.

Dyane and Larry took the little boy's body by jeep to Jipmer, the big hospital on Madras Road. I carried Auralice, his distressed little sister, back home. We had a tragic burial. People from all over Auroville gathered silently around Dyane and Larry's home. I still hear Larry's hammering echoing through the space as he nailed the little coffin shut.

When we had dug the well near the bakery, the villagers had implored us to behead a chicken and drip its blood in the well as soon as we struck water, to appease the spirit of the well. If we failed to do that, the spirit would seek revenge. With our usual Western arrogance, we had rejected that barbaric idea. We surely couldn't tolerate any such superstition in Auroville. Now the villagers muttered that they had known all along something bad would happen.

As life was settling back to normal, we heard about an English woman named Margaret who was a midwife. She had just arrived in Aspiration, one of Auroville's larger settlements. She used guided meditation in her delivery practices and was delighted to be able to practice her art with women who were aspiring to be spiritually conscious. We met and made an arrangement with her that as soon as my labor started, Daniel would go fetch her by motorbike.

On Sunday, September 15, 1974, I woke up noticing the first contraction. I soon realized they were occurring at regular intervals of about ten minutes. Daniel set off to fetch the community motorbike to get the midwife and, on his way, to tell Patricia at the Matrimandir workers' camp to please come and be with me.

After Daniel left, I stepped outside. Sundays always felt special, the land being steeped in silence. The workers were all in the village. I was alone as far as the eye could see. The kombu stood ripe in the fields heavy with grain, gleaming in the morning sun. What a perfect harvest day to have my baby, I thought, and felt so blessed. I circumambulated our hut and the grove behind it and ate some bitter leaves from a neem tree, well-known in India for its purifying properties. I felt sanctified and ready.

Patricia arrived with a little bouquet of pink roses, which Mother had named "Surrender." With mugs of tea, we made ourselves comfortable in rattan chairs in the shade behind the hut. For most of that day, I sat with my best friend, the little roses on my ample belly, looking out over the waving fields, being deeply at peace, riding the contractions.

I heard the motorbike in the distance, and shortly after, Daniel arrived with Margaret. By late afternoon other friends from our little community arrived. We watched the sunset. I was still sitting outside when suddenly my water broke. With some help, I hauled my heavy body up into our hut. I got down on the bed and asked Daniel to sit behind me so I could lean into him.

After each powerful push, I was able to lean back into the security of his embrace and rest deeply. When the baby was coming down, I felt a sharp searing pain and knew my vaginal wall was tearing. The midwife didn't think it was, however, and she encouraged me to keep pushing. Usually, babies are born headfirst and face down. My baby came out face up, and right there between my legs, I beheld the sweetest most beautiful little Buddha face. With the next push, its little body slid out of me. She uttered the purest high note, like a little bell singing. No crying. The midwife announced, "It's a girl!"

As soon as she was laid on my body, she opened her eyes wide. She looked around the hut and at all the people as if she recognized she had just come home. Her whole body was a deep shade of pink. That color lasted for more than a week. The name Surrender Rose came to me, but, chuckling, I realized that was quite out of the question. We named her Aurelia, the Golden One.

The first three weeks of her life were a heaven of sweet bliss. She was the most exquisite little being, so fine and lovely, so at ease in my arms. How I adored nursing her and seeing her slowly reach satiation and drift into sleep, her little mouth letting go of my breast, lips glistening with milk, continuing to make sleepy suckling motions until she would drift off completely. I would just linger there in utter bliss, gazing upon her delicate sweetness. And, how I loved watching Daniel when he held her and talked to her. We were a family.

Unfortunately, the morning after her birth, when I stepped outside to pee, I experienced a sharp burning. This continued for weeks. I must have torn. Because our hut was open, I never had enough privacy in the daytime to examine myself and at night it was too dark. I finally went to visit Liesbeth, one of the other young mothers in our community who had a closed-in shower. I had a good look. I was shredded. I decided to go to the French hospital in Pondicherry to get myself stitched up.

But, before I got there, another drama would radically change life as I knew it.

The Attack

One early evening, when our sweet Aurelia was just three weeks old, Daniel and I had a meeting at our hut with all of the villagers who worked in our community. It was already dark. The hut was crowded, and some of them were squatting on our porches. I was sitting with the baby on my lap with my back to one of the porches when I was suddenly overcome by a physical sensation of sheer terror. I broke out in goosebumps all over and my hair was standing on end. I felt something threatening behind me and flung my head around to see. But I only saw the impassive faces of our workers against the black backdrop of the night, nothing to cause any alarm.

After everyone was gone, Daniel left too. He was going to visit Iris at the Matrimandir nursery because their son Mitra was ill. I found myself alone with Aurelia in our hut. I had forgotten about my earlier fear, but I instinctively moved my mattress in front of the cradle as if to protect our baby. I turned the kerosene lamp down as usual, low enough so it wouldn't spread any light, but visible enough to reach for when needed, and went to sleep.

I was in a deep sleep when I heard some sounds in the hut. "Daniel?" No response. "Daniel, is that you?" No response. Still half asleep, I vaguely wondered if someone else from our community had come into the hut. "Peter?" Silence. Suddenly I realized, Danger! I bolted upright and saw the silhouette of a skinny figure standing motionless bent over me. I burst into an unearthly scream. I screamed for my life, knowing that the nearest hut was three fields away. In the middle of my screaming, while the figure continued to stand there bent over me, I heard only one tiny little sound from my baby behind me.

Finally, I saw a lantern moving in the distance. So did he. He darted closer and demanded hoarsely "Kasi koode" (give money). I saw he had a mustache but still couldn't make out his face. Then, I felt a hard bonk on my leg, followed by a loud clattering of something heavy on the floor. He leapt out of the hut and ran into the night.

I quickly reached for the kerosene lamp to turn up the light. I had two stab wounds just above my right knee. The flesh was bulging out of them, although there was hardly any blood. On the floor lay one of the large iron tridents from the Kali temple! Since it was regularly smeared with oil and colorful pastes and decorated with rotting marigolds and jasmine, I knew it was rusty and dirty. Since I had a baby to nurse, I commanded my body in no uncertain terms, "You can't get infected!"

Peter arrived and was shocked, of course, too. We realized I needed to disinfect and bandage my wounds right away. I didn't have what was needed. Now Peter had to walk across all three fields back to our kitchen to get the first aid kit, leaving me alone again. I was amazed that Aurelia was sleeping through it all. I began to worry about Daniel having to walk back through the night from the nursery since my intruder had escaped in that direction.

Peter returned with Jaap and the first aid kit. They were both quite disturbed. While I was taking care of my wounds, I urged them to let go of their fear, since I was expecting Aurelia to wake up to nurse. I did not want her to be exposed to any frightening commotion. She soon awoke, and I nursed her peacefully. Not long after, I was relieved to see Daniel coming home safely.

The next morning, the news of the attack spread like wildfire, and the villagers came thronging to our hut. They were profoundly shocked and very concerned for me. They told me that if such a thing would have happened to one of their women, she would not have survived. They were also positive that it couldn't possibly have been someone from their village since they were all way too terrified of the Kali temple. In the dark, I had only been able to see my attacker's silhouette. I told Radhakrishna that the man had a skinny, spindly body, just like Loganathan, one of our watchmen, but that this man had a moustache.

Our baby seemed alright. For some reason, Daniel felt it was inappropriate for him to return the trident to the Kali temple himself. He felt that whoever was in charge of taking care of the temple should do it. That would have been Loganathan. I didn't particularly appreciate the delay. Daniel stuck the trident in the dirt in front of our hut. We cleaned it up, rubbed oil all over it and stuck fresh marigold flowers on its prongs, hoping to expel any darkness associated with it. We waited. Loganathan never came. My wounds did not get infected and healed in three days.

Several days later, while our sweet baby was sound asleep, Daniel and I were sitting on our front porch in the evening, quietly talking. When I had to pee, as usual I stepped behind the hut to relieve myself. Just then the moon was rising and in its silvery light, I saw the creepy, stooped silhouette of a figure loping by the trees. Gripped by fear, I hollered with a deep voice that came out of my gut, "Who is there?" The figure ran and disappeared into the darkness.

Daniel came around and asked what was happening. Breathless, my heart still pounding wildly, I stammered, "I saw him. He was right there. I saw his silhouette against the trees." "Are you sure?" was Daniel's unfortunate response. I felt instantly devalued. His mistrust created a breach in the support I had felt from him till then.

After my pursuer's reappearance, I began to live in terror. I had weathered the attack with a great deal of inner strength not wanting to disturb my baby. Apparently, my attacker was not satisfied with a job half done and was coming back to finish me off. I decided it was time for me to go to the French hospital in Pondicherry to get myself stitched up and take a break from what had become an intolerable situation.

We Almost Lose Her

In the late afternoon, I arrived with my baby at Cluny. The nun who checked me in took a look at my vagina and shook her head in disbelief. She got a mirror and showed me how the inner labia had torn and there was a tear all the way up the vaginal wall resembling a jagged crack in a rock face. She promised to make time to help me later that evening and allowed me to stay for several days to recover. What heavenly rest it was to be in a comfortable bed with my baby by my side in a safe place where I was completely taken care of.

Reluctantly, I returned to our hut under the cottonwood trees. The community hired extra watchmen for night duty. Life seemed to have resumed its normal patterns. Daniel and I had begun a handicraft project to help create some income for Auroville. He would cut fine leather into small panels, and I taught young women to crochet them together into vests, purses and pouches. We were also crocheting bikinis. Our hut had turned into a little workshop. I loved having the women sit on the floor of our little hut, crocheting and chatting away.

Still, there would be times in the late afternoon or early evening, when I was alone again with Aurelia and plagued by fear. I never walked past our trees in the direction of the Kali temple from where my attacker had taken the trident. I also felt deeply betrayed. I had lived with complete trust in Mother's protection. How could such a terrible thing have happened to me?

Aurelia started to suffer from colic and diarrhea and cried a lot. Other young mothers in the community told me that babies often show symptoms like those. They told me that mother's milk was the best medicine and that I could give her some ginger ale. I shouldn't worry. Since I'm not the type who worries anyway, I took them literally. However, over the next few months, the diarrhea continued, and her crying became more and more inconsolable.

I would carry her and walk her around and try to soothe her for hours on end, all to no avail. Sometimes, I was so worn out by her endless crying that I would hand her to someone else to carry her for a while. I didn't know that she was in constant pain and wondered instead if she was unhappy with me.

One morning, I woke up after a restless night during which she had cried and fussed a lot, and I found her diaper full of blood. Daniel and I were both deeply shaken and exchanged a look I will never forget. Our eyes acknowledged that we might lose our baby. Having a great aversion at the time to Western medicine, we decided to try homeopathy first. Daniel got on the morning bus to consult the homeopath in town, planning to return as quickly as possible.

Mid-morning, while Daniel was still gone, I laid down exhausted to nurse her and rest. When I woke up, her whole body was rigidly arched back. She was unconscious with her eyes rolled up into her head and more blood in her diaper. I jumped up, quickly grabbed a few essentials and ran to the village bus to take her to Jipmer Hospital. One of our young men from the village came with me to get off at Jipmer and attempt to catch Daniel on the bus coming back.

Desperately holding my sweet little girl in her rigid coma, I rode on the rickety bus to the hospital. To my horror, she felt cold. In a state of utter panic, I ran with her to the emergency room. Gratefully, Daniel arrived soon after. When a doctor came to examine her, he gingerly inserted his little finger into her anus, which instantly released some poop but did not awaken her. She was diagnosed with septicemia (blood poisoning) and put on intravenous antibiotics, with tubes going into her stomach and a drip in her little hand to keep her hydrated.

Aurelia lay comatose for three days. I stayed by her side around the clock and slept on the floor under her bed. Daniel came every day. I frantically tried to squeeze as much milk from my breasts as I could, bending over a little sink in the room, hoping to keep my milk flowing. There was no breast pump to help me. On one of those days, two nurses came in and told me they had to take some blood from her. They explained that they could only draw enough blood by going into her groin. As they were preparing things, I heard one of them talk about an air bubble in the line. I had heard once that if an air bubble reaches the heart, it can be fatal. Instead of talking to them, I freaked out silently until I could no longer control myself. I ran out of the room. As soon as I had closed the door behind me, I lost all control and screamed, running through the hall. Sobbing, I flung myself against a wall. I glimpsed the startled faces of nurses and patients. In a few minutes, our doctor came rushing over, asking me kindly what had happened. "I thought the nurses were killing my baby," I stammered.

It's only now, decades later while writing this story that I realize they were *drawing* blood and not *giving* her anything. I had been struck with terror but was unable to protest, even when I thought they were killing my baby. That's how strongly I was conditioned from my earliest experiences, in the war and in the camp, to keep absolutely silent, even when I was terrified that all of us were getting killed. However, the internal pressure had been unbearable and the best I could do was run out of the room and then erupt.

In the afternoon of the fourth day, one of our Kottakarai Aurovilians, Judith, came to visit. She brought an energy of sweetness and light and flowers for Aurelia. She blessed the baby, touched her head and gently spoke to her and to us of hope, of the beauty of life and of the Mother. Aurelia visibly relaxed, and so did we. Over the next few hours she slowly, slowly returned back to us.

We were then moved to a regular ward. No matter how hard I had tried to keep my milk flowing during those long, fearful days and nights, I had nothing left. My breasts had dried up. I implored the surgeon to help me, to give me hormones, anything that might help. He looked quite mortified as he had to tell me, "I am so very sorry, but there is nothing we can do." Apparently, Western medicine had no solution for this problem.

As soon as Daniel came to visit, I asked him to stay with her. I ran to catch the bus into Pondy to see the homeopath. After I explained my problem, he said reassuringly, "Ah, we call that Agalacteria. I will give you two doses of a remedy. Take one tonight before you go to bed and, if the milk does not come in by midnight, take the second dose." By eleven o'clock that night, sleeping on the floor under Aurelia's bed, I was awakened by the milk shooting into my breasts. I was able to nurse her until she was one year old.

Reflecting on the possible cause of her intestinal obstruction, I remembered how she had let out a tiny sound when I was attacked and had screamed. Her insides must have frozen in fear.

My Mother Comes to Visit

Before all this drama unfolded, my mother had been planning to visit us to be with me and meet her new granddaughter. We had not seen each other since I left in September of 1971, three years before. It so happened that her arrival coincided with the very day we left the hospital. Of course, she knew nothing of our ordeal. Daniel and I decided that I would go and stay at Parc Guesthouse with our baby. It was the same ashram guest house in Pondicherry where I lived when I first got there. That way both the baby and I could relax and recover in a hygienic environment, and my mother would certainly be more comfortable. After all, in our hut under the trees, we had no electricity, running water or even a bathroom. Since Daniel needed to help me with the move and get us settled in at the guest house, we asked Dutch Pieter to go to Madras to meet my mother at the airport.

Arriving in India for the first time can be a harrowing experience. My mother had stood in front of the airport, fending off taxi drivers and porters who were ready to grab her luggage, anxiously looking for Daniel in vain. After some time, a tall Dutchman approached her, introduced himself and explained the situation. Exhausted from the long flight and disturbed by the confusion upon her arrival, she and Pieter boarded the bus to Pondicherry. A quiet form of revenge white people experienced those days in India, was getting relegated to the very back of the bus. It was the most uncomfortable seating. You were bounced and shaken violently as the bus roared over potholes and veered dangerously to avoid the myriad obstacles on the road. The trip lasts for three hours. My poor mother became car sick and vomited

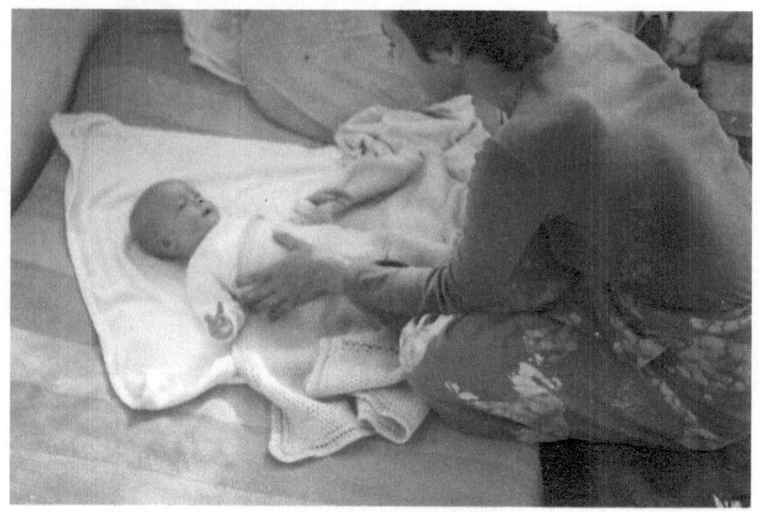

My Little Angel

all over herself. When she arrived at our doorstep, although she was happy to see us, she was a miserable wreck.

In a few days, all three of us recovered beautifully, each from our own ordeal. My mother had brought some baby toys. We tied a colorful wooden toy to the sides of Aurelia's mosquito net so it could dangle over her to amuse and intrigue her. I have a few photographs of her taken barely a week after we had come out of the hospital. Amazingly, our sweet little Aurelia had already plumped up into a healthy and happy baby as if nothing had ever been the matter.

Before Aurelia's birth, having been quite close to many villagers in my little clinic, I discovered that I had picked up a variety of critters in my hair. I surely did not want to be that unclean with my newborn and decided to shave my head. One morning, I took scissors to my hair and cut it all off. Then I asked Daniel

With my mother at Mahabalipuram

to give me a shave. I was surprised how wonderfully cool it was to feel every little breeze on my exposed scalp.

A few weeks later, Daniel did the same thing and even shaved his ample beard. From photographs, my mother had expected quite a different-looking man. She was a bit perturbed by Daniel's naked face. Even I had been startled when I first saw Daniel shaved clean. You really have no idea what someone's face looks like when it's been so fully overgrown. I was surprised by the masculine chin and strong jaw lines, where before he had appeared so soft and gentle.

Of course, my mother was shocked by the life-threatening illness Aurelia had experienced. I carefully omitted telling her about my attack. She would be going back to Holland, and I certainly did not want her to worry about my safety. We made short trips into Auroville, so she could see where we lived and meet Patricia and other friends who lived in different parts of the community. My mother and I had a lovely time together. My old resentments seemed to have evaporated, and it was good to feel close to her.

When it was time for her return, we decided to take her by taxi back to Madras Airport. On the way we stopped in Mahabalipuram to see the ancient coastal temple, which had at times been fully submerged in the ocean. The temple was dark and dank, the stone floors and statues worn by centuries of worship, but especially by the wear and tear of the ocean. I have a picture of us leaving the temple. My mother looks very serious and windblown, and I am holding my baby close, wrapped in a little blanket as if to protect her from the darkness.

I wept when my mother left.

The Truth Sets Me Free

I was dreading the idea of returning to our hut. I expressed my desire to Daniel that we move to another part of Auroville. Even though he was sympathetic, I did not feel that he was really supporting me in this nor did he put out any energy to make such a move happen. Of course, both of us were also committed to our work and life in Kottakarai. I returned with my baby girl to live in our hut. Several months went by in which I struggled with my fear. I was often alone with Aurelia. I still couldn't walk past our tree grove in the direction of the Kali temple.

During one of my trips into Pondy—I had left Aurelia in the kind hands of Dosai-amma (who usually took care of her when I wasn't there)—I ran into an elderly French lady who had been living in the Ashram for a long time. I had made a delightful connection with her when I first came to the Ashram. Her head was shaved, she looked very Zen. I had always sensed her wisdom. When she asked me very kindly how I was doing, something gave way inside of me, and bursting into tears, I blurted out, "I was almost killed, and my baby nearly died!" She wanted to know all the details. I shared everything with her. Then she said quietly, in a knowing kind of way, "This was karma. Your blood needed to flow. It's because of Mother's protection that it was just a little blood, and your life was spared." I knew in my bones that she was right. I felt so relieved! In my distress, I had wondered why I had not been protected by Mother. My faith had been shaken badly. Even though I did not know any of my past lives' karma at the time, her explanation gave me a sense of the bigger picture involved and the rightness of it. I moved into acceptance.

One beautiful Sunday morning, I am walking outside with my baby Aurelia in my arms. Nobody is around. Everything feels profoundly peaceful. Something sparkles in the air like a golden benediction, and I find myself turning towards the forbidden Kali temple. I know in my soul that this is the day to overcome my fear and that we are completely protected by Her grace.

I carry my sweet child to the temple. We are filled with light. As we arrive in front of the old rectangular, low-ceilinged and much-feared sanctuary, there is Loganathan, squatting by the side of the temple, messing around with some ceremonial ashes. He looks up and I see his moustache. He didn't used to have one and I had not seen him since my attack. Our recognition is immediate. "Ah, it is you!" We look into each other's eyes. Time stands still. Not a word is spoken. We both know the truth.

No fear, no anger, no need to accuse, just a great luminous clarity. I nod at him in acknowledgment, smile and walk away in grace, my baby in my arms. I am free.

Loganathan

When I realized it was Loganathan who had attacked me, I instantly understood his motives. Priests and scholars for temples in India are members of the Brahmin caste. There was at that time no Brahmin in Kottakarai village. Loganathan, an extremely poor and ignorant man, who sometimes worked as a watchman in our community, tended to the temple and led the poojas. How he came to fulfill this function, I do not know. Clearly, in his ignorance he had become an ally to the dark forces that were associated with Kali, the Goddess of Power, Love and Death.

In the beginning of Daniel's and my relationship, we had gone together to spend a day in town, visiting the Samadhi and enjoying a nice Indian meal in one of our favorite restaurants. Upon our return home that night, we found our hut ransacked, our possessions all over the floor. Some items were missing, like bedcovers and other simple household items. Since we owned nothing of value, it was no big loss. However, we felt horribly violated. Of course, there was no clue as to who the culprit was.

Several months later, on a Sunday morning, Daniel and I decided to walk to the Matrimandir. On passing the Kali Temple, we ran into a small group of Tamil men. Gabriel was there, the French-speaking cook whom I remembered fondly from my days of working at the Matrimandir Worker's Camp kitchen, and, standing by his side, Loganathan.

After some pleasant greetings, I noticed that Loganathan was wrapped in one of those blue and white checkered bed covers, just like the one that had been missing from our house. Without thinking, I stepped right up to him and turned over a corner of the fabric and saw my laundry number! "Ah," I exclaimed, looking him straight in the eyes, "this is my blanket!" He squirmed in discomfort. Then, while sliding the blanket off his body, he stammered, "Please take it." It looked terribly worn and dingy. "No, thank you," I replied. This was my first insult to him, in front of his friends.

Loganathan's wife and her little children came to the clinic regularly. I treated her children's scabies and runny noses. One day she came in with her baby, surrounded by shouting women who accused her of having flung her baby against the wall. She complained that she did not have enough milk for her baby, and it wouldn't stop crying. She was obviously in dire straits. I began providing her with formula milk for the baby. A year later, out of gratitude, they named their next baby after me, Anjali.

Then, during one of his watchman shifts, Loganathan had borrowed a flashlight from Daniel, which he would not return. We had asked him about it numerous times and got pretty annoyed with him. We were rather poor ourselves and could not just go out and buy a new one. I felt especially indignant. Here I was helping to feed his family and he did not even have the courtesy to return the damn flashlight.

One morning I was alone in the clinic with Radhakrishna, the young man who used to help me, when Loganathan himself showed up. Suddenly, I had it with him. I flared into a fury and laid in on him about his despicable behavior. "How dare you come here and ask for anything, if you can't even return Daniel's flashlight?" I might as well have slapped him in the face, that is how my furious words lashed at him. My second insult!

Surely, being insulted by a woman and, a white woman to boot, in front of another man, was tremendously humiliating. In the rage and darkness of his soul, it must have been inevitable that he turn to Kali for revenge.

The Sacrifice and the Release

Rajili, one of our most reliable and senior watchmen, lived with his young wife Boomadevi, whom I had befriended during my time at the Matrimandir Center, and their baby Tushita, near Larry's bakery where they were both employed. Rajili had been one of the main voices encouraging us to sacrifice chicken blood to the spirit of the well, in which Aurolouis had drowned. Ever since that terrible event, Rajili had been getting drunk and ever more disturbed. He would ramble to Larry about what the spirit of the well was telling him. It was difficult to take him seriously because his drinking was out of control and his talk seemed to be that of an alcohol-addled brain. He seemed deeply frightened and warned Larry about what the spirit of the well was telling him, that he needed another life, this time not by drowning but by strangulation.

One night, after we had just fallen asleep, I awoke to his desperate voice outside of our hut, calling, "Angela! Angela!"

I didn't have it in me to deal with him in what I suspected to be his drunken stupor. I couldn't respond and kept quiet until he left.

The next day, his young wife was worried. Rajili had disappeared. He had been very upset and couldn't stop talking about the threat from the spirit of the well. For three days, we heard nothing. On the third day, after leaving the clinic, I noticed a hush hanging over the village square, small groups of dejected villagers scattered around the place. One of the village elders approached me with an ominous look in his eyes. He whispered, "Rajili," while moving his hand around his neck and up, indicating that Rajili had hung himself. "Hurry, hurry," he said, "his mother and Boomadevi are over by your kitchen."

I hurried through the gully and the Palmira grove to find Andai Amma, his old mother, crumpled down on the kitchen floor. Daniel was with her. Boomadevi lay sobbing under one of the palm trees. Villagers gathered around the scene told me that the police had come to Kottakarai to announce that Rajili had been found hanging in the Kali temple of his birthplace, South of Pondicherry. I went straight to Boomadevi and knelt by her. As I reached out to her, I suddenly knew we had to get into action. One of the things I had learned from Mother was that the souls of people who commit suicide may be at the mercy of vital forces of darkness who continue to torture them. I took Boomadevi by the shoulders, looked her straight in the eyes and told her we had work to do. She snapped to it, as if she too, knew.

Off we went to our hut which was directly on the path to the Kali temple. There we gathered some things to do pooja for Rajili's spirit. I took a picture of Mother, we picked some flowers, got a lemon, candles and incense, and headed straight to the temple. Since he had chosen to hang himself in a Kali temple, surely this was the place to go. I had no thought of the dark entity in the temple. We were on a mission. We opened the gate and walked resolutely up to Kali's statue, her red tongue sticking out, a garland of skulls around her neck, and proceeded with our offerings and prayers to the Mother, asking her to take Rajili's soul into the light.

Afterwards, we just sat there for a while in silence. Then, Boomadevi told me that Rajili had talked to her about needing to sacrifice himself for the spirit of the well. He had told her not to grieve. No wonder she had responded so quickly to my command to stop crying, that we had work to do. He had even indicated to her the exact spot where he wished to be buried: directly behind our tree grove facing the Kali Temple, with the Matrimandir in the distance. We were to plant rosemary and holy basil on his grave. When it was time to go, we left Mother's picture in the temple.

The police had demanded that some family members go to the Pondicherry morgue to identify the body and then come to the police station to speak with them. We understood that in case of suicide, the police always investigate to make sure no crime was involved. It soon became clear that fear of the police was so great that neither his mother nor anyone else of his family dared face them.

Daniel borrowed a van from the Matrimandir workers' camp. Boomadevi had the courage to come with us and the three of us took off into Pondy on the gruesome mission. An attendant led us into a large cold room with many cement slabs, some of them with bodies. We were led to one particular slab and there he lay... Rajili, his head turned upward and sideways (as he had stiffened while hanging), a smile of rapture on his face. Speechless, we gazed at his astonishing beauty. "Roombo ajagaay" (very beautiful), I whispered to Boomadevi. She nodded. Together we stood breathless for a while, in awe of the beauty of Rajili's deliverance and sacrifice.

The attendant was puzzled and questioned us whether Boomadevi really was his wife. Clearly, he expected any woman who recognizes the body of her deceased husband to burst out wailing. Then he told us to go to the police and return with a permission slip to take the body with us.

Arriving at the police station, we were led to the chief of police. A burly man in uniform with an impressive-looking moustache, a striking look-a-like to Stalin, indicated for us to sit across from his desk. He began to grill us and seemed hell-bent on proving that a crime must have been committed. How come his wife wasn't crying? Daniel and I shamelessly used our authority as whites to convince him that we were speaking the truth. I could hardly believe my eyes when I noticed a little nameplate on his desk: Stalin. However reluctantly, he finally agreed and stamped the permission slip to go pick up Rajili's body.

There was only enough room on the floor in front of the back seat to lay his body down. The whole trip back I had to try my utmost to keep my feet lifted, not to step on his body. We delivered him to his mother's hut in the grove above the village and laid his body on a narrow bench outside. The carpenters of Matrimandir were going to make him a coffin. Feeling the need for some official to be present, Daniel sent a message to Shyamsundar, Mother's secretary for Auroville, to attend.

After a few days, it was clear that no one was coming and it was high time we got the body in the ground. The whole village gathered around in front of his mother's house. Now Rajili's body had to be picked up and placed in the coffin. Nobody moved. I stepped forward to do the job and seeing that no one else stepped forward, ordered a few men to help me. They approached reluctantly. His body had become unpleasantly soggy but it took just a few seconds to move him. Then we walked in procession to the grove behind our hut, where a grave had been dug exactly where Rajili had indicated.

Everyone gathered around the grave and the coffin was let down into it. Suddenly, out of the crowd, Loganathan stepped forward to do the ceremony. I had not seen him since our encounter by the temple. After walking around the grave, praying and sprinkling holy water, he produced a plate with prasad, Indian milk sweets which are usually handed out to all participants after a ceremony.

He turns to me, calling out my name, "Angela!" and comes over to me to offer me the first prasad. I accept. As he moves around the crowd, offering prasad to all, I gaze up, becoming aware of a great release. The very air seems to sparkle, the leaves on the trees shimmer with pure joy. A great lightness of being seems to descend on the land.

In the days and weeks following Rajili's burial, the area in and around the temple came to feel perfectly ordinary. It was unmistakably clear to me that the entity which had inhabited the Kali temple had been released, never to return.

I never saw Loganathan again. A year or so later, I heard that he and his family had moved to a different village and that their baby Anjali had died. It seemed the laws of karma had been at work.

A Terrible Accident

In August of 2021, living in California, I am reading *Better to Have Gone: Love, Death, and the Quest for Utopia in Auroville*, by Akash Kapur. Akash grew up in Auroville himself and later married Auralice, daughter of Diane and Larry, who were living in the Kottakarai community when I was there. He describes the remarkable story of Diane and Johnny, their love, their faith and their eventual death.

I remember walking by Diane's two-story hut one day to haul water from Jaap's well when I heard Johnny Walker and Diane laughing and giggling up in the loft. Clearly in love, they sounded so very happy.

On July 12, 1976, a month and a half before giving birth to my second child, I was outside our hut in the early morning and watched Diane come bicycling by at a furious pace towards the Matrimandir. She had recently begun to work at the construction site. I commented to Daniel, how incredibly strong and powerful she looked, like a horse.

Later that same day, a shockwave traveled through Auroville, Diane had fallen from the scaffolding and had been taken to Jipmer Hospital. A small group of us, stunned by the shock, got on the village bus to the hospital. We were allowed to visit her, one at a time. Nothing had as yet been done to help her. The report was that she had broken her back and her jaw.

I came to her bedside. Diane looked devastated. Her face was a wreck. Heavily pregnant with child, I bent over her, trying not to show how shocked I was to see her like that. She looked at me in desperation and, through all her broken teeth, cried out, "Mudder!" To my utter dismay, I thought she said, "Murderer." I stood deeply and unaccountably accused. It hit the same place of the inexplicable guilt I had felt as a child. Later, I realized that she had called "Mother!" Diane ended up paralyzed. I was quite sure that if she hadn't been at the top of her physical prowess, she would not have survived.

Undoubtedly, all of us wondered how such a terrible thing could happen at the Matrimandir, where we all felt Mother's energy so powerfully present.

Later, we heard that Diane felt she had been pushed even though no one had been in her vicinity. She then tumbled down all the rungs of the scaffolding, one by one until crashing down some fifty feet below on the cement floor.

I remembered the story of Andai Amma, Rajili and Vijayrangam's mother. Since her hut had been right at the center of Auroville next to the construction site of the Matrimandir, it seemed obvious that she couldn't remain there. She had been asked and undoubtedly urged, to please move back to Kottakarai where she was from. She adamantly refused. To my shock and disbelief, a number of Aurovilians working at the building site eventually decided to simply burn down her hut. I had heard the tale of how the old woman had erupted in fury, shaken her fist at the Matrimandir and cursed the site. Many of us felt that Andai Amma had occult powers. I felt in my gut that the accident was the direct result of the curse from Andai Amma.

Gordon Korstange, one of Kottakarai's Aurovilians, recently published his memory about a startling experience he had with her when he was in charge of the food distribution in our community. He writes:

> Andai Amma, the old woman who had been a fixture selling foodstuffs to travelers under the banyan tree at the center of Auroville, had been moved out of her hut and taken into the Kottakarai community. She came to the workshop one day asking for her allotment of rice. It was not distribution day and I told her so but then she erupted, like a sudden squall
>
> comes the carrier of skulls,
> Kali, glutton of worlds . . .
> I stare stupidly at the fiery eyes,
> for I do not know the words
> to speak to that presence
> smoldering under the wrinkled skin
> and I close my book, lose the place,
> get up to fetch the rice.

Sometime later we heard rumors of Diane having been moved to another part of Auroville and that she was only allowing Johnny Walker, her sweetheart, and a few of her men friends to tend to her. She adamantly refused any women around her. It was very strange to not be allowed near her and help take care of her. It felt quite disturbing to me, adding weirdness to the shocking event.

After ten years, Johnny, being Diane's devoted caregiver, died. He had been terribly ill for some time and had refused Western medicine. When Diane was given the news, she immediately proceeded to poison herself with toxic seeds of the Datura, growing in their garden. Datura is one of the most common means of suicide in the surrounding Tamil villages. She was determined to follow Johnny into the afterlife. The next day both bodies were displayed side by side for what must have been the strangest and darkest memorial in Auroville.

Ludar Comes to India

My father and I continued to correspond. He was studying Sri Aurobindo with a passion and asked me numerous questions about Mother. He had always been an eclectic philosopher with deep roots in mystical Catholicism. He grappled with the notion of an embodiment of the Divine Mother since that is such an unfamiliar notion in Western culture. We only have Mary, and she is hardly represented as an empowered female. The highest spiritual status a woman can achieve in the church is that of a Mother Superior of a convent. I understood his suspicion.

He decided to come and see for himself what Mother's presence was really like. Being highly sensitive and intuitive, he figured he would sense the truth about her and what she was really all about when he got there, even though she was no longer in the body. He was sixty-six by this time. I watched his lone figure walking through the shimmering heat from the village through the fields to our hut.

Just setting foot on Auroville's red earth had transfigured him. By the time he stood in front of me, he was deeply moved. "It is all true," he said softly. "You were right. She is good!"

During one of our many intimate conversations, he shared with me how, before WWII, he had once received an occult initiation during which he was given the name Ludar, from the Latin *ludare—to play*. I felt it did reflect his playful nature, his resonance with the *Glass Bead Game* and his skill as a magician. From then on, he would introduce himself as Ludar.

One quiet afternoon, we were both sitting in rattan chairs in front of our hut overlooking the fields, sipping tea and chatting, when in the distance we saw an enormous snake undulating at high speed in our direction. We watched mesmerized. When it was about fifty yards in front of us, I recognized it was a gigantic cobra heading home to the jungle behind our hut. I was sitting precisely in its line of motion. As it approached at full speed, I simply lifted my legs, and without hesitation, it sped underneath my chair towards its home. After a moment of stunned silence, we both burst out laughing. My father looked at me with astonished admiration. I hadn't even flinched.

The cobra is sacred in India. In Tamil it is called the Lord Snake—Sami Paambu. You will see it wrapped around Shiva's throat, showing Shiva as master of life and death. No one would think of killing a cobra, especially not this one living in Kali's grove. Later in my life, I would realize "Snake Medicine" in the Native American tradition. This giant snake rushing between my legs right under me surely was a worthy introduction to that medicine.

Toward the end of Ludar's visit, he surprised me with, "I've decided to come and live here. I want to be near Them, close to the Source, to prepare for my Bardo." (The "Bardo" is a Buddhist term for the transition of the soul after death.) He planned to go back to Holland, get rid of all his possessions and say good-bye to everyone. With his small pension he would have enough financial security to live here quite well. "I'm planning to rent a flat in Pondicherry. I don't want to live in the Ashram, that is too confining for me," he said. "I also won't live in Auroville, since I don't want to belong to any group anymore. This is *my* time." Naturally, we loved the prospect of being near one another.

After finalizing his affairs in Holland, he said goodbye to my mother and his friends and came to live in a new suburb of Pondicherry. He rented a small, clean home, got himself an amma to help with his household tasks, and befriended a boy to run errands for him and for whom he provided an education.

Whereas in Holland, my father had often looked a bit shabby and overweight, in India Ludar became slender and dressed impeccably in white tailor-made suits. He became quite the gentleman of leisure. Without financial worries, and with his daily needs taken care of, he could now freely focus on his inner life. His open-minded, warm-hearted and deeply spiritual nature won him many a friend in Auroville and the ashram. I had never seen him so happy, relaxed and well-groomed. He seemed to naturally gravitate to the Tibetan refugee community in Pondicherry and made friends with the monks. He purchased a dark red hand-made carpet from them for my mother. It now embellishes my living room. He also found his way to the leprosy colony, where he became a regular visitor. He had a deep and abiding love for the outcast.

During one of his visits to us, Daniel invited him on a trip by bullock cart to meet his friend, Tupten, in another part of Auroville's green belt. I was happy seeing the two of them leave on a little adventure. It gave me a feeling of family, the feeling I always seem to be longing for.

Sometime after the birth of our second daughter, Ludar sent us an invitation to come and visit him with both the children. He arranged for a taxi to come and pick us up. I was happily looking forward to this special day. It would be our first family outing with the children. On the appointed day, a taxi appeared around the trees, and we all got in. As the car started up, Daniel shocked me when he mindlessly cracked a joke. "Monsieur and Madame Lapin," he chuckled. "Mr. and Mrs. Rabbit." I was devastated. With one fell swoop, he destroyed my little dream of a happy family event. Apparently, Daniel felt a family outing was quite beneath his dignity. I shut down. His remark hung like a shroud over my day. I felt deeply disappointed, unable to speak.

It felt like a re-play of the nun in boarding school coming to offer Sunday treats. I was all happy and excited to get a little treat when she barked at me, "No, you can't have any. You've been bad!" So close to happiness and it gets whisked away from me, both in the past and in the present. Surely, Daniel hadn't meant to deal me a devastating blow. He was just having fun. Here was another replay of my past, feeling terribly hurt and not able to express myself.

Over the next few years, whenever I went into Pondy, I would visit Ludar. We were always thrilled to see each other and laughed a lot. We enjoyed our deeply loving and spiritual bond.

Tara, Star Child

When Aurelia was around six months old, I felt drawn to go back to the clinic, which Radhakrishna had continued to run.

Dosai Amma, the dosa lady from the village, had come to help me around the house and with the baby. I felt comfortable leaving Aurelia in her care. I was happy to return to the satisfying work at the clinic. When I came walking back home in the heat of noon, Dosai Amma would be greeting me with the baby on her hip. Those morning hours may have been too long for Aurelia to not have me near her. She would be eager to come into my arms. Then, because I was tired from the whole morning working in the clinic, I would have to rest and give her back to Dosai Amma. Daniel had constructed a little hut across the field where either one of us could retire to meditate or rest. My heart would ache leaving my sweet baby behind again, crying. But our life settled into a pretty comfortable rhythm.

In November of 1975, two months after Aurelia's first birthday, Daniel and I made love. Afterwards, I stepped outside into the night to pee. Upon entering back into our hut, I had the sudden experience of a small spiral nebula exploding in my womb. I stopped in my tracks. As I stood there in our doorway in the dark, I heard Daniel's quiet voice from our bed on the floor, "Are you pregnant?"

I wasn't quite ready for another pregnancy. It just felt too soon. I could not feel immediately welcoming. I then worried that my lack of enthusiasm might negatively affect the newly growing child inside of me. I did my best to accept and adjust to the unexpected guest choosing to grow in my womb.

At times during this pregnancy, I would spontaneously ask this being growing inside of me, "Who are you?" and "Where are you from?" In the last months, I would be startled by sudden explosions in my belly, getting kicked and punched violently in

Pregnant with Tara

all directions at once. My due date was mid-August. I had such a sense of the power of this child, I thought surely it was going to be a Leo boy. Mid-August passed and I kept getting bigger and bigger.

Around that time, when I was quite heavy with child, Auroculture surprised me with a visit. She was an Austrian woman whom I had befriended in the ashram, one of those remarkable people so intoxicated with the Divine that they become quite eccentric. Every evening, she would gather the hundreds of blossoms which had decorated the Samadhi during the day, take them to her apartment in town and compost them. Then she would bring this special compost to the gardens in Auroville to enrich the soil with Mother's and Sri Aurobindo's energy. Even her chosen name was strange. Who on earth would call themselves Auroculture? What "culture" was she referring to? It only now occurs to me that it may have referred to her desire to help cultivate Auroville's soil.

We were delighted to see each other and sat down with a cup of tea. She then proceeded to tell me a most remarkable tale, which I remember verbatim.

> Sometime last year, a woman in the ashram asked me, since Mother was no longer available, would I please go and meditate by the Samadhi and bring down a new name for her. I agreed and when I next sat and meditated there, I opened myself to receive a name. I had a powerful experience and the name "Tara" came through. I immediately understood that this name had nothing to do with the woman who had asked.
>
> I returned to meditate by the Samadhi and opened myself to whatever being had been communicating this name to me. Tara came through and told me she was a being from the stars who had never been to earth and that she wished to incarnate here.

Since Auroculture was not in a situation to conceive, she had proceeded to walk at night under the stars through Auroville, calling for Tara to come down. In November, she felt Tara had incarnated. She began to make regular trips into Auroville, visiting pregnant women in one community after another, hoping to find her. She hadn't. Finally, she heard that I was pregnant, and she trekked out the distance to Kottakarai.

The more her story continued, the more I resonated with it. Hadn't I kept wondering where this being came from? The spiral nebula experience upon conception could not have been a more powerful indication that maybe, indeed, it was Tara from the stars who had exploded into me. When I referred to the baby as a "he," Auroculture immediately corrected me. "Oh no," she said, "It's a she!"

I laughed and responded, "Well, if it's a she, surely it must be Tara." Auroculture had no doubt. When she went on her way, she asked if she could come and visit in a few weeks to see the baby.

As the birth approached, a deep fear took hold of me. I had an ominous feeling about the delivery to come and was also beginning to get anxious because I had not yet found a midwife. Two young French midwives came to visit from another settlement in Auroville and, smiling happily, were telling me that there was no reason to be afraid. Secretly terrified as I was, I couldn't handle being told blithely not to be afraid. I did not accept their offer. Just a few days before the delivery, Paula, an American midwife, showed up and was willing to help me.

On August 27, 1976, my contractions started early in the morning. Paula came over. Very quickly I moved into violent contractions. I lost control completely. The baby was coming down with such force, I felt like a train was rushing through me. The water hadn't broken. The midwife tried her best to tear the membrane to help slide the baby out. No such luck. Finally, she said, "I don't think you're really giving it your all."

"Oh, really?" I thought. "I will show you!" And, with a few massive pushes, the baby came crashing out of me.

"It's a girl!" Paula exclaimed. She was born with the hood. Her silent face tightly covered in the amniotic sac was a disquieting sight. When Paula pulled the membrane from under her chin over her head and turned her to me, her little wrinkled face looked just like Mother's had at ninety-five. Right there, from between my legs, she gave me a dead-serious, piercing look. I felt terribly put on the spot. It was frightening. Deep in my being, I felt as though I stood accused. Then in one smooth move, Tara was

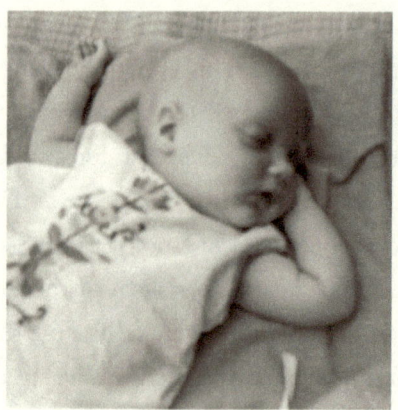

Baby Tara

brought over to me. In the few seconds it took for her to land on my body, her little face plumped up to perfection. She resembled one of those perfectly adorable Hummel babies I remembered from German postcards.

I had torn so badly that a doctor was sent for to stitch me up. By late afternoon, she finally arrived. When you get stitched up directly after the birth, the tissues are so numbed that it can be done quite easily. Now, she had to give me several shots of anesthesia and, along with the stitching, it was more than I could bear. I howled in pain. If I had torn just a bit more, I would have had to go to the hospital. It left me feeling quite resentful of the midwife, who, while everything was already happening so fast, had urged me to push even harder. Don't ever tell me that I can't do something. I will prove you wrong.

But, most of all, I felt crushed by the terrible accusation I experienced when Tara gave me that first penetrating, serious look as if I was being evaluated and found wanting: my childhood dread, seemingly confirmed in that most vulnerable moment.

I couldn't share my disturbed feelings with anyone, so ashamed I was. I had to hold it all in and felt so very isolated again, a perfect repetition of my inability to express my terror when I was only three years old, and nobody knew.

During the first few weeks of her life, our little Tara was profoundly peaceful. She mostly kept her eyes closed or just barely opened when she was awake. She had a healthy appetite and drank greedily. After each nursing, she would fall sound asleep and radiate an extraordinary silence. When, together with an Indian friend from the Ashram, Auroculture came to visit, I was sitting with Tara sleeping in my arms out on the back porch. They knelt in silence and adoration in front of her. I felt like the kings had come to visit, honoring the Christ child and bringing gifts.

When she was three weeks old, I carried her outside, like I did every day. As I strolled with her under the big cottonwood trees behind our hut, for the first time she opened her eyes wide. She looked up in wonder and surprise. "Oh, this is what it looks like down here," she seemed to say.

Ludar came to visit to see the new baby. He quietly entered our hut where she lay peacefully asleep in her beautiful cradle. When I wanted to move the mosquito netting aside so he would be able to better see her, he waved away my gesture and knelt in silent reverence by her side. He was deeply moved.

Within a few months, I began to worry that I did not have enough milk for my little Tara. She would drink with a vengeance, and I felt I couldn't quite meet her hunger. When she was three months old, I decided to try and give her a bottle with formula to see what would happen. I was shocked when she emptied the bottle in seconds. That's when I knew she needed more than I was able to produce. I then fed her a bottle every day, resulting in my own production steadily diminishing. By month six, she was completely fed by bottle.

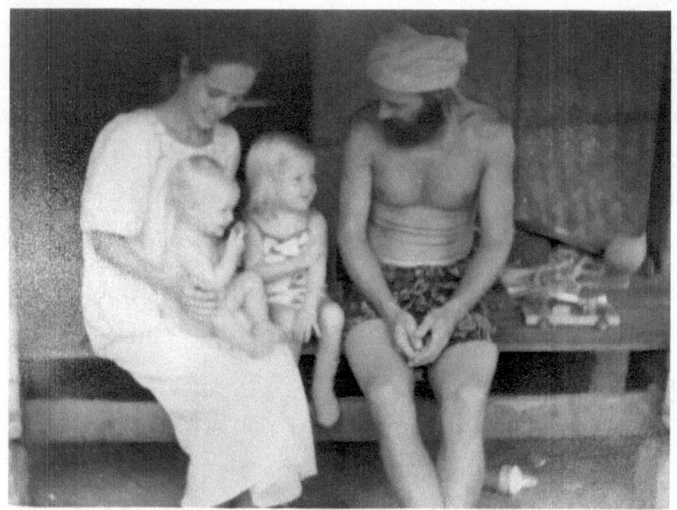
Our little family in front of our hut

Part IV

California

We Move to California

In the fall of '77 we received a letter from Daniel's father that would change our lives. He wrote that Daniel's mother was not well enough to travel, they hadn't seen Daniel in ten years, and we had their only grandchildren. He then announced that they were sending us tickets for the whole family to fly to America for a four-month visit with them. It was an offer we could not refuse.

The American consul in Madras (Chennai) had strong objections to granting me a visa, "You have children with an American man. You're going to like it there. I am sure that you will not want to come back. Of course, I could marry you two, then there would be no problem." Since Daniel was still legally married to Iris, and a divorce could only happen in California, that was not an option. The consul explained that his previous job had been with immigration in the U.S., and he was determined not to allow potential immigrants into the country. We were unable to convince him how important life in Auroville was for us and that we had no intention of leaving. Only when I brought him a letter from my father confirming that *he* was living in Pondicherry, did the consul reluctantly give his consent. We left everything behind in our little hut, convinced as we were that our life belonged there.

It so happened that Iris and Constance, with their little daughter Hira, were already visiting family in California. Mitra, Daniel and Iris's son who was by now eight years old, was coming with us. Aurelia was three and a half and Tara one and a half.

In February of '78, Daniel and I with the three children embarked on the long trip across oceans and continents. I saw my country with its extensive delta passing by below us. We landed in New York, then continued on to Los Angeles.

Exhausted from the long ordeal, we were met at the airport by Daniel's parents. After a lot of enthusiastic hellos and introductions and adoration of the children, we finally drove off in the back seat of their red station wagon. I barely dared look outside. It hit me how afraid I was of America. Memories came back to me of Kennedy being shot and his killer getting murdered in front of our eyes on TV, then the assassinations of Martin Luther King and Robert Kennedy. I feared this violent country, where the best and most beautiful people get killed.

Having lived in a simple bamboo hut without paved roads or transportation, without electricity and in the first years even without water, the high-rise city and massive traffic of Los Angeles was overwhelming and intimidating. I kept my eyes closed for most of the drive until we got to South Pasadena with its tree-lined streets and large mansions surrounded by lush gardens.

We pulled into a stately driveway with formal French gardens accentuated by Roman statues. In front of us rose a massive Italian pink palace overgrown with ivy. We entered through large sculpted front doors into a white and black checkered marble hallway. On a pedestal in its center stood a large Buddha head. Antique tapestries and works of art decorated the walls. Two red-carpeted flights of stairs curved on either side of the entryway to the second floor.

Daniel's father, Lyman Augustus III, was a tall, imposing, renowned heart and lung surgeon with a booming voice and a lively bounce in his step. He offered us a hearty welcome with a wide sweep of his arms, "Please, make yourselves at home!" Daniel's mother, Jane, took over from there and guided us upstairs. She was fairly short, white-haired and a bit plump. Her face was very white, with round pale blue eyes. Her skin was entirely covered in a web of fine wrinkles. She seemed a bit nervous with our invasion, but she was a most gracious hostess. She took us up to the second story of the west wing and showed us our quarters.

Our spacious bedroom, the "green room," had two large beds—one for us and one for the girls with an adjacent bathroom. Here we discovered one of Jane's artistic abilities. She had painted the entire bathroom in a perfect imitation of Gauguin's jungle paintings, a tiger peeking through lush greenery and a colorful toucan perched in the branches. Our suite was completed with a rococo-style sitting room.

On the other side of the same wing, Mitra was given the "Napoleon Room," which was fully decorated in imperial French reds and blues. His massive bed was hung with heavy striped draperies. French lilies were everywhere you looked. He had his own bathroom. Clearly, he was welcomed like a little prince. I can hardly imagine what that must have seemed like to this boy who had been born in a hut in Kerala and grown up on the red earth of Auroville where he freely roamed around half-naked.

After we had refreshed ourselves and rested a bit, we went downstairs. A large table was set in the stately dining room. Between the dining room and the kitchen, we were shown a small anteroom where all the various special sets of dishes and silverware were stored—three walls of cupboards full. Then, Father Lyman proudly pointed to a large case exhibiting his war trophies: some of Hitler's personal silverware and other treasures which he had been able to confiscate when in Berlin at the fall of the Third Reich. I was profoundly shocked. It was clear to me that my father's history was to remain an absolute secret.

Daniel's younger brother, Lyman IV, who continued to live at home, joined us for a sumptuous dinner, with elegant dishes, crystal wine glasses and silver candelabras. We had entered a high-class, elegant world, so very different from our primitive existence in Auroville, but one that lived somewhere in my own family's background. The elegance was also a part of me, and I enjoyed the luxury.

Over time, I learned that Daniel's father had been a surgeon on the battlefront during the American invasion in Europe. He loved talking about his experiences in the field, and how he had developed his greatest skills as a heart-and-lung surgeon, having to be utterly creative when dealing with open chest wounds under those dire circumstances. In the front hall was a framed photograph of him—the very image of the "American Hero"—proud, with steely blue eyes, absolutely sure of himself and on top of the world. I carefully kept my father's dark secret out of sight.

The next day started a daily routine with family breakfast in the kitchen where Jane was queen. However, as long as father Lyman was at the table, his affable presence and loud voice dominated the space. After he left, mother Jane would start with incessant, nerve-wracking monologues criticizing anything and everything. I quickly understood how Daniel had become such a quiet person and how he had learned the often-maddening art of tuning out. After a while you did not really want to listen and, certainly, no one could get a word in edgewise.

After breakfast, we ventured out onto a stone veranda on the South side of the mansion, with steps leading to a gorgeous, perfectly manicured lawn surrounded by flowering shrubs and large trees. In a far corner, a big fountain splashed into a rocky pool with Neptune sculpted in the rocks behind it. Father Lyman's workroom and sumptuous library were in the East wing and their bedroom and her boudoir on the floor above it.

The children seemed to adjust effortlessly. Gramsy, as they called Jane, took much pleasure in getting the girls pretty dresses. Some of them she sewed. Out of sheer habit, I still let them run around naked. The California weather was warm as well. It was a bit challenging for Jane. When she was expecting gardeners or other workers, she would whisper urgently in my ear that I should make sure the girls would be dressed.

Gramsy arranged a preschool for Aurelia to attend. We all went to witness their Easter celebration. The children went on an egg hunt and afterwards the children sat around little tables that were nicely decorated and enjoyed cookies and treats. When it was time to leave, of all the children Aurelia was the only one who came up to the teacher and thanked her so very graciously. The teacher looked at us, delighted with our little girl's courteous behavior.

About two months into our stay, we were in for quite the unexpected turn around in our lives. During Aurelia's first three years in Auroville—after her terrible episode in the hospital when she was only three months old and we nearly lost her—her immune system had been severely compromised. She had suffered from diarrhea, impetigo, boils, whooping cough—you name it. She had never been completely well for more than three weeks at a time. Now, I watched her running around, robust and healthy. It struck me—as if being hit in the head with a two-by-four—she did not even have so much as a runny nose. In fact, I had not even thought about her health.

This startling awareness turned everything upside down. I realized we could not possibly go back to India, not for her and not for me. I went to Daniel and presented him with the facts. I simply said, "We can't go back." I could feel what a difficult decision this was for him. Clearly, we had no other choice. He could only agree. So it was that we decided to stay in America.

Finding a New Home

Lyman and Jane were thrilled with our decision. In fact, I always suspected that this was their secret hope when they invited us for a four-month visit. However, when we decided to stay in the U.S., Daniel and I were both quite clear that we did not want to live in the Los Angeles area. We just did not feel at home there. We planned a trip around six of the Western states to see if we could find a community of like-minded folk and a beautiful environment where we might want to settle. We had contacts all over the country with people who had either lived in or felt connected to Sri Aurobindo or to Auroville. We planned to visit some of them while camping out along the way.

Father Lyman lent us his station wagon. Mitra went to stay with his mother who was in L.A. at the time. I made a comfortable play and sleeping area for the girls in the back, with blankets and pillows and their newly acquired stuffed animals and off we went. Daniel wanted to show me California's beautiful coast and decided we would drive all the way up Hwy 1 to Santa Cruz, where our friend June lived.

Driving along Big Sur, my heart leapt when I spotted a sign that read "Esalen Institute." When studying psychology in Amsterdam, I had trained in Fritz Perls' Gestalt Therapy with a woman who had studied with him at Esalen. I knew the institute was at the very forefront of psychological and alternative healing approaches. Just seeing its name felt like a promise for my future, however nebulous that still was.

We stopped at Julia Pfeiffer State Park. It was my first experience among the redwoods. I soaked up their majestic abundance and the dappled light falling through the tall trees, the refreshing sound of a rushing creek at our feet, while our darling little girls happily clambered about. I do not recall ever having felt this ecstatic in nature before. I felt showered with grace and beauty and breathed in the fresh air as if I had been parched—such a contrast with the dry hot barren plateau we had lived on for years.

I still remember driving into the Santa Cruz area, which I would eventually call home. Before coming into Aptos, the town just south of Santa Cruz, a gorgeous view opens out through the trees onto the Monterey Bay. We had a lovely visit with June and her family.

We loved exploring Santa Cruz. I was particularly charmed by the cobblestone courtyard with coffee shop, nestled in between brick walls overgrown with vines, behind the old Bookshop Santa Cruz. What luxury and freedom we felt browsing in the bookstore and enjoying a fresh brewed cup of cappuccino in the courtyard. Not only did we feel completely at home among the local population of relaxed people with their long hair and easy clothes, but it felt familiar to me as if we were in Amsterdam.

Then we crossed the country eastward through the majestic Sierra Mountains, the vast Nevada desert and the bizarre Utah landscape into Colorado. We went to visit an Aurobindo center in Boulder and enjoyed the hospitality of the people there. We picnicked by a creek amidst abundant wildflowers. I still have some lovely pictures of our two adorable blond-haired girls playing among the blossoms. However beautiful we found Colorado, we quickly realized that the summer seasons were brief and long cold winters did not appeal to us. Daniel's interest in gardening and growing food would be seriously hampered by a three-month growing season.

From there we crossed the mountainous lands to meet friends in Santa Fe, New Mexico. We both found the artistic and free-thinking lifestyle appealing, but I had quite enough of

Daniel with our girls in Colorado

living in the desert. Daniel and I agreed that Santa Cruz was by far the most appealing place for us. I loved the prospect of being near trees and close to the ocean.

It took us almost a year before we were able to move. In South Pasadena, we had little choice but to settle back in with Daniel's parents. I began to feel quite oppressed in the stilted atmosphere with his mother at the helm. I missed the magic of Auroville, where every part of the land had felt sacred as if inhabited by the Divine Presence. Here, even the most beautiful gardens looked like the artificial décor of a stage. Empty. I had no soul connection with the people or the place and felt as though I was living in exile.

Daniel made a few trips to Santa Cruz by himself to see if he could find a suitable place for us to rent. This was easier said than done. I hoped that we might find a home and garden just for our own little family, which might fulfill my old childhood dream of family life. Daniel said he was willing to look for that but he much preferred that we try and create a small community. He found a large, old farmhouse with three acres of fertile land on Ocean Street Extension, just outside of town. There he would be able to garden to his heart's content and we could gather a small community around us. I was secretly disappointed, even as I understood and also shared that ideal.

Through our friend June, Daniel had already connected with some young people who had visited Auroville and were eager to start a small collective experiment in Santa Cruz.

We loaded up a moving truck with any furniture Jane was able to spare and made the long trek north. When I saw the farm, my heart sank. Paint stains and cobwebs covered the windows

Farm house in Santa Cruz   Me on Ocean Street

and the place creaked with age. The land was neglected too. It would require quite a lot of maintenance and upkeep to meet some minimal standards of cleanliness and aesthetics. So, together with the others, I threw myself into cleaning, scrubbing and decorating with what little means we had.

The main house was a two-story building with a large living room upstairs, four bedrooms, two walk-in closets, a bathroom, and balconies in front and back. Downstairs were a couple of inter-connected low-ceilinged spaces, as well as a small side room, a large community kitchen with a walk-in pantry and a bathroom. In the back of the house was a cabin with a sauna, and to the right a converted garage, close to the street. Behind the cabin was a chicken coop in the shadow of a large avocado tree. An enormous pine tree stood in the front yard with a long swing suspended from one of its lower branches. Over the years, our little community consisted of between six and nine adults and two or four children.

Ocean Street Extension is a dead-end street a few minutes out of town, with small farms and orchards, ending in the woods

With Daniel and friend on the farm

along the San Lorenzo River. The farm was situated on three acres of floodplain. As a result, the soil was marvelously fertile.

Daniel started to prepare a generous size garden. I planted roses around the house. We had inherited an old pony with the property, Mr. Jackson, and acquired chickens and a goat. For the children it was paradise. They were free to roam outside, climb the avocado tree, swing from the branches of the old fir, visit the chickens, play hide-and-seek among the luscious tall stands of corn Daniel planted. Besides being an avid gardener, he was quite the artist. Not only was he skilled in working with leather, he did beautiful woodwork, fine calligraphy, played the piano, especially the joyous ragtime, and regularly I would find snippets of paper with a few lines of poetry scribbled on them.

Reluctantly, I adjusted to living communally, again. I did believe that it was much better for the children to have a variety of role models rather than just one set of parents. It was certainly convenient that I could at times go about my own business because other adults were always around to look after the children.

When Aurelia was five and Tara three, I remember watching them with delight as they were running around naked in the rain and splashing in mud puddles. With a pang, I realized that was the age at which I had been ripped away from my family to live with strangers in the severe and stark environment of a Catholic boarding school. I saw how young they were, and carefree, but also how small and vulnerable, and how much they needed the safety of home and my loving care.

Our house was a carefree welcoming place. The children were freely running around. Our little Tara was an adorable child, with her sweet round face and blond curls. She had such a loving nature. We hosted a refugee from El Salvador, and this little one just climbed onto the man's lap and put her little arms around his neck. He was greatly comforted.

However, just like in Auroville, Daniel was mostly absent here as well. He was either off on odd gardening or construction jobs, trying to earn a living or disappearing into the garden. Often, he was simply nowhere to be found. Then, I would feel quite lonely and wished to have more closeness with him. The women we lived with once remarked to me that I was really like a single mother because of Daniel's near-total lack of involvement in the children's daily care. However, I was happy that he was always kind to them and to me. I did not really know what a father could be like since I had no real experience with that.

Fortunately, the girls have lovely memories with him. They felt inspired and nurtured by his connection with the land, his creativity and his loving kindness.

For myself, I was used to doing life on my own and putting my feelings aside. Being lonely in relationships and among people was all I knew. I did not dare complain to Daniel or demand anything of him. I was too afraid that he might get annoyed with me, and I might lose him even more.

I was also often frustrated by the lack of participation from the young people we lived with. Regardless of endless schedules we put together during our monthly community meetings for housekeeping, cooking and cleaning, most duties were easily forgotten. Fortunately, they did take their turn in cooking, which allowed me marvelous quiet times outdoors in the late afternoon when the golden light played over the fields and trees. But by default, and much to my chagrin, I had become the house mother. To all appearances, however, our life was a happy one.

One day when the girls were in school, Daniel invited me to get stoned with him. I hadn't partaken for a long time. He took me by the hand and guided me to a quiet spot in the grass behind the chicken coop. There we laid down in sweet surrender, when he removed my sandals and took my feet into his hands and began to lick and nibble each of my toes. When his tongue dipped in

Daniel and my wedding

275

the hollow between them, I felt his pleasure and between each set of toes my body would erupt into a sweet orgasm, one after the other. Such delight.

Meanwhile our friends Constance and Iris also came to live in Santa Cruz with their two little children, together with Mitra, who now moved freely between our homes.

When we were living in Auroville, we had made friends with Arky and Ginger, a couple who were traveling through India and the Middle East to purchase oriental rugs for their store in San Francisco. After settling in Santa Cruz, we went to visit them in the city. We brainstormed with them about ways Daniel and I could make a living in this country. They understood that we were not very well equipped to fit into ordinary society. They told us that the Bay Area really needed a professional hand-washing and restoration service for fine and antique oriental carpets. The only professional repair and restoration was done in London. Businesses who proclaimed to do hand washing were not too reliable.

Arky and Ginger showed me a fragment of an antique carpet, priceless because of its age and unique color and design. It had been handmade long ago in some remote village in Persia, now carefully stitched onto linen and mounted onto a frame so it could be displayed like a painting. They had a trunk full of these fragments. Did I think I could do that kind of work? Having once knotted a carpet back in Holland and recreated the Gobelin upholstery for my grandmother's rocking chair, I was quite convinced that I could. She gave me a piece to try preserving and mounting it. They were so satisfied with the result that they gave me a handbook on the technique of carpet restoration and from then on, I was in the business of restoring and repairing oriental carpets.

Daniel and Constance started a hand-washing business called Talisman, which is still going strong to this day. Iris and I worked on the repair and restoration. It was quite wonderful for me to have a quiet focus amid our rather chaotic community. After a damaged rug had been carefully cleaned, its original colors and patterns shining again, it was most satisfying when it would come out from under my hands in all its original beauty.

In a mansion across the street from our farm, lived Jasper Rose, a tall dignified looking Englishman with a shock of white hair, and his wife. They were both fine watercolor artists. One day, during a neighborly chat, I mentioned about my carpet restoration. Their eyes lit up. Their dog had chewed a large hole in the beautiful oriental rug in their living room. Daniel took the rug to Talisman to be cleaned. I then recreated the foundation

Restoring oriental carpets

and knotted the pattern back matching as closely as I could the original colors. It is quite tricky because the colors have to be carefully matched with the original and, to blend in seamlessly, the knotting needs to be made to look just as aged as the original. The result was marvelously satisfying. The owners were quite impressed. In appreciation, Jasper offered that I choose one of his fine watercolors. I picked an exquisite painting of white roses in a ceramic vase on a tablecloth with shells strewn around it, all in various shades of white. He signed it for me and wrote, "Angela, loveliest of rug repairers."

A Last Week with My Father

In the spring of 1981, I traveled with six-year-old Aurelia to Holland to celebrate my mother's seventieth birthday. It was my first return to Holland since I left for India ten years before. It so happened that my father, who was still living in Pondicherry, would be in Holland a few months later for a small surgery. He was seventy-two years old and had already had three heart attacks. With him going back to India and me back to the United States and neither of us having much money to travel, we both knew this would be our last chance to see each other in this lifetime. I decided to extend our visit to spend a last week with him.

At that time, Hanna, a playful and artistic Dutch woman, had become a part of our Santa Cruz community. She was exceedingly fond of our little Tara and the two of them often spent time in her bus up in the Santa Cruz mountains. I trusted she would be a good substitute mom and I left Tara in her and Daniel's care.

My brother, Reinier, picked us up from Schiphol airport with a bouquet of tulips for Aurelia. He was instantly smitten with his gentle, gracious little niece and showered her with compliments.

My mother's seventieth birthday was a big event. It was held in a grand historical restaurant surrounded by a park near the Rotterdam harbor. Her sisters had come over from Germany for the occasion. Annelies, my father's youngest sister, and most of my Dutch and German cousins were there, as well as the entire musical community in Rotterdam who had been around my mother over the decades. The highlight of the event was my mother's performance on a splendid grand piano. She played some of her all-time favorite classics by Chopin, Brahms and Schubert, but also more modern pieces by Fauré, Poulenc and Andriessen. She was in top shape and performed fabulously. I so loved hearing her play again after all those years. She beamed with pleasure at the enthusiastic applause and bowed stately as a queen.

Reinier and I at my mother's 70th

Aurelia blossomed under the affectionate attention of all my aunts and cousins. We spent a week in Amsterdam visiting my dear friend Nol, who taught her to play chess. He, too, was quite smitten with her.

Towards the end of our three months' stay when I was expecting my father's arrival, I rented a cottage in a beautiful part of Holland set amid heather and woods. I had just readied the space when he arrived with a friend who had picked him up from the airport. He looked fabulous. His skin was a deep bronze from the Indian sun, he had grown himself a silver-gray wavy beard and had lost the extra pounds he had before. The three of us spent a magical week together. Ludar adored his sweet and bright little granddaughter and lavished her with his kind attention. She remembers how he taught her to read the clock. One morning he quietly waved her over to the window. "Come and look, Aurelia," he whispered and showed her the millions of dewdrops twinkling like diamonds in the early morning sunlight, turning the entire forest into a magical fairyland.

With Nol and Beth in Amsterdam

One evening, after Aurelia had gone to bed, he suggested we take our shoes off and spend a few hours in silence. The candles were lit, and the cottage felt like a monastery. We shared a profoundly sacred space together, so peaceful and intimate. To our delight, we noticed that we had the exact same well-shaped, slender feet, our second toes longer than our big toes. He had very sensitive feet. I did not remember ever having seen him barefoot before.

Knowing that this was our last time together, we spoke at length about his death. He was well prepared. We were clear with each other—nothing was left undone or unspoken. He was very clear about his wishes. "After my death, don't bother about my body," he said. "It is nothing. Don't transport it. Just get rid of it." After his surgery, he planned to visit a few friends in Germany and then return to his home in Pondicherry.

One morning, he was puttering in the kitchen, when I came out of the shower and on an impulse decided to wrap my towel around my waist only. When he turned and laid eyes on my

Ludar visiting my mother from India

breasts, he gasped, "Oh... how beautiful... thank you!" His gratitude and joy were overflowing. I was pleased to have offered him this small, innocent gift.

When it was finally time for my father to leave, one of his devoted friends, a doctor himself, came to pick him up to drive him to the hospital in Arnhem. We gave each other our last embrace, our hearts overflowing. I can still see him walking to the car, opening the door, and, turning to me, waving his hand in a final blessing and a joyous fare-thee-well. The air shimmered with delight, a loving acceptance of the inevitable in our hearts. We were complete in this lifetime.

However, it took me many more decades to process and gain clarity and relative freedom from my childhood difficulties and the underlying complexity of my relationship with my father, and the darkness of his past. None of that work had really begun by the time of this last farewell.

My Father's Death

Exactly one month after our return to California, at five in the morning, I woke up to a call from my brother in Holland. My journal entry from that day reads:

July 25th, 1981, at 5 a.m., Reinier calls me. My heart pounds as I answer the phone. So early in the morning cannot be good news.

"What is it, Reinier?" I ask. "Angela, something terrible has happened." I hold my breath. "Our father died this morning at 5 a.m." I fall into silence... "Oooh..."

My brother seems terribly worried how I will take the news, knowing full well how deeply I was bonded with my father.

Reinier does not realize how beautifully my father and I had made completion just a month before. He also has no comprehension of my inner spiritual resources, and even though I felt the initial shock, I am completely at peace with his death.

Ludar died of his fourth heart attack. Reinier tells me that our father was in Germany visiting with a dear friend of his, at her parents' home. They had just spent a lovely evening in deep conversation. Shortly after they had gone to bed, she had heard him knocking loudly on the wall and found him gasping for air. In the hospital, at some point during their efforts to revive him, she noticed him making a small hand gesture to stop.

I reassure Reinier that I'm alright and so is our father. After hanging up, I stay motionless. From a picture in the hall, Mother smiles at me ever so sweetly. Everything is as it should be. I urgently need to pee. Is that ok, right after hearing that my father died? I laugh and hear him laughing. Yes, life simply continues. I go to the bathroom. The moment I sit down to pee, he is there in front of me with a big smile on his face. His love and sense of humor about the situation fill the space. I stay there for a while basking in the pleasure of his presence. Then he is gone, and I burst into tears. Now I don't have my daddy anymore. I am overwhelmed with the feeling that I am his child, now a bit more alone in the world. We were so connected with one another. He called me into this life, and I came. Always we had this strong, warm, and mystical bond of love from lifetimes shared.

I go back to bed and tell Daniel. He is immediately awake and present. He gives me a knowing smile. We lie together quietly talking about him, reverberating in the mystery of death. Our sweet Aurelia comes and crawls into bed with us. I carefully share with her that my father has died and that everything is fine. Soon she begins to cry. I hold her and comfort her and try to reassure her. Her crying turns into heart-wrenching sobs. She sobs and sobs, until her whole body is heaving in distress. I ask her, "Why are you crying so much, sweetheart? Are you so sad?"

"Nooo… I'm crying for you, Mommie!" Oh, my dear child.

"I'm ok, honey, really," I reply. "His love will be always with us." I rock her for a long time.

Later that day as I'm walking through our old farmhouse, I look outside and glance up into the tall fir tree. High up on a branch, my father sits like the joker blowing bubbles, relishing his freedom and his ability to surprise me.

Over the next few days, I have several conversations with Reinier. My mother is on a cruise ship in Norway with her sisters. He cannot reach her. He is calling the embassy and trying to reach customs where she might cross back into Germany to see if they can intercept her. He is frantic because he is the only one there to take care of everything. I try to calm him down and explain that our father did not want any hoopla around his death; to just dispose of the body. It was nothing to him. But Reinier cannot let go and continues to try and move heaven and earth to get my mother back for the funeral in time.

He probably really needed her so as not to be alone with his own emotions and have to make all these big decisions by himself. My brother had a strong bond with my mother and stayed close to her all his life. She did not get the news until the day after the burial. The truth is, however, that my mother did not really care about my father anymore. It was nothing to her to have missed his burial.

It turns out that the local graveyard had no room for non-residents. The family of Ludar's friend agreed to bury his body anonymously in their family grave. My brother and my father's friend were the only ones walking behind the casket. His body truly disappeared without a trace, just as he wished, buried anonymously in some German village.

My brother wrote this obituary letter to family and friends. He wrote in German since half of our family does not speak Dutch. I translate:

3.6.1909 Münster, Germany—Lived: Yes!—7.25.1981 Behringsdorf (Nüremberg)

My good father—Willem van de Loo, Ludar to his friends—has taken leave of us forever. He came therefore from his beloved India to his loved ones in Europe. Saw his Ellen, his children, grandchildren, and friends.

His heart, his great, warm heart stopped beating on July 25, 1981. He was staying with friends in Behringsdorf, near Nüremberg. We have buried his earthly remains where he was, quietly—the way he wanted it.

The last time I saw him was just a week earlier, recovered from a successful surgery. Together with my son: Three generations for the first and the last time together! I saw them—seventy-two and fourteen years old—walking off hand in hand. In a ray of sunshine. Together, grandfather and grandson. An afternoon stroll. I could not wish for a more beautiful image of his farewell.

And a farewell it was. He himself would say, "I have left my body in peace."

Without pain—because no heart attack can compare to the pain he has suffered...

Without care—he was completely prepared, glad and without a trace of fear...

Without bitterness—because he knew no hatred, only forgiveness, he loved you, me, all...

His guiding proverb was: "Ama et fac quod vis—Love and do as thou wilts." He loved! Gave his love. Those who could receive it, understood... And he did as he pleased!

Immeasurable goodness—what he received in return was too little. And for the one error, beguiled and misled by false prophets, he bore inhumanly heavy penance and suffering.

He found true peace at last when his inner warmth and wisdom found resonance amongst his European and Indian friends in Auroville and Pondicherry. There he shared his spiritual wealth with those who understood and loved him. There he shared his meager earthly possessions with the poorest of the world. His last dimes were for the lepers...

Great, good, rich, warm, beloved Ludar—father, enjoy your well-deserved rest, live (!) in your long-awaited peace!

Those who knew you, know how grateful you were for each greeting, every kiss, the smallest helping hand. Therefore, you do not need to thank anyone again. Nevertheless, I do so in your name: My gratitude goes to each and every one who in their own way has been there for you, has done for you, has meant something to you.

Utrecht, July 1981. Reinier

My Healing Begins

About eleven years into my relationship with Daniel—it had been a long time since I had been intimate with a woman—I began to long for that beautiful, nurturing closeness. When I talked with Daniel about it, he seemed comfortable with the idea that I would find a woman lover. None of the lesbian women who lived in our small community were particularly appealing to me. Then there was Martha, a bit masculine with a compact body, short curly hair and a serious demeanor. She came and visited us for years and, since she worked for a flower grower, always brought me large bouquets of flowers. Later, after we became involved, the women in our community chuckled that I had never been aware of the real reason for the flowers. They had always known what a crush Martha had on me.

Over time our conversations deepened. We spent more and more time with one another until it seemed natural to be in her safe and nurturing arms. She offered me the emotional safety to start the process of healing my childhood wounding.

She listened with genuine interest to the stories of my childhood, the loneliness, the boarding schools, the nasty nuns. I cried the tears I never shed when I was little when I had to be "a good girl" and be quiet and not disturb anyone with my emotions. Often when I felt that, surely, she must have had enough and that I was taking up too much space, she would reassure me, "No, no, don't stop, don't leave things under the table. Just go on." Never had anyone turned to me with that much willingness and capacity to listen, and encourage me to have my feelings and express them.

Her listening stood in stark relief to my old reality. When I had been twelve, after seven interminable years of isolation and oppression in boarding schools, where I carried the terrifying knowledge of my father's death sentence as a huge dark secret inside me, I had come home to my mother who never once asked

With Martha on the farm

me how it had been for me all those years. Now that we were together and all that was behind us, we were just going to be happy.

Of course, most everyone in her generation had no idea that the war and its aftermath would leave scars on the psyche, carrying wounds in desperate need of healing. The entire post-war adult population, reeling from the unspeakable horrors they had lived through, collectively moved into that bizarre decade of the fifties where denial was the unspoken rule, and we were all "fine and pretty." My mother had mastered that pose.

In my early twenties, when I first felt safe enough to talk to a friend about my years in boarding school, I was surprised when I started to cry. This would occur again and again as I shared bits and pieces of my story. Always the tears, each time breaking up a bit of the walls of defense I had constructed around my inner despair and loneliness.

Now, in the safety of Martha's presence, some of my feelings began to surface. I raged against the nuns, jumping on the couch, morphing into a huge Tyrannosaurus Rex with mighty haunches, crushing those hateful nuns into black and white dust under my heels.

Once, coming home from my time with Martha, I wanted to share with Daniel some of the feelings I had been able to disclose to her. "Why would you want to go back to that?" he asked in utter astonishment, and "That seems kind of silly." I was shocked, baffled by his lack of comprehension. The "silly" particularly hurt. It dawned on me that Daniel had no space or patience for my emotional life at all. Until then our relationship had been rather uneventful and harmonious, probably because we had both been fairly dissociated from our feelings. His dismissive and belittling attitude put a definite wedge between us and drove me further into Martha's arms.

I entered a period of deep soul-searching. I was in my early forties. I cut my hair which had been long most of my life. I took off my wedding ring. I was aware of Jung's *coniunctio* concept and had the clear realization that it was my time to individuate. I needed to get married to myself. Then, an odd thing began to happen around my name. At a parent meeting, I introduced myself as Angela and was suddenly addressed as Andrea. Curiously, this happened again and again. People would call me Andrea. I had always loved my name Angela and had never considered changing it. During those same weeks, someone had written the name *Andrea* in big letters on our community bulletin board.

I decided that I wanted to find myself a ring which would symbolize my commitment to myself. I drove up the coast to the

Soul-searching on the farm

old Davenport Cash Store, where I had often seen interesting jewelry from all over the world. I looked around and spotted a silver ring with a double-headed snake entwined on itself. I was afraid it would be too intense of a symbol. I asked the woman behind the counter to lay the ring aside for me. "I need to think about this. I'll come back in an hour." Down to the beach I went. When I returned, a different woman was tending the store. I asked her for the ring that had been put aside for me. I told her my name was Angela. She looked and looked. Finally, she picked up the only package she found. She turned to me puzzled and said, "Andrea?" Lightning struck and I knew that I had found my ring and that Andrea was my name.

I appreciated the androgyny of the name. *Andros* is man in Greek. The name beginning and ending with *a*, just like my old name, indicated male/female balance. I placed the accent on the middle syllable, *Andréa*. In Angela there had been nothing much in the middle, now the center of my name indicated strength.

In the meantime, Daniel admitted he had a crush on Lisa, who had come to do work at Talisman, his carpet cleaning business. She was a tall, lanky, beautiful Buddhist woman. I felt that it was only fair, now that I had Martha, that he should explore a new relationship for himself. I really liked Lisa and I was happy for Daniel to have found her.

After some time, we rearranged our community so that Lisa could live with Daniel and Martha with me and we could each take turns, as couples, caring for the children. We were motivated to keep us all together so the children would continue to have the stability of our home. I was happy that we were all open-minded and willing enough to give this experiment a try.

Being confronted daily with the love and interest Daniel showed for Lisa was harder than I expected. I noticed his desire to be with her in ways he had never shown towards me. Then, one evening, I was in the upstairs bathroom and happened to see them with our girls in the cabin behind the house where they were living. I saw the four of them, like one happy family, sitting around the table playing games. He had never given us that, either. Sobbing, I turned to Martha and said, "I can't do this anymore. I need us to go and live by ourselves. This is too painful."

Martha owned a two-bedroom Victorian home in the nearby town of Soquel and, after discussing the issue among all of us, we decided to move there. Living with Martha felt like entering the safe haven I had needed for so long. Here was a quiet home with a garden, a walnut tree, roses, a white picket fence and a kind, understanding woman with whom I felt safe and loved.

She even looked a bit like my mother. The first few months of living there, I spent many hours resting deeply on a chaise lounge under the trees in her garden. I had not known how exhausted I was, physically and emotionally, from living in the ongoing chaos and stress of our communal home.

Then I resumed the repair and restoration work of oriental rugs which I had begun when living on Ocean Street Extension. Martha would leave for work at a very early hour, and instead of sitting quietly with my work in the center of our lively little community with my children around me, I was now alone at home spending hours focusing my skill and attention on carpets. The awareness of my "healing hands" and of having such deep love of helping people, came to the forefront. I realized it was time to get serious about developing my healing skills and start working on living bodies instead of carpets.

Since I needed to make a living, it was not clear to me how to make that transition. One day, Martha and I were driving on Highway 1, when the car in front of us which had already moved onto the off-ramp, merged back onto the freeway. Martha swerved to avoid a collision and we were hit from the rear by a car in the fast lane. Her car was totaled and both of us ended up in neck braces. Having been the passenger, my injuries were rather serious. I was not able to handle the weight of the carpets. I saw my chance! The car insurance covered my loss of income for some time, and I suddenly had the space to pursue a healing career.

Becoming a Healer

I enrolled at Twin Lakes College of the Healing Arts in Santa Cruz. I was forty-one. Their basic course was massage, to which other healing modalities could be added. In a conversation with the director, I told her that some years before I had followed courses and had been certified in Polarity Therapy. I would prefer to combine Polarity with other forms of energy healing. Since I planned to be independent and work from my home, I explained that I did not like the idea of having strangers undress in my space. She agreed to make an exception for me. I chose to focus on Jin Shin Do Acupressure, since that modality specifically addresses the emotional body. I added a course in hypnotherapy so I could learn to help people access underlying issues.

In hypnotherapy class, we practiced with one another. One assignment was to invoke our Shadow. One of my fellow students did a trance induction and asked me to visualize myself in a special place. This is what I wrote in my diary afterwards:

I'm on a high, steep mountain in a small, shallow cave near the top. There is no path. I am all alone, blissfully sitting in the light enjoying the immense view of the sky and the plains far below, forests and meadows halfway down with deer running freely. No one can come here, it is too steep. I experience myself in my thirties with long hair, dressed in a very fine long, white and blue skirt, a beautiful light blue embroidered blouse, sitting cross-legged.

She asks me, "Is there anything you would like to do?"

"Yes, I should like to dance."

I turn into a dancing goddess, like an ancient Indian statue, full-bodied, naked, dressed in beads only, my arms raised, I make slow circular motions, my feet stomp, anklets tinkle, toes pointed up. *I feel solid and strong. But, I would prefer to dance for someone. Dance for God... too impersonal. I see Krishna, a blue statue, playing the flute on a path in a meadow below me.*

I protest, "Here I am making all these gods and goddesses appear, while I am supposed to meet my Shadow."

Krishna begins to turn black. He changes into a large male figure in a long black cloak, his hands gloved in fine black leather. He is tall and standing so close to me that I can't see his face. He feels profoundly benign. He moves closer until I can feel his body warmth and the texture of the black wool. An overwhelming feeling of care and protection radiates from him and from his cloak. My face now rests against his chest. He wraps his cloak around me and holds me close. Tears stream down my face. I have never been so safe. He is father, valiant knight, protector, caregiver and lover. His tall, black phallus enters me effortlessly. We merge in union. Delicious, sensuous feelings pervade my body. My arms are up around his neck.

I am told: "Look at his face."

As my face turns up to him, he cradles my head with infinite care. He looks like a North African Buddha. His features are very dark and strong, with full lips and a strong straight nose. A velvety bronze light glows in his large, almond-shaped eyes. I can look into his eyes forever. They look at me with pure goodness.

"What is his name?"

Silence... then, "Antar."

"Where did he come from?"

"He came through my heart."

"Look for a path."

He moves a little behind me to my right. I see a sand-colored path all the way down the mountain, leading to the plains below. Suddenly a wreath of gray clouds moves in front of the sun and obscures my view. Nevertheless, I am willing to go down. Hand in hand with my powerful protector, we start walking down the

path, regally. I know my session time is up. We will continue. I will
be completely safe and protected. I emerge, feeling a new strength.

Apparently, my psyche decided I wasn't quite prepared to meet my Shadow and gracefully brought forth my loving and protective Inner Male first.

About the name Antar—when I had been in love with Hedi, the beautiful North African young man from Tunisia, he had shared with me a poem translated from Arabic, called Antar. When I got pregnant by him, I said, "If it is a son, we will call him Antar." He had burst out laughing, "You can't do that! People will think it ridiculous. It would be like naming him Hercules in your culture!" So, here was Antar, my powerful Inner Male.

During our next hypnotherapy class, I firmly intend to encounter my Shadow. As soon as I go into trance, I find myself standing solidly planted on the ground, facing East. The Sun is rising. A big black Nothing comes closer and closer, trying to crush me. It pushes me back a little but I stand firm. I am not afraid. First, it reminds me of my recurring childhood dreams when large concentric circles used to get bigger and bigger and come closer and closer. At the very moment I would be annihilated, I woke up in a sweat, terrified. Then, I remember a dream I had years ago, which I share with my fellow student:

> *Daniel and I are walking through a deserted, barren land. I am*
> *pushing a baby carriage. People are fleeing the area and warn us*
> *that there is a wild, ferocious dog attacking anyone crossing that*
> *land. He bites them right in the stomach and kills them. He is strong*
> *and mad with fury. No one has any defense against him and he*
> *kills everyone. Somehow I am convinced that we are safe, maybe*
> *because we are together, or that I can't imagine it could happen to*

*me. We walk on. Suddenly, a huge, wild dog appears in front of
me. He leaps at me and sinks his teeth into my clothes. I can feel
them pressing towards my heart. Instantly, I know that I have no
way of rescuing myself by any other power but love and with great
compassion, I tenderly stroke his head and neck, talking soothingly
to him. I feel him respond to my touch until he purrs and curls up
in my arms. That's all he needed. Love and Touch.*

*I am strong and look him directly in the eyes. All of a sudden,
he attacks and sinks his teeth into my heart. I gasp but stand firm. I
know I have to love him. I stand there and slowly and deliberately
begin to move my arms around him. I feel the stiff, bristly hairs
standing up all over his back. He must be terrified. I make sure
that I am completely sincere and make not a single phony move.
I just continue to hold my arms very lightly around his shoulders
and then, slowly, ever so tenderly, my hands begin to stroke his
neck and throat. He relaxes just a little and takes his teeth out of
my heart. He is certainly not yet at ease, still baring his front teeth
and snarling. I am keeping him like this. My session time is up.
I feel his big, heavy body against mine. I promise I will hold him
and love him the best I can.*

It was abundantly clear to me why my Shadow figure was like
a feral dog/wolf, because of the profound neglect of my suffering
child-self. My childhood had been like a barren desert with no
one to take care of me. What a relief to bring this terrified and
raging part of me home into my heart. Little did I know at the
time that this was just the beginning of my healing process and
that, later in my life, I would have to delve much more deeply
into the loneliness, fear and shame of my early childhood. Over
time, I realized that healing such deep issues is never a simple,
one-time event but rather becomes a process of a lifetime.

Around the time of my training at the healing arts college, a group of alternative healers, psychics and astrologers was gathering every Tuesday morning for breakfast, education and networking at a local restaurant. I became a regular participant at The Healing Connection, where I began offering my work to start building my practice. I had transformed the front bedroom of Martha's home into an office. Through this outreach and the subsequent word of mouth, my practice grew pretty quickly. I felt I was finally completely in my element and loved the work.

My Healing Practice

I described my practice as *Body-Mind-Soul Integral Healing with Intuitive Touch, Process Acupressure and Hypnotherapy.* Early on, I happened to work with a client who was an incest survivor. Our work was very useful to her. She also participated in a local institute which offered support groups for survivors of child sexual abuse. By word of mouth, the majority of my clients were dealing with those particular issues during the first decade of my practice. These were often heart-wrenching sessions for both the clients and myself. I became deeply grateful to have had kind and loving parents. It was horrifying to realize that parents could be so cruel to their own children. I felt that whatever I had suffered as a child was nothing compared to what these women had endured.

Right from the beginning, I also saw quite a few therapists and psychologists who found their way to me. Some called me a therapist's therapist.

In the late eighties, I attended a weekend workshop by Arnold Mindell at UCSC, the University of California at Santa Cruz. Mindell grew up on the streets of New York, became a physicist, then underwent psychoanalysis and studied at the Jung Institute in Zurich. Jung appeared to him in a dream, telling him to take his work into the body. That is when Arnie began to develop his Process Work. He referred to the subconscious body as the *dream body*, observing and evoking the secondary processes behind our communication. What we communicate consciously is frequently accompanied by unconscious body movements. He developed many techniques to help the person amplify these and become aware of the underlying messaging. It was his first and possibly his only comprehensive presentation of the many techniques he had developed. For three days, he taught, and we practiced. I soaked it up.

With my first client that following Monday, I implemented some of the techniques I had learned. He was astonished at the process he was able to access in himself. When I told him I had just learned it, he said, "You are old at this!" I did feel that Mindell's process work fit me like a glove. It added beautifully to my work.

My practice evolved into a blend of Jin Shin Do Acupressure, Polarity and Reiki, and of Arnold Mindell's Process Work, Aminah Raheem's Transpersonal Integration, hypnotherapy, guided meditation, deep listening and healing touch, sprinkled with a healthy dose of laughter. In the beginning, when insight would come to me while I was having my hands on a person's body, I would hesitate to speak my thoughts, but after it just came out of me and my clients would respond positively, I gave myself permission to speak these unbidden insights and began to trust the process.

I felt moved to do some volunteering work and was particularly drawn to assist the dying. I applied to the local hospice and participated in their volunteer training. It became some of the most satisfying work I have ever done. I noticed how often people were exhibiting a fair amount of anxiety on their deathbed and that during my time with them, they would relax and I could guide them into opening to the great mystery of their upcoming transition. I remembered how a local astrologer wizard had once told me, "You stand in the doorway between worlds."

Throughout my life, I have loved to be present for the dying. It's a time when the veils are torn, superficialities fall by the wayside, and the essentials of life come to the fore. I noticed how many of us only learn to receive when all else has fallen away and we can no longer rely on our *doing*.

I created a brochure to explain the essence of my work. I wrote that every session becomes a creative process, supporting and facilitating each individual's unique journey towards healing, happiness and enlightenment. Some of my clients called me a Midwife of the Soul. Deep nurturing and re-mothering became my special gifts. I believed in the power of the gentle, the wisdom of the body, the Divine essence within and that the Truth will set us free.

It became painfully clear to me that many of us simply had not received enough nurturing and respect as a child. Some of us were neglected, others were raised in fear. We experienced emotional, mental or physical abuse. Most of us at least had to be good to be loved! We have all suffered from the poisonous pedagogy described by Alice Miller, a German psychotherapist, in her books *For Your Own Good* and *Thou Shalt Not Be Aware*. She also exposes the insidiousness of the old German pedagogy which created fertile ground for Nazism to thrive. In my brochure, I wrote:

"We became alienated from our true original Self. This may well be the root cause of most human suffering. When we cannot freely be who we truly are, we are disconnected from the natural flow of life and love.

When those early experiences of neglect and abuse are brought into the light of loving awareness and a person allows themselves to receive safe, nurturing touch and attention—without which no child can grow to be whole—deep and lasting healing begins to take place."

I invited some of my clients to write a testimonial. These are some of the responses I received:

Andrea has deepened and broadened her skills and her presence to a level commensurate with the most excellent practitioners I know... She is a healer of the highest order.
—RN, PhD.

Andrea mediates the energy of the creative feminine. Through her intuitive and nurturing touch, she gently enables her clients to experience deep healing of longstanding conditions.
—Jungian Psychologist

For years my essence had been locked away and the key had been lost to me. Within moments you found the core of my being and over the months you have taken me gently by the hand and, with an infinite amount of love have led me back to my own spirit... Your constant caring has helped me birth a new, courageous self... Your smile, your vibrant, warm penetrating eyes and your loving, healing hands take me beyond my boundaries into the sphere of the Great Mother where all is possible.

—O.T., incest survivor

I am not easily impressed and have a strong 'b.s. detector!' I experience you as deeply authentic and have always trusted you. Working with you has helped me move and change in ways I was unable to do with any other therapies or processes.

—Attorney

All my major changes have taken place from being in your presence. It works because of your love.

—DNFT Chiropractor

You open my eyes. You help me become aware of things that I would not otherwise perceive.

—Anonymous abuse survivor

Past Lives

When I had read Yogananda's *Autobiography of a Yogi* back in Amsterdam and came across the notion of reincarnation, I experienced an immediate *kerching*! Everything suddenly seemed to make sense. When I looked within, I felt I knew that I had been around "ever since we crawled out of the mud."

Then, when I saw The Mother, somewhere in my consciousness there was the sense that we had known each other six thousand years ago, which might have placed us in Mesopotamia.

I have frequently had vague realizations of a lifetime as a mother superior in a convent in France and have met quite a few women with whom I either had unresolved conflict or an immediate sense of knowing one another. I am sure I had many lifetimes as a Christian woman. And, when I lived in India, I felt that my soul was half Indian.

I heard about a woman in Santa Cruz, who loved to meditate. In one of her deep states, she had the experience of Sri Yuktesvar (Yogananda's teacher) coming through. Since then, she offered private and group readings where you had a chance to ask him questions. During one of those evenings, I asked him if there was a past life that I should know about, that was still influencing me. He was quiet for a moment then asked me if I was sure I wanted to know. "Yes," I said.

> You were born to a woman who was a poor seamstress. You were four years old, and it was your job to take care of your baby brother. One day you were walking with him on a country road when you saw a horse-drawn carriage approaching.

The moment I heard him mention that I felt a powerful fear, my body full of apprehension. He continued.

> The carriage stopped in front of you. Several men jumped out and grabbed you. They hauled you into the carriage. You saw your baby brother falling face down in a puddle and drowning.
>
> You were kept in a dirty bunker. You were abused and died there when you were seven, starved and covered with sores.

The drowning of my baby brother hit me the hardest. I had been responsible for him and had been devastated about failing to protect him. I carried that guilt into my next lifetimes.

I experienced a deep understanding and a release of those feelings of guilt I had carried around inside of me ever since then.

When I did past life regressions with some of my clients who had inexplicable symptoms in this lifetime, they would frequently stumble upon a particularly violent death in a previous life. The knowledge would bring great relief, and their symptoms would usually disappear.

I came to understand that when the psyche carries unresolved trauma from the past into this lifetime, a similar trauma will occur early in this life to trigger the healing process. For myself, I saw how the guilt I acquired by association with my father was the perfect trigger to send me on my healing journey to this moment.

Later that year, I traveled with a small group of friends to Santa Rosa, north of San Francisco, to participate in a weekend with Gangaji, an American spiritual teacher in the lineage of Ramana Maharshi. That evening, I sat on my bed in the hotel room and sank into deep silence. When I opened my eyes, I saw myself in a mirror across from the bed. I saw my face shifting at high speed into hundreds of faces—male, female, young, old, of many different cultures. I knew these had been my many lives.

A Painful Realization

The kindness, safety and quietude Martha offered me had marked the beginning of my healing process. Living with her was like a refuge for me. However, Aurelia and Tara were never happy there. Martha's mother had died when she was only five years old. The presence of my children with me, their loving mother, right there in her home, became deeply disturbing to her. Just like my mother, she would often have a disgruntled look on her face and withdraw. She was displeased with any level of noise. My nine and eleven-year-old daughters were a lively bunch and were used to expressing themselves freely.

Our small communal life on Ocean Street Extension had been a carefree and happy drop-in scene for many. Friends and family of everyone who lived with us had always been welcome. At Martha's, I became more internal myself, and I felt that I had to protect Martha's need for quiet. I had to control my children's natural exuberance. Suddenly, they had to behave no matter what, just like I had to in my own childhood.

I often took them out to dinner to escape the stifling atmosphere in Martha's home. Instead of the happy family energy we had always known, my girls were now fighting and bickering with one another, and even dining out was not a pleasure. Also, I noticed that they never brought their friends over.

When the girls both started menstruating within weeks of each other, they happened to be with Daniel and Lisa at the Ocean Street house. Naturally, they turned to Lisa. I only found out about this big change in their lives when they asked me for provisions while staying with me. It broke my heart. I was their mother and I hadn't been there for my daughters at that critical transition. I was also deeply disturbed and puzzled by the loss of my daughters' trust. I began to feel painfully alienated from them.

Slowly the situation in Martha's home became more and more intolerable. I did not know what to do and felt quite trapped. Under ever-increasing internal pressure, I finally gathered my courage to talk with Daniel and Lisa about my impossible situation. Torn between guilt and embarrassment—guilt for surely this would prove I was a bad mother and embarrassed to have to ask them—in tears, I managed, "Would you please accept having the girls live with you full-time?" Knowing full well what a huge thing it was to ask them, and how unfair it would seem, I begged for their understanding.

It was a most disturbing situation. Daniel and Lisa were quite shocked. I felt terrible. They took some time talking with one another. I believe we all felt we were backed against a wall. A few days later they invited me to have a joint session with a therapist they trusted. At some point the therapist asked me to step out of the room. When I came back in, he mentioned that Daniel and Lisa felt particularly pressured because of my tears. I was startled. I then worried that they felt I was trying to manipulate them. However, they did accept my proposal and from then on Aurelia and Tara lived with them in our old haunt on Ocean St. Extension. I was immensely grateful to both of them, but especially to Lisa, who was willing to take on the responsibility of full-time mother. I was convinced that it would be a much better situation for the girls.

I tucked my shame down where all my other shame lived and at least was able to proceed with my life and my healing practice in reasonable peace.

In the spring of 1991, I took both my girls to Holland for my mother's eightieth birthday. It was lovely for us all to visit my mom. The three of us also spent wonderful days with Paul and Doortje, my old friends from my days of studying psychology in Amsterdam. Doortje had become a child psychologist, working with adolescents, and Paul worked at an institute in Amsterdam designed to support survivors of the Holocaust! My daughters felt very close to Doortje. Tara especially had intimate conversations with her. I had no idea how to restore the broken trust with my daughters and didn't know even how to talk with them about our difficulties, not only because they were so closed to me, but I was so confused myself. I was deeply grateful for Doortje's ability and willingness to be emotionally supportive to both my girls during their difficult times with me.

I enjoyed Paul and Doortje's happy family home in Huizen, beautifully situated in one of the finest areas in Holland, surrounded by a heath and woods. The house had a thick thatch roof, French doors to an enclosed garden, beautiful wooden floors and a large family kitchen. As long as I have known them, they always had a large Leonberger dog. Their three children with spouses, numbers of grandchildren and their many friends are always welcome. Enjoying their lifestyle again after so many

Alessandra and me visiting Paul and Doortje

years, I recognized with a pang how I really wanted to live my own life like that, open-minded, openhearted and creating a beautiful and welcoming atmosphere in my home.

I knew then that my life with Martha had to come to an end. The lovely shelter her home had provided me with had turned into a prison. I had to recreate my life and my home according to my own values and realize the vision of how I wanted to be in the world. I was forty-nine years old. With the help of some of my healer friends, I was able to get clear that I needed this change for myself and that I didn't need to express any disappointment with Martha. I was grateful for what she had been able to give me.

Regaining My Freedom

Upon my return home, I wrote a letter to my circle of friends and clients with a vision of what I was looking for. Because I had felt so enclosed, number one on my list was the desire to sleep under the stars. I found a cottage from heaven. It was part of a Hacienda-like estate owned by one of my clients, in the Larkin Valley area, just south of Santa Cruz. The elegant cottage had high ceilings, bay windows, hardwood floors, and a large bathroom with deep blue and terracotta Mexican tiles. Shaded patios and arched columns overgrown with bougainvillea and climbing roses gave it a Mediterranean feel. Hummingbirds dashed around. Owls hooted in the night. The cottage was high up on the hill above the main house, with a view over a vast expanse of trees all the way down to the bay. I could not see any homes nor hear any traffic noise and the two large bay windows provided me with blissful nights sleeping under the stars. Friends would remark on my astonishing powers of manifestation. I didn't know about that, but I was grateful to have been graced by such good fortune.

Feeling free to have my children again was such a joy. They loved it too. They did keep their main living quarters with Daniel and Lisa, but we were reunited and free to enjoy each other. I seemed to be regaining some of their trust and we had a few good conversations, for which I was very grateful. They explained to me how with Martha I seemed to have become a completely different woman from the mother they had known. Now we turned up the music and danced and laughed and played games to our hearts' content.

It was then that Aurelia was able to talk with me about being in Junior High and the shame she felt when she realized her mother was a lesbian. Of course, homophobia still ran rampant among students. She had felt too embarrassed to bring any of her friends home to me. She also believed that there was no point in confiding in me because, surely, I would not understand anything about her feelings towards boys. I was stunned. If she only knew!

Tara had been gaining weight for a few years and I noticed that at times she would refuse food, saying that she wasn't hungry. At some point, she actually talked with me about her weight problem. With great remorse, I must admit that I had absolutely no idea about what could be done and didn't even have the awareness that there might be professional help somewhere. Having grown up myself without anyone to turn to for help, ever, I didn't recognize that option.

I came across some products that were supposed to help with weight loss and having seen good results with people who used them, I provided Tara with these. All I knew to counsel her was to love herself, no matter what.

Rent for the cottage was high, but my healing practice bloomed. Even though the drive from town was long, my clients loved coming to my charming Mediterranean paradise. For those few hours at my home, they felt as though they were on vacation.

I relished my newfound freedom. I don't believe I had ever felt this ecstatic in my whole life, free to be myself, unencumbered by anyone else's limitations. What joy it was to create my own space. Living in beauty is such a source of happiness for me. At night I would tune into the stars before drifting off into dreamland, and in the morning I opened my eyes to the beauty all around me.

About three weeks into my stay, I was sleeping in one of the bay windows, when a sudden noise right next to me startled me awake. My eyes flew wide open and there, just a foot and a half away from my face, a great horned owl perched on the window ledge looking right at me, its wings spread wide open against the window. My heart raced. I was startled and awestruck. After some minutes had passed, I really had to pee and reluctantly left my visitor to go to the bathroom. When I returned, he was gone. It was three o'clock in the morning. The next morning I saw six scratch marks from his talons on the window ledge. I felt I had been graced with owl medicine for my love of the night and, hopefully, to grant me the wisdom and compassion I longed for.

Maurice

In May of that year, 1992, I celebrated my fiftieth birthday in my beautiful new home. I felt at the peak of my life. I celebrated with my daughters and friends, who shared poetry and songs. We had my favorite Princess Cake. Flowers were everywhere. A friend videotaped the event. The only thing I felt missing was someone to be close with. I had begun to feel the desire of having a man in my life again. I hadn't been with a man since I left Daniel six years earlier.

Looking around in my social circles, which consisted mostly of new age and alternative healer types, the men all seemed way too nice, boy men really; not appealing to me. I wanted a *real man*, a man like my father, broadminded, big-hearted, solid, sexual, intelligent and fun. I imagined we would each have our own lives and then spend a day or a weekend together every couple of weeks or so, enjoying each other sexually and otherwise.

I decided to put an ad in the local newspaper. On Friday, September 4, 1992, this was my ad as it appeared in the Santa Cruz Sentinel:

> I am thrilled to be fifty, in love with life, wishing to share the juice, the joy and all the dimensions of being with an extraordinary man.
>
> Free in body, mind and spirit. Healthy, N/S. The depth of your soul matters more than the color of your skin. Commitment only to the truth of our beings.

I received a few letters. Only one of them caught my attention. The letter looked kind of frumpy and was clearly typed on a rickety old typewriter. He wrote that he had found my ad while looking in the dumpster for an old newspaper to clean his paintbrushes. He was a poet and a painter. He only smoked while sitting at his typewriter. The letter was signed with a flourish: Maurice. Here was certainly a different kind of man with a sense of humor and his French name was charming. I gave him a call and was immediately struck by the full deep tone of his voice. We talked easily for an hour. He was very funny. When I suggested we meet in a coffee shop somewhere, he wanted me to come to his home in Ben Lomond, a small town along the San Lorenzo River about half an hour from where I lived. I said that I didn't think that was such a smart idea. He responded, "My door opens in, and my door opens out."

The relaxed conversation, the laughter and his unusual response led me to agree. We set a date. A few days later he called and asked for a few more days because he was trying to clean his house for me and needed more time. I laughed. We decided to meet on September 14. He said that was his birthday. It felt like serendipity.

On the appointed day, I took the long drive from Larkin Valley to Ben Lomond. I turned on the radio. Who but Grover Washington would croon his romantic *Just the two of us. We can make it if we try, just the two of us. You and I.* It's a long song and it accompanied me for the rest of the drive. It felt as though I was being groomed for a great romance and my heart was already aflutter. As I turned into the parking lot in front of the small apartment complex, I caught a glimpse of a portly man who quickly disappeared back into his apartment as soon as my car came into view. In that very first glimpse, he actually reminded me of my father!

With a bouquet of flowers for his birthday, I knocked on his door and there he was: a big scruffy dude with thick glasses which made his big brown eyes look even larger, a large head with an unkempt bushel of long dark gray curls, beard and moustache, wearing a freshly washed but stained shirt stretching tightly over his ample chest. With a generous sweep of his arm, he welcomed me gallantly into what truly was the most trashed-out place I had ever set foot in. It had taken him three days to clear a path through the mess to the one easy chair for me to sit in and another path through the bedroom to his bathroom which had recently been scrubbed with lots of bleach, and to somewhat straighten out his kitchen. The dingy walls were hung with paintings of Alaskan snowscapes with bloody Inuit hunting scenes. A rickety easel covered in paint stood in a corner of the living room. An old bike was lying buried under piles of clothes and trash in the bedroom. A note on his kitchen cabinet read: *Take your meds, Stupid!*

None of it seemed to matter to me, in fact, I found it all quite amusing as I took in this fascinating man. I peered into his big brown eyes as if seeing into the depth of his soul. I felt completely engaged in getting to know him. We both laughed heartily at the absurdity of the situation. He offered me tea. We talked and mused and laughed. We went for a walk under the redwoods behind his place, when I noticed how unsteady he was on his feet. He walked with a cane and explained to me that he had six metal pins in both of his ankles since he was run over by a truck as a young man in the U.S. Army when stationed in Germany. We seemed to naturally enjoy each other's company and light-hearted banter. Here was a jovial, big-hearted, unusual man alright, and I was irresistibly drawn to him. I drove home singing.

I understood why he had wanted me to come to his home. He didn't drive and he looked like a street person who did not belong in any kind of social setting. Two days later I made the trek to Ben Lomond again. He welcomed me with open arms and a sonorous *Hi Baby*. As soon as the door closed behind us, we fell into each others' arms like hungry lions, as if we had, at last, found the love we had been waiting for. We kissed and hugged and moaned and were lost to the world. That evening back home poetry began to flow from me to Maurice:

You touch me so tenderly
my eyes brim with tears
and all is soft and warm
inside me.
I weep at your defenseless face
no varnish on your soul
no place to hide…

A few days later I received a response in his inimitable style:

It's really quite an impact: you! You bring me flowers. You send me poetry. I find it exhilarating, Andrea, to actually be pursued by so gracious a lady as yourself, even more I appreciate your subtle aggressive spirit.

Come then dear lady. Give us pause that we may embrace, for us to feel the heartbeat, for you to give me suck of your breast, to inhale the fragrance that is you… Maurice

His words touched the depth of my womanly core. I was lost, like a butterfly in a vat of honey. Our love catapulted us into torrents of poetry and desire. I felt as if my soul was naked before him. Within a week of meeting him, I received this poem:

Andrea, love-dancer, she of fine graceful step
Come to me dear lady,
Hearken to the whispers of your yearning heart
Reach-claim my hand
So we may walk together...
With the courage of your warrior's heart.
For now your silken fiber shall be set upon life's spindle
To spin yet another turn
To a far and fragile thread to weave.

During the months that followed, I basked in the depth, the warmth, the poetry of his love. Then his stories came tumbling out. His mother was, as he described her, a Colombian whore, "Men loved my mother and my mother loved men." She left him and his father when he was only five.

At age eighteen he was stationed in Heidelberg, Germany with the U.S. Army. One day, drunk as a skunk, he was run over by a truck which crushed both of his ankles. Six metal pins held each ankle together. That was the end of his career in the military. Next, he found himself homeless, roaming the streets of Seattle, when he was told there was a boat in the harbor sailing for Saigon. They were looking for men to go fight in Vietnam for $6,000 a month. Being angry, hungry and homeless, he jumped at the opportunity. Upon arrival in Vietnam, he became part of a group of mercenaries under the command of an ex-SS officer. They did the dirty work. Once a month they'd have the choice to fly to Tokyo, Paris or Cairo for their entertainment (hotels, alcohol and brothels), all expenses paid.

In the midst of all that insanity, Maurice fell in love with Simone, a French-Vietnamese girl. Together they dreamed of the end of the war, of getting married and living in Marseille, her father's hometown. Then his commander told him that Simone was suspected of being a spy for the Vietcong. Maurice knew what would happen to her. Bodies of traitors were regularly displayed, stuck on poles around their compound. His superior knew how much she meant to him. He gave Maurice the grace of a last night with her. While he couldn't save her life, he had the option to save her from humiliation and torture before dying a gruesome death. During their lovemaking, while she orgasmed, he drove a pin into her brain, killing her instantly. Maurice regularly woke up screaming. It broke my heart to imagine the agony he must have endured. One night he showed me a few weather-stained photographs he still had of her—a beautiful young woman with wide-set eyes and soft, even features.

After the war, Maurice disappeared for a few years into the Alaskan bush, licking his wounds. He had contact with Inuits and admired their rugged lifestyle, which inspired his paintings of the Alaskan snowscapes with bloody hunting scenes. Hungry and cold, he finally emerged from the bush and spent years pursuing the Veterans Administration for assistance, based on his accident in Germany, which he finally received. Just a few years before we met, he got his little apartment from the Housing Authority and there he hibernated, painting, writing, smoking, "growing crusts over his soul," as he put it.

For me, having grown up loving my father, who suffered unspeakable loneliness and fear on death row, praying with all my little girl's heart to save him from the firing squad, I seemed to be particularly predisposed to love this isolated man who was starving for love and companionship, who had become embittered and had given up any hope for love or happiness. With all my heart, I wanted to prove to Maurice that he was good and lovable, and deserving of happiness.

I told him about my experiences in India with the Mother and brought him a photograph of her, all with the desire to bring light into his darkness. Referring to my first experience with Mother, he began to call me the Hibiscus Carrier. When I came to visit him a few weeks later, I noticed he had placed a cloth over Mother's picture. Curious, I asked him about it. "Her light is too intense," he said. "She is blinding me. I had to cover her up."

When I invited my girls to meet him up at my cottage, we had dinner together and played games. He was utterly charming to them. When he mispronounced Tara's name and she pointed it out to him, he gave her a bow and a big smile and said, "A rose is a rose by any name." I was happy and relieved that we were all having a fine time together.

In the meantime, in Maurice's unbridled imagination, he invariably convinced himself that I could not possibly be spending my nights alone at my home. Surely a lusty lady like myself, as he phrased it, would have orgies galore and have him as a treat on the side. He could not imagine that I was truly interested in him and that there was no one else. He confessed to me at some point that he had scrambled up the hill behind my cottage one evening to see for himself. He had been able to look into my windows from his hideout and had felt quite foolish seeing me there enjoying a cup of tea and quietly reading all by myself.

However, it did not abate his suspicion and his ongoing paranoia began to be disturbing.

One day, while visiting him in his apartment, he complained of a severe headache. Natural healer that I am, I placed my hands on his broad head trying to give him relief. He closed his eyes and let out a deep sigh, relaxing completely. Suddenly, he began speaking to me in a different voice, "Hello there, dear lady." He proceeded to talk to me about Maurice in the third person. From my healing practice, I was familiar with other parts of a person coming forward as an important part of the healing process, so—even as I was taken by surprise—I was also excited to be having this conversation. "Who are you?" I asked.

"I am First Lieutenant Richter. I was Maurice's commander in Nam. We used to call him Smokey back in those days…" I can't remember all he told me, except that in the end he wanted me to know about Maurice's generosity, which he would never tell me himself. Apparently, from his small monthly allotment from the VA, he was making donations to a few charities. We easily spoke for half an hour. When he finished, Maurice stretched and gave a big refreshing sigh as if waking up from a deep restful sleep. "Oh, baby. I feel so good! What did you do to me?"

I laughed, "That was quite an interesting conversation we just had!"

"Huh…? What are you talking about?"

At first I thought he was putting me on, but he did not remember a thing. Now, I was shocked and frankly, a bit frightened. I had never experienced a true multiple personality, someone who has no recollection of what another of his personalities said or did. I recounted my experience with Richter to him. He couldn't believe his ears. Confused, he tried to accuse me of making it all up, but he couldn't deny that Richter was his man in 'Nam and that his nickname had been Smokey. It was disturbing for both of us. Nevertheless, he had experienced great relief and his headache had vanished. I would learn that when the headaches came on, some part of him needed to come out and talk, and these sessions became a regular occurrence.

Sometimes Smokey himself would appear, a brazen, unruly nineteen-year-old out in the bush, wondering what the hell a beautiful lady like me was doing with him, where I came from and if he could mess with me. Once at my home in Larkin Valley, Smokey became so aggressive, I was worried he might force himself upon me. I was happy to be lovers with Maurice, but I wasn't about to let this immature brat have his way with me. It was time to give him a reality check. I managed to talk him into coming with me to the bathroom. When I guided him to the mirror and he saw his scruffy, old, gray-bearded face, he screamed in terror and was greatly disturbed. I had to keep him from running away panicked. He was in no state to start driving. It took all my love and soothing skills to calm him down.

Between his bouts of distrust, accusing me of lying and making crank calls at all hours to check on me, and having to manage his frequent psychic disturbances, I began to feel quite overwhelmed and drained, to the point that I knew I had to separate myself from him or it was going to cost me my health and well-being. I wrote in my journal:

> The specter of your fear slithers around my house like a thief in the night.

With my heart still full of love for him, separating from this big, loving and foolish man was an excruciating dilemma. When I finally told him I couldn't do it anymore and he would have to leave me alone, I planned a trip to Lake Tahoe with a woman friend to pray for clarity and to get away for a few days.

Arriving at the hotel, there was a message for me on the answering machine. It was a hang-up call. During the first two hours, we were there trying to relax from the drive, hang-up calls kept happening, until I got furious. It could only be Maurice. I called him. The phone rang and rang until finally, he picked it up with a weak "Huh?" I yelled at him to leave me alone and quit bugging me. His voice was slow like molasses and seemed to come from far away. He had difficulty speaking.

"I... don't... know... what... you're... talking... about... I'm... sleeping..." He sounded weird, incoherent. I didn't trust him and still furious, I yelled at him some more, what the hell was he doing. With a fading voice, he mumbled about taking whiskey and a bottle of painkillers. Fuck, now he's killing himself. Enraged, I hollered at him to get up and get his act together, and don't dare calling me again.

I don't know where those calls came from, that infuriated me so. He actually did not know where we were. If I hadn't called and hollered at him, he might well have died. Later I found out that he had staggered to his bathroom and taken a cold shower, then slept for a few days. I couldn't help thinking then that an angel had intervened to save his life.

The next few days I roamed through the woods, desperately praying, begging Mother for clarity. My soul felt torn to shreds. How could I leave this man I loved, yet who was killing me?

Did I really have to bear this cross or was I allowed to let him go? Nothing came until, finally, I got this message, "Learn to dance with the bear." I accepted. "If this is what I must do, I will, come what may," I told myself.

On the way back, after dropping off my friend, I stopped by to see him and communicate my renewed commitment. He was sitting motionless in the field behind his apartment with his head hung low, the image of despondency. When I walked up to him, he thought I was a ghost. "I'm here. I love you. I'm not going anywhere." I took him by the hand and led him back inside to the bed. We quietly laid in each others' arms to rest. I surrendered to our togetherness. Shortly after, I received this poem:

> You came to me upon the whim of random chance.
> You poured a rich and splendid light
> into my body, mind and heart-spirit.
>
> From which I gained a cognition of who I am,
> lain fallow for near a decade: you gave me love,
> care, sweetness, the richness of your embrace,
> a fragrance of tomorrow.
>
> Then came that Friday which came as a wild savage fist,
> and then Saturday came with your voice across the miles
> to awaken me from the lethal consequences of my own error.
> Had you not called, even now I would lay upon a steel tray
> In an autopsy room. Slit from groin to chest cavity:
> Disemboweled for the sake of bored inquiry. Placed then
> Into a plastic bag, eventually fed into the earth or an oven
> To become rendered into ashes then become I, fertilizer
> for the weeds which grow upon a pauper's grave: forgotten!
> Oh Silky, Silky, I do love you humbly, with devotion,

but I cannot match your fierce spirit.
Fly then from me, oh gracious and loving Silky.
Give me leave to seek my tiny cardboard dreams.

I couldn't accept his offer. It seems that once I love a man, I feel a commitment in my soul to stand by him come what may and I was convinced that this great love of ours would heal his self-esteem. Surely this crazy, warm, funny, heartfelt man was worthy of my love.

Even though we were happy to be reunited and I felt more at peace because I had gotten off the fence and placed myself squarely in the relationship, his self-deprecation and his suspicious mind kept creating havoc and continued to torment me.

Nevertheless, my commitment was solid. It became clear to me that for us to have any peace of mind, we should live together. I became willing to sacrifice my sweet paradise in Larkin Valley. One of my clients, whose mother had died recently, told me that she and her husband were preparing her mother's house for rental. When I asked her about the layout of the house, it seemed to be made for us. It was a large U-shaped four-bedroom house on the upper west side of Santa Cruz, the master bedroom with bath in one wing, which could be Maurice's quarters, and three smaller rooms on the other side would work well for me. A large living room, hallway, kitchen and bathroom separated the two wings. My bedroom opened with French doors to the garden, there was a room for Tara when she came to stay with me (Aurelia was already in college) and the front room would serve well for my healing practice. It had a deck and large garden in back and a garden in front with a thick hedge sheltering us from the street.

Financially, it was a stretch, but between the two of us, we could just manage to afford it. When all was packed and loaded, I circumambulated the cottage, weeping. I had never wept leaving any place before. Taking a few deep breaths, I said farewell and expressed my gratitude for the two lovely years I had been allowed to live there. Then I drove off, courageously entering yet another phase of my life, for better or for worse.

We did enjoy creating our home together. It was much larger than either of us had been accustomed to. The living and dining rooms were one long open space, bigger than my entire cottage had been. I used the fireplace to create an altar with Mother and Sri Aurobindo's pictures. Maurice loved his room which had a big brick fireplace and French doors to the garden and his own bathroom. From there he had direct access to the garage to use as his art studio.

I created a lovely healing space in the room next to the front door, an ideal situation to receive my clients. A bower of wisteria blossoms framed the window and created a charming, almost dreamlike sense of protection. Tara and I were excited that, for the first time, she had her own room in my home. She would still spend most of her time at Daniel and Lisa's, but at least she now had a real room of her own with me.

A few days in, we had barely unpacked and decorated, when Tara brought a friend home from school—I happened to be out. As they entered the front door, Tara talked excitedly to her friend about showing her room in her new house. Overhearing her, Maurice immediately barged in that this was not *her* house, this was *his* house and she shouldn't have any pretensions. When I came home, Tara was very upset. When she told me what happened, I felt like my world collapsed.

Shocked beyond belief, I flew at him in a rage. How *dare* he speak to my daughter that way. I felt murderous. My rage and accusations did not even seem to touch him. I was dismayed at his territorialism. I had not seen this coming and now it was too late. Exhausted from the move, and financially stripped to the bone, I saw no way out. I couldn't imagine and didn't have the energy to upheave my whole life again, right then and there. With a sinking heart, I decided I had to try to make the best of it.

However, when we were on our own, Maurice and I enjoyed a sweet time together. He lavished me with affection, something which had been sorely lacking in my life. I lapped it up like a dried-out sponge submerged in life-giving waters. His quick, sparkling wit kept me in stitches. He longed to do nice things for me and complained about my self-sufficiency, which tended to pre-empt his desire to be helpful. He decided to make me coffee every morning. It became his little ritual to show me his appreciation.

Sitting together in the intimate hours of the evenings, his words of deep adoring love were like the Song of Songs to the Beloved. Under the warmth of his gaze and the power of his words, I opened to him like the hibiscus I had carried to the Mother and bloomed into radiant ecstasy. Never before had I felt so truly seen, known and adored in the depth of my womanly soul.

I've often thought that it was precisely because he had multiple personalities, that when he was in his heart, love filled his universe and mine, with the downside, of course, that when he was in his crazy mind, he had no access to his heart, as I would eventually find out.

One morning, I found him feverishly typing away and asked him who he was writing to. "I'm writing a letter to Tara," he said. When I looked over his shoulder and read his angry accusations, I was horrified. "You can't do that!" I exclaimed and tore the letter from his machine and destroyed it. "Don't you ever dare write to her!"

He told me why he felt the need to write to her. He couldn't tolerate that she was leaving crumbs on the kitchen counter every time she had a snack and that, in his words, she was just sitting on her ass reading and not helping me. He was furious at her lack of respect for me. He seemed fully convinced that he had every right to call her to task. I tried to make him see that he often behaved exactly like she was. I had to clean up after his mess in the kitchen several times a day and he sat on his big fat ass all day long reading. At least, she was coming home after a whole day at school and reading. I tried to show him how he was projecting onto her, to no avail. He seemed to have no capacity for introspection.

A week later I got a phone call from Lisa. Tara had received a terrible letter from Maurice. Tara was very upset and had been talking with her dad about not staying with me anymore. I flew at Maurice in such a rage as I had never known. Instead of listening and responding, he simply stood there smiling at me, urging me to calm down. I was losing my mind at my inability to get through to him. "Come here, baby, calm down," he tried to hush me with a deep voice and took me in his arms to comfort me. Insane with rage, I snapped and bit him violently in his ear.

He jumped back yelling, accusing me of violence, still showing not a trace of comprehension. I stormed out of the house and took off into the woods of the nearby Pogonip. Even as I was running away from him, in the end, I had nowhere to run to. Many hours later, I quietly returned home. I was beat.

When Tara returned a few days later, I told her how very sorry I was about what had happened and that I thought she was making a wise decision and that it was probably best for her to stay with her dad from now on. Sadly, I learned later that she thought I was asking her to leave. It created a rift between us that may never completely heal. Truth be told, I did weigh the rest of my life with this man I loved against the two years left of her being in high school and decided it was a sacrifice I needed to make. Shamefaced, I've learned over time that healthy mothers choose their children over their men. I was not one of them. Around that time a book became popular titled *Women Who Love Too Much*. I knew that was me.

With just the two of us in the house, a fairly peaceful time ensued. My practice was going well, and Maurice was reinventing himself as an artist. It turned out that he was fascinated to read about ancient Roman times and warfare. One day I caught a glimpse of our past life connection. He had been a Roman soldier and I was one of the early Christian women in Rome who had to practice her faith in secret, in fear of the brutal persecution of those times. We loved each other. He vowed to protect me. When I was betrayed, we both knew I would be thrown to the lions as a public spectacle. Before they could take me captive, he killed me out of mercy to protect me from such a horrendous fate. I could see the stone-paved alley and the doorway to the home in which I lived in secrecy. The 'memory' made sense of how madly we loved each other and also that he had to repeat the same mercy murder in this lifetime with the woman he loved during the Vietnam War.

When he would be in a particularly happy and affectionate mood, he would often quip with a twinkle in his eye, "Will you marry me?" I kept laughing at him, dismissing the very idea. Over time, however, he became more and more serious. He also continued to have bouts of paranoia about me having other lovers or leaving him. Slowly my resistance wore down. Since I was, after all, fully committed to my relationship with Maurice and, again, to reassure him and barter for peace of mind, I finally agreed.

Because we had found each other through an ad in the Sentinel, we called the paper to inform them of our wedding. Shortly thereafter we received a call from Peggy Townsend asking if we would be willing to do an interview. She would also bring a photographer. And so, our story got published:

Their Love was Born in a Dempsey Dumpster

Last September, Maurice Egan found himself rummaging through a dumpster near his apartment in search of some paper to clean his paintbrushes.

As he dug through the refuse he spotted a copy of the Sentinel's Spotlight section "crumpled between a box of Fruit loops and an empty coffee can" and he opened it.

As he glanced through the pages, he spotted a personal ad that began: I am thrilled to be fifty," and his interest was piqued.

On a whim he replied.

Maurice and I

"I had very few responses, probably because I wasn't asking for anything romantic," said Andrea van de Loo. "His was the only one that spoke to me."

So the bodywork practitioner called Maurice and the two met.

Sunday they will be married in the garden of the home they share on Laurent Street.

"She lifted me out of the gutter and brought me to paradise," said Maurice, who is an artist and a poet.

"I looked into his eyes and saw who was there under the crust," said Andrea. "I saw a man who was real and very raw—a jewel in the rough."

We held the wedding in the garden under an arch decorated with flowers. I had found a lovely ivory silk dress at the Goodwill. Sara, a friend of mine, was the minister. Maurice's only friend, his lawyer, was his best man. All my friends and my beautiful daughters were there. My mother had flown in from Holland and when all were seated, she took me by the hand and walked me

Our wedding, with my mother

out of the house through the crowd over to Maurice. I flushed like a shy bride being walked to the altar. Even though it was my third marriage, I felt that for the very first time, I was getting married as my true self. My friend Lynne with her beautiful voice sang *La Vie en Rose*.

During the ceremony, my friend Joanna asked the question of all who were there: *What is it that you want most of all in your life?* I turned inward and one single prayer rose from my heart: *All I want is to be with you, Mother!* It struck me that on the very day of my wedding, what I really wanted most of all was a spiritual union with the Divine Mother. I was in bliss. We spoke our vows. After our rings were exchanged and we kissed, we danced tenderly to Beethoven's *Moonlight Sonata*.

About three months into our married life, Maurice surprised me with the statement that sex had become physically painful for him. Even though our heartfelt loving was as passionate as before, over time he suggested that "a healthy woman like yourself

328

shouldn't have to do without sex" and that I should take a lover as long as I kept it secret from him. He made the offer very lovingly and I much appreciated his heartfelt generosity. However, I knew very well that I could never live with secrets, and he wouldn't be able to cope with me having a lover.

And so, I found myself living a monogamous life in celibacy. I knew in my bones that if I would ever choose to leave him, all hell would break loose.

Later, I wondered if, knowing full well that eventually a non-sexual marriage would become intolerable for me, he was setting himself up, unconsciously, to be abandoned again, as he had been abandoned by his mother when he was a young boy.

Part V

Psychedelics

An Anaclitic Session

In the spring of 1996, I received a surprise phone call from a local psychiatrist, known as Dr. Bob, who had experienced my healing work himself. "I wonder if you might be willing to meet my best friend and shaman, Hara Ra. He is looking for a nurturing female therapist or healer to do a very particular kind of work, which cannot be discussed over the phone." My interest was piqued. I felt honored by the request and agreed to meet Hara Ra for lunch.

Hara Ra's appearance was quite unique for a man in his fifties. He was tall and wore bleached hippie jeans with a light blue denim shirt stretched tightly around his ample figure. He sported a neatly trimmed Manchurian moustache. A gray pony-tail was held together with a maroon-colored ribbon. He moved brusquely, guiding me through the restaurant. We found a quiet spot in the garden. I could see he was nervous. Sweat was beading on his forehead.

"For years I have pursued healing," he plunged right in, "to no avail. My mother was a paranoid schizophrenic, and my father was a mean, critical, self-centered bastard. For the first nine years, I was their only child. I grew up terrified and in extreme isolation. It was in 1983 when I read Stanislav Grof's *LSD Psychotherapy* that I found, for the first time, an accurate description of my unhappy state of being (The Basic Perinatal Matrix II). I have pursued psychedelic therapies ever since, with very limited results. When I read about anaclitic work, I knew instantly that, if anything could help me, this would be it."

To his surprise, I knew about anaclitic work. When I was studying psychology at the University of Amsterdam in the late sixties, I had read that some female psychiatrists in London had experimented with patients who would be nude, wrapped in a light blanket and held by them throughout their LSD experience, hoping to mend their injured mother-child bonding. He said that he had been looking for a suitable woman therapist or healer ever since and that he was at the end of his rope. I told him that I offered safe, nurturing touch and presence to my clients. "I have called it re-mothering." I suggested that we start with a few of my regular sessions. Then we'd take it from there. He readily agreed.

Hara Ra was a most unusual client. One day, he was lying on my healing table. His eyes were closed. I had my hands on him trying to run some peaceful, nurturing energy into his body, when he startled me by saying, "Try to relax. Your lips are tight!" I noticed it was true, I was holding some tension. I relaxed. Without ever opening his eyes, he approved, "That's better!" I was a little spooked by his uncanny psychic perception.

After several sessions, he made it clear that he was ready to proceed with the anaclitic work. He thought that the use of MDMA, popularly known as Ecstasy, would be more appropriate for his purpose than LSD. MDMA is an empathogen, not a psychedelic per se. It calms the amygdala and produces a profound heart opening. For a period of four to six hours, the user is actually free of fear. It fosters a deep trust and wonderful tactile receptivity. I had personal experience with both materials, and I readily agreed with his assessment. His psychiatrist friend would be present to hold a safe space for both of us. The session was to take place at Hara Ra's home. A preliminary meeting was set up between the three of us to go over the details and clarify our intentions and procedures.

I was aware of the crucial importance of this work for him. The early imprint of his mother's neglect was having a devastating effect on his ability to take care of his health. He had already become diabetic. Some years ago, after he impregnated a woman and had decided he would stay with her to have the child, friends had promised him that when he would hold his newborn son in his arms, he would experience a love he had never known. Instead, when his infant was placed in his arms, he froze. To his great dismay, he had been completely unable to bond with his son. Nor had he ever been able to establish a satisfying long-term relationship. His moods were predominantly sad or grumpy and he was left with very little energy or enthusiasm for life.

I felt motivated to do my very best to try and provide him with what he needed. I looked at my natural limitations and realized that I was generally happy to be completely focused on a client during my healing work for about an hour and a half to two hours. Then, I was usually quite ready to call it quits. I decided I should partake of the MDMA at the same time as he, which would allow me to be fully present with him for the session's four to six-hour duration.

When the three of us gathered at his home, I opened the conversation with this offer. His eyes lit up with appreciation, maybe even admiration. Later, he told me that he knew at that moment that I had the necessary courage for the work.

I was dismayed to see the condition of his living environment. The house was small and dark. Boxes were stacked high in the living room. Neglect was everywhere. Where would I nurture this big infant? Surely not in such a mess. He suggested the east-facing bedroom as the most comfortable place. He invited me to take a look and tell him how I wanted the room to be. I told him flatly, "You've got to clean this up. Move all the boxes out of here and hang some beautiful fabric in front of those shelves and then put some flowers on the dresser." Months later, he chuckled to one of our friends how "his mom had told him to go clean his room!"

When Dr. Bob asked him what he would like to accomplish with the session, he said, "I want to feel alive. Right now, when I look inside at my life, I see an empty grave."

The big day arrived. I prayed for my heart and soul to be fully present, to be the most loving mother I could be for this man. I felt a bit nervous as the hour approached. I was happily surprised to find that his home was about as clean as could be expected, but the bedroom had been completely transformed. A colorful batik of an Indian Goddess covered the shelves. A large bouquet of flowers on the dresser gave the room a festive air. We both took our medicine and the three of us sat and chatted for a bit. The atmosphere became relaxed. We were entering the sacred. Hara Ra and I strolled out into the garden.

I had asked him to wear shorts for the session, but as the medicine came on, I felt completely trusting of him and realized they were unnecessary. I told him so. "Good," he smiled gratefully. When it was time to go in, he removed his clothes and lay down in the middle of the bed. I wedged myself next to him, took him in my arms and we settled down for the experience. Dr. Bob was sitting by our side.

I felt my mother heart opening and becoming deeply empowered. I turned to Dr. Bob and addressed him as the father of our child. I waxed on about the miracle of expecting this baby together—how happy we were, what a lovely boy he was going to be, and how much we were going to love and care for him. I proceeded to recreate his life from its very beginning, from conception itself. For the next few hours, I held my big baby, gazed into his innocent eyes, rocked, stroked and comforted him, held him to my breast and cooed sweet nothings into his ears. Quietly, he received it all.

Towards mid-afternoon, he drifted off into a blessed sleep. Dr. Bob and I retired into the living room to drink some tea and ruminate about what had transpired. At one point, I heard a little sound from the bedroom, and much to my surprise, I jumped up and ran to see if "my baby" needed anything. I realized with a bit of a shock that my mother hormones had truly kicked in.

Bonding with My Shaman

We entered a completely unknown territory. Nothing had prepared us for what followed. We were both fully aware that we became bonded as mother and child. We trusted the process and decided to follow our intuition and go with it. I told Hara Ra that he could call me any time he felt lonely or in need of comfort, and I would come over as soon as I could. This we did.

After a few weeks, the three of us sat down for a debriefing. When Dr. Bob asked Hara Ra if he would look inside and see what happened to his empty grave, he turned inward. "It is gone!" he said. None of us had expected that. We had hoped that maybe it would be partially filled or somehow changed. We were overjoyed.

A month or so after the session, Hara Ra chose to go on a vision quest to Mount Shasta. Near the mountain, he discovered a quaint little pagan store where he found the perfect drum. Alone on the sacred mountain, he partook of psychedelic mushrooms and played the drum till deep into the night. Later he said he had 'found his voice.'

During that same weekend, back home in Santa Cruz, I suddenly felt myself again. The cord had been cut. The entire mother/child formation vanished in an instant. When we saw each other after he returned from his trip, he had felt it too. The change had happened simultaneously. We confirmed our new reality, wondered at the mysterious nature of our process and were also happy to be free again.

I visited him regularly. What a pleasure it was for me to have in-depth and intelligent conversations with this insightful and brilliant man. The pleasure seemed to be mutual. With each conversation, I felt my psychological understanding deepening and appreciated the gems of wisdom he would casually toss around. "Trust the process" was one of his favorites and he lived by it.

One day, just before I left, he casually leaned against the doorway, one foot crossed in front of the other, looked at me and said, "I've been thinking carefully about this. I would like a relationship with you and, I'll accept whatever you are willing to give me, even if it's just one lunch a month."

Warding off the very idea, I crossed my arms in front of my face. "No, no. I can't go there." "And why is that?" he asked kindly.

"I don't want any problems with my marriage."

That seemed to be the end of it. Even as we continued our visits and sometimes relaxed in his hot tub, he never physically approached me nor did he in any way try to convince, seduce or cajole me. His respect for my integrity, his powerful clarity and unwillingness to manipulate, elicited a deep trust in me.

Around that time, friends of mine, all alternative healers of sorts, were planning to attempt purchasing Paraiso Hot Springs in the Santa Ana Mountains. We shared a vision of creating a healing and retreat center within an hour's drive of Santa Cruz. We went to visit the ancient Indian grounds which, in the early 1900s had become a popular resort with the wealthy from San Francisco. There were hot pools, an Olympic-sized swimming pool, quite a number of cabins and a yurt all set in an idyllic, rustic landscape of hills and oak. The property was owned by an aging alcoholic woman who wanted to sell. She was wooing us with promises but would never follow through. Rumors of hexes and mishaps floated about the property. Something was wrong.

When we planned to go there for another round of brainstorming and to gather in ceremony, I asked my new shaman friend if he would be willing to join us. Maybe Hara Ra could divine what was going on with the land, and with the old witch and do something! He agreed. We all spent a few magical days up there and relaxed in the warm waters. I was sharing the yurt with some of the other women.

While we were hanging out by the pool, Hara Ra asked if he could give me some feedback about something he had observed about my personality. I agreed. The moment I heard his observation about my need to please others, I turned inward to see if there was truth in what he was saying and pondered my underlying problem. I acknowledged what it made me realize about myself and thanked him. Later, he commented that he had never seen anyone accept a critical observation without first getting upset or becoming defensive. It must have added to his respect for me.

On the ride back through the beautiful scenery, I am driving, we are relaxed and we were talking. Suddenly, he makes a silly remark, "You don't have a sister, do you?" Uh oh... I understood the unspoken implication. Silence dropped between us... as they say in French, *Il y a un ange qui passe*. We lightly skipped over that one and continued our journey home.

At times, Hara Ra would talk about the healing work he offered to people. He had become a guide for psychedelic therapy work. He expressed his longtime desire to have a female companion to assist in this session work, especially for women clients and for couples. When he invited me to begin training with him, a bright light beckoned in my mind's eye to evolve my healing skills in a way that would far exceed what I had been able to offer until then. Already I would take clients deep into their process and help regress them to the source of their emotional or psychic trauma, whether it had occurred in early childhood, in the womb or in previous lifetimes. I believed that facing old traumas in safety, and bringing loving attention to them, would initiate a profound and significant healing process. Psychedelics would bypass the ordinary mind and allow unprecedented access to the inner workings of the psyche. They create a fluidity in which new patterns can be established and long-lasting healing might occur.

"To become a journey guide," Hara Ra explained, "one has to travel those pathways oneself." Even though I was familiar with acid from my early years in Amsterdam, I would need to have a therapeutic session with The King, as he liked to refer to LSD. He would sit for me. He suggested I would fast beforehand and that I would be in the nude, devoid of any outer contraptions or barriers. It was late August of 1996. I looked for an auspicious date and decided on September 29th, the day I had left Holland for India twenty-five years before—my first major transition.

A few weeks before that day, our group had planned another trip to Paraiso Hot Springs. I asked Hara Ra if he was interested in coming again. The energy between us had become more intimate. He wasn't quite sure yet if he wanted to go but talked about the possibility of renting a cabin. I would be welcome to share it with him. Still remaining loyal to Maurice, I declined and said I would share a cabin with one of the other women.

The next morning, I was at my desk doing paperwork, when the phone rang. It was Hara Ra, "I've decided to go to Paraiso and rent a cabin," he said. I don't know what he did energetically, but my body spontaneously erupted into orgasm. I was blown away. I didn't even know such a thing was possible. It definitely got my attention. During some quiet time alone that evening, I turned inward. The truth was that my relationship with Maurice had already been non-sexual for a couple of years. I asked my body if it was willing not to have sex for the rest of my life. "NO!" it shouted, loud and clear.

While Hara Ra drove us through the farm fields into the rolling hills, I told him what had happened. "I've decided to share the cabin with you if that's still ok with you?" He broke into a happy smile and became quiet. Then, he asked ever so tenderly, "And what does little Angela think about this?" I was deeply touched. Tears of happy gratitude rolled down my cheeks. All I could do was smile at him through my tears. I was speechless. He didn't just want sex from me, he wanted to make sure that even the most tender and possibly frightened parts of me were on board. What a man! And so our sweet and crazy romance began.

We arrived early at the hot springs and after setting ourselves up in the cabin, we lay down together. Though he was welcoming, he stayed strangely passive. Thinking that he didn't know what to do, I took the initiative. It was not very satisfying. Over the course of time, I learned that he wouldn't rush into anything but rather have us relax together and allow whatever passion might arise, if any. This kind of sexual engagement was quite different from anything I had ever known or experienced.

The Turning Point

September 29th arrived. It is 1996. I am fifty-four years old. My LSD session would take place at Hara Ra's home. I carefully explained my plan to Maurice and, dear man that he was, he gave me his favorite blanket to comfort me on my journey. It was soft and furry, dark brown with a large golden lion on it. I arrived at ten in the morning. As before, Hara Ra's bedroom was spotless and had been made beautiful. I had brought photographs of Mother and Sri Aurobindo. With flowers and candles, the dresser was transformed into an altar. I laid Maurice's blanket on the bed to have his love with me, too.

I partook of the medicine. Hara Ra turned on a joyous piece of music by Rafael "Music to Disappear In." I looked at the Mother's photograph. She was radiant. I saw her smile, nodding her approval. I took off my clothes and laid down on the soft, warm blanket. Hara Ra went off to the kitchen to fix himself a cup of tea. He was still out there when I suddenly came on. My body moved as if on its own and I found myself kneeling on the bed, face down into the brown furry blanket, full-on into an astonishing experience. Head first, I was worshipping the Great Mother's furry yoni, from where all life proceeds. "Ooh! Hara Ra! Come, quick," I shouted. I was so excited, I wanted him to know about this blissful start of my trip. He came right away and I shared my experience with him. At five o'clock that afternoon, he found his cold tea sitting in the kitchen. He had not wavered from my side all day!

A few hours into the session, I became aware that Hara Ra had been pacing the floor for a while. Suddenly, he stopped in his tracks and declared, "You have a secret!"

"Oh, no," I groaned, "not THAT!" I knew.

There is only one big, ugly secret. It is clear to me that I am at a point of no return and agree to take the plunge into the abyss of my subconscious. It seems I drop out of time and space. Everything becomes profoundly still... Slowly, my right shoulder lifts off the bed as if moved by some involuntary force. Something is hidden behind my back... As my upper body lifts up, I look behind me and gasp: I see a mass grave with white corpses...

The Holocaust. My terrifying guilt exposed. I reel with the impact. Hara Ra is right there, holding the space for me, unflappable.

After a little while, I move to sit in front of Hara Ra, facing him. I look into his face and see a great wizard. Gray eyebrows curling fiercely over kind, penetrating eyes. Goodness seems engraved in the very texture of his face. He is strong like a mountain, not phased in the least by whatever drama I am going through. Just present, strong, kind and exceedingly skillful. In his gaze, I understand the error of my child's mind. I hadn't been able to differentiate myself from my father, nor could I differentiate his war crimes from the mass murder of six million Jews. The horrifying images of the concentration camps I saw in the newsreel when I was twelve had blended seamlessly in my young psyche with the inextricable bond of love for my father, who had participated in that monstrous system. In my confusion, subconsciously, I instantly felt guilty by association.

Hara Ra

Somewhere later in my session, I re-experienced my birth, particularly, the cruel "hold the baby upside down by its feet and slap her on the back" routine of those days and the cold metal scale. My experience of those first moments, before I was given to my sweet mother, was the feeling of being among strangers. The doctor was a stranger and I didn't want to have anything to do with those mean old women (my grandmother and her old friend). More importantly, where was my father, to whose call I had come?

Hara Ra's presence feels like a great boon to me. Never has any man paid such kind and unwavering attention to me, with only my very best interest at heart. I have never trusted like that. Towards the end of the session, I gladly fold myself into his arms to be held.

My first therapeutic LSD experience resulted in an essential turning point for my psyche. I became aware of the deep subconscious shame of being the daughter of a Nazi, and of the horrifying sense of guilt by association for the unspeakable atrocities committed in the concentration camps of WWII.

Jumping ahead. It is June 2021. The Western world is slowly recovering from the COVID-19 epidemic while white people are inherently deemed different and more valuable than all other people of color.

This is the time of Black Lives Matter, fifty-three years after the assassination of Dr. Martin Luther King Jr. and thirty-four years after James Baldwin died. The cold-blooded murder of George Floyd has erupted in a global movement to awaken all of us to the great lie that white people are inherently different and more valuable than all other people of color.

Scientific research is beginning to clarify that the entire notion of race is a questionable creation, especially of white male superior thinking. It started centuries ago when European explorers began to discover other parts of the world and found great resources to pillage and make them very rich. We began to justify seeing ourselves as the peak of creation and the darker your skin the easier it was and continues to be to consider you intrinsically less valuable.

This same cultural belief of the superiority of one race over another was the foundation of Nazi Germany's belief in itself as the superior race, resulting in the horrendous persecution and murder of millions: Jews, homosexuals, gypsies (the Sinti people) and the mentally and physically disabled, and of course anyone trying to undermine "das Reich."

And, these last years, to my great distress, the United States is being seduced by another power monger to "Make America Great Again," and it seems nearly half of the population prefers to believe the lies perpetrated on African Americans, LGBTQ+ folk and immigrants alike—to distort history and obliterate the dark side of the American psyche.

My Marriage Blows Up

I had arranged for Maurice to come and pick me up after my session that evening. When he came to the door, he barged right in and headed straight for the bedroom. He wanted to see for himself what might have been going on there. I was grateful we were both dressed and had made the bed.

Once at home, in our front hall, he looked at me and was startled by the light in my eyes. "You're on fire, baby!" and, concerned, he guided me to my bedroom. (I usually slept by myself since he snored loudly.) We sat on my bed for a while, and I knew I couldn't withhold the truth any longer. I turned to him, and holding his face between my hands, I said, "You know how much I love you, don't you?" trying to establish the truth of our love first, hoping that he might have a space in his heart for my new reality. Then I told him that Hara Ra and I had become lovers. Turning away from me, this was the first thing out of his mouth, "Frankly, that is kind of a relief!" A moment of truth.

We lingered for awhile in mellow feelings of palpable love. Then he wished me good night and went off to his own quarters on the other side of the house. I was still quite wired in the aftermath of the acid trip and couldn't sleep. Soon I heard a clunking and banging in the house that wouldn't stop. I finally got up to see what was going on. Maurice was packing his bags. Disturbed, I asked, "What are you doing?" "I'm leaving," he stated, "and first thing tomorrow morning, I will be contacting my lawyer." I should have let him. It would have saved me a lot of grief. But no, I couldn't tolerate such an abrupt ending and convinced him to stay. Surely, we could work things out together. He relented.

I had already made plans to go and visit my mother in Holland that fall. I felt disturbed to leave so shortly after my fateful revelation to my husband. When I discussed this with Hara Ra, he startled me with the advice to make sure not to leave any important personal belongings in the house. I did secure my jewelry but couldn't imagine what else might be in jeopardy.

I first flew to London where Tara happened to be on vacation, so we would have a few days to visit. I called Maurice from her friend's house where we were staying. He told me he had written to the Immigration and Naturalization Service (INS) about me giving LSD to my clients, to get me deported. Much to my daughter's embarrassment, I screamed at him, helplessly, that he could not do that. I don't think I had ever felt so powerless in my life. My visit with my mother was largely overshadowed by my fear and distress about Maurice's vengeful state of mind.

Upon my return, hoping against my better judgment that we might at least somewhat repair our relationship, I found to my horror that he had destroyed everything that was precious to me. A whole drawer full of photographs of my childhood, my daughters' quaint birth certificates from a village registrar in India, all the letters I had written during my trip overland through the Middle East to India which my mother had carefully saved for me, and worst of all, the fairy tales my father had hand-written to me as a child in boarding school from his prison cell, illustrated by a cellmate. All was gone.

When I questioned him about it, he grinned with evil satisfaction, pointing to his fireplace. Ashes were piled high, showing small remnants of papers and photographs. My rage at him was as desperate as it was useless. The loss pierced me to my core and kept haunting me for a very long time. He had exacted his revenge.

I went to stay with friends and would only come home to get my mail and phone messages. One day, when I came into the house, he came right up to me, standing way too close for comfort. He was shaking in his boots. "I want to kill you so bad!" he growled under his breath. I knew I had to leave.

I called the movers and arranged for them to help me pack everything and put things in storage. I called Maurice to notify him of my intent, requesting that he not be home. He agreed. However, I knew very well I couldn't trust him not to be there since he loved nothing better than causing trouble. I called the police to protect me.

Hara Ra offered me $20,000 to help me through this time. I could spend it however I deemed fit. He acknowledged that he was helping me buy my freedom. I knew Maurice was going to be homeless. Early on in our life together, he had sold his old Volkswagon van and had been relying on my car. I sent Maurice an $8,000 check to buy himself a car that he might be able to sleep in. Unfortunately, even though he and I had been married for three years and had continuously struggled to make ends meet, it only added to his insane suspicion that I had lots of money and had been stealing from him.

Determined to get a chunk of my imaginary fortune, he took me to divorce court. Hara Ra had provided me with a lawyer. When she and I met Maurice in front of the courtroom, he said with an evil grin on his face, "Can you hear the music?" so convinced was he about taking me to the cleaners! We were counseled to go to mediation first. We tried that, but since he couldn't believe that I had no resources, we had to go in front of the judge. In the courtroom, in a last desperate attempt to destroy my life and get me deported, he told the judge I was giving LSD to my clients. The judge was not impressed and, since there was no property to be divided, the case was dismissed. Maurice then appealed and we had to go through the whole thing one more time.

Obstreperous as he was in his deluded state, he refused to leave the house, and our landlady, a previous client of mine, had to evict him. Convinced of his rights, he then took her to court also, twice. All over town, he spread tales to whomever he could corner about what a terrible woman I was, "a liar and a common thief." The whole dreadful experience wore me down to the bone. I was devastated. This crazy man I loved, and who had loved me so deeply, was stomping all over my tender heart like a mad bull.

I wondered why I had to experience this public shame and humiliation, and realized it was exactly what I had dreaded since my childhood. Shame and humiliation about my father's past had hung over my life like a shroud. And here again, it was caused by a man I loved.

Love is Action

The terrible disruption with Maurice resulted in an ever-closer bonding with Hara Ra. He was completely supportive of me throughout my ordeal. In fact, he respected my heart's grief because, as he said, it made him appreciate the depth and loyalty and capacity of my love.

Life with Hara Ra became an adventure, both good and bad, or to be more exact, fabulous and excruciating. If I was dedicated to truth, he taught me to apply the principle of transparency in our relationship. During our first three months together, especially in bed, I felt like I was in the classroom.

"Don't do anything you don't really feel like," he would say. "I've learned the hard way that whenever a woman does me favors or gives me sexual pleasure without really wanting to, I invariably end up paying the price!" If we were in the middle of lovemaking and I might begin to feel tired, or my body hurt, or some feelings would come up, he urged me to just say "Stop." Whatever was really going on would need our attention. He explained how the internal process is always the most important thing in the moment. When I expressed my concern about how frustrating that might be for him, if he was sexually aroused, he simply countered, "Whatever comes up, will go down by itself. It is not your concern."

So, he wanted me to accept a "stop agreement." I couldn't imagine ever being so rude as to just say, "Stop!" In fact, I thought it was a bit hilarious to ask that of me, having been so thoroughly conditioned to be polite and considerate under all circumstances, to be a lady, no matter what. However, I did understand and appreciate the principle. I accepted his plea to be honest and to speak up when I needed to. I practiced it as faithfully and courageously as I could.

Over time I learned to pay attention to myself and to speak up when something was going on inside of me, when feelings or memories would get triggered or my body simply had enough. He never failed to respond. What a novel idea to not be responsible for a man's sexual satisfaction. This radical notion went against my entire childhood formation of wanting the man I loved above all else and therefore doing whatever would be in my power to please him and keep him with me. Risking a man's anger or displeasure had been completely counterintuitive. Hara Ra never did get angry with me.

A few months into our love affair, Thanksgiving was approaching. Since I was living at a friend's home, I couldn't invite him for a festive dinner, and he didn't even have a dining table. I cooked up a plan which I intended as a sweet surprise to him. I asked him to pack an overnight bag and just let me take him somewhere for a few days. I drove us up the coast and past San Francisco. As we drove amongst the dense grove of trees down into Green Gulch Zen Center, I could barely contain my joy. Hara Ra became very quiet. We installed ourselves in one of the Center's fine guest rooms and rested from the trip. Now it was time to get dressed and join the guests for a special Thanksgiving dinner.

Barely able to speak, he cringed with shame and embarrassment. He couldn't do it. Apparently, he just did not feel comfortable amongst the kind of people one could expect to attend such an event, the intelligent, educated, well-groomed upper-middle-class people from the Bay Area enjoying the simple luxury of Thanksgiving dinner in a Zen monastery. Had he known of my plan, he would have warned me. I was deeply disappointed and quite shocked to be faced with the depth of his social anxiety. Close to tears but bravely, I went to the dining room where, amidst a happy crowd of celebrants, I piled up two plates of the delicious spread. We quietly ate in our room.

We spent the evening processing our feelings. He commiserated about the extreme isolation of his childhood. He grew up in a small mining town in Montana where his father owned the mine. He had never played with another child when he was suddenly thrust into kindergarten and stood there completely bewildered, not knowing what to do. In third grade, he had once gone to another boy's home to play after school and came home later than usual. He was taken out into the backyard and scrubbed from head to toe with Pine-sol. "That'll teach you that we don't mingle with those people."

Hearing these shocking stories, I wanted nothing more than to comfort that little boy inside of him with all the sweetness of my heart. All through his school years, he felt he was treated like a weirdo. Being brilliant didn't help. The shame and fear, the alienation, never left him. We snuggled for hours.

The next day we walked through the gardens to the beach, picked up a to-go lunch at the dining room and returned home.

Since leaving my home, my healing practice was on hold. My friend Jane had invited me to share her apartment. It was on the second floor of a small senior housing complex in one of Santa Cruz's old historical neighborhoods. She had given me her bedroom, which—social and political activist that she was—she had dedicated as a refuge. When someone was in need, she would offer up her bedroom and move herself into the living room. I was glad and grateful for the safe haven she provided me. Slowly, I began to recover from the onslaught of Maurice and began to feel ready to start looking for a place of my own again.

It had been clear from the beginning that Hara Ra and I would never live together. Knowing himself, he had said early on, "I am not living together material and our lifestyles are way too different. Let's not ruin a good thing." I completely agreed.

In the meantime, rents in Santa Cruz had kept rising and I found out that a halfway decent one-bedroom apartment, where I would use the bedroom for my office and live, eat and sleep in the living room, would cost me a minimum of $1,200 a month.

Even when my practice had been in full bloom, I could barely afford $900.

I discussed the situation with Hara Ra. He surprised me with his offer to guarantee my rent up to $1,200. Not wanting to be beholden to anyone, I hesitated and said, "You understand that I may never be able to pay that back."

"I am well aware of that," he smiled. "I have thought about this very carefully and I am willing and able to take that risk."

So, I started the search for a suitable place, which turned out to be rather discouraging. Even as I can live simply, I do have a pretty high sense of aesthetics and I found most places to be rather dismal.

For Valentine's Day, I invited Hara Ra over for breakfast in my friend's kitchen. She was visiting family at the time. I remember sitting across from this dear man at the breakfast table, the morning sun coming into the second-story kitchen window, when Hara Ra with a twinkle in his eye, caught me off guard. "Yesterday, as I was walking down my street, I noticed a house for sale just across the street from me." He said he picked up a piece of paper posted on the property and crunched some numbers. "When I realized that the mortgage payments would come to about $1,200 a month…" Before he could finish his sentence, I knew where he was heading and gasped in disbelief. I felt an energetic anchor dropping down through my body all the way into the earth. I had never owned a home, neither had my parents. I knew that he would only speak this way if he had already made the decision. As he continued his proposal, I blushed in happy confusion.

I expressed my fear again that I might become beholden to him. He reassured me that he really did not want to have any power over me and offered that my name would also be on the title. Then he explained that he firmly believed that if I had security, I would blossom and, naturally, he would benefit from my blossoming. That made sense to me. Then he said, "Love is not a feeling. Love is action." I was struck by the power of this lesson and have never forgotten it. We looked at the house across the street from him, but an offer had already been accepted.

He suggested that I would contact a real estate agent and go look at the homes first. If I liked one enough, we would go and look at it together. He wanted to be sure to buy a house for me that would truly make me happy and came up with an original yardstick to measure the happiness potential of a particular home, "How high is it on the orgasm scale from one to ten?"

I looked for homes with a garden. We saw quite a number of homes and, because I was eager to get one, I frequently imagined that the home we were looking at would work just fine for me. However, he had time and patience and wisdom. When he asked me how high it scored on my orgasm scale and I would say "Oh, I think a seven," he dropped it immediately. No ifs or buts.

One day, my agent said he had discovered a condominium which had been listed for quite some time. It was a free-standing two-story, three-bedroom home within Hara Ra's budget range. I went to see it with my agent. The downstairs had an open floor plan. A dark-blue tiled kitchen connected to a dining room with French doors to a backyard. A stairwell rose in the center of the space. Light poured down through a large window at the top of the stairs.

The moment I entered the master bedroom, I fell in love with it. It was large. A fireplace with brass trim and shiny black tiles gave it elegance. French doors opened out to a small balcony set into the walnut tree in front. My heart soared that such a palatial room might become my bedroom. The bathroom was also in black tile. Two bedrooms on the other side of the hallway, where one could function as my office and the other would be a guestroom, completed the house. A double garage sat in front. The house was quiet, light and spacious. It felt like a dream.

That evening back in my room, I consulted the *I Ching*. I don't remember the hexagram, but when I read "The man and the woman are in harmony," my body spontaneously erupted into orgasm. I laughed. When I reported this to Hara Ra the next morning, he twinkled all over. We made an appointment with our agent. After a brief tour through the house, we sat down with him. Without hesitation, Hara Ra said, "OK. We're buying. Let's make a proposal."

When we were handed the keys to the house and saw it empty, we realized it needed quite a bit more work than we had anticipated. Hara Ra urged me to postpone my long-awaited move so that we could paint, refinish the wood floors and replace the carpets while the house was empty. I enjoyed picking out colors and an off-white Berber carpet. I loved creating my new home. After I moved in, I had the entire deck which covered most of the backyard removed and enjoyed designing a brick patio with steps curving down from the French doors, and began to prepare the garden from scratch. Hara Ra generously shelled out extra dollars to accomplish all of that. I invited Aurelia and my friends for a plant-my-garden, housewarming party.

I picked up my healing practice which I had sorely missed, and so, life took yet another turn...

Our Psychedelic Relationship

Now that I was settled in my new home, Hara Ra suggested we celebrate this new phase of our relationship with an MDMA journey. He explained that the experience of that substance, which is an empathogen rather than a psychedelic, could go in two different directions. Either we would sit and talk and communicate deeply and truthfully from the heart or we could lie down together and tune in to the sensory delight of being intimate. Contrary to popular belief, MDMA, which is better known as Ecstasy, does not lend itself very well to sexuality. As the word empathogen indicates, its very essence is the opening of the heart to trust and empathy which are its domain. I chose the latter.

With the candles and a fire lit, and a pitcher of water at hand, we made ourselves comfortable in my brand-new bed. We began gazing at one another and relaxed. Time disappeared and slowly we melted into the indescribable sweetness of no defense left. We touched and talked and smiled with exquisite tenderness. Experiencing this powerful man in utter vulnerability, absorbing and inhaling his sweetness, and relaxing ever so deeply into the trust of his kindness and his absolute honesty, I found myself opening like a flower. Gratefully, I felt myself coming home to him, snuggling into his ample, soft and furry body, his benign gaze upon me. I felt a deep sense of belonging.

Sometime later, we decided to share another MDMA journey, this time focusing on communication. For a while, we sat in intimate silence in his living room, when I realized how deeply I trusted this man. After all my marriages and other attempts at finding someone who I could truly partner with, I realized that I had found my mate. I looked up and said, "Will you marry me?" His eyes lit up in happy surprise and agreement. It was clear that I wasn't talking about a legal document but about an inner commitment between us. It sealed our relationship right then and there and, for a long time, we stayed in a celebratory mood, reveling in the joyful surprise of having found one another.

Ever since reading Grof's *LSD Psychotherapy*, he had turned to working with experienced psychiatrists in this field, as well as on his own, with a variety of substances in a never lagging attempt to overcome his depressions, his deep-seated unhappiness and his all-pervasive sense of separation from humanity. Every few months or so, we explored another psychedelic substance together. He seemed to have access to a cornucopia of different materials, each one with its own special qualities.

Hara Ra had befriended a number of luminaries amongst the psychedelic intelligentsia, amongst them Alexander Shulgin, chemist extraordinaire. Shulgin singlehandedly developed a great number of psychedelic specialty molecules. He would experiment with them first on himself, then, if he was pleased with the result, would invite a group of friends to partake, to verify the value of the particular material. Together with his wife Ann, he then wrote about them, revealing all their chemical formulas, so that no government would ever be able to contain or prevent other chemists from producing them, thus assuring the availability of these mind-expanding materials to all those who wished to explore consciousness and the multi-faceted nature of reality. We traveled to Marin County once a month to attend the so-called Friday Night Dinners where we met the Shulgins and a variety of psychiatrists, psychologists, anthropologists, Tibetan Buddhists, tantrikas and other exotic explorers of consciousness.

We put these materials to the test for two-fold purposes. First of all, to heal our own psyches from our traumatic childhoods, we would take turns "sitting" for each other, holding space and guiding the process along whenever necessary. Or, we would partake together to deepen our connection and clarify our communication. Hermit that Hara Ra was, we usually saw one another only a few times a week and that was mostly on my initiative. We rarely even spent the night together. When we would go on a psychedelic journey, he would also stay the night, which then satisfied my longing for continuity with him.

For me, these journeys became the high points of our lives, taking me beyond all my defenses into a rare and precious closeness with this man I loved. They also opened me into amazing mystical experiences, dissolving me into timelessness and allowing me to linger in ineffable beauty and spaciousness where all traces of separation vanished, and I became one with the universe.

❀

Song of a Luscious Wench

Of a woman in her divine glory
of jubilation in the cells
of sweet juices flowing
like waterfalls,
meadow creeks,
glistening, shining,
rushing, moving.

And then again so still,
reflecting
earth and sky.
In this body of mine
so little earth,
so much light.
Just particles floating
in space,
in the breath of
the Great Mother God.
No need for anything,
but the sacred fire of
my own sweet breath
moving through me
on streams of quiet bliss.

Our Attempt at Tantra

Even before we ever got together, Hara Ra and I had been interested in tantra. We decided to go to a weekend workshop at the

beautiful San Rafael Civic Center built by Frank Lloyd Wright. I was excited to finally be with a man who had the interest to explore a higher form of sexuality with me and who could afford to take us there financially. We also planned a trip to the Mendocino coast afterward to celebrate our relationship.

We enjoyed the workshop and the teachings. We were taught about the significance of the G-spot for women and the prostate gland for men. Both these areas can hold past emotions of rejection, lack of safety, fear of intimacy and the like. Gently stimulating these areas can help release these emotions and can apparently produce amazing pleasures. We were given practice assignments to help each other to release any past traumas which might arise and explore how much sexual pleasure could be had from the stimulation of these spots.

After the first day of teaching, the men were instructed to make their women feel most special by buying them flowers, running a hot bath for them and lighting candles. After the woman would feel all warm and toasty and special, the man was supposed to invite her to bed and gently begin stimulating her G-spot. He would then be completely present for whatever emotional reaction or sexual pleasure might arise.

As we drove to our hotel after class, I noticed Hara Ra was forgetting about the flowers. When we were almost at the hotel, I asked hesitatingly, "Were you planning to get me some flowers?" He growled under his breath, swung the car around and pulled into a Safeway parking to buy "the damn flowers." When we got to the hotel room, he tossed the flowers on the bed, turned to his suitcase and got completely absorbed in whatever he was doing. I found myself standing in the middle of the room, rather forlorn. What about the hot bath? I lingered around and became more and more uncomfortable, feeling confused and neglected. He was supposed to make me feel like his most special woman on the planet and I didn't even seem to exist.

I finally reminded him of the bath. He dropped what he was doing, turned on the faucet with a short "There," and returned to his business.

Over time, I came to realize some of the peculiarities of my man. He had very limited available energy, which only diminished over the years as his health deteriorated. He was particularly short on social energy, and I came to understand that after a whole day in the midst of people in a workshop setting, he didn't have anything left and just had to withdraw to recoup himself.

The next night, after a full day of teachings, the women were supposed to explore the man's prostate. Hara Ra was overweight and a neglectful diabetic, so his body really wasn't that attractive to me. I also hadn't quite recovered from my disappointment the night before, so the situation was not really appealing to me. Because I did not have the courage to confront him, the whole thing went underground and I "forgot" about it. I did my best to be kind and loving to him, but my heart wasn't in it.

I was relieved when we traveled to the coast for our next adventure. We drove up to an old hotel, directly on the cliffs overlooking the Pacific. The high-ceilinged, old-fashioned room had a spectacular ocean view, the surf churning wildly on the rocks below. There was a delightful air of festivity between us. Hara Ra was in great spirits. We tumbled laughing onto the bed. Usually, he was quite the passive man, waiting to see what would arise and because of his weight I would tend to climb on top of him. Now, without foreplay of any kind, he came over and into me with a mighty force. He seemed to be in his power at last and all I wanted was to honor him and give him what he needed. I felt small and fragile under this big man and a bit frightened. In fact, the way I would describe it to myself later was that I felt as if I got fucked by Genghis Khan.

Here again, having not yet overcome my fears of disappointing a man, I was unconsciously terrified that I would lose him if I complained or asked for anything to be different. I did not dare express to him that I didn't feel safe. Those feelings got tucked away, too.

For years we wondered what happened to our sexuality. In spite of our love for one another and all of our good intentions, it just wouldn't take off. We began discussing the possibility of other options to bring some more excitement and satisfaction into our lives.

One of my long-term fantasies had been to be intimate with two men who would also love each other, and of course, I would be happy with a woman, too. Hara Ra was also bisexual. We decided to invite other people, men or women, into our relationship.

Together Forever

Quite some time into our relationship—he must have waited till he felt quite secure about us—Hara Ra and I were spending the morning lounging in his bed when he announced there was something he wanted to share with me.

"I've been somewhat reluctant to tell you this, but you should know that I am a signed-up cryonicist. Upon my death, my brain will be frozen at liquid nitrogen temperature to be preserved for the possibility of revival in the future."

"You did what?" I exclaimed horrified. A long time ago, when I was still living in Holland with my parents, we had read about some rich man in America who had been frozen after his death and we had found it thoroughly macabre.

I didn't even have adequate words to describe my aversion. I felt an instinctual revulsion, imagining a dead body being preserved and, worst of all, imagining it being brought back to life after god knows how long. After I had calmed down and we sat in the living room with a cup of tea, he explained his motivation.

"I deeply resent the fact that the insanity and neglect of my early childhood have left me so emotionally scarred." Then he explained that as a senior in high school, he had become acutely aware of being different from other people. They seemed to enjoy being with each other and were comfortable in each others' presence. If ever someone would accidentally touch him, he would automatically shrink away from them. At twenty-three, studying physics, he fell in love for the first time. "I didn't know what was happening to me and I was afraid I was going insane," he told me. In his desperation, he approached a professor of psychology whom he admired. The man kindly explained what he was experiencing and encouraged him to approach the girl. When he did, she immediately turned her back on him in disdain. He sank into a deep depression. "That's when I decided to take on psychology as my second major."

Recently, he had come across a research article in the prestigious *Scientific American*, stating that men who have been abused or neglected as children have a noticeably smaller corpus callosum, the central part of the limbic system which functions as a relay station between the left and right hemispheres. He had finally found proof of his theory that his limbic system was irreparably damaged and that he simply did not have the capacity to bond.

When he first came across cryonics, he was greatly intrigued. He looked into it and decided that, considering the exponentially accelerating progress of science, there had to be at least a small chance that it would eventually become possible to revive and even repair the cryonically suspended brain. If some 300 years from now, medical science might have advanced to that point, surely it would then be possible to repair his injured limbic system. He explained, "What I want more than anything is to have a full experience of being human. With one caveat: I do not want to lose one iota of the brilliance of my mind." He assumed that the diminished capacity in his emotional brain had caused an increase in his neo-cortex, seat of his intelligence.

Even though he had such powerful intuitive and shamanic sides to him, he would not believe in reincarnation. For him, death was the end. If there was even a nano-possibility of a successful resuscitation, he wanted to have that chance.

Since I had a deep respect for the man, I was open and interested to hear him out. He described his fantasies about being alive in the future, which definitely included the possibility of traveling to the stars. Since he was only intending to have his brain frozen, he figured that his memories, his sense of self and his intelligence would be downloaded onto a motherboard and from there the information from his brain would be uploaded into a number of cloned copies of himself. These would then go out and travel the world and the cosmos, gather a great many experiences and meet one day "at the end of times at the Hard Rock Cafe on the other side of the galaxy." It sounded pretty fantastic to me, but it was a pleasure to listen to him. Later, he would add that he wanted one version of himself to be the wonderful loving man to me we both wished he could be.

Slowly, over time, after listening to his intentions and visions, I began to respect his choice. I learned that a team would be dispatched to wherever he happened to be dying, to do the initial preparations before his body would be shipped to Alcor, the cryonics company in Scottdale, Arizona, where his cranium would be suspended in liquid nitrogen. Because I would be the one nearest to him when he died, I wanted to make sure the suspension would be done as well as possible. That's when Hara Ra gave me the Alcor brochure.

I started reading and was impressed. Here were some very bright minds at work. They weren't trying to sell anything or convince anyone that cryonics was going to work. Instead, they looked at the many difficulties and obstacles and approached each one of them with scientific rigor and honesty. The more I read, the more intrigued I became. What if there really was a possibility of being revived in the future? Would that not be a fascinating adventure?

With every turn of the page, I began to see the intelligence, the possibility and the radical adventure of cryonics. The logic of it seemed inescapable and I realized the amazing potential of not having to start over again through rebirth. What if I could continue to progress in wisdom and compassion, wouldn't I become a greater gift to the world? I then realized that I might want to participate in this extraordinary adventure.

This began some deep soul searching, inner conversations with Mother and Sri Aurobindo, and tuning in with my body. I struggled with all of my concepts. Then, I remembered things Mother used to say, to not be attached to your convictions, that one must be willing to surrender even the most spiritual of concepts to the Truth as it unfolds inside of you.

Mother's own journey was to bring Divine consciousness into her cells, to transform her body and to defy death. Her cells were learning to be in a constant state of opening, becoming transparent, plastic, peaceful, releasing the old habits of pain and suffering and death. She said that the collective belief in death was one of her greatest obstacles.

When I turned to Mother, in the photograph on my wall, her smile lit up. She seemed delighted as if we were becoming a team on an exciting journey towards cellular transformation which may eventually lead to actual physical immortality. When I turned to Sri Aurobindo, this is the message I received: attempt to integrate all scientific, technological and spiritual avenues. The spiritual must and can completely embrace science and science must attempt to explore the spiritual. Both Mother and Sri Aurobindo fully embraced science and technology. I felt their support for me in this adventure.

When I asked my body how it would feel about being frozen, it was immediately delighted. It exclaimed, "Yes, of course, I prefer ice over death. I always prefer LIFE!" In death, this body is recycled into fire or earth. In ice, it will be suspended,

367

With Hara Ra

its information kept intact, until life is restored. If that does not come to pass, my cells will simply have been consumed by ice, rather than fire. At least, I will have contributed to the science for the development of these techniques.

When I told Hara Ra about my decision to pursue cryonics for myself, in addition to my desire to assist him, he was utterly surprised and delighted. We were now joined at the hip, so to speak. I offered to take the Alcor training for transport technician. He bought a life insurance policy to cover my suspension. I chose for the full-body option, rather than the head-only one. I know too well there is wisdom and information in my body, and I love my body. Also, the idea of my head having to be severed for a cranio-suspension was too gruesome.

In 2002, Ted Williams, a famous baseball player, died and came in the news because his son had opted to have him cryonically suspended. Other family members disagreed and took him to court. Our local paper, the Sentinel, carried an article about the scandal. Hara Ra emailed the paper that we were a couple of local cryonicists, and we would be happy to talk with them. We had a wonderful conversation with a reporter. The photographer took some pictures of us. The next day an article appeared on the front page with the headline, "Together Forever, Local couple hopes to be frozen through cryonics and see the future." It showed a large photograph of Hara Ra and myself walking hand in hand on the little woodsy trail behind my house and another delightful picture of the two of us embracing. I had never seen Hara Ra so happy.

A Sweet Seduction

I used to love going to the Kiva, a small nudist paradise tucked away in the heart of Santa Cruz, within walking distance of my home, with lovely gardens, large communal hot tubs and a sauna. One afternoon, after a satisfying day of work, I took a toke and, happily stoned, sauntered over to the Kiva for some relaxation. To my delight, there was no one in the sauna. I lay down on my towel and drifted into a fine state of bliss when the door opened. Out of the corner of my eye, I glimpsed an absolutely gorgeous, young black man. I quickly closed my eyes again.

There was my dream body. I remembered my experience in hypnotic trance when I met my inner male who was a gorgeous, tall, black Buddha kind of figure. Being well aware that I should not be projecting my desire onto this harmless young man, I said rather sternly to myself, "No, this is not for you," and decided firmly to leave him alone. After a little while I sat up and saw him sitting across from me, his eyes closed, a splendid erection lying in his lap.

The moment came when we happened to open our eyes at the same time. He smiled and said in a soft voice, "Wow, the energy is so very nice in here!" I heartily agreed with him. After some silence and some small talk, he quietly offered, "Could I rub your feet?" Seeing his kindness—he felt like such a gentle being—I happily responded in the affirmative. He came to sit next to me and lifted my right foot on his knees, closed his eyes and concentrated on giving me a lovely foot rub. I drifted further into bliss when I became aware of the velvety touch of his member as it brushed lightly against my foot. Slowly, his hands moved up to my knee, asking if that was ok and then a little higher, again asking my permission. "Sure," I happily agreed. When he was done with both legs, the air was heavy with eros.

I decided this was enough heaven for me and it was time to set my boundaries. I sat up, shifted myself back into social propriety and with my voice rather businesslike, "That was very nice of you and, that's enough, thank you very much."

He looked a bit startled. "I didn't hurt you, did I?"

"Oh no, everything was very fine. I enjoyed it very much. I just feel this was enough. Thank you again."

We sat in silence for a few minutes, when he ventured, "I wouldn't mind giving you a back rub, if that's ok with you…?" My mind did a quick flip. Am I really going to refuse the pleasure? I'd be a fool if I did. I giggled and admitted that a back rub would be very nice indeed.

He came to stand by my side and started to gently rub my back. Now his velvet erection was quietly lying in my lap as if he didn't notice. It was quite a thrilling sensation. I could hardly believe my good fortune. His other hand started to wander across the front of my body, even as he kept asking permission. By now, I was putty in his hands.

Just then, the door opened, and someone else came in. I tore myself out of my trance and quickly motioned for him to sit down. Shortly afterwards, he left the sauna. I stayed for a while, then went out into the garden. I saw him sitting on one of the massage tables, clearly waiting for me. I walked over to him, smiling and we started to talk.

His name was Devon. He was thirty-five years old and single. He lived in San Jose but loved to come over to the Kiva to relax. We had an easy, comfortable conversation. We both were quite clear that we were interested in being intimate with one another. I told him that I was in a committed relationship but that we were open to having other lovers. I still felt some caution was advised. After all, I did not know this young man and did not want to make a decision without Hara Ra. I asked Devon if he would be willing to meet my partner for dinner to see if he would agree for us to become intimate. He was okay with that and gave me his phone number.

The next morning, I bounded over to Hara Ra's house. I told him of my delicious encounter. Since he knew of my experience of meeting my inner male under hypnosis, he immediately understood how irresistible Devon would be to me. He agreed to meet him for dinner. We met at a Thai restaurant. Since our ages and our education levels were so vastly different, the conversation was unremarkable. Devon did the honorable thing and paid for our dinner.

On our way home, Hara Ra remarked that he felt Devon to be quite harmless, and if the young man could give me pleasure, then to please go ahead and enjoy him. Mostly, he seemed reassured that Devon was no competition for him. For me, that was never a question. In my eyes, no one could possibly compete with my shaman.

Soon, Devon became a regular visitor. His kind and gentle personality, his youth and his innocence, were a delight to be around. We would hang out together in my kitchen, talking and laughing, while he was happily doing my dishes and cleaning everything in sight, because he liked doing things for me. Physically, he was a dream come true. His tall, gorgeous, well-shaped body in all hues from light bronze to dark chocolate, his ebony black, silky soft, generous wand, brought me wonderful pleasure and he seemed to be enjoying himself equally.

Because the sexuality between Hara Ra and me was not all that satisfying, and we were both bisexual, we had already expressed an interest in a threesome. With that idea in mind, he would sometimes come over for a visit when Devon and I were together, to see if anything of the sort might develop. However, when we broached the subject, Devon got rather disturbed. He turned out to be quite homophobic and any closeness with Hara Ra was out of the question.

One time, I was able to convince Devon to put his reluctance aside and let me have the pleasure of Hara Ra watching us during our lovemaking. Reluctantly, and feeling quite shy about it, he allowed it to happen. We were in my living room. I sat on the couch, and he knelt between my legs. Hara Ra was sitting at the table. As we proceeded, I realized how I longed to have eye contact with my powerful mate while getting sexually ecstatic and I asked him to come closer so I could really look into his eyes.

Upon reflection, I am quite sure that feeling unseen during most of my childhood, and definitely never feeling safe to be vulnerable in front of my caregivers, there's some amazing power for me in getting aroused while gazing into my beloved's eyes, for my entire being to be so revealed and seen at my most vulnerable. However, I do realize I was using Devon for my own purposes and that it was a fairly crooked way to get there.

Over time, Devon shared stories of his life with me. He was severely abused by his father and like so many black boys, had landed in juvenile hall. He had trouble in school because he was dyslexic and suffered from attention deficit disorder. He was on Supplemental Security Income (SSI) and received mental and financial support from Social Services. I noticed that when we got stoned together, conversation was easier, and when I gave him some Ritalin, he would suddenly be delightfully fluent and have access to his inner processes. I wanted very much help to him.

Off and on, Devon would disappear for a while because he was too depressed. I began to wonder whether I really was of any help to him.

Once, after he had been gone longer than usual, I got a threatening letter in the mail from the Medical Board. They had received information that I was giving drugs to one of my clients (with Devon's full name) and was not licensed to do so. I was asked to make a statement so they could determine whether to pursue the issue. I showed the letter to Hara Ra and he talked with his doctor friend. Both of them were very concerned that I might be in serious trouble.

I simply wrote the truth: that Devon was my delicious lover and had never been my client. Because of his dyslexia and his difficulty communicating, I had sometimes offered him cannabis and Ritalin, which seemed to give him ease and fluency of speech which was helpful in our relationship. I added that I was concerned that he did not seem to get the proper medical care for his ADD.

I never heard from the Board again.

However, it became painfully clear to me that my relationship with Devon and the ways I had tried to help him heal were not only ineffective but maybe also inappropriate. His depressions had not diminished and the incident with him giving my personal information to his case manager had betrayed my trust. Much to my regret, and with a heavy heart, I had to say goodbye to Devon.

A Healing Friend

From amongst our psychedelic friends, we received an invitation to a party on a houseboat in Sausalito. The party was on one boat with live music and dancing and the neighbors' boat was available if you felt the need for some quiet time. I danced on the deck for hours, the evening lights shimmering on the dark water and the myriad lights of San Francisco sparkling across the bay.

When I got tired, I went exploring on the boat next door. It was quite spacious, with a bar, a large living room and a somewhat secluded area where I sat down to relax. After a while, a white-haired gentleman approached and asked if he might join me. We enjoyed a quiet conversation. I shared with him about my healing work with psychedelics. He seemed quite interested.

A few months later, my phone rang. "Hi, this is Stanford… I wonder if you remember me?" a voice on the other end said. I had to admit I didn't. "We met at that boat party and sat and talked for a while," he added. "I happen to be coming to Santa Cruz and wonder if I might invite you out for breakfast?" I've always been game for being treated to a meal, so we set our date. I expected that he might be interested in doing some psychedelic work with me.

We enjoyed our breakfast and chatted about nothing in particular until I began to wonder what brought him to seek me out. He hesitated, flushed a bit and stammered trying to find words.

"Maybe you want to talk about working with the medicine?"

"Uh, no, that's not it. Uh… I… I have been thinking of you ever since we met," clumsily suggesting that he was attracted to me.

"Oh…," I laughed sheepishly, taken by surprise.

All during breakfast I had a queasy feeling in my stomach, to the point of feeling a bit dizzy. When I mentioned this to him, he said he did craniosacral therapy and that he would be happy to give me a session. Back at my house, we went upstairs to my healing room, and I lay down on my table. First, he focused quietly, then laid his warm hands gently on my forehead. He worked slowly and I relaxed deeply. All along, I felt my body responding to the marvelous, sensuous quality of his touch. A pleasant warmth emanated from his hands, beautifully comforting and nurturing me.

At the end of the session, I commented on how wonderful his touch was. "It really caught my attention," I chuckled. I hadn't even considered being intimate with him before that. "Maybe we can get close." Stepping back from the table, confused, he mumbled about having to make a sudden shift from attending to me as a healer, not wanting to cross boundaries. I appreciated his awareness and suggested we go and have a cup of tea in my garden, so we could have a conversation. Slightly giddy, he followed me downstairs.

When we settled in the garden with our tea, we talked about our relationship situations. It turned out, he was in a long-term, non-sexual marriage, and even though he would not want his wife to know about it, he felt free to explore his options. Always on the lookout for someone to share with Hara Ra, I asked him if he had ever enjoyed being sexual with men. He said he had been approached a few times, when he was young, but hadn't really cultivated that part of his sexuality. Then, I boldly asked him if he had ever been penetrated. He looked startled. Then we both burst out laughing at my audacity. No, he hadn't but he was open to exploring a threesome with my partner.

We agreed to meet with Hara Ra and get tested for STDs first. When Stanford was able to return a few weeks later, the three of us met in my living room. It quickly became apparent how different these two men were. Hara Ra led with his mind and his wit, whilst Stanford was a much more heart-centered person. He also suffered from ADD and, faced with Hara Ra's brilliance, he became virtually incoherent. When Stanford excused himself for a moment, Hara Ra told me he was quite bored and wanted to go home. I understood. When Stanford came back into the room, Hara Ra got up and excused himself. "Please go ahead and enjoy yourselves," was his parting wish.

And so, this gentle man and I began a long, erotic friendship. Since he was also a healer and had steeped himself in metaphysics and spirituality for most of his life, we developed a very open intimacy, bringing healing to each other's childhood wounds and traumas. Stanford had grown up with a severe and controlling mother, which turned him into a frightened little boy with a stammer. Of course, I had lost all nurturing parental care at the age of two, had lived under frightening circumstances, and then had been submitted to the severity of the nuns. When one of us would regress to helpless, childlike vulnerability, the other would become the all-loving nurturing and soothing parent. We would cradle each other to our hearts until we felt safe and comforted. Our sexuality was a wonderful blend of sweetness, healing and pleasure.

He was the very opposite of Hara Ra and lavished me with attention.

My Brother's Life and Death

Brother-sister love is a singular thing without any demands. Reinier and I always loved each other and that love never faltered no matter how far apart we were. The only time we lived together was the year after our time in the camp when we came to my grandmother's house. I have fond memories of him as a young boy with his big brown eyes, his soft face and his big ears sticking out. Whenever he paid attention to me or showed me some of the little treasures he kept in his pockets, he made me feel so special. According to my mother, he had been very fond and proud of his newborn baby sister and loved watching when she was taking care of me.

In 1947, my mother had dropped us off at boarding school. She told Reinier to look after me. I was five, he was three and a half years older than me. She must not have realized the near complete segregation of boys and girls in that school. So, my brother became burdened with the unfair and impossible responsibility of taking care of his little sister. The rare times I got to see him were in the chapel when he was an altar boy. Otherwise, we were only together when my mother came to visit every few weeks on a Sunday afternoon.

I got to live at home when I was twelve, whilst he was still in a Catholic boarding high school. He would only be home during his vacations. We'd all celebrate his homecoming, happy to share our meals, go to church and play endless games together. We would finally feel like a complete family.

Once I created a package for him with a few things he would like. I used my father's address label, which showed his Insect Control business, and sent it off. During his next vacation, Reinier told me how very upset and embarrassed he had been when he found the package sitting on his desk in the classroom for everyone to see that his father was not a director of the Unilever, Oil and Margarine factory. This was the lie he had spun all those years. Boarding with boys of respectable families, he felt the need to be proud of his father and was terrified anyone would find out who his father really was.

After high school, Reinier was drafted into the Dutch army for a couple of years. Then, he went to study German at the University of Utrecht. He had quite a flair for languages and for writing. All the main cities in Holland have their own dialects, some of them quite pronounced. He would have us rolling with laughter by switching from one heavy accent to another.

After he was discharged from the army, he traveled as a working student on one of the large Holland America ships for a round trip to the United States. On board he met the head stewardess. When she introduced herself as Grace, he was reminded of the most romantic couple of the time, Prince Rainier and Princess Grace of Monaco. Grace was quite a bit older than my brother. He was so flattered by her attentions and by that ever so romantic serendipity, that they became engaged shortly after their return to Holland.

Before introducing her to the family, he warned us that she was "a few years older." When she arrived, we were all a bit shocked. Grace seemed quite older, not very educated nor particularly attractive. We had hoped for a more appealing match for my handsome and intelligent brother. Shortly afterwards, when I was living in Paris, I received a letter from Reinier, telling me of his decision to marry Grace. I knew in my soul that it was a disastrous and hasty decision and wrote him a long letter begging him not to.

The next summer, after I had come home again, Reinier and Grace got married. During the ceremony, we learned of her true age: she was a full thirteen years older than my brother. Before long, they had a son. To complete the royal romance, they named him Maurits, after the Dutch crown prince.

However, Reinier soon found that he had married a fanatic Christian woman. She went to church a lot and nagged and bullied him frequently to give his heart to Jesus. This went deeply against his grain. Not knowing what to do with his feelings, he became an angry man. When Reinier finally succumbed to having an affair with one of his young, hot colleagues, he realized how intolerable his marriage had become.

The only time he came to visit me in Amsterdam was during that affair. Just like myself, he had grown up in emotional isolation and didn't feel he had anyone to turn to. The stress was killing him. He desperately needed to talk with someone about his impossible situation. I was grateful that he trusted me. He divorced Grace. He opted for the boy to be raised by her, realizing he would most likely lose his son to her closed-minded Christianity.

In the meantime, Reinier became quite a successful journalist. While working for international affairs at the Utrechts Nieuwsblad, a regional newspaper in Holland, he made a few trips to Africa, a continent he came to love. In South Africa, he managed to charter a helicopter to interview Bishop Desmond Tutu, who was at the time in hiding in the bush. He also wrote a series of articles on the problematic situation of lepers in Uganda. His articles on leprosy were carried by all the major newspapers in Holland. The series earned him a highly coveted national award for journalism.

After his divorce, he got to enjoy his newfound freedom. During one of his vacations, he was in a bar in Lisbon where he met an attractive Portuguese woman named Dulce. He confided to me that he had the sexual experience of a lifetime. A few months later, back home, there was a knock on his door. Dulce had followed him to Holland. Even though he wasn't ready to give up his freedom, she convinced him to accept her into his life. They had an elegant wedding with local dignitaries in attendance.

Because both of us had grown up without proper parenting, neither of us had learned we had the right to say "No!" and became fearfully codependent in our romantic relationships. Reinier became Dulce's willing slave. Her needs were inexhaustible. Appearances were all-important to Dulce. After everything had been bought for the house, she insisted on having two little dogs. My brother hated dogs. It was not enough. Finally, she convinced Reinier that she would only be happy with a child. Since, after a botched abortion in Portugal, she was unable to have children, they would have to adopt.

Against his better instincts, they adopted a little black girl from Brazil who had been left in the hospital as an infant.

Reinier

They chose Brazil so that mother and child would share the Portuguese language. My brother had also become fluent in that language. When Reinier first held the darling two-year-old with her big brown eyes in his arms, he was instantly smitten and became her adoring father. While Alessandra was coddled and adored when she was young, what ensued was a sad story of a dysfunctional family, with too much alcohol: Dulce became a dictatorial, disapproving mother and my helpless, angry, easy-to-manipulate brother tried to cope with the impossible situation by working, drinking and smoking.

In the mid-nineties, when I was in my fifties and living in California, I planned a trip to Holland and told Reinier that I wanted only one thing: to spend three days just with him, no matter where. In the middle of his chaotic family, we never had personal space. I longed to talk with him about our shared early life. I was painfully aware that my brother continued to live with lies, in fear that the truth about our father's past would catch up with him in his public life and destroy his career.

To my delight, he immediately agreed and arranged for us to stay at a spa hotel in a small town in Germany, Frenswegen, the very place near the border with Holland where we had stayed towards the end of the war and had found refuge with a customs officer and his family in an abandoned convent. It was there that my mother made the fatal decision to travel back with three little children into Holland to be near our father when German troops were already fleeing in the other direction.

Frenswegen was a charming town with centuries-old cobblestone streets, little shops and restaurants everywhere. We relaxed in the mineral spa waters and talked and talked. He was greatly relieved to be able to talk freely about all that had been oppressing him: his fears of discovery of our father's dark past, the extreme dysfunction in his marriage, and the many ways in which he felt manipulated and disempowered—his inability to stand up for himself—and his grave concern for his daughter.

At last, I shared with him my first terrifying memory of standing in a courtyard in the midst of a group of dingy-looking women, an angry man shouting somewhere in front and the ominous feeling that something was terribly wrong with us. I had feared for our lives. He immediately recognized my memory. It was roll call on the morning after our little sister Almuth had died, he told me. I was relieved to finally understand what had happened then and also realized how strange it was that I had never told my mother of that first frightening memory, wondering if she could explain the experience. I think I must have been convinced that she wouldn't have known or would not have wanted to talk about it.

I also shared with him parts of my healing journey and tried to explain to him the internal freedom that comes with having a safe place to express your emotions and let go of your painful secrets. I reminded him how much he liked and respected my friend Paul, whom he had met a few times and whom I knew to be a fine psychologist in Holland specializing in war trauma. After many hours of intense conversation, he agreed that he would contact Paul. However, he would wait until he retired. It never came to be.

Shortly after our visit, he did have the courage to divorce Dulce, which allowed Alessandra and her papa to enjoy some much-needed peaceful and fun times together. He also found his first love from high school again, Constantine, both of them now divorced and with grown children. I never saw him so happy. Reinier was about to retire, and he and Constantine were looking forward to years of love and the freedom to travel together.

Then, I received one of the rare phone calls from Reinier. He told me that he had been diagnosed with emphysema and expressed his relief that it wasn't cancer. He had smoked heavily his whole life and had feared cancer for years. Soon, however, his health started to deteriorate. We now talked on the phone rather frequently.

At the beginning of December 1999, some three months into my brother's retirement, I got a worried call from Alessandra, who had just turned eighteen. She told me that her dad was in a lot of pain, but he didn't want to go to the doctor. The next day, she called again. She had found him moaning on the floor not able to get up. He thought he had back problems and did not seem to connect it with his illness. I urged her to call the family doctor, who came and diagnosed a lung embolism. He had Reinier taken to the hospital straight away.

Constantine arrived just as he was wheeled into surgery. Exhausted from the pain, Reinier whispered to her, "I can't do it anymore." He died on the operating table. Later, we learned that his lungs and all around his heart were riddled with cancer.

I had already made plans to travel to India and return to Auroville that coming January, so I changed my flight to be present with my mother and Alessandra and participate in the memorial. It was strange to see Reinier's lifeless body in the open casket, as is the tradition in our country. My mother was grieving terribly. Their bond had been so strong. Reinier had been her closest ally.

Remarkably, Reinier had been planning for years exactly how he wanted his memorial to be. He had selected all his favorite music. The church in Utrecht was packed with some 300 people. His coffin stood raised on a dais under the cupola. The event opened with the majestic First Piano Concerto by Brahms, played by Emil Gilels, then the ethereal "Litany" by Arvo Pärt took us into silence. Some officials and people from his newspaper spoke. Then Pink Floyd's "Wish You Were Here" boomed through the high-ceilinged space. Reinier's son from his first marriage, Maurits, spoke. Then I did. My sad mother sat small in the front row. When, towards the end of the ceremony, Ali Farka Toure's joyful music erupted, I caught a glimpse of Reinier dancing wildly, like an African shaman, in the space between his coffin and the cupola—an exuberant outburst of joy and freedom.

Afterwards, the family gathered at Reinier's house. I got to meet Maurits' evangelical wife and three of his four children. Their new baby had not been brought along. When his wife showed me pictures of the newly born, I felt deeply moved. "What a beautiful soul!" I exclaimed.

Since it was just before Christmas, we made plans to celebrate the holiday together at Maurits's home. The next day, my mother got a call from Maurits. He and his wife had made "the difficult decision" that they could not invite me into their home. They were afraid that I would adversely influence their children because of my unorthodox spirituality. They had been particularly disturbed by what I had said about the beauty of their baby's soul since the baby had not yet been baptized and was therefore still "of the devil." It was a nasty bomb to drop in the middle of our grief. We were shocked beyond belief. My mother was furious. My heart, broken open as it was by the sudden loss of my brother, felt dealt a vicious blow. My mother, Alessandra, and I decided that none of us would celebrate Christmas at Maurits' house.

Revisiting Auroville and Finding a Soul Brother

In January of 2000, shortly after Reinier's death, I went back to Auroville for the first time after having left in 1978. I had made a reservation for a few days at Quiet, a Healing Center on the beachfront, outside of Auroville, to allow myself to settle in and recover from all the stress around my brother's death and from the long journey to India. I had made no other reservations because when I used to live in Auroville, I had experienced the magic of how we would be "guided by the force." I trusted I would find a place to stay in Auroville soon enough to be closer to the center of the township.

At Quiet, I was given a small bamboo hut on stilts with a view of the ocean. A beautiful little spot that reminded me of the way we used to live in the "old days." I enjoyed a wonderful massage, walked along the beach and felt refreshed by the gentle ocean breeze while reclining in my hut.

During a communal lunch, a group of us were sitting around wooden tables outdoors and I was asked about my connection with Auroville. As soon as I told them that my name used to be Angela and that I had lived in Kottakarai in the seventies, a man looked at me and said, "A very special friend once brought me to visit you in Kottakarai…!" I stopped in my tracks.

"Aah," I exclaimed. "My father?" Indeed. Mikael, a young American/Israeli who had met Ludar shortly after arriving in Pondicherry, had become a close friend of his. My father had brought him to our hut to introduce him to me and see our way of life.

I barely remembered the occasion, but it felt very special to meet Mikael again, especially since he had been so close to my father. We agreed that we wanted to spend time together and made plans for me to visit him at his house in Shanti, one of the smaller communities in Auroville.

While browsing in Pour Tous, the Auroville community store, I met a friend from the early days. She mentioned that someone in Sincerity, a small settlement close to the Matrimandir, was looking for a house-sitter on short notice. This is the Auroville I knew. Everything happens as if by magic. Two days later I moved in and had my own comfortable home right in the heart of Auroville.

When I lived there in the seventies, we could see the Matrimandir silhouetted against the sky from anywhere across the barren plateau. The heat emanated an immense power which felt like the very pressure of Mother's Force. Now, in the year 2000, some thirty years into Auroville's existence, over three million trees had been planted and the entire area had developed into a jungle. The heat was heavy with moisture, which I found difficult to tolerate. You could not see the Matrimandir anymore unless standing right beside it. Auroville, in its physical manifestation, had changed beyond recognition.

However, the Matrimandir, which Mother said would be the "Soul of Auroville," was now completed and stood shimmering golden in Auroville's center, a massive globe rising out of the red earth. Even the meditation hall up high inside the gigantic structure was now complete. A large, perfect crystal sphere, created by Zeiss in Switzerland, had been placed in its center, supported by Mother's and Sri Aurbindo's symbols laid out in gold. A beam of light from the sun, directed by mirrors, streamed from an opening high up in the ceiling directly onto the crystal. The walls of the huge, high-ceilinged room and the twelve tall pillars were all tiled in white marble, imported from Italy. Soft white carpet covered the floor. Mother had specifically indicated that there were to be no distractions, no sounds, no flowers, no incense. She wanted Aurovilians to experience Divine Consciousness in complete silence.

I went to visit the Matrimandir and slowly walked up the ramp. I put on the white socks that were provided by the entry into the meditation hall. I entered the silent room. Seeing the crystal stopped me in my tracks. The large crystal sphere was of such sublime perfection that it seemed barely there as if manifesting a realm between light and matter. It made me think of Mother's personal yoga, inviting her very cells to receive and manifest the Divine. She, too, had at times seemed translucent. I immersed myself in the great silence.

It was a special joy to recognize some Tamil Aurovillians from the past. To my surprise, I found myself still able to speak a bit of Tamil. I had no idea that I would remember some of that unusual language.

I went to visit Mikael in his beautiful, artistic home in Shanti, which he had designed and helped build himself. Thick, white-washed mud walls with oval windows incorporated a tree into their side. A tiled patio encircled the house, a small creek running through it. It was surrounded by flowering trees and shrubs. A little paradise.

I had brought some 2C-B with me, a fine, short-acting psychedelic, and Mikael was delighted to partake. It opened us to a deep, heartfelt conversation. He spoke enthusiastically about my colorful and unusual father. Their meeting seemed to have come about by divine guidance. Mikael considered Ludar not only a very special friend but also his spiritual mentor who gave him direction to explore and study Sri Aurobindo's Integral Yoga, but also to continue his schooling in dance and the healing arts, and to immerse himself in Tantra and the Kabbalah.

Apparently, Ludar had taken on quite a few students, both from the Ashram and from Auroville, and took his mentorship seriously. Mikael had noticed a file cabinet where he kept notes on all of them.

When I asked Mikael how he came to know that my father had been a Nazi, he told me how he met Ludar shortly after arriving at the Sri Aurobindo Ashram. Their attraction was strong and immediate. "We were meeting on a much higher plane than our old identities," he told me. At some point, Ludar had simply mentioned his Nazi past and during their time together he shared some of his experiences. "It was never an issue between us," Mikael said. They were both well aware of him being a Jew, but it was never an obstacle between them.

Hearing about this experience reminded me of Rumi's famous words, "Beyond right-doing and wrongdoing, there is a field. I will meet you there."

Mikael shared a memory of Ludar warning him how he had been trained to kill with a knife if suddenly attacked. He should never startle him from behind because of this reflex. Ludar told him that besides having had to commit unspeakable acts, he had also secretly tried to help quite a few people.

Mikael chuckled and said, "To this day, I sometimes get a kick out of telling people that my guru was a Nazi, not only that, he was even with the SS!" We both burst into hearty laughter.

To this day, I mostly avoid speaking of my father's past. Even when I have made a new friend whom I have come to trust, I still feel apprehensive to reveal the awful secret. Since Mikael is also a Jew, to hear him share about his powerful connection with my father, and how much he loved him, was quite redeeming for me. After having just lost my only brother, who had been so profoundly burdened by our father's past, I had found a real soul-brother, with whom I could share the love of this outrageous man, my father.

My Dilemma

After returning from my travels to India and with Hara Ra's powerful support, I felt ready to contact the Ministry of Justice in Holland in 2001, and requested documentation about my father's death sentence and his subsequent acquittal. Several months later, I was surprised to receive a personal phone call from a high-up official at the State Archives in The Netherlands. He said, "I have your father's file here in front of me. I want to speak with you and warn you about it. It is a very large file, indeed. I have to tell you that it contains pages and pages of the most horrendous allegations I have ever seen." My heart cringed.

Then the man spoke straight from his heart, saying, "If you were my daughter, I wouldn't want you to be exposed to this. I believe it would be harmful to you and to your daughters to read these files." I gratefully accepted his advice and dropped my request. The very system which had sent my father to death row was now extending its heartfelt care to me.

Two years later, when the US went to war in Iraq, I was shocked to be seeing so many Americans waving their flags and expressing pride in their national superiority. I got motivated to write my story. Now, the necessity of knowing what crimes my father was actually charged with became clear. I imagined myself at book readings being accosted by animosity and accusations about painting a loving picture of my father, the Nazi criminal. Even worse, someone might access the archives, get all the horrific details and come to confront me with them in public.

At the same time, I was afraid that reading the files would be an onslaught on my psyche and forever alter my relationship with my father, this man I have loved and whose love saved my heart from withering during the long and lonely years of my childhood.

I also felt that the truth would be impossible to come by, because, as my father had explained to me, he was the fall guy; a man who stood hated and accused not only by the Dutch but also by his SS comrades who were taken captive because of him.

I always felt that I *knew* my father. I resonated so deeply with the great compassionate and spiritual soul I knew him to be and his big warm heart, that his stories of having love for the people he tortured were completely coherent with my perception of him.

During my next visit to Holland, I asked my mother carefully whether she thought my father might have tortured people. "Oh, no, your father was such a kind man," she replied immediately. "He would never harm anyone." My mother remained convinced of his innocence, even though she had been in the courtroom and witnessed all the horrific accusations which led to his death sentence. Besides, my mother knew of my father's inclinations like no other. She had shared his bed and his sexual fantasies. She had been the recipient and witness of his sadomasochistic games for many years. Her belief in the kindness of his nature added another level of coherence to my own perceptions of him.

Shortly after my return from Holland, I found the courage to ask for the court files. I reached out to the same man who had warned me about them. He sent me the documents right away.

They were indeed horrendous and deeply disturbing. I spent time with Hara Ra to help me process the terrible information. With the court papers was a copy of a ten-page hand-written plea note my father had provided to his defense attorney.

The note starts with, "I do not wish to defend my actions, because these are indefensible. But, I wish to give the High Court insight into the circumstances which could provide some explanation. I will agree with whatever punishment the Court feels it needs to impose on me and I completely accept, from my inmost conviction, even if that be the death penalty."

He explains that he had not wished to write about his sexual aberrations, but that his counselor had urged him to do so. He writes that he acquired these disorders during his teenage years at the hands of an older man who was eventually persecuted and imprisoned for child sexual abuse in Germany. From *my* perspective, it started when he got whipped by his father as a twelve-year-old boy in front of his eighteen-year-old brother, with a rhinoceros whip from Africa. In the letter, he admitted that the sexual tortures he had perpetrated on their group's prisoners were no other than had been done to him.

He then writes about the immense agony he experienced during those last weeks of the war (which is when all the alleged crimes took place), worrying that rumors he had heard might be true, of the Dutch having already killed my mother and his children. He had no way of contacting us. He had not been in his right mind.

In 1952, my father was indeed exonerated on psychiatric grounds and considered not responsible for his actions. In 1954, his parole was extended for another two years, never to be revisited.

Getting Out of Control

During my psychedelic forays, both with Hara Ra and by myself, I frequently processed my early childhood fears and isolation. Over the years, I had become aware of being quite dissociated from my emotions. I discovered that smoking marijuana would help me get in touch with my feelings and allow me to process whatever difficulty I was facing.

Hara Ra and I never lived together. Often, after we had a satisfying visit, he would return to his home and seem to just forget about me. This frequently triggered my abandonment issues. About three days into not hearing from him, a feeling of desolation would come over me. If I then took a toke, I would enter a stream of awareness and journal about my current upset and my childhood distress of abandonment, freely raging on the page. Over the years, I filled stacks of notebooks, convinced I was doing my inner-child healing work.

I was also convinced that the idea of marijuana being addictive or a so-called "gateway drug" was propaganda from the government. In my experience, it was a sacrament and a gift from Mother Earth—harmless, healing, sacred, and most enjoyable. From the very first toke, I would experience a deep breath of relief and relaxation; a lovely sense of well-being would come over me. I would relax on my couch and listen to some fine music, sit in my garden and merge with the beauty and magic of my roses, or soak the sunshine into my body and float off into dreamland. I would feel like I was finally coming home to myself, in a longed-for sense of union. It seemed that without cannabis in my system, I was in a constant, unconscious state of internal pressure.

I also noticed that, after a toke, I would not be afraid to boldly speak my truth and my anger to Hara Ra. Since I remained in awe of his brilliance and his psychic powers, he had become somewhat intimidating to me. To his relief and mine, I could, when stoned, counter him with a resounding "Fuck you!" if whatever he said or did was obnoxious to me. Then, we would both burst into laughter. He liked being met with my force.

He loved unmitigated honesty and my direct expressions of anger, because, he explained, "I then know exactly where I stand."

The more I got stoned, the more I got in touch with my emotions. I seemed to regress ever deeper into processing my childhood. After a few years of regular marijuana use, I actually felt I had liberated my two-year-old and was proud of it. Later, I would realize that a liberated two-year-old in a sixty-year-old body is not a pretty sight, nor was it a pleasant experience for my loved ones to endure, especially not for my daughters.

I also began feeling entitled to have my pleasure as I saw fit. My old sex and love addiction came roaring back, although I thought of it then as a sign of being empowered and liberated. Over the course of four or five years, I accumulated seven different lovers, all men. I made a couple of forays into erotic relationships with women as well. These were emotionally much more involved and complicated than my affairs with men. None of them panned out well.

Hara Ra and I had come to identify our relationship as polyamorous, but I was the one with all the extras. I was always hoping that one of the men or women I became close with would be interested in a threesome with Hara Ra. Except toward the very end, no one ever came near him. Over time, our relationship began to feel quite out of kilter.

My getting stoned also started to seriously interfere with our intimacy. Marijuana made me exceedingly talkative, if not manic, and I just could not shut up long enough to allow a quiet soulful closeness with him to unfold. Then I would be even more aggravated about our lack of intimacy. I was in a downward spiral.

Some six or seven years into all of this, I got deeply depressed. I suffered lots of back pains and spent thousands of dollars on chiropractors and acupuncturists. I felt easily overwhelmed, and I cried a lot. By this time, I understood that I was self-medicating with marijuana. In addition, when I was hurting, I would take Vicodin. When I was getting too excited and needed to calm down, I would use GHB (gamma-hydroxybutyrate). I could not sleep anymore without taking a Lorazepam. "Better living through chemistry," Hara Ra and I used to say. My healing practice was disappearing. My whole sense of well-being and self-sufficiency was coming to a grinding halt.

I was now seriously worried about my dependence on marijuana, but when I discussed it with Hara Ra, he would invariably ask me if it was interfering with my quality of life. "Oh no," I would answer, "It is helping me. It makes me feel better, it comforts me, it gives me energy, it helps me to understand and process my feelings." Neither of us really knew anything about the nature of addiction, so we could not see the denial, the rationalizations, the insanity of continuing to believe this herb was my ally.

Whenever I would decide not to smoke for the day, or not before 4 p.m., I would obsess about it until I felt that denying myself the comfort of a toke was abusive. I never once made it until 4 p.m. And, quite to my embarrassment, when visiting or going for a walk with a friend, I would talk endlessly about marijuana—whether to use or not to use, how I was feeling, how much I needed it, what it did for me—as if there was nothing in the world more interesting or compelling to discuss or even think about than smoking pot.

Aurelia came to visit me one day. I was deeply steeped in misery. She had brought a recording of her teacher, Sogyal Rinpoche, reciting a poem. With the chanting of the great Vajra Guru mantra in the background, *Om ah hung benza guru pema siddhi hung*, I heard him speak to me, *"Rest in natural great peace this exhausted mind, beaten helplessly by karma and neurotic thoughts like the relentless fury of the waves in the infinite ocean of samsara. Rest in natural great peace."* I wept. I was profoundly grateful that my sweet daughter had brought me this gift. However, nothing really helped me shift.

Then, there came the moment when I could no longer stand not being altered with my clients. Knowing full well that this was inappropriate, I would start a session without it and soon find myself utterly bored. I could not stand listening to what seemed their endless and pointless complaining. I would excuse myself, run downstairs and quickly grab a toke. Then, in my altered state, I would happily crash through their boundaries to enlighten them about their problems, convinced that I was now much more effective. It often seemed to work like a miracle. However, slowly but surely, most of my clients disappeared. I became ever more dependent on Hara Ra's resources. He was not pleased.

It was on a spring day in 2005 that he called to come and talk with me. I made tea and we sat in my garden. We were both quiet for a while. In an even tone, he began, "You remember how I told you in the beginning that if my principal would ever drop below $130,000 I would no longer be able to support you financially?" It was the line he had drawn for himself because he never wanted to run the risk of becoming homeless again. "I have been watching my resources drop continuously due to the crash

397

of high tech. I know this is going to be hard for you, but I can no longer sustain you financially. We will need to sell your home."

My heart dropped, but I knew he was right. I quietly accepted my fate. By that time, I only had a couple of clients left. It was obvious to both of us that I was not going to climb out of my hole anytime soon. The unknown was looming large.

My Year from Hell

Just before Hara Ra's announcement that we needed to put my home on the market, I had been diagnosed with a prolapsed uterus. Surgery was scheduled in May of that year, whilst I was moving blindly into an uncertain future. I figured that I better take a break from marijuana and stopped cold turkey. Within days I felt so clear and peaceful, I assumed I was free of my obsession.

The surgery went very well and, for once, Hara Ra showed up like a real husband. He was with me when they rolled me into the operating room and again when the surgeon came by for a post-op check-in.

Hara Ra had already suggested that I wait a month to recover from surgery before beginning the process of putting my home on the market, so, for the month of June I still had my beloved home space.

Sometime during that month, a friend who was using marijuana medicinally came to visit. His living situation prevented him from preparing his special brownies in his shared kitchen. He was aware that I had quit but asked if I would be willing to let him use my kitchen to bake the brownies. "Sure," I said.

"Go right ahead. I am not wanting any, so that should be just fine." Slowly, the delicious fragrance began to fill the air. When the brownies were done, they looked so appealing. "Oh," I said. "It has been three months. Surely one brownie would not hurt." I happily partook.

The effects were quite fabulous. I went for a solitary walk along the creek behind my house and found a spot in the dappled light amongst the trees where I lay down and bared my post-surgery belly to the sun. I rested, enjoying the penetrating, healing warmth. I was thinking how fine it was to come back to the magic of the herb. Strolling back, I spotted three crows in a tree overhead. As I stopped to greet them, four more flew across the creek to land in the same tree. I lingered blissfully with the seven crows and felt like I was receiving crow medicine. I then realized it was Friday, the thirteenth.

I felt so blessed by the magic that I could not imagine ever wanting to live entirely without marijuana. So, I decided I would get stoned one day a month and be sober the rest of the time. The thirteenth of every month was going to be my witching day. A week later, I figured that getting stoned once a week would be fine. Then, a few days later, I was unhappy about something and knew that a toke would take care of whatever was bothering me. Within two weeks, I was back to daily use with more vigor than ever.

From among my alternative healing friends, I had found a kind and competent real estate agent. I spent hours with her to prepare my home for showing. We had the good fortune of a rising housing market and, in August 2005, the house sold for more than three times the value we had bought it for. Hara Ra agreed that, after we paid back the mortgage, I could invest half of the remaining sum as a little nest egg.

Then came the harrowing labor of getting rid of most of my beautiful possessions. I did not want to put things in storage and increase my cost of living, so I had to part with much that was dear to me. Most of my artwork, a lot of my furniture and my fine quality bedding went to friends who came and picked what they liked. Thankfully some of them helped me with a few yard sales. I finally managed to get the house empty and clean. I was exhausted to the bone.

At the same time, I needed to find a place to live. I heard that a couple of women in my circle of friends had a large room for rent. I was quite apprehensive about living in someone else's home, but I had no other options. I barely knew them, but I was grateful to have a place to land. They told me that theirs was a drug-free home. I respectfully argued that my marijuana use was like a sacrament to me, that I used it for sacred and healing purposes only. I do not believe they agreed, but they chose not to argue with me.

The spacious room was in an old Victorian home with high ceilings and tall windows. I have always enjoyed creating my living spaces. Putting my heart into decorating my new room served as a good antidote for the loss of my beautiful home. I arranged my bookcases and my grandmother's rocking chair, an oriental carpet on the floor, art on the walls. I sewed long wine-colored velour curtains to give a finishing touch to the space. I was pleased with how the room had gotten both an intimate and a stately effect. One of my friends said it felt like a room that could have belonged to Jung's wife.

I did not feel right, however. My mental state became more and more disturbed, and I was constantly lost in my emotions. I smoked all the time. Hara Ra was distancing himself from me more and more because he did not like being around me when I was stoned. The more I suffered, the more I self-medicated. I became a real drama queen and had no idea that my use itself was propelling me into a downward spiral. I was stuck in a hopeless loop.

Nevertheless, I still believed that marijuana was helping me heal. In my altered states, I realized that I was suffering from self-judgment, from having been made to feel wrong as a child. Internally, I was always defending, accusing, blaming, and shaming myself. I could not imagine anybody really caring about my suffering, or, if they cared, that their empathy could even make a difference. I found myself in a total no-win situation. Also, my mind's repetitive refrain reflected my ongoing frustration with Hara Ra's absences: *Will he call me? Shall I call him? Weren't we going to do something? Does he even remember me? I doubt it!*

I feared that a separation was in the making. I knew that Hara Ra had made me heir to his estate. When I asked him if he might want to change his will, he thought for a moment, then answered with a cryptic, "It's ok for now."

September 21, 2005, was our ninth anniversary. To celebrate that day, a fun young couple from our polyamorous circles invited Hara Ra and me to visit them in their beautiful home up in the Santa Cruz mountains. After a lovely dinner, Hara Ra sat on a couch next to me which was unusual, given the amount of physical distance he typically preferred. He even put his arm around me, which was a first. I wish I could remember the exact words he said to me because they moved me deeply. He expressed his profound gratitude to me, for who I was and for the quality of my love and the years of companionship I had given him. Never, he said, had a woman been able to tolerate him for any length of time.

Little did I know that the worst trauma of that year was yet to come.

Hara Ra's Demise

Hara Ra had been suffering for an unknown number of years from diabetes, which had been discovered in the early nineties during one of his rare doctor's visits. Over the years, his energy had been steadily diminishing. He was now battling an infection under his foot. Only once did he agree that I take him to an urgent care doctor to look at it. The doctor did a half-ass job at cleaning it out and sent him home with antibiotics. I went to his house every day to keep the wound clean and renew the bandage. It would not heal. Slowly his leg turned an ever-deepening crimson from the knee down. He refused to go back to the doctor.

On a Monday morning, shortly after our anniversary, I came to visit him. From the small sofa, in the midst of his messy living room, he announced, "I don't really feel like doing anything anymore." I stopped in my tracks. One word reverberated through my being: Death! By the time I had made us tea and we sat together, the thought had gone underground and we just visited for a while.

On Thursday night at 2 a.m., my phone rang. His voice was soft and sad, "I'm not feeling very well. I wonder if you would not mind coming over for a bit." I jumped out of bed and raced over to his house. I found him in the hot tub in the backyard. When he wanted to get out, he could barely do so. Shaking all over, he curtly denied my offer to give him a hand. Once he was out, he was quite unsteady. He motioned me to get out of the way and with sheer willpower barreled himself into the house to sit down. His leg was swollen and had turned a dark scarlet. He was sweating and in constant tremors. Emphatically, he declared, "I do NOT want to go to the emergency room." After we had visited for a while, he thanked me for coming over and suggested I go back home and get some sleep. I promised I would check back in with him the next day.

It was late afternoon the next day when I called him. His phone was busy. I called a few more times. By 7 p.m. I decided to watch a movie, *Crash*, of all things. It was close to 9 p.m. when I called again. The busy signal put me on full alarm. I jumped into my car and drove full speed to his home. The whole house was dark and cold. I called out to him. No answer. I could not find a light switch that worked, since half the electric circuits in his house were not working. He had managed to light the house with a complex network of extension cords. All the doors to the outside were wide open. I stumbled around, calling for him. I finally managed to turn on the light in the bathroom. Then, across the narrow hallway, I saw him, naked, in his bedroom, slumped against the door, an empty cardboard box on his legs, unconscious, breathing hard. Clearly, he had lost consciousness while moving things around. I ran to the phone in his office. It was off the hook. So was the one in his living room.

The plan had always been to first call Alcor, the cryonics organization, to prevent him from ending up in the emergency room. However, Alcor was all the way in Arizona. I called 911 in a panic. When they arrived, I was asked if he was on medication. I answered he was on all kinds of medications. Right there they tried to pump his stomach, fearing a possible overdose. Dragging his body through the narrow hallway, they told me to bring all his meds and follow them to the emergency room.

I looked around. Medicine containers were everywhere, in the bathroom, in the hallway closet, in his bedroom. I had no idea which ones he was taking. I frantically grabbed handfuls of pill bottles and rushed to the emergency room. They had already diagnosed renal failure due to the massive infection in his leg. Even though he was comatose, it was clear to me that he was now conscious. I leaned close to his face and said, "Hang in there, my love. You cannot die now. I will try to get Alcor here as soon as possible. I love you."

They wheeled him out to take a CAT scan. As soon as he arrived in the ICU, they hooked him up to dialysis. I went home to get some sleep. The next morning, I was told that the CAT scan did not look too bad and that as soon as his kidneys would be cleared, they were fully expecting him to regain consciousness and improve.

Alcor technicians arrived from across the Bay area. These were all cryonicists themselves who had volunteered to be trained to prepare a body for transport, just like Hara Ra and myself had done a few years before. For a successful cryonic suspension, it is of the essence to get the body's temperatures to drop as quickly as possible upon death since ischemia (cell death) sets in immediately.

The two most critical things to be accomplished are the cooling of the brain by placing the body in an ice bath and at the same time to keep the heart pumping artificially, so the blood keeps circulating and can carry the necessary medications and chemicals designed to protect cellular structures.

Together with a few of the Alcor volunteers, I met with the funeral director at the cemetery across the street from the hospital. He agreed to prepare the death certificate as soon as death was pronounced so we would be allowed to transport the body across state lines without delay. He allowed us to store the necessary equipment at the cemetery.

All this time I felt helpless. It felt like the world was caving in on me. I kept trying to figure out what had happened the day I found him. When it was warm enough, he usually walked around the house in the nude. Clothes for him were just an obstacle. So, to find him naked was not unusual. The fact that all the doors were wide open to the outside meant that he must have collapsed in the middle of the afternoon because as soon as temperatures dropped, he would have closed the doors. He hated to be cold. He usually had the heater blasting. Since he had dropped an empty cardboard box on his body while he fell unconscious, he had obviously been putzing around the house and had pushed himself to keep going, even as he must have become progressively weaker. I wondered if he had taken both phones off the hook because he did not want to be bothered, or maybe he had intended it as an alarm signal to me. It certainly worked that way. I was mortified that I had not reached out to him sooner, and that consequently he had been there slumped on the floor, propped against the bedroom door for hours in the cold before I found him.

In the meantime, he remained on dialysis in the ICU. Members of the Alcor volunteer team came and went since there was nothing to do while he was still alive. Hara Ra's psychiatrist friend, Dr. Bob, who was himself a signed-up cryonicist, came up from Los Angeles. When he saw the condition of Hara Ra's leg, he knew that if he were to survive, his leg would have to be amputated. Knowing Hara Ra as well as he did, he also knew this was not something his friend would be able to tolerate. He bent over to him and whispered in his ear, "It is okay to let go, I'll see you on the other side of the dewar," referring to the cooling cylinder in which bodies and heads are preserved with liquid nitrogen.

Over the weekend friends came to visit. The couple who had helped us celebrate our ninth anniversary spent some time by his side. When they left his room, the young man reported that, when he told Hara Ra that he regretted not having a chance to get to know him better, Hara Ra had blasted him with such a powerful burst of energy, it made him stumble backwards.

I had a similar experience. One time I had come to his side and noticed that his hand was lying all crooked. I gently picked it up to try and make him more comfortable. Angrily, he yanked his hand away from me. The shock of it affected me deeply. I felt so inadequate and helpless already. Now he was angry with me. I was utterly miserable. Even as Hara Ra never opened his eyes or spoke again, apparently his awareness and his psychic powers were in full force.

After several days on dialysis, the doctors were puzzled why he was not improving and planned an EEG on Monday morning. The results of the EEG were so encouraging that the doctor saw no reason why Hara Ra would not recover. Five days into feeling that his death was imminent, my heart leaped and I shouted incredulously, "You mean I can get him back?"

On Tuesday morning, the medical team decided to take another CAT scan to compare with the one that had been taken upon his arrival. It took all day to get the results. I had to wait till evening to be told that there was quite a lot of damage to his brain and he would not make it. Finally, I had clarity and it was time for me to take action. I did not want him to die in the ICU. The occasional presence of Alcor's volunteer transport team seemed hopelessly inadequate and I knew much precious time would be lost for his optimum cryonic suspension. I was determined to move heaven and earth to get an emergency transport for him to Scottsdale, Arizona, before his death.

I spent the next day on the phone. I called all over the country to make arrangements. I chartered a medical evacuation plane for the next morning at 9 a.m. A couple of medics would be on board to keep him ventilated. It was going to cost $8,000. I got hold of a good friend of his, a wealthy fellow cryonicist, who offered to pay for the transport. I arranged for an ambulance to take us from the ICU to the nearby Watsonville airport. I called Alcor to let them know we were coming. They gave me the name of a nearby hospice to take him to. I managed to arrange for his admittance there and for an ambulance to pick us up at the Scottsdale airport. When it was all done, exhausted but greatly satisfied with my accomplishments, I returned to the hospital that evening.

When I came into his room, he was deeply unconscious, and his body seemed to be under enormous internal pressure. He was beet red. His stress was palpable. Horrified, I accosted a nurse, "What is going on? He looks like he is about to explode." She told me that they had discontinued his dialysis and as a result, his potassium levels were off the chart, which would most likely give him a heart attack. "You can't let him die now!" I shouted. "I'm flying him out to Arizona for his cryonic suspension tomorrow morning. Is there anything you can do to keep him alive?" Fortunately, there was. He got hooked up to a bag of Maalox which would bring his potassium levels back up. I stepped outside for a bit to recover from the sudden panic.

Anna, a woman from the Alcor team, whom I had not met before, showed up in the hallway. I remembered that Hara Ra had once told me how he had wished to meet her. He knew that she had recovered from a serious bout of cancer and had been close to death herself. Where most cryonicists were in the scientific geek category, we expected her to be more fully human, a woman with a heart. She was. It felt good to connect with her. After we talked for a little, I invited her to come in with me so I could introduce her to Hara Ra.

When we entered his room, his whole body had mercifully calmed down. He looked peaceful. Even though I did not expect him to be conscious, when we stood on either side of him, I said, "Hello my love. Anna is here. She is the woman we had wanted to meet from the Alcor team." Then, I turned to her, "May I introduce you to Hara Ra? He is my great love," and in a burst of enthusiasm I gushed, "He is such a fabulous man!" When I looked at him again, I saw a big smile on his face. "Oh, you are here! You can hear me!" I exclaimed as I felt my heart leap. "Hara Ra, listen to this. I have good news! I have chartered a med-evac and we'll come to pick you up tomorrow morning at nine to fly you to Arizona." His smile widened from ear to ear.

I felt so redeemed. For a week I had been helplessly watching his gradual demise and finally, I had been able to take action and carry out his wishes. I left him that night with a "Now you hang in there, my love. I will see you first thing in the morning."

Hara Ra's Suspension

On the morning of Thursday, October 13, 2005, Hara Ra was hoisted onto a gurney and wheeled out of the ICU into an ambulance, which took us swiftly to Watsonville airport. A small plane stood ready to take us to Scottsdale, Arizona. At each transfer the men were grunting and heaving to get the unwieldy gurney with his heavy body moved into place, his body being shaken around violently. In the very small space right behind my seat, two medical personnel sat by his side taking turns keeping his ventilation going by hand pump for the hours it took to get to Arizona. I sat with the pilot in the cockpit.

Once in Scottsdale, I called Alcor to announce our arrival, only to find out that they had just finished another unexpected suspension and were not ready for the next one. Their instruments needed a day to get sterilized! I was furious and shouted, "What do you mean? I bring him all the way here and you are not ready?

He is not going to make it through the night. I am taking him to the hospice near you and you better get ready fast!"

It was about four in the afternoon when we were welcomed at the hospice. He was moved onto a bed, and we finally had some space to relax. He looked physically very stressed but otherwise peaceful. I sat by him and we talked, or rather I talked with him. Off and on I would check in with Alcor and was assured that they were getting their transport truck, which was fully equipped to accomplish the first part of the procedure, ready. They were expecting to have the truck in the hospice parking lot by evening.

In the past, we had considered that his suspension would happen quite a bit sooner than mine, his health already being poor. Since technology advances by leaps and bounds, my resuscitation in the distant future was also more likely to happen before his. When I thought about the possibility that his might not be feasible, I arranged with Alcor to preserve his DNA separately. I was imagining that with as yet unimaginable medical technology, I might then be able to conceive of him. When I told Hara Ra that Alcor was almost ready, I said, "Alcor will also preserve your DNA. If I am revived before you and for some reason, your resuscitation is not feasible, I will try to grow us a little Gregory!" A big tear of gratitude pooled in the corner of his eye. Gregory had been his given name.

The night before I had called Jesse, a fine and brilliant young man who had come under Hara Ra's mentorship during a difficult time with his mental health when he was just a teen, and with whom I had also done a number of healing sessions. I had given Jesse an update on Hara Ra's condition. First thing in the morning he had tossed a bag in his car and driven non-stop from

Dallas to Scottsdale and made it just in time. He came to Hara Ra's side and let him know he was there.

Alcor personnel finally arrived with their truck. They wheeled an ice bath mounted on a gurney next to his bed. Everything was ready.

Shortly after that, the nurse announced that Hara Ra was close to death. Everyone stepped out of the room to give us privacy during his last moments. Jesse stood by the foot end of his bed, and I was by his side. I kissed him goodbye and said softly, "Everything is ready, my love, you can go now... No more suffering..." A breath, a pause, a small breath and then silence... The nurse came back in and confirmed his death. Immediately, the room filled with a whirlwind of personnel. We all heaved his body into the ice bath. I had grabbed his feet. Some of his decaying skin came off on my hands. Ice bags were quickly placed all around him. I had a last glimpse of his dear face as an ice bag was unceremoniously tossed upon it. I could not help chuckling inside. No sentimental ceremony here. Time was of the essence. We were doing exactly what he had wanted. They got a heart pump going to ensure the circulation of the meds through his brain and literally ran him out of the building to the awaiting truck.

After all that commotion, I closed the door and turned to face the silent room and the empty bed. I felt an enormous energy in the room. As in a trance, I approached the bed and laid down on it. Right away I felt the colossal pressure of him bearing down on me. All I could do was to spread my arms and lie there, flattened out, and accept him.

When Jesse and I finally sat together, he shared with me that he had seen Hara Ra leaving his body in a radiance of colors bursting from his forehead like a golden sun streaked with orange and blue. Then Jesse had felt a great force entering his body and heard Hara Ra's voice, "Here are the emanations. Take them while they are fresh!" We both burst out laughing. It was so exactly like what Hara Ra would have said, ever down to earth and practical. He used to imagine that there would be several of him in the far future and he liked to call those "emanations" of himself.

When we stepped out into the night, I was struck by the quiet splendor of the full moon. Jesse drove us to a local hotel for a well-deserved night of sleep.

The next morning, we stopped by Alcor. We were told that his suspension had gone remarkably well. They had used a new medical cocktail to prevent cell damage during the gradual lowering of the temperatures to minus 320°F, the temperature of liquid nitrogen. Small sensors had been placed on the inside of his skull and no cracking was heard. In the past, they used to hear the cracking of cells as they were lowering the temperature. This would of course imply damage. Not hearing any cracking had never happened before. It was the most successful suspension to date. Everybody was elated with the success.

My Obituary for Hara Ra

Most of us knew him as Hara Ra. He was born as Gregory Yob on June 18, 1945. He left his body and was cryonically suspended on October 13, 2005.

After five days in diabetic coma at the ICU in Santa Cruz, California, with the help of his good friend Ken Weiss, I managed to have him airlifted to a hospice near Alcor in Scottsdale, Arizona, where he died that evening. Alcor was present and started preparations immediately. His dear body was swiftly moved into the ice bath and wheeled to the truck within minutes. It seems to have been the best suspension performed to that date. New advanced chemistry was used, and no cracking was observed during cool-down except for some small ones toward the very end.

The promise, even if infinitesimally small, of cryonics to transport him into a future where he might be repaired from the emotional and psychological damage he experienced during his childhood, is what gave him hope and vision for a future in which he might experience life and love to the full human potential.

His was such a potent spirit with a far-seeing eye. He truly was a Future Man, a fine artist and a visionary. Under the grumpy exterior, which sooner or later almost everyone who knew him would bump into, lived a brilliant mind, a compassionate heart and a delightful childlike playfulness.

In his early twenties, he experienced a spontaneous Satori, a sudden state of awakening. He became an integral part of the natural coherence of everything, which lasted for three days solid. It gave him a foundation for the pursuit of Zen and for non-ordinary states of mind.

Hara Ra's favorite poet was Cold Mountain who lived in seventh-century China. He deeply identified with him. This must have been his favorite verse:

For the hundred years of human life
the Buddha preached a twelvefold canon
but compassion is like a wild deer
and anger is like the family dog

you can't drive the dog away
the deer meanwhile prefers to run
to tame your monkey mind
listen to the lion's roar.

He was the creator of the very first computer game, *Hunt the Wumpus*. He designed interactive computer art of ever-changing mandalas, called the Fool, intended to entrance the player into altered states of consciousness. He also invented the concept and application of Comfort House, a place entirely wired to sense the visitor's emotional states and physical movements and to respond in kind, intending to evoke in the visitor the spontaneous experience of harmony and of feeling connected with the universe around him.

Expecting future scientific leaps, he wrote *The Anatomy of the Electric Creation*, in which he imagined a seamless interface between human and machine with the possibility of creating and experiencing infinite realities and expanding consciousness to actualize a global mind.

Out of the sheer necessity of his own suffering and with great determination, he pursued to understand and heal his condition. No psychiatric evaluations really fit him, until he came across LSD Psychotherapy by Stanislav Groff, MD. He subsequently worked with some of the finest psychiatrists in the land, exploring therapies with MDMA, LSD and Ketamine. He knew at the time that anaclitic work would be his best hope to heal the lack of bonding he suffered in infancy at the hand of his unfortunate mother. It was in his search for an anaclitic healer or therapist that he found me.

LSD became his ally. It was during an acid session that he received his shamanic initiation, lasered into him, across space and time, from a place deep in the Amazon. That's when he took his shamanic name, Hara Ra. The hara is the Japanese term for the second chakra, the creative center below the navel and Ra is the Egyptian Sun god. He would translate his name as "the Belly of the Sun." With a gleeful twinkle in his eye, he would call himself a Neo-Neuro-Cyber-Shaman.

Gregory definitely was an avowed scientific materialist. More than anything he wanted the truth, real, unmitigated, down to earth, about everything. At the same time, he had to accept the fact that he and others possessed unexplained psychic powers and abilities. He had a unique capacity to tune into a person's hidden processes and get to the core of things within minutes, often facilitating surprising breakthroughs. Having explored altered states of consciousness and experienced his own occult shamanic initiation as a psychic reality within himself, he knew there were realities for us to experience which did not fit the scientific model. He surmised that our psychic abilities to intuit and to experience the numinous and the unseen were the results of an evolutionary process in the software of our brains.

Cryonics was a centerpiece of hope and vision in his life. He was deeply engaged with the future possibilities for mankind and was determined to do whatever it took to be able to participate in it. One of the highlights of our relationship was when, on July 12, 2002, the Santa Cruz Sentinel published a very positive front-page article with a picture of us walking hand in hand into the future, entitled "Together forever: Local couple hopes to be frozen through cryonics and see the future."

It was our dream to be reunited in the future when both of us could be psychologically and physically restored and even enhanced for the fulfillment and enjoyment of our love for each other. His aspirations, however, went far beyond that. In his spirit, he saw himself as a guardian of the earth. He was extremely motivated to contribute in the future to humanity achieving world peace. For his personal satisfaction, he imagined having multiple manifestations of himself with at least one copy of him going off exploring the stars. He would joke about all of his many selves meeting at the Hard Rock Cafe at the end of time.

In the last few years of his life, he dedicated himself to establish a clinic in a country with more liberal and humane attitudes than the United States, for the realization of Vistasis, a facility which would offer legal arrangements for cryonic suspension by appointment, to avoid the injury of ischemia to the brain inherent in the natural dying process. It was in that context that he adopted his new name Gregory H. Coresun. H. for Herald, Bringer of Good Tidings, Coresun, as an adaptation to his shamanic name Hara Ra, the core of the sun.

See you in the Future, Love of my Life. Andrea

Together Forever

The man who stirs my womb is dead,
Yet so alive and present in his photograph.

Silently you smile at me.
Your kind and penetrating gaze
Touching my soul
Awakens my love.

On our soft lips linger
The long patient kisses
When we floated together
In the timeless space
Of non-doing

Just hanging there
As if suspended
In the sweetest dream.

Grieving

Jesse offered to drive me to LA the next day to visit with Dr. Bob and his wife Nancy. I was grateful to be with them, because of their friendship and appreciation for Hara Ra. It felt good to have a place to bring my grief. Full of empathy, Bob directed me to his little stash of marijuana and mushroom butter of which I gladly partook. I spent time in their garden walking a small labyrinth, grappling with Hara Ra's death and my loss. I attempted to surrender and imagined communicating with him all at the same time. My heart ached. I felt shredded.

I could not tolerate being sober and snuck into Bob's private stash over the next few days. I was too ashamed to ask him for more but was unable to leave well enough alone. My altered state made me behave in ways that later embarrassed me. One evening, one of Nancy's best friends came to visit. I was expecting to have space for my grieving process with them. Instead, they talked about all kinds of stuff and Nancy kept looking things up on the Internet. At some point, I could not stand it any longer and

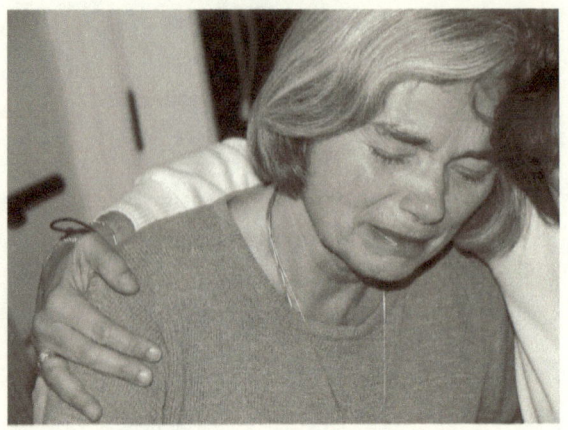
Grieving

blurted out, "Could you turn that laptop off, please?" They all looked shocked. It became an awkward situation. I went to bed that evening feeling quite confused and embarrassed.

Jesse drove me back the six hours to Santa Cruz. Together we entered Hara Ra's house. I had not been there since I had found him comatose some ten days before. We got all the bedding washed, dishes done and trash taken out, and created a semblance of a home. The roof in the living room was leaking. He had constructed a dripping system with a rope coming down into a bucket. Mildew was blooming on the ceiling. The kitchen sink was barely draining, and half of the house was without electricity. In a moment of sheer disgust and fury, I took a marker pen and wrote in large graffiti on the wall *warthog burrow*. Jesse and I had a good laugh.

Then life alone began. I found Hara Ra's will. It turned out that I was sole heir and executrix of his estate. Even as I felt extremely alienated in the home where I was still renting rooms, since I knew my marijuana use was barely tolerated, I could also not imagine living in that shabby, run-down, overstuffed house that was now mine. When Hara Ra and I had discussed the matter, expecting full well that I would outlive him, I always urged him to start getting rid of stuff. He had simply waved away my concern. "You won't need to bother with all that stuff," he'd say glibly. "Just sell the house as is with everything in it. It'll be torn down anyway and that'll be the end of it." I never really trusted that scenario.

Feeling quite lost, I would walk along the ocean on West Cliff in Santa Cruz, bawling my eyes out and shaking my fists at him, despairing. After one such walk, I returned to his house and sat quietly on the back deck, where we had so often visited one another. In the silence, I realized my refuge was right there. Without this house, I had nothing. Owning a little home on the West side of Santa Cruz within walking distance from the ocean was nothing to scoff at.

I decided to move in and make the best of it. I asked Pancho, a handyman from Mexico whom I had known from the time I lived in Larkin Valley, to start emptying out the garage and the house. He and his son hauled off at least five truckloads full to the dump. They took home many carloads of equipment and tools in trade for some of their work.

One of Hara Ra's computer geek friends came and spent a week cleaning out his office, the boxes and the closet, and left me with just one computer and a printer. I felt a bit conflicted since I knew the man was a pathological hoarder, but he was happy to take off with several carloads full.

It was good to sleep in Hara Ra's bed. Often, I felt him sitting kindly and quietly by my side, so much love between us. It was a relief to no longer be subject to the limitations of his personality. It seemed that finally we could just totally and completely love one another and be together. Our unexpected closeness was a great comfort to me. During the day I would see him everywhere. In the rocks by the ocean, a bird flying overhead or a butterfly dancing into the yard.

One afternoon, I was soaking in his hot tub; I had a strong sense of his presence. Because I was now stoned most of the time, I did not trust my perceptions. The moment I asked him if it was true, if he was really there, the hot tub motor kicked in with a bang. It was set to turn on in the evening and never came on in the daytime. It felt like a clear confirmation that he was indeed present.

Then one morning, I had a terrifying experience about the horror we had shared in our past lives. Never had I felt that Hara Ra and I knew each other before. With a number of significant people in my life I have had the sense of a shared past lifetime, sometimes with particularly vivid glimpses of memory. I had been somewhat puzzled how this strange man had appeared in my life as such a strong presence. I did have a recurring vision of seeing him as a powerful polar bear at the peak of his strength running over the ice, his golden-white fleece waving around his massive body. He fell into a deep crevasse in the ice and fought with all his might, attempting to melt the ice with his considerable body heat, to no avail. That's where he perished.

He himself felt a strong association with Cold Mountain, the Chinese hermit poet, who wandered the mountains scribbling his poems on the rocks, only once in a while to appear in some remote monastery.

Three gods in one

That morning I woke up and went into the kitchen to make myself some tea… There he was. Larger than life. He stood across from me in the exact pose and appearance of a stone statue he had owned that combines the figures of Krishna, Ganesh and Hanuman. The figure stands in the typical Krishna dancing pose one foot lightly placed in front of the other. It has Ganesh's ample belly and trunk and the heavy brow of Hanuman, monkey god, servant of Ram. There he stood. His sudden presence took my breath away. "Oh my god, there you are," I stammered. We stood there for a while in silence.

Suddenly, terror strikes me. I flee back through the house, through the bedroom to the outside. I'm panting with sheer terror. Before going outside, I sit down on the bed, my heart pounding. I make the decision to follow the fear. I must understand.

I see us in a cherry blossom garden of the imperial palace in ancient China. I am standing upright, brave, a fragile, elegant figure teetering on small feet, a basket with my newborn infant by my side. He is head of the imperial guard at the peak of his power and stands across from me in front of the garden wall. I am a high-ranking personal attendant and friend to the mother empress. I was married to one of the guards. I had given birth to an illegitimate child. Tradition required that the child be killed in front of me, and I beheaded. It was his duty to perform the gruesome task. We silently gaze at each other, facing our unavoidable fate. Behind his severe demeanor, I feel his great compassion and admiration for me. His heart is breaking. With one swift move he cuts the infant in half and almost with the same stroke severs my head from my body, skillfully saving me as much pain as possible. He leaves the palace and disappears into the mountains never to be seen again. There he roams and eventually perishes in the snow and ice.

In that moment, I came to understand so much: His bitterness, his power, his isolation, the depth of his love, his acute refusal to follow anyone's orders, his complete self-determination, and his great dedication to understanding the human condition, especially violence. I understood my great love and respect for him, and the deep-seated fear and awe which would sometimes arise in me and which hit me that morning like an avalanche. I also understood why we had not been allowed any glimpses into our shared past. The horror was too great. It took me quite some time to settle down.

Through the months that followed, I continued to feel very close to him. Six months into my grieving, I felt a shift, a certain distancing, as if he had ascended to another level. Exactly a year after his passing there was a distinct detachment, a spaciousness, a sense that he was moving into the light beyond my reach. I understood it as the natural course of things and was at peace. I was grateful he had lingered with me for this long.

❀

Anandaloka ~ House of Bliss

I am in the house of my love.
In the deep security of being
the beloved in my own sweet form
I recline in your warm embrace
and smile in quiet bliss.

The journey home seemed endless.
Sometimes I despaired
I thought I was lost
wandering, often running
through the interminable
dark woods of my childhood
through the wreckage of the Great War
and its dreadful aftermath.

With great determination
my little self has been fluttering
up against the bars
of the unseen self-erected cage
always trying to find a way out.
My wings are worn and tattered
My mind and body exhausted
From the myriad attempts at freedom.

You had to die to give me life.
Now in your eternal presence
Your dear blessed head pressing

Tenderly between my breasts
We belong, you and I, and
give each other a home of love.

My heart is your home
Your home is my place,
this humble little home
you gave me in your death.
All are welcome here
who are of good will.

Spiraling Down

During 2006—I am sixty-four by now—in the depth of my grief and misery, and being stoned most of the time, I did manage to have the house remodeled while I lived in the bedroom. How that hovel got transformed into a little jewel of a home is still astonishing to me. I had come across a young contractor with an interest in design and the kindness to work patiently with me to get things just the way I liked them, no matter how disturbed I often was.

My daughter Tara, who by then was thirty years old, had quite a strained relationship with me since the debacle with Maurice. No matter how hard I had tried to make my amends to her, there was a painful distance between us that we couldn't seem to bridge. She would rarely spend any time with me, and I easily felt rejected. I couldn't accept that our mother-daughter bond could not be healed. She did not want to talk about anything anymore, because, as she stated to me, that didn't work.

She came home from Vermont that Christmas. Since it was clear to me that neither of my girls liked being around me when I was stoned, I promised myself and them that I would stay sober over Christmas, no matter what.

One evening, Tara was visiting with me and had a dinner date with a friend, which fell through. I was looking forward to having some time with her. Next thing, she's on the phone trying to find other friends to go out with. She couldn't even stay with me for one dinner. My heart sank. I couldn't cope. I fled into the garden and took a toke. When I came back in, I had the courage to talk with her about my feelings, but at the same time, I felt terribly ashamed about having broken my promise.

Over the coming weeks, I spiraled down fast. My integrity was in ruins, and I felt exhausted to the bone, overwhelmed and profoundly depressed. Everything was too much for me. First thing every morning, I had to smoke. Tears would run down my face from the pain of the hot smoke burning my throat. I also had to smoke more and more to feel any effect.

Spiraling down

I finally decided I had to do something. I understood that my problem was in my mind. So, the brilliant solution I came up with was to drop a high dose of acid. Maybe that would give me the spiritual awakening I needed. I pulled out my stash and figured I would measure out 350mcg of the fine liquid acid I had inherited from Hara Ra.

I took a wild ride through space and time. I found myself in the year 2035, where I saw Carl Jung and Hara Ra together in Switzerland, concocting a homeopathic dose of LSD as the perfect remedy for me—this little slut in Amsterdam, alternately whore of Babylon. Seeing Hara Ra alive in the future, I thought he had been successfully revived from his cryonic suspension. Ecstatically, I exclaimed, "Oh my God! It worked! You came back!"

After hours of insanity, I was completely overwhelmed with the loudness and speed of everything happening in my delusions. It felt as if three megaphones were simultaneously blasting in my mind, and I was unable to turn it down. I became desperate for silence.

I thought that if only I could submerge under water, everything would finally be still. So, I decided to drown myself in the hot tub. I called a couple of friends, Dr. Bob in LA and a friend in Menlo Park, to tell them what my plan was, to reassure them that it was the right thing for me to do. Of course, neither one of them agreed with me, but there was nothing they could say to deter me. As usual, I was completely convinced that I had the right answer.

I stepped fully clothed into my hot tub and went under. I hate getting water up my nose. I hadn't thought of that. The moment

I went under, I came up coughing and snorting, and went back into the house, deeply discouraged.

In the meantime, Dr. Bob managed to get a hold of Aurelia, who was thirty-two at the time and living in Santa Cruz. She jumped in the car with Paul, her fiancé, and came to my house. To this day I am dismayed at what she must have gone through on the way to my home, not knowing whether she would find me alive.

They spent hours with me, while I was spewing a never-ending stream of nonsense. Since my father's grandfather had been the director of the Dutch Bank in the West Indies, I was convinced that there was a vast fortune for me in Holland and I was as rich as the Queen. The least I would do was buy them a fantastic house. At some point, I noticed an old friend of the family had arrived, a therapist. It was late in the evening. She asked me what time I had dropped the acid. I told her, "10 a.m." I wasn't coming down. After more hours passed, when I finally did quiet down some, I wanted to get more acid, convinced that it was exactly what I needed. Aurelia stood like a mountain. I couldn't get past her.

Around 2:30 a.m., Aurelia suggested we go for a walk. "Sure," I said, "that sounds great." No sooner were we outside, when I heard her click open the doors to her car and she said, "Let's go for a drive." Paul drove and she and I got in the backseat together. I felt like a little kid. We were driving in the middle of the night through the silent streets. "Are we going to the movies?" I giggled. When I noticed we were driving on the freeway and realized they were taking me to the emergency room, I hollered, "Turn around! Don't take me there!" Paul didn't say a word and kept driving. Then Aurelia got on her cell phone with the emergency room announcing our imminent arrival. I was startled to realize they were expecting us.

When I got out of the car, I saw two police officers standing by the entrance. Something in me collapsed. I couldn't imagine making a scene in public right there in front of the emergency room. I became meek like a lamb and followed my daughter into the waiting area. Unbeknownst to me, Aurelia, who had enough of my drug use, had brought my entire stash with her. When she placed the little box on the counter, a cop took one look at it and said, "That's three felonies right there!" He looked over at me, a meek, gray-haired, exhausted old lady looking like a drowned cat and just shook his head. Fortunately, nothing came of it.

In the early morning, I was wheeled over to the Behavioral Health Unit—the mental ward—and placed under a three-day hold because of my threatened suicide. I was grateful for a safe place to rest my exhausted body and mind. A psychiatrist came to see me once. To my surprise, he asked me if I wanted to overthrow the government. I must have expressed some of my rebellion against the state of affairs in America during my delusions.

Apparently, he had spoken with both of my daughters and asked them if they thought I might be bipolar. He suggested that I start on a mild dose of medication. Certainly, addiction had made my moods quite volatile and I often swung between ecstasy and misery, but I didn't think I was bipolar. However, in my state of meekness, I agreed.

On the last day of my stay in the hospital, Aurelia organized an intervention. A small group of my best friends met with me in a room in the hospital with Tara on speakerphone from Vermont. Aurelia told me she had found a high-quality rehab clinic in Santa

Cruz and that they had a bed for me. Would I be willing to go? "Yes," I said. I didn't know anymore what to do with myself. I knew I needed help.

The next morning, January 21, 2007, Aurelia came to pick me up. We went to my house first to remove all of my various stashes and paraphernalia, and then to gather the various things I thought I might need. Then she drove me to Janus, the twenty-eight-day residential rehab clinic. I chose that day as my recovery date since the days in the hospital were not of my volition. And so, a new part of my life began.

Part VI

Recovery

Rehab

On meeting with the director and a few counselors for my intake, one of my first remarks seemed to surprise them. I said, chuckling, "I certainly never expected to find myself among the drunks and addicts of Santa Cruz!" I did not understand the looks they gave each other. Later, I realized both my ignorance and my arrogance. Almost everyone working in a rehab setting is in recovery themselves.

Then they wanted to see what I had brought with me. I put an assortment of teas and supplements on the table. Again, they seemed surprised. No, I could not bring all of that, they said. After arguing for one or two of my favorite teas and for a few supplements I thought were essential for my health, they allowed me to keep some. These would be kept under lock and key in the office.

Even though I had already detoxed for three days in the hospital, they suggested another three days of detox before beginning the program. At the end of those days, I could decide if I wanted to make the commitment to the twenty-eight-day program. The tab at the time was $6,000. Fortunately, I still had enough from Hara Ra's inheritance that I could afford treatment.

I was offered a small dark room with a single bed. Together with a few other newcomers, we received daily instruction about the nature of addiction so we could verify for ourselves if that indeed applied to us. Everything I heard was true for me. I had lost all control over my marijuana use. I couldn't stop. I had to have it, no matter what. I always had a good reason to use. My use had become more important than anything else. I had become terribly isolated. It had made my life completely unmanageable. As I was listening to these teachings, I proved to myself "beyond the shadow of a doubt" that I had indeed become an addict.

I also understood why they called addiction a disease and not a moral defect. I realized how much addiction completely undermines your common sense and your ability to control yourself, putting you in a state of helpless bondage to your compulsion. It really is a disease of body, mind and spirit. Marijuana had become my everything—my Higher Power, if you will—and I was its slave. My body couldn't handle it anymore, my mind couldn't give it up, and I felt as if I had lost my soul. I understood that I was not responsible for having become an addict—no one decides to become an addict. However, I was now responsible for my recovery.

While gaining these insights, I realized that these people actually had a solution for my problem. This gave me hope that I could be freed from my insane obsession. All I needed to do was listen and be willing to take direction. I understood the main directive in recovery was to find a power greater than myself because I had truly lost the ability to overcome my difficulties on my own. Since I had no more answers, I clung to this glimmer of hope as the drowning cling to a life raft. Later, I would hear one of the numerous acronyms to help people deal with that difficult "God" word: *Gift of Desperation*. I had definitely been "blessed" with that gift.

The staff seemed surprised when I decided to stay for the twenty-eight-day program. I joined the group for the morning session and people began to share. Here were serious alcoholics, meth and heroin addicts—people I had never known or been around. I looked and listened and realized that I was safe. These men and women were suffering just as I was. There was no more room for any pretense. We could all be real since we had no social personas or egos to uphold. We all knew why we were there. Every one of us was on a downward spiral to hell and in desperate need of help.

I was assigned to counselor Rhonda, a tall slender woman with long straight auburn hair coming down to her waist. She asked me to write an acceptance letter, to describe how I knew I had a disease. I did. Amongst the many insane and embarrassing behaviors I was beginning to recognize, I described how my compulsive use had ruined my precious relationship with Hara Ra who was now dead. Rhonda asked me to read it out loud to the group. It was a rather emotional experience for me. Later I heard that there hadn't been a dry eye in the house. Previously, the group had scoffed a bit incredulously at my being in rehab for "just" marijuana addiction. I was now fully accepted as one of them.

I was moved to room with another woman. The whole place was rather funky. The outdoors where we could hang out during breaks consisted of a relatively small parking lot with a couple of picnic tables, surrounded by some trees. Large coffee cans served as ashtrays for the smokers—a majority among us. All through the day we were on a strict schedule with set times for waking up, meditation, breakfast, clean up, etc. At 3 p.m. a supervisor would accompany us for a daily walk to the nearby beach. Group sessions and meetings were held every morning, afternoon and evening. In between, we got to see our counselor and complete our writing assignments.

One of my assignments was to make a list of all psycho-active materials I had used and the frequency with which I had used them. I think there were twenty-three different substances on my list, and on estimating the frequency of the use of each one, it came out to be many more than I had been telling myself. At the top of the list was marijuana, combined with daily use of one Vicodin for pain killer and a lorazepam to help me sleep. Interestingly, since I knew Vicodin was addictive, I never used more than one a day. I had not believed marijuana was addictive and so had happily indulged until it was too late.

I had noticed two large banners, one with the Twelve Steps and the other with the Twelve Traditions of AA, displayed on the wall in our communal living room. Being quite averse to rules, I hadn't even felt like reading the Twelve Traditions. One day, after my mind had cleared enough, I was drawn to read them carefully. Imagine my surprise. I was profoundly impressed with the wisdom of these "traditions" to prevent any kind of authoritarianism to develop in AA (Alcoholics Anonymous). Having lived in a community, I knew that large egos were always a problem in any kind of organization. One of the traditions reads, "Our leaders are but trusted servants; they do not govern."

Members of recovery fellowships, like AA, NA (Narcotics Anonymous) and CA (Cocaine Anonymous) bring meetings and literature to hospitals and institutions to share their experiences of when they were in their addiction, what happened to create the turn-around and how their lives had improved through the Twelve-Step recovery. These visits were the highlights of our week. Here were people who had suffered just as we did. Clearly, they were just fine. They had recovered from their addictions by working the Twelve Steps with a sponsor, going to meetings regularly and doing service. I was particularly touched by the ones who had found a deep spiritual connection and were learning to practice surrender. It's what I had so much wanted to accomplish ever since I had seen Mother, now some thirty-five years ago.

One of the suggestions on how to listen to people was to listen for the similarities, so we would identify with them, rather than the usual cultural habit of focusing on our differences.

During one of these meetings, a young woman came to share her story. She was covered in tattoos, with a mop of bleached hair and numerous piercings. I wondered what I could possibly have in common with her. She described having been in and out of prison numerous times. She told us that when she stood before the judge for the eighth time, she suddenly heard a voice inside of her saying, "Stop fighting." That is when her recovery started. Her words hit me like lightning. I became acutely aware of how, on some deep level inside of me, I had always been defending myself. I, too, needed to let my guard down and stop fighting. I felt a wave of deep relaxation flowing down my back as all my cells settled down into a new place of trust.

On Sundays we were allowed to have visitors. When Aurelia came to see me, walking up and down the parking lot, she confronted me about my use of psychedelics. I felt a great deal of resistance to include them in my commitment to abstain from drugs and alcohol. I was convinced they were not addictive and avoiding them would affect my work with clients. She insisted. After she left, I took a good look at my habits and realized that my use of psychedelic materials was completely intertwined with my pot use. I already understood that my only chance at recovery was my complete and ruthless honesty. It was difficult to let go of what I considered to be my sacred work as well as my identity as a Medicine Woman, but I realized it had to be done.

One of the shocking things we were told is that, according to statistics, only 5–10% of us would be able to stay sober in the long run. I looked around and was deeply worried for everyone, but I could not imagine that would happen to me. Then, a man was admitted who had been sober for nine years and relapsed. He was smart, well-educated and had taken his recovery very seriously. He had been greatly involved with the program and had even taken numbers of sponsees through the steps. After several years, he believed he was fine and had moved away from the program. Here he was, back in rehab. I recognized myself in him. In fact, I figured that I would be an enthusiastic participant for about six months and then I would surely feel that I had things under control. After all, I am smart and motivated, right? Seeing him scared me good!

Throughout my time at the clinic, I was an emotional mess. Often, I could not sleep, or I'd wake up in the middle of the night, restless. So much for marijuana not being addictive. Clearly, my brain chemistry was out of wack. I was in complete upheaval. One day, Rhonda spotted me, crying. When she asked me what was going on, I described my distress. She said, "Just sit with it. This too shall pass." Clearly, there was nothing else to do. So I sat on an outcropping bulge on one of the trees surrounding the parking lot with my feelings. Slowly, I calmed down. During my first year in recovery, I would learn the power of acceptance, again and again.

After two weeks of seclusion, we were driven to a variety of Twelve-Step meetings. One of the main reasons why the anonymous recovery programs work so well is because they help you become an integral part of a community you can reach out to for support. We were directed to take phone numbers from members in these meetings and then call them the next day. Most of us believed that we were different, that we didn't belong and that we were basically on our own. We felt uncomfortable asking for help. But, we were told that people in recovery loved to hear from us, that supporting newcomers helped them to stay sober.

So, one morning, in deep distress, I called a woman whose phone number I had collected. I cried and blubbered into her ears for what seemed a long time. She listened and had all kinds of good suggestions. At the end, she said, "You have no idea how helpful your call has been for me!" Really? I thought, surprised. Apparently, what we had been told was true.

In the last week of my stay, Rhonda, aware of how deeply troubled I kept being, told me to write an essay about what my upcoming life could be, free from addiction. This assignment was a brilliant suggestion. It took me out of the miserable merry-go-round in my mind and into imagining my future full of clarity, creativity and peace of mind. I also needed to create a plan for my recovery before graduating. I created a list of meetings I intended to go to and stated my plan to get a sponsor and start working my steps. I already had a list of people I could call if I needed support.

During my last day at the center, I felt quite terrified about going home. Again, Rhonda spotted me and called me in. Realizing that my future-tripping was creating all that fear, she suggested, "Why don't you meditate this evening and bring yourself completely into the present." That evening, in the midst of everyone milling around, I sat down with my notebook and talked myself into silence. This is what I wrote:

Remember this moment is the gift
right here, right now.
Remember you are a child of the Mother and She provides.

Then I remembered what Mother had told us and I wrote:

This is what She told me:
"Be simple, be happy,
do the best you can
and leave the rest to the Divine."
Let go and breathe…
Trust the wisdom that surrounds you.
You only need to show up today,
right here, right now,
this breath,
trust,
relax,
surrender…

In the silence that followed, I heard a clear voice behind me to my left, "*I am here.*" It was life-changing. I was ready for my graduation the next morning, and my return home.

❀

Through the Dark Night

Lifetimes of turning around the ancient tower
of searching for a Father God—
finding Her in my own true self
the great benevolent Mother of Life.
Turning to Her again and again
she is the lifeline to my soul
her photograph inviting me
Again and again to gaze
Ever more deeply in myself.

For decades I kindled the ardent flame
to become like Her.
I did not really know how to accomplish
this mysterious surrender thing.

Exploring psychedelic states
I entered the Heart of God
dissolved into the Elysian Fields
of indescribable delight.
I drank from the cup of bliss unalloyed
And thought I had found the answer—

Until I slowly, inexorably plummeted
into the dark of night
my natural energy wasted
my brain chemistry depleted,
my sense of being in the world distorted.
My isolation became
my private prison cell
an underground bunker without exit.
My mind battling with a fury

against its own windmills
until I collapsed.
I overdosed on acid
And after a day and night of sheer insanity
my daughter came to the rescue.
Via the emergency room,
a three day hold in a Behavioral Health Unit,
I landed in rehab
soul-dead,
a little puddle on the floor.
No answers left.

Through that dark and downward spiral,
my ego crushed
my sense of self destroyed, I found
a strange and motley crew
of sufferers like me
who wove a net of humble love,
tolerance and honesty around me.
It was there, at the bottom of the well,
that I found myself belonging with mankind.
No longer striving to be like Her
the Great Divine Mother
or fretting that I was not good enough
but learning to be just one
small creature amongst many
opening my heart to whoever
comes straggling through our doors
having lost all
and finding hope and love and
a shared humility in simply being
of service to one another.

No teachers, no doctrine, no rules.
No great enlightenment to attain.
Just being, simple, small, kind, me
With you.

The 12 Steps

During one of the last days of my stay in rehab, someone mentioned a 7 a.m. daily AA meeting downtown, called Sought Through Prayer. At the very moment I heard of that meeting, it hit me like I got punched in the stomach. I knew instantly that I needed to go there after my release. Some anger flashed through me at the idea of having to get up that early every morning. But, the direction I received at that moment was unmistakable. The meeting's name refers to the eleventh step: *Sought through prayer and meditation to improve our conscious contact with God, as we understood Him, praying only for knowledge of His will for us and the power to carry that out.*

So, after my return home, I made it a habit to be at STP every morning at 7 a.m. It started my day with much-needed structure. STP was a large meeting with some sixty people, men and women, young and old, gathered in the community hall of Calvary Church, in downtown Santa Cruz. Every meeting had a secretary. The position was rotated every six months, so no one gets to feel they "own" the meeting. The secretary would open the meeting, read the preamble and various suggestions. The most significant suggestion was that each person would have three minutes to share and we were "to refrain from giving advice or directing comments to any individual at meeting level." This format created a remarkable sense of safety. You would have a chance to speak without being interrupted or having to worry about people's reactions. I learned to listen very attentively to each person, my mind open to being taught, while holding back on comments. Just sitting quietly, listening and watching the meeting unfold became like a morning meditation. Nothing was expected of me. I could just sit and be still and open. Over time it helped me to quiet my mind and become peaceful.

Then there is the fascinating tradition of anonymity. Over the years in recovery, I realized how brilliant that suggestion is. The moment you step into a meeting, you leave your last name and any social status at the door. In the room, everyone is equal, there to save our lives and our sanity. When you come into the rooms of AA, you have not much ego left to stand on, anyway. Humility and tolerance are two central guidelines.

In the midst of a society where we need to assert our identity and stand out in one way or another and therefore tend to compare ourselves, AA offers the remarkable suggestion to focus on the similarities between us rather than the differences. It shifts your gaze. In fact, between my daily experience in the AA meeting and working the steps, I found the relief of not needing to be a significant *anybody*, of letting go of my identity, of just becoming one among many.

Pretty soon, to my amazement, I realized that the Twelve Steps would possibly guide me to the surrender I had aspired to ever since I met Mother in 1972. Regardless of the intensity and sincerity of my desire to live only by and for the Divine, I had never been able to accomplish anything remotely resembling surrender. How *do* you surrender your ego, had been my puzzled question. Yes, there had been all kinds of spiritual experiences and inspiring literature, but I did not seem able to change myself. Now, in AA, I found twelve specific steps I could take, one at a time, to hopefully accomplish exactly that.

It begins with Step One, *We admitted we were powerless over alcohol* [marijuana in my case] *and that our lives had become unmanageable.* Over time, I came to be grateful that I had become addicted because I would never have experienced my powerlessness so viscerally otherwise. I am smart and tend to be quite competent. Since I grew up without people to turn to, I had no idea I could ask for help and had become very self-sufficient. Accepting powerlessness—what a perfect beginning to become willing to surrender to That which is greater than I.

Step Three says, *Made a decision to turn our will and our lives over to the care of God as we understood Him.* Here was a point of choice on how to apply my will. I remembered how the right use of the will is central to Sri Aurobindo's Integral Yoga. From *The Twelve Steps* and *Twelve Traditions*, I quote, "Our whole trouble had been the misuse of willpower. We had tried to bombard our problems with it instead of attempting to bring it into agreement with God's intention for us." I knew I had done exactly that and with a vengeance.

To my great relief, the clause *as we understood Him* removed dogma and definition out of the God idea. It still had a masculine pronoun, but I understood the limitations in consciousness around the time that AA originated. It was in the 1930s when Christianity was still dominating the culture and the notion that the Divine could be any other than *He* was likely inconceivable at the time.

Bill Wilson and Dr. Bob Smith, AA's founders, both hopeless alcoholics, turned for help and inspiration to various Christian scholars and mystics. The wisdom to be found in Christianity does pervade AA's literature and tends to lead to the misperception that AA is a Christian path. It certainly can be, if that is your path, but this particular clause and a careful reading of Bill's prolific writing on how AA needed to be open to everyone, even to the atheist, assured me of the open-mindedness of the program. After leaving the Catholic Church at eighteen, I had become quite allergic to Christianity and its righteousness about being the only path.

Bill Wilson was able to get sober after he had a massive spiritual experience when he was utterly hopeless and doctors had given up on him. He was about to be institutionalized. It proved to be a life-changing event and he never drank again. After an American alcoholic had been treated by Carl Jung for a full year and relapsed shortly after his return to the States, Bill wrote to Jung, who responded with a letter explaining that, "His craving for alcohol was the equivalent on a low level of the spiritual thirst of our being for wholeness, expressed in medieval language: the union with God." Jung's letter confirmed to Bill Wilson the need for a spiritual conversion for most alcoholics (addicts) to have a chance at recovering from the hopeless disease of alcoholism (alcoholism = addiction).

Many of us in meetings struggle with the loaded word *God*. People try to make it palatable by inventing rather creative acronyms. Some of my favorites are the *Gift of Desperation* and *Group of Drunks*. This reminds me of the frivolity and hearty laughter that often explodes in a meeting. It can puzzle the visitor, but we have found such immense relief from our suffering that we cannot help but laugh at ourselves and make fun of who we were when we were in our disease.

In most recovery meetings the Serenity Prayer is recited by the group:

> God, grant me the serenity to accept the things I cannot change, the courage to change the things I can and the wisdom to know the difference.

Every time I joined in this collective prayer, I found myself carefully reflecting on its meaning. I would invariably realize that the only thing I could change is my attitude, my thinking and my reaction to things. It began to steadily undermine my need to try and change others or change any situations I did not particularly like.

I heard people talk about acceptance on a daily basis. I had never considered acceptance particularly desirable. Don't I want to change and better myself, you, and the world? But willing as I was to do whatever it would take to keep me sober, I accepted the suggestion. I began to practice acceptance in all things great and small. I remember when I went to be with my mother for her final days and had to be on the long flight to Holland, rather than trying to alter my state as I had done before, I practiced accepting everything—the long lines, the waiting, the hassle with luggage, and the many hours sitting in a tight space. To my surprise, I found that I remained completely relaxed and was even able to enjoy the whole experience.

In fact, I believe that acceptance is the single most significant and transformative spiritual principle I learned in AA. It changes everything.

I also heard frequently that if I had a problem, to give it to God and pray for it. It sounded a bit trite until I had a striking experience. During the first few months back home, I became aware that I woke up every morning feeling disgruntled, without any notable cause. I decided to give this a try. I sincerely prayed for relief. The next day, driving to my meeting in the morning fog, I realized the simple truth that the sun shone behind the clouds. It gave me some perspective. The following morning, I realized that my brain chemistry was still out of balance, which was only logical and would settle over time. It was nothing to worry about. A few days later, I realized I had forgotten all about it. I have not woken up disgruntled since!

I understood the importance of finding a sponsor to guide me through the steps. I would hear people laugh sometimes how they had such a terrible sponsor in the beginning: themselves. The suggestion is to find a person "who has what you want." I carefully looked around for a strong woman who seemed particularly grounded in her spirituality. I was drawn to Katie, a blonde, middle-aged woman who worked in sales. I loved her joy and often admired the clarity and conviction with which she expressed her faith and described how she dealt with life's problems. I asked her and she agreed. Katie wanted to see me once a week and, in between our visits, I was to work on the step I was on, one at a time.

It took me a full year of learning to be patient with myself and to be meticulous with my attention to every aspect of this transformative work. Every step offered a surprising experience. I particularly remember what it was like for me to do Step Four, *Made a searching and fearless moral inventory of ourselves.* Step Four frequently hampers people because it requires such honest self-examination.

Step Four's work format is presented in four columns. In the first column, you simply list everyone and everything you are or have been angry with. That part was easy. In the second column, you write what they did that hurt or angered you. In the third column, you list how their words or actions affected you. In the fourth column comes the most critical part of this exercise: What was my part in this difficulty? Having been raised with a generous amount of Catholic guilt, I thought, "Great, now I get to be guilty for the many ways in which I got hurt?" I was especially thinking of the times I was raped.

When I came to that question, I looked inside and asked myself what part I had in those painful events. I realized that I had come from a deep place of need for attention and affection because my father had been completely absent during my younger years. So, whatever men offered me, dinner out, a gift, anything, I was happy and eager to accept. Then I would find myself in dangerous situations where men were able to overpower me. I realized that "normal" girls might not have been so ready to fall for their seductive approaches. Rather than feeling guilty, this realization led me to have compassion with my young self. It turned out that every step created significant relief inside of me and a gradual letting go.

From my perspective, Step Seven, *Humbly asked Him to remove our shortcomings*, is at the heart of AA's spirituality. When I was ready for Step Seven, I felt confused and excited. How could my difficulties be removed? What kind of miracle was in store for me? When I brought my confusion to Katie, she smiled and said, "Read Step Seven slowly." And I read, "Humbly... asked..." Instantly, I understood that my changes would not be *my* doing. I did not have that kind of power, but I could humbly ask my higher power (whatever concept of the numinous resonated with me). I felt like the ground was pulled out from under my ego. My firm belief that I was alone and help was not available, was no longer true. It was a radical, life-changing moment. I became humble.

❀

Out of My Loneliness I Have Come

Out of my loneliness and the illusion of self,
having to prove my validity or a heart to defend,
I have come to the well in the center of the village.
The family of all to which I belong.

I have come to be with you
to hear your song and to sing my own.
We are learning to listen as
the mystery speaks
through each one of us.
At this new dawn, we recreate the garden.
We are learning to forgive the past.
We have realized that we cannot do it alone
And, there is no one in charge.

My voice like yours is small.
Humbly and sincerely, I bring my
tender heart, my aging body and
my joyous spirit into the circle.

My reward is your smile
and the knowing that you are
my sister and my brother,
my source of wisdom and delight.
We see each other and we care.

Our human family is returning to its roots
and evolving into a wholeness
we have never known.
Praise be to the smallest one of us.

Shame and Oblivion

At some point in this process, shame came fully into my awareness. I went to see one of my fine healers, Phil, and explained to
him how deeply rooted shame is inside of me as a result of my
father's history. The words had barely come out of my mouth
when I burst into tears and fell sobbing in his arms.

After I got on the table, Phil started running healing energy
through me. Suddenly, I saw my father. He was younger than
I remembered him, in his early forties, the age he would have
been right after the war. Phil asked me if there was anything I
wished to say to him. I looked around inside and simply said, "I
love you." It did not feel that meaningful because our love had
always been beyond dispute. But then I felt myself entering a
soft, young, sweet space and I heard my child-self whisper, ever
so gently, "I forgive you. I forgive you. I forgive you."

The depth and innocence of this forgiveness was beyond anything I could have imagined. In the weeks following, I felt ever so light and free. Just thinking about it made me smile.

Not long after this event, I participated in a healing workshop. We all laid down on the floor and were guided to enter our heart or soul center. This is the place behind the heart which Mother named the psychic being, the individuating part of our soul which participates in our evolution of consciousness throughout our lifetimes.

When we were asked to identify one particular aspect of our shadow-self that bothered us the most, I chose "obliviousness." Throughout my life, whenever I have become aware that in my words or actions, I have been oblivious to someone else's feelings and have made mindless comments that hurt them, I invariably have felt mortified and beat myself up for being so "stupid," "unconscious" and "unaware." I then wonder what's wrong with me, how I can possibly be so negligent, and when will I ever learn.

The guide suggested that we go inside and find the place in our bodies where this particular shadow has its home. I found that it lived in my neck, just where my neck joins my shoulders. The area felt dense and impacted. Her next suggestion was to make a connection between my heart and this shadow place. As soon as I imagined that and opened my heart to this place, I was flooded with compassion and understanding. Unable to process the terror I had faced as a young child, apparently, I had formed a shield to protect myself from the outside world. That shield took the form of obliviousness. It had made me a bit blind… I forgave myself and felt a deep relaxation throughout.

Love Swallows Me Whole

Living ever more vividly
surrounded by my loved ones
who have already transcended,
I savor a love that surpasses
all tribulations big and small
of life on earth.

Even those gaping wounds from the past
are healing and dissolve
in the warm glow of this love.
I release my clinging and see
these are just ripples in the pond.

When I dive into the waters of life
I swim with the fishes and I am free.
No more up or down
the good and bad dissolve
like mirages
in the ocean of love
one with all
nothing left to defend.

My little heart opens in innocence.
Without walls of protection
there is nowhere to strike.

Love swallows me whole.

Through the Veil

Towards the end of my stay in the rehab facility, an alcoholic named Chris had come in for detox. I had never seen such a run-down man. He looked like human refuse, so miserable and forlorn. Just seeing him made me sick to my soul. I talked with one of the counselors about him. I was told that they all really liked Chris and that he was a very good man who suffered from post-traumatic stress disorder from his years as a firefighter. He had been through their program several times before and had great difficulty staying sober. I got the impression that he was considered a "hopeless alcoholic." During my last week there, I came to know him as a dear heart, a deeply caring human being.

Shortly after my graduation from the program, I returned to Janus for an AA meeting. Afterwards, I saw Chris standing by himself in the parking lot, looking quite forlorn and distressed, talking on his cell phone. I went over to him to say hi and we talked for a bit. Nothing was going right for him. He was having no luck getting into a sober living environment where addicts and alcoholics can try to get back on their feet with the support of other recovering folk. So, he was going to be living on the street again.

I gave him my phone number to call if he needed some support and wrote down his. After I left him, I drove into town for a bagel. I picked up a copy of the free local paper and in it, I spotted this quote by Hafiz, "Ever since love heard your name, it has been running through the streets trying to find you." I wrote the quote on a postcard and sent it to him.

Several weeks later I gave him a call to see how he was doing. He was so surprised. "Nobody ever calls me," was his sad remark. A few months later, he called me. He sounded deeply despondent and obviously drunk.

"I'm so sorry to bother you," he mumbled, "but you are the only person who ever cared enough to give me a call." I asked him where he was. I found him sitting on the sidewalk behind a downtown garage, utterly despondent. I asked if I could bring him back to Janus, but he said the county would not pay for him to be there anymore.

Taking a deep breath and with a heavy heart, I said, "Ok, I'll take you home with me so you can detox there." I just could not leave him like that on the street. I would not have offered my home unless I instinctively felt what a good and kind man he was.

For the next few weeks, he slept on my living room floor. I nursed him back to health, urged him to eat, wash his clothes, shower, and slowly try to get his life back together. I learned that he had been a firefighter for a long time and still had nightmares from his experiences. His colleagues used to call him the Angel of Death because, whenever they were called to a rescue, he would know beforehand if the person had already died. He had been living on the streets for the last ten years.

Chris was very respectful of my space, helping around the house and even offering to cook. I trusted him completely. After having reasonably detoxed, I knew he had to get back out on the street. I offered that he could stay at my house two or three nights a week to catch up on his self-care and rest.

We grew to care about each other. He had a quick-witted mind and made me laugh a lot. Over time, an attraction was developing between us, but it was clear to me that we were not appropriate relationship material since we really had nothing in common. So, I resisted. A few months into this, just as we were wishing each other good night and I turned towards my bedroom, I heard him mumble under his breath, "I want to kiss you so bad!" I could not resist. I turned on my heels. We kissed. So, we began being affectionate. However, I continued to resist becoming sexually intimate.

One evening, he said, shyly, that he needed to talk with me about something. After some encouragement, he stammered that he was in contact with someone in my home who had a message for me. The tone and choice of words he then shared were unmistakably Hara Ra's. I was astonished that he had the psychic receptivity to receive verbal communication from the other side. It was comforting to be able to speak with Chris about Hara Ra.

One day, after Chris had been out on the street for some time, he called to say that Hara Ra had asked him to take me up to the Pogonip, the woods near the college campus just outside of town. On a previous walk there, Chris and I had discovered a magic grove with "stone people," an entire village of figures created by some creative spirits, by balancing small stones on top of one another.

It reminded me of a hike Hara Ra and I once took in Arizona's Chiricahua National Monument where gigantic rocks are stacked, looking like stone giants. On the way back from that hike, Hara Ra had begun to pant quite heavily. His heart was racing. We had to stop every few minutes. As the sun was starting to go down, it was obvious that he was not going to make it out before dark, if at all. So, I told him to stay put and promised to return with help. I hiked back as fast as I could. I drove for a while through the deserted park. Just before dark, I found a ranger and we quickly drove back to the head of the trail. No sooner had we arrived when, to our surprise, we saw Hara Ra walking up the trail as if nothing was the matter.

That night in our motel room he shared what had happened. He had tried to keep going but could not and was faced with the possibility of dying there. Entirely alone in the vast silence among the stone giants, he had begun to sing to them. He let his voice ring out and felt that he was received. The welcome of the powerful stone beings re-energized him and he had walked back up the trail with a new zest for life.

Hara Ra's spirit had instructed Chris to take me up to the stone people in the Pogonip. Chris told me it was there that Hara Ra wanted to ask for my forgiveness. I immediately objected, saying that there was nothing to forgive. Chris curtly admonished me to allow the man to do what he needed to do. When we got out of the car, Chris gave me mythical instructions. I was to walk in front of him in silence. I was not allowed to turn around. I was supposed to take the long way to the grove rather than the shorter climb, so as not to get hurt.

Walking silently ahead, sometimes perceiving glimpses of Hara Ra by my side, I entered a different realm. When we arrived, I sat amongst the stone figures and became quiet. Sunlight dappled through the trees. Chris respectfully stayed a distance away. I did not hear anything, but my eyes rested on a stone figure of a mother and child. I understood Hara Ra was healing. Then I received his desire for my forgiveness for the ways he had caused

A sweet hug with Chris

me suffering. Chris called out to me to express my forgiveness out loud. I did.

As Chris was becoming more and more attracted to me, he said that he was receiving messages from Hara Ra to not give up on me, that I simply was not ready. One night when he came home, the erotic tension between us was so powerful, I invited him to lie down with me. With great urgency, we fell into each other's arms. My resistance broke and I brought him up, over and into me. We made love in wild abandon. I exploded into the greatest orgasm of my life. My whole body shuddered. We both screamed. Waters burst forth out of me like a waterfall. Even my feet were wet. I had never experienced female ejaculation. Right then I sensed Hara Ra's joyful bubbling laughter rising above me. I had finally achieved, through Chris, what he had always known to be my sexual potential.

Chris and I had a few sweet years together. As I had known, we did not match culturally, socially, or spiritually, but most of all, and sadly so, he could not stay sober. I finally had to let him go.

Later, I had another experience "through the veil." After entering recovery, I kept feeling that cryonic suspension was not right for me. I was aware that it would be nearly intolerable for my daughters. Also, truth be told, I realized that I would much prefer to have a peaceful death. Yet, I felt torn because of the promise I had made to Hara Ra.

Then a friend introduced me to a shamanic healer, Elana. The moment I entered her space, I felt a kinship in the atmosphere with Hara Ra. I laid down on her massage table. "Let me tune in," Elana began. After a silence, she said, "There is a man in the room who wishes to speak to you." Oh… Hara Ra… I knew. Then, she said in his words, "It is time for me to move on. You are okay now. My love will always be with you."

I asked him how he would feel if I were to have a natural death and forego the cryonic suspension. "You are free," was his answer. I instantly recognized the truth of this. Then I saw him ascending. My last glimpse of him was seeing his feet rise into the sky.

Opening

Walking in the early morning
awakening of the world
along the softly lapping bay
the clean expanse of beach
laid out before me
in a gracious curve.
The whole creation shimmers
with your light.

The shell of my heart
is opening
softly exposing
your reflection
like the moon.

Farewell to Hara Ra

Having made the decision to not proceed with cryonic suspension
for myself, I needed to make sure that some important information would be available to his revival team. I also wished to leave
a love letter to him. Alcor offers storage of vital information for
the suspended person. I wrote:

My Beloved Gregory,

You left your body on October 13, 2005. You died from
multiple organ failure from septicemia caused by a massive
streptococcal infection in your right leg due to diabetes. I
had found you comatose in your home five days earlier. You
came in and out of consciousness during those days, but never
opened your eyes or spoke again. I flew you from your death
bed in the ICU of Dominican Hospital in Santa Cruz, still
alive, to a hospice near Alcor in Scottsdale, Arizona. You
died that evening and were immediately prepared for your
cranio-suspension. It turned out to be the most successful
suspension Alcor had performed to that date.

It had been your explicit wish to be cryonically suspended
to give you a chance, however small, to be able to have a
full experience of the joys and love of life, to be able to fully
manifest your unique creativity, to see the future, to travel
the stars, to participate in and contribute to the building of

a world without war. As an avowed scientific materialist, you did not trust in the possibility of life after death, or of reincarnation; therefore cryonics seemed the safest route into the much-desired future.

You imagined since you had opted for a cranial suspension, that upon revival the information from your brain would be uploaded and you would be asked questions as to your desires for any repairs or adjustments you might wish to have installed in what would undoubtedly be a clone or several clones of your former physicality (unless you would be kept 'conscious' in a virtual reality). In fact, if those options were to be made available to you, you would wish a number of copies of yourself. At least one of these, with all your brilliance and creativity intact, to travel the stars, and one of you would have a thorough healing of your limbic system, hopefully without loss of your remarkable intelligence, to be a fully enjoyable and loving husband to me.

Your emotional injuries from early childhood had been profound and irreversible, no matter how hard you tried. Your father's rage, your mother's terror, your childhood isolation and neglect, all resulted in a significantly impaired limbic system which prevented you to be able to deeply bond on the emotional and physical planes. Your love and loyalty to me were enormous, but we both suffered from your inability to provide the closeness and comfort and pleasure I longed for.

Jesse, your student, and I were by your side at the moment of your death. Jesse, having the ability to see other planes of reality, saw an outburst of golden light with orange and blue burst from your forehead. Then he felt the impact of a massive force and heard your voice, "Take the emanations while they are fresh!"

Alcor personnel rushed in. We all lifted your body into the ice bath which stood by your side and whilst an ice bag was unceremoniously tossed upon your dear face, you were wheeled at great speed out of the room, into the hallway and out into the waiting truck, leaving Jesse and me alone in the room. I turned around and felt a great energy in the room. I walked over to the bed and laid down on it. It was still warm from your body. Immediately a massive force, like a huge elephant, descended and penetrated my body. All I could do was lie there open, my arms spread wide, flattening out, receiving you into me. So much for death being the end-all!

Your best friend, Bob Newport, had worked hard to help achieve your suspension, flying to Santa Cruz, drawing meds, working with the hospital and Alcor as a coordinator. He told me he is looking forward to "whatever possible relationship Hara Ra and I might have in the future. I still miss him, his wit, his intelligence and his implacable intransigence and loving heart." If you ever get to read this letter, he will probably already have been revived and meet you on that side of this amazing experiment.

I was broken with grief over your loss, but felt you close to me many a time. I often felt and could almost see your sweet and tender presence sitting at the edge of my bed, soothing and comforting me, enveloping me with your love. It was so very healing. Now that your material personality had dissolved, I got to receive the full presence and benefit of your amazing love.

About a year and a half after your passing, I had a session with a shaman woman. I was drawn to her because her space reminded me distinctly of you. Soon into the session, she said there was a man in the room. I knew it was you. Through her, you spoke to me, "You are now well enough. The time has come for me to move on. My love will always be with you." I told you about my reservations regarding my own suspension since it was incompatible with my desire for a peaceful death in the presence of my daughters. "You are free," you replied. The last thing I 'saw' were the soles of your beloved feet as you ascended.

I then ended my Alcor membership. My daughters were relieved when I told them.

I realize that if and when your brain is revived, it is unlikely that you would have any memory to resonate with my experiences with you after your physical death since these experiences would not have involved your physical brain.

I placed $25,000 in a 'perpetual fund' to accrue into a significant amount for you, if and when that time arrives. Your son Mapachi, for whom you provided a suspension contract with Alcor, in the hope that in a future lifetime, you might heal your relationship with him, has not been in contact with me and at this point has no awareness of this arrangement.

Even now, many years after your passing, your love is often near me, quite tangibly. I recovered from my marijuana addiction and am happy, healthy and well. I adore being a grandmother to Aurelia's two little boys.

I am deeply grateful to you for your gift of love to me and for leaving me your material wealth. I have remodeled your old home into a small jewel of a refuge and often sit in our garden, at peace, smiling at the nasturtiums and feeling you close, my Mate.

I love you forever and as you can see I never lost you in the first place. Who knows how, when and where we will continue to meet.

Be well, my Beloved.

My Mother's Passing

A half a year into my recovery, mid-2007, I happened to call my ninety-six-year-old mother, who was living in an elder care facility in Delft. I found out she was down with a bladder infection and was given antibiotics. She sounded depleted. I got the feeling that she was done with life and just wanted to die.

Decades earlier, when my mother had visited us in Auroville, I had promised that I would be with her when she died. She had been happy about that agreement. Now, I called her regularly, waiting for some clear indication that it was time for me to go and be with her. In early August, I got a call from a nurse saying that my mother had gotten too weak to get up and that she called frequently for assistance throughout the night. My mother seemed anxious, the nurse said. I had never known her to be anxious. It was my sign that it was time to go.

I booked a flight. When I told my mom to "hang in there," that I would be with her shortly, she let out a sigh of relief. I explained that I had three weeks to be with her. Aurelia's wedding had been scheduled for August 30th and I wanted to be back in California before that. We both felt that was plenty of time.

When I arrived, it was clear to both of us that she was on her deathbed. Having been a proud and self-reliant woman, she seemed thoroughly confused. "What can I do? What can I do?" was the one puzzled complaint she repeated.

"Just relax, Mom," I suggested. "Relax and let go. Nothing left to be done, but to let go." "Oh, you can talk!" she muttered, annoyed. She would not have any of it. I was completely at a loss how to help her in her passing. It seemed her soul had become inaccessible, even on her deathbed.

I had been aware for decades that she had shut down emotionally and spiritually. After my father came home from his ten years in prison, I am certain my mother expected we would "live happily ever after." There had been a modest inheritance waiting for my father, a welcome nest egg. In his efforts to create work, he used it to start a small business. He bought a small car. Since he grew up in a well-to-do family where money had not been a problem, he had never learned how to budget. I remember how deeply shocked and disturbed my mother had been when I came home from school one day after she had found out that all the nest egg money was gone.

In addition, my father's propensity for sexual fantasy continued to be as active after he came home as it had been before the war. In a rare moment of intimacy, when I was well in my fifties visiting my mom, she admitted to me that "being a little sex slave" was of course "quite fun," but that she had actually just wanted a "normal man with real sex." Instead, she told me, when she and my father were intimate, his fantasies would invariably turn to young men. I could feel how deeply disappointed she had been.

Also, after the war, independently of one another, both of my parents converted back to Catholicism and became deeply religious. I remember sitting next to my mother during Sunday mass. I was always so moved to hear my mother's beautiful alto voice ring with such depth of devotion.

Over the years, however, she had lost her faith. I believe it was partly due to the Catholic Church abandoning Latin, which removed much of the beauty and mystery from their rituals.

465

Still, I suspect it was her resentment of my father's endless spiritual monologues—while at the same time disappointing her in so many ways—that had turned her off. She had once shared with me how much she had loved her spirituality, how close she had felt to Jesus, and complained how it had all disappeared from her. Now, she said, she did not care anymore.

So, I was quite at a loss how to help her with her transition, which we were expecting at any time. After she had stopped eating, I would moisten her lips and try to keep her comfortable. During my last few days before having to return to California, she did not give any more signs of life, except for soft breathing. The nurses and I were surprised that even though she seemed already gone, her death wouldn't come. We wondered whether her pacemaker kept her heart beating.

When the day of my departure arrived, I told her I had to leave, and I kissed her goodbye. As I was walking away from her, I spontaneously turned and exclaimed, "Come fly with me!"

In the middle of the night, on the plane high above the Atlantic, I suddenly had the visceral experience of my mother flinging herself into my arms, terrified. As I held her, I saw my father sitting like a burnished golden Buddha in the sky, completely still, just being there, waiting for Ellen, my mother, the woman he had adored, wounded and disappointed. I understood that she had to face him and face her one great sin; her grave disillusionment in him had caused her to close the windows of her own soul. My father and I quietly held her soul in the great love of our beings until she saw and understood. All was instantly forgiven, and she was free. Three days later—a day

Ellen, beautiful

after Aurelia's wedding—I got the call that, finally, her heart had stopped beating.

That morning, I mentioned in my AA meeting that my mother had left her body. After the meeting was over, I walked out into the beautiful early morning sunshine. People were expressing their sympathy to me. Then, I raised my eyes into the morning light and saw her coming to me. When I got into my car, there she was, sitting next to me, pouring her mother love out to me. I leaned into her and felt her holding me like the little girl she had so loved. I felt cherished and restored. Love and forgiveness, a perfect completion with my mother.

In mid-September, I returned to Holland for my mother's memorial. Her music partner, Phil, had found a centuries-old little church in the countryside for the ceremony. Since she had donated her body to the medical profession, we did not have her body. I placed a photograph with flowers and candles in the front of the church to create a small altar. Friends and family gathered. My friends Paul and Doortje and even my dear Beth came to be present for the occasion. Phil played the piano. I spoke of her, her gifts, her hardships and her life, and people shared their memories.

Afterwards, I met with an old friend of my mother, Marie. They had been close, both during and after the war, and my mother had lived with Marie's family whilst my father's trial was happening in Scheveningen. Marie shared with me that my mother had traveled to The Hague to be present during all my father's court hearings, where she witnessed him being accused of the most heinous of crimes. "After one of these hearings, your mother came home looking ashen and completely defeated," she said. "I have never seen anyone looking so beaten down. She had not looked anyone in the eye and disappeared upstairs into her room. She never spoke of what happened that day."

Ah, my sweet mother, you never spoke of this to me, either.

My Fear of the Angry Dutch

A few years ago, I heard from my friend Lowie in Holland that a book had been published about the Dutch collaborators with the Nazis during WWII. It was published after a botched process of canonization of Cardinal Johannes de Jong, initiated by the Catholic Church. This process is the first step on the road to declaring sainthood. Cardinal de Jong was ordained cardinal of the Netherlands shortly after WWII. The process involves a thorough examination of the life to determine that no essential flaws should prevent the declaration of sainthood. It was discovered that Cardinal de Jong had been involved behind the scenes to get my father a psychiatric re-evaluation, resulting in the court's decision that he had not been responsible for his actions and therefore had been set free. It resulted in the dismissal of the canonization. The news created a huge uproar in the Dutch press.

Lowie sent me the excerpt of the book in which my father's full name appears, along with a description of the atrocities he committed. He is, understandably, depicted as a monster. Reading the excerpt hits me straight in the gut. It made me feel terrified about the possibility of having to face the angry Dutch with the publication of my book. How can I possibly stand in front of them and share my love for my father? I can hear their voices shouting... accusing...

Lowie reminds me that this depiction of my father's evil actions presents a one-dimensional view of him. It fosters a black-and-white, good-vs.-evil thinking, rather than looking at the complexities of these attributes within each one of us. Listening to his kind and wise words, I could feel Lowie standing by me with great spiritual strength and clarity about the purpose of everything being revealed, to deepen people's understanding and compassion.

Not long after this conversation, Lowie told me he had become involved with Neeltje, who is a psychic. Together they had tuned into me for healing. She had "seen" that my past with my father seemed like a screw that had tightened in my belly. I was struck by the accuracy of her perception from halfway around the world. Ever since Lowie told me about the publication, I had felt a dull tightness right at my belly button. The pain persisted and sometimes made me double over.

During one of our conversations, Lowie mentioned his frequent experiences of Ludar's presence and guidance. I expressed to him how curious it was that I hadn't felt his presence for a long time. He responded, "Ludar is too ashamed to come near you." Then he mentioned how Neeltje could feel my strength. She said she was convinced that my father would not have made it without me.

Weeks later, I went with a friend to Harbin Hot Springs, an outdoor spa about three hours North of Santa Cruz, to celebrate Christmas. The first morning there, it was still dark, and we decided to soak in the oversized hot tub with a few other early risers. Breathlessly, we watched the sun rise slowly until the golden light fractured in brilliant shards through the branches. There she was, the Great Mother in all Her Radiance. What a numinous beginning to this Christmas day.

When I went to sign up for a massage, I couldn't decide which practitioner to choose. So, I scheduled myself for an hour and a half in the late morning. Fate assigned me to Sunheart, an old sundrenched hippie. When he asked what I needed, I mentioned the knot in my stomach. He starts working on my body. Pretty soon I wonder what is going on. I am lying face down. He seems to just grab my body here and there, all over the place, without rhyme or reason. This is not what I expect from a massage, which is usually peaceful and harmonious. This is sheer chaos. I find myself on the verge of getting irritated but choose to accept and see what happens. He does explain that this is what my body is calling for.

Well, in the end, I came laughing off the table! My body felt in complete disarray. I exclaimed to Sunheart, "You have deconstructed my old matrix!" I found myself moving ever so freely as if all my body parts had become unscrewed and loosened. I couldn't stop laughing. The tightness in my tummy was nowhere to be found. When I saw my face in the mirror, my eyes were like two gleaming dark coals of fire. Ever since I had to stand still and silent during that terrifying headcount in the courtyard of the camp, when I was barely three and my baby sister had died the night before and I knew something was terribly wrong with our family, rigidity had begun to lodge in my body, only to be fortified by having to face angry, controlling Catholic nuns during the rest of my childhood, while my feelings had been completely ignored.

Back home and having to take my car to the dealer, I got a ride on a shuttle. When the driver found out that I was Dutch, he happily reported knowing an elderly Dutch gentleman, named Jaap, who had lost his wife a few years ago. He was living on his own and not in very good health. I spontaneously offered that he could give my phone number to the gentleman. I would be happy to meet him. I didn't have any Dutch-speaking friends in Santa Cruz at this time. Barely had I made my offer, when the driver volunteered that this man had terrible experiences during the war and had told him how, when the war ended, he had gone after collaborators to kill them. It caught my breath. I feared what I might have to face when meeting this man.

It was good to have another chance to talk with Lowie. He just laughed at the serendipity of my encounter and reminded me that this was presenting itself as an opportunity for my own growth and understanding. Then he told me about "bijltjesdag," the "day of axes." One day after Holland's liberation, the Dutch took to the streets and killed as many collaborators as they could lay their hands on!

Jaap did indeed call and we made a date for me to visit him at the beginning of the New Year. Slowly, I came to a place of acceptance of whatever might arise. I gratefully practiced some of the principles I had learned in the Twelve-Step program, to not take things personally, to show up for this man and not make it about me and to keep my heart open.

I drove onto a beautiful spacious property with meadows and trees. There were several buildings, so I was a bit confused and glad when I heard his voice calling to me from a balcony. I found my way up some stone steps through a garden and up the wooden stairs to a deck where a fairly tall, slender, not unattractive older gentleman welcomed me. He walked unsteadily into the house and complained about having lost his balance. After we sat down with a cup of tea, he started telling me about his wife. They had lived there together for sixty years. He missed her very much. He had built the place himself. He was grateful that his son, who was looking after him, lived in another house on the property.

When he started to talk about the war, I asked him where he had been living. In Delft. Then he enquired about me. I told him I had been born in Driebergen in 1942 and then lived in Apeldoorn. He quickly figured that I had been too young to remember much, and we left it at that. Long tales unfolded about the terrible difficulties he and his family had experienced. His father died of starvation during the hunger winter. Inside of me, I stopped in my tracks. This kind man had lost his father whereas mine got to live. I questioned my preoccupation with my own story. He was seventeen during that last war year. They were rationed to receive one potato and one small black cube of bread per person per week. He would bicycle into the surrounding farmlands to try and scrounge what he might. I imagined that his father probably gave up his little bit of food for his children.

The Gestapo were always searching to round up young men. Jaap's family had created a hiding place above the ceiling and moved a heavy cupboard under it to make it more difficult to access. One day the Nazis came. They never rang the bell, but banged on the door and forced their way in. He and his brothers managed to hide. He was asthmatic and had to force himself to be still. The officers seemed a bit in a rush and after looking around just started shooting randomly through walls and ceilings. One of his most traumatic experiences was having been forced to witness the execution of a number of young men who were accused of being members of the resistance.

He mentioned that only a few years ago he had found himself shaking and sweating for days, being practically unable to get off the couch. When he was taken to the hospital, he was diagnosed with PTSD. He said, "I can't stop my thoughts, all those memories and images keep running around and around in my head!" It is more than sixty-five years after the war! He was now taking medication, which helped a bit. When we were ready to say goodbye, I gave him a friendly hug. He said maybe we could go out for lunch someday. "Yes, that would be lovely!"

I feel humbled and grateful to this man for helping me to open my heart, my compassion and understanding for the suffering of the Dutch people at the hands of those like my father. With my own internalized fears of the wrath of the Dutch, and having to live with the shame and secrecy around my father's participation and his death sentence, I hadn't had much space to consider what a terrible time it had been for the people in Holland.

Of course, I had known about it. I know I will need to foster that compassion if I am to face the publication of my book with any kind of equanimity.

Whenever I complete a chapter for my book, I read it to my women friends in our writing group. We gather twice a month. After I read this chapter to them, one of the women asked if I would like to feel my father's presence. I looked inside and had to say that I didn't know. After we had our meditation and wrote for half an hour, we listened to each other share what we had written. I found myself sitting forward and deeply listening with my heart. Suddenly it felt as if I was my father leaning forward and listening. I could see and feel his face looking through mine with such love and appreciation for each one of them. I felt immersed in his warm, benign presence.

For days, I continued to feel glimpses of my father's loving presence shining through me. I have a feeling that opening my heart to the Dutch who suffered in the war has somehow made me more whole.

Evil Men

One morning, I listened—in ever mounting astonishment—to a radio interview with James Dawes, author of *Evil Men*, "a searching meditation on our all-too-human capacity for inhumanity."

Here was a man who approached war criminals as human beings like himself who might have done similar things if he had been in their situation, without any finger-pointing. After listening, with bated breath, I found myself reeling with emotion.

I finally felt that I was not alone. I immediately ordered the book from our local bookstore and felt compelled to write him.

> Greetings James,
>
> I am sitting here, sobbing with relief and gratitude and a whole mix of emotions I can't even begin to describe after hearing your startling interview on the 7th Ave Project on KUSP in Santa Cruz. I deeply admire your willingness to introspect and reveal your innermost thoughts and feelings about what is probably the most abhorrent issue humanity has to deal with.
>
> I was born in Holland during WWII. My father was a Nazi who was sentenced to death for war crimes; torture, to be specific. He was actually released after ten years. I knew him as a profoundly loving and compassionate man whom I loved more than anyone. I have been burdened with shame and guilt my whole life. I am in the process of writing my biography to show the world how perfectly beautiful and loving young people can be seduced into the "glory of war" and end up committing heinous atrocities, the suffering of which spreads out through families and loved ones in all directions (victims and perpetrators alike) and through the generations.
>
> I am immensely grateful for your courageous work and have already ordered your book from our local bookstore.

I spent the rest of the day alternately sobbing and resting. For the first time, I had heard someone speak with emotion and compassion, sincerely attempting to understand how and why perfectly ordinary human beings can become monsters, preventing easy labels such as "evil men" to conveniently distance ourselves from them. He talked about the title of the book being both a statement and a question.

I experienced this emotional meltdown because he acknowledged and addressed the core issue of my life with such amazing kindness and understanding. It broke through my deeply rooted and often unconscious shame and isolation in a whole new way. He accomplished with his research and writing what I hope to accomplish at least to some extent with my book.

Let me quote from the book's cover:

> Drawing on firsthand interviews with convicted war criminals from the Second Sino-Japanese War (1937–1945), James Dawes leads us into the frightening territory where soldiers perpetrated some of the worst crimes imaginable: murder, torture, rape, medical experimentation on living subjects. Transcending conventional reporting and commentary, Dawes's narrative weaves together unforgettable segments from the interviews with consideration of the troubling issues they raise. This book is not just about the things war criminals do. It is about what it is like, and what it means, to befriend them.

I received a heartfelt reply from James. Clearly, he understood the turmoil in my psyche, the conflict inside of me between my father's crimes and my love for him. He appreciated that I was writing my memoirs and hoped I would send him a copy when published.

A Vision Quest

My friend Elke shared with me that she had participated in a vision quest and how transformative that experience had been for her. When I was invited to her birthday party, I met Chayim Barton, a local psychologist, who led these vision quests together with a friend of his. He shared about the gifts of awareness that come to people on those quests. He explained that participants would first gather several times in his office to gain clarity about the procedures and to tune into their intentions. Every participant would be sent out alone into the desert for three days and three nights, fully fasting, with only a gallon of water per day.

It is 2008. I am one year into my recovery and feel that such an amazing opportunity for renewal and spiritual quest would be perfect timing for me. Even though I am a bit fearful about being alone in the desert for three days and nights, I am more apprehensive about the idea of fasting. Having experienced hunger in my early childhood does not make fasting sound appealing. But, I feel drawn and sign up.

A small group of us seekers gathered in Chayim's office. It's a beautiful space with windows looking out over a canyon of wilderness. He runs these quests together with his friend Bryan, who is also a therapist. The two of them have gone on many trips to the wilderness together and have led these groups twice a year for over a decade. Since it is springtime, we will be going to the Joshua Tree Desert. In the fall they lead these quests on Mount Shasta. Chayim drums for a while. We tune in and begin to share about where we are in our lives, what our intentions are and whatever fears we may have.

We learn that during the three days and nights alone in the desert, we will only have our sleeping bag, a pencil and notebook and one gallon of water per day. On the last day, we are to create a circle of stones for a ceremony during the night when we are supposed to stay awake. The only task we are given is to receive a spirit name for ourselves.

A few weeks before the trip, we are instructed to spend a full twenty-four hours alone in nature. "Do not have a goal," Chayim says. "Do not feel you need to get anywhere, just linger where you are, allowing yourself to be drawn wherever." He suggested we walk in slow motion, remain silent and pay close attention to the plants and animals we come across. We should also meditate on what our highest intention for the Vision Quest would be.

I choose to go camping at Henri Cowell State Park. The night is very cold. When I do my morning ablutions, a bumble bee buzzes loudly in the bathroom. When she is finally quiet, I recognize how my own mind has been buzzing and I become quiet. When I come back to my tent, I notice the bee is firmly planted on my glove. I gently set her free. I spend the day wandering ever so slowly through the chaparral and white sand dunes into the shade of the tall redwoods down by the river. I meet a deer and we quietly gaze at one another. Then she continues to graze peacefully. I am in the sacred. I am clear that my intention is to be free of my past and of my sense of separation. During a last get-together before we leave, we share our intentions with the group. At that time, I explain the shadow I have carried from my father's past as a Nazi.

In April of 2008, eight of us seekers and our two guides travel in a few vehicles for some seven hours to Joshua Tree National Park in Southern California. From the parking lot, we walk for quite a stretch through the sandy desert. I notice various rock formations and the scruffy-looking Joshua trees. Some of the men help me carry my water. Chayim and Bryan clearly know where they are going. We veer away from the path and find a beautiful circular space for our opening ceremony.

We are instructed: "When hungry, drink water. When achy, drink water. When frightened, drink water." Then, we are sent out on our own and told, "Let yourself be drawn to find the spot where you want to settle for the quest."

I work my way between a rock wall and some dense brambles and find myself in a beautiful valley, created by the sudden floods which occur in this desert. It is called a wash. The ground is dry, sandy and rocky, a wide stream bed strewn with the tiniest of wildflowers and surrounded by large rock formations. I am pleased to see a tall rock face which promises to offer me blessed shade during the heat of the day. There are no paths coming into this wash and I love realizing that there is no chance anyone will wander into my space. I will be entirely alone. It adds a huge sense of safety.

On the first day of my solitude, in the cool of morning, I walk to the edge of my world. The passage between the rocks narrows until the wash drops down steeply. I can go no further. I lean on a large round boulder, pressing my belly into its comforting coolness, looking out over the wash as it continues down below. Large rock formations surround the valley. They create the impression of tall ancient beings frozen in time. Down below, small rocks seem to be carefully placed in a circular pattern on the valley floor. It looks like an ancient ceremonial site. I am in silent awe.

Silhouetted against the sky, some large rocks look like a great figure with a huge boulder on his back, like the Earth Father carrying great burdens. His powerful impassive gaze looks out over the world. Then I notice that his arm gently holds and guides what looks like a young girl, standing at his knees, as if protecting her from danger.

Behind him and a bit lower are two large figures. I see a bound man guarded by a hooded monk whose face is hidden, Death. I immediately realize that the bound man is my father. My voice rings out over the valley when I call his spirit name, "Ludar, Ludar, Ludar!" I wait in the silence. From under the large hood a face peers from the dark.

For years I felt that my father is not free to move on. Now, I wonder what he needs. Gazing upon the ancient rock formations and contemplating my father's immovable presence, with Death as his captor, the understanding comes to me that he will remain in the earth's atmosphere until all those he harmed find their resolution, in life or in death. At the very moment the thought arises, I am startled by a loud whir. A tiny, brilliantly colored hummingbird dashes and hovers right in front of me, as if saying "Yes! Yes! That's it!" Later, a friend of mine tells me that according to the ancient Aztecs, Hummingbird was considered a messenger from the ancestors.

In the late afternoon, I venture back to the same place. Just as I enter the narrowing between the rocks that leads to the lookout, I am startled by a loud high-pitched rattle.

I freeze. Not far across from where I stand, on a small ledge in the now sunny rock face, a rattlesnake in full alarm raises its head, looking directly at me. My heart races. I quietly step back a little and apologize for having disturbed her space. I bow to her in Namaste with deep respect. I wander back to my spot for the night. I sleep under billions of stars.

I spend the days in resonance with the life around me. What I normally perceive as the inanimate world turns out to be fully alive and conscious, from the dry ground, the tiny desert flowers to the rocks. The rocks feel especially present and in direct benevolent communion with me. I write in my little notebook and spend time reviewing all my relations. When I get tired, or achy, I drink water. Just as they had suggested, every time it helps.

Early in the morning of my third day, I return to the same site. I know that the snake is asleep in the cool of morning. I sit myself down at the Edge of my World and am overtaken again by the majesty of the occult world I am beholding. Looking up at the Ancient Father in the early morning light, the young girl has morphed into a little angel. She has a chubby belly and strong fat thighs. She leans confidently into her powerful father, sucking her thumb. Two chubby little wings sprout from her shoulders. Angela, little angel! I smile, I weep. It's me, my child-self, safe with her Heavenly Father.

In the afternoon, after having strolled around for a while, I return to my place and sit down on my pad, leaning against the

Great Father

rock face behind me. It is hot. I am a bit tired and drink some water, gazing out over the wash. Out of the corner of my eye, I notice a small movement in the sand. When I look, it stops. I keep looking closely. It starts to move again with slow sideways curves. I realize it is Rattlesnake. I am not afraid. I know that if I keep quiet, I have nothing to fear.

She slithers directly towards me. Then I see that the corner of the tarp on which I am seated is slightly lifted off the ground. Ever so slowly, not to startle her, I place a small rock to keep the tarp down. I'm fine with her coming to me, but really do not want her to get under me. She comes closer. She comes right up to me and slowly slides over the corner of my tarp, just inches away from my body. We gaze at each other for a moment in quiet recognition. Then, ever so slowly she disappears into the shrubbery on the other side of my spot. I stay in deep silence. I realize my spirit name: Silent Snake.

That night in my circle of stones in the middle of the desert, under the magical splendor of billions of stars, I make a little fire with the dry twigs and scraps I have gathered during the day. Deep into the night, I suddenly become aware of my father having joined me by the fire. He is sitting to my left, in the East. I see his gold tooth gleaming in the light of the fire as he smiles at me. I am awash with his warm and loving presence. We laugh with deep heartfelt happiness. It is so good to be together. All is well. The shadows of the past have been illuminated, understood and forgiven. All that remains is the warm glow of our love.

A powerful gale starts blowing. Ruach, spirit breath, blows through all the nooks and crannies of my world to cleanse and dissipate any further clinging to the shadows of my past.

The next morning, upon returning from our individual spaces into the common area, we all look like radiant gods. Our guides have placed bottles of water behind some shrubs, so we can wash up and refresh ourselves. They have prepared a marvelous meal of fruits and salad to break our fast. Then we gather in a closing circle. We take turns sharing our experiences.

Being well aware that both our guides are Jewish, I share the redeeming experience with my father, first how I understood that his spirit is still lingering in the earth's atmosphere for his redemption. Then, how we sat together by the fire in the night. Only joy and love between us. Chayim closes the circle by addressing each one of us. When he comes to me, he looks softly and lovingly into my eyes and says, "Our ancestors make peace!" His words impact my psyche like an earthquake, creating a great opening. Then I kneel in the center of the circle and speak.

"For three decades," I say, "I have known about vision quests. It is only now that I was ready. I am so grateful to have been guided to go on this quest with the two of you as our guides. Both of you are Jews. You have been graciously witnessing my process with my father, trying to free myself from the shadows of his horrendous past."

Chayim comes and embraces me in the circle of our little tribe of seekers. Heart to heart we stand there, in the middle of the desert in Southern California. I weep for joy and gratitude to him, for that moment, for myself, for my father, for the release and the forgiving, for peace amongst all our tribes and for a brighter future for mankind.

❁ Silent Snake Full of Love

Having lived long and much and many times,
I have run out of the need to be something or someone;
anything other than a kind, somewhat intelligent, somewhat wise,
loving and generous soul amongst many,
anchored in the Great Love, the Source,
a particle of the Great I Am—
always looking for That in you and you and you
and smiling at That in you and you and you,
to widen and deepen and awaken
that marvelous, mysterious, joyous
Presence in and amongst all of us.

I am and unfold, Silent Snake Full of Love,
gently undulating in my core, quietly
carrying the vibrations of the Great Silence
from which we spring, into the life
of all my loved ones, in and out of bodies,
bringing the unseen gift to all,
to be a quiet anchor for the ones who are still a bit lost,
offering the ground of being, a refuge and a constant,
ever changing reflection of the One Great Love.

Another Round

Some years into my recovery, I continue to attend and enjoy
Twelve-Step groups on a daily basis. Here, I find myself belonging
amongst the rough and tumble crowd of addicts and alcoholics
aspiring and attempting to live a life of love and tolerance, where

the sharing is raw and honest and the desire for a spiritual life is a down-to-earth simple path of action without any pretense, without teachers or dogmas.

The other day we pondered the topic of fear. One of our members mentioned that when he finds himself alone at home, he sleeps with a gun under his pillow. That's how afraid he is. Another man, I'll call him Rob, whose harsh grating voice is almost painful to my ears, but who moves me often to tears by how honestly he struggles with his barely controllable rage, tells us that he had been in the Gulf War and in Bosnia and that he chooses not to own a gun. "I know only too well that the combination of me and fear and guns is bad news. I'll defend my life at all costs. In fact, I'm still trying to stay away from the images of my past."

I immediately see him blindly firing rounds at the slightest threat to his life. My insides take a nose dive. I start to weep, quietly. I keep very still. I also feel my love for this man and compassion for his pain. All during that day the disturbance keeps making itself felt deep in my psyche. Rob's presence, his demeanor and his voice are staying with me. I don't know what to do with it.

Two days later, just before Thanksgiving, I wake up with a pain in my chest. I take some herbs and go back to bed hoping I won't get sick just before the holiday. The next morning, I decide to call Jasmine, my acupuncturist of many years, and am glad she can see me that afternoon. As she is checking me out, she asks, "I wonder if you have been anxious lately?"

"Hmmm... anxious? Let me take a look... oh..." I remember my recent disturbance. Jasmine listens closely as I tell her what happened. She knows me well. "Ah, that's your memory of war. Your little girl got frightened." I burst into tears. Comforting me, she strokes my forehead. I sob. "It's good. Let it out... What a great opportunity for healing for both of you," she says.

Driving to my meeting early on Thanksgiving morning, my heart is beating loudly in my chest because I realize that I have to share my feelings. I am afraid. I'll have to tell the group about my father. My shame will be exposed. I've learned from my daily attendance to the meetings that every disturbance in the field is an opportunity for growth and when I bring my feelings, especially my fear and my shame, into the fellowship, somehow healing occurs.

Rob is sitting in his usual spot. I usually sit fairly close to him. I choose a chair on the other side of the room today. My heart beats in my throat as the secretary opens the meeting and we go through our preamble and prayers. We read the chapter on Tradition Twelve which states that anonymity is the spiritual foundation of our fellowship. I am struck by the line "We still thought we had to hide from public distrust and contempt." Right!

I look around the room. Since it is a holiday, the meeting is mercifully small and most faces are familiar to me. One woman I know well and who is always very kind to me comes in late and my body relaxes a bit, feeling safer by her presence. As the sharing begins, I wait for an opening and then I jump in.

"I'm Andrea. I'm an addict/alcoholic. My heart is beating in my throat. I am afraid. I have never really shared with you about my past. The other day the topic of war was brought into this room and I've been triggered ever since. Some of us have experienced war as an active participant. I was a child in World

War II at the receiving end of it. Our family life was completely destroyed. Then my father was sentenced to death for war crimes because he was on the wrong side. I was six years old when my mother told me. Before ushering me back into the boarding school, she said, 'Don't tell anyone!'" I burst into tears. "I've lived with this dark secret all my life." The room is dead-silent. I can't speak anymore... "That's all. Thank you," I manage to whisper.

The kindness and sympathy of the people in the room washes over me. A woman next to me touches my arm. Another one brings me tissues. The meeting continues. I'm safe. I did it. It's ok. Afterwards, surrounded by hugs and words of appreciation and encouragement, I see Rob walking towards me. When the crowd parts, he takes me into his arms. We hold each other. I sob against his chest. Then I am at peace. Yet another round of healing in myself and in my little world has taken place.

❀

A New World

Going inward,
I see my grey sleek wolf's belly
moving forward on long legs striding,
free, clear, unassuming.
My natural strength moving me forward
into the clear space ahead.

Walking in natural grace
my path in the wilderness.
One amongst many,
solitary but not alone.

Emerging from the ashes of my past,
an inner knowing seems to lead me
to the birthing of a new world.

Coming to Terms with Tara

My oldest daughter, Aurelia, and her family continue to live in Santa Cruz. This is where my children grew up and I will probably live here till the end of my days. For many years, Tara, my younger daughter, has been living and teaching high school in Vermont. Ever since the debacle with Maurice and even after having tried desperately to offer my deep regrets to her, she has kept herself distant from me.

For years, I have made myself available to give Tara rides to and from the airport when she comes to visit—my little scheme to at least have that time with her in the car. We do see each other at family events, but outside of those visits in the midst of family, she does not choose to spend time with me. I can't help but feel rejected.

The birth of Aurelia's second son, Ezra, was expected just before Christmas, 2010. Tara planned to come for a couple of weeks during her winter break. She and I can both assist Aurelia, especially by taking care of little Theo, her firstborn.

As usual, Tara does not communicate her travel plans with me. Then I hear from Aurelia that Tara thought of asking a friend to pick her up from the airport. It hurts. I am suddenly hit, deep in my body, by a flash of black hatred: you are NOT my daughter! I stop in my tracks, startled by the vehemence of my feelings towards my own daughter. I feel two distinct urges, one to immediately do away with it as completely unacceptable and wrong, the other a perverse desire to spiral down in that blackness of disowning her and reveling in the revenge. I realize I had been unable, no matter how hard I tried, to fully accept her distance and have judged her inability or unwillingness to forgive me. I have some work to do before she gets here.

During the meeting of my AA home group the next morning, the speaker dwells extensively on his relations with his relatives, on the injuries from the past and the healing that occurred during his recovery. It feels like an invitation to address my fury with my daughter. As I have mentioned before, when I speak of my difficulties at group level, it invariably brings relief. I take a deep breath and share about my recent experience with my daughter. I get pretty choked up. After the meeting, one of the members reminds me to pray for Tara. Good idea!

The next day, I attend another meeting, and the topic is "judgments." I listen closely. Clearly, I am in disagreement with my daughter and judge her for continuing to reject me. Someone speaks of "mercy." I recognize that I have judged her passive-aggressive behavior and figure that underneath such behavior surely there must be fear. My heart softens and I take a sweeping look at the many years that I have caused her suffering.

First my separation from her dad; then my impossible choice of partners, Martha, who could barely tolerate being around my children; Maurice, who insulted her and created a deadly rift between us; only to be followed by my relationship with another difficult person, Hara Ra; and my years of marijuana use when I became more and more demanding and sometimes even got furious with her. I look at all this history with a dispassionate gaze. These are the facts. I am not judging or shaming myself anymore. I come to a great acceptance of the results of my actions and drop any expectation of her changing how she feels or behaves toward me. I experience profound relief.

Later that morning, I attend a baby shower for Aurelia. Her women friends, most of them young mothers, have organized this sweet event to honor her and bring their blessings for a good birth. One of them reads from Kahlil Gibran's *The Prophet*, the section on children, reminding us that our children are not our children, that "they are the sons and daughters of life's longing for itself."

I remember my father telling me that when Reinier was born, he hung a saying over his crib, *Werde der Du bist*. (Become who you are). I grew up with that knowledge. So, I knew from the beginning, from before their births, that my children would not be here for me. They came through me to become who they are and to fulfill their own purposes.

Later that day, pondering all this in relation to Tara, in a flash of pure joy I realize how marvelous it is that I will get to see this beautiful, extraordinary young woman and will be blessed with her presence, however briefly. My heart floods with gratitude. The old mother-daughter conflict seems to be dissolving.

A few days later, I get a rare telephone call from Tara. "Do you still have your Dutch passport on which Aurelia and I traveled from India to America?" I have to disappoint her. When my passport got renewed, my daughters each got their own EU passports. The old one was not returned to me.

"What do you need this for?" I ask her.

"I would like to travel with Dad and Lisa to India in January and I need a birth certificate to get a visa from the Indian embassy."

My daughters' birth certificates had been unique documents, handwritten and coffee stained from the registrar's office in Vanur, a small Tamil town near Auroville. They were some of my prize possessions which, in his madness, Maurice had burned. I hear myself say to her, "That was such an unforgivable act." She responds with a halting silence.

After we hang up, I realize that from my perspective the unforgivable act was Maurice's, but from my daughter's perspective, the unforgivable act must have been mine. I chose that crazy man and brought him into her life. Seeing that situation through her eyes opens a space inside of me to fully accept her as she is and understand her injury at my hands. I weep for the harm, the pain and suffering I have caused my child.

Tears flow as I accept and forgive and grieve all at the same time—her precious heart, her vulnerability, her distances and my shortsightedness; my blindness and the fact that I failed her. Through all of the changes I chose to make after leaving Daniel, I had put my needs before hers. I shall do for her what I can.

I find the registrar's office of Vanur on the internet and email her:

Hi Tara,
    Progress: I just found the registrar's office of Vanur online and submitted a request for a copy of your birth certificate. The official policy states that all birth/death certificates are kept in their files. The trick will be if they can find it...
    It was interesting to hear myself say last night that the burning of your birth certificate was an unforgivable act.

Then I saw that from your perspective, it was the result of my choices and I realized anew how deeply you were harmed at such a tender age at my failing to place your needs before mine, and it wasn't the first time. I am very sorry to have expected your forgiveness!

I am so very grateful to you, Tara, that you have had the grace to keep accepting me in your life and that we can continue to love each other and that I actually get to see you occasionally and experience the joy of being in your presence.

I love you so much, Mom

I get a response from Vanur that all documents from that time had been destroyed by moisture and termites. So, unfortunately, I have to disappoint her again.

Part VII

Healing

Healing Little Angela

About a decade into recovery, I began to feel the need to work the Steps on a deeper level. I was quite aware that my difficulties were much older than my addiction and were rooted deep in my childhood.

In the fall of 2016, I attend a presentation on ACA, a Twelve-Step program for Adult Children of Alcoholics and Dysfunctional Families. Towards the end, the woman presenter says, "We were taught not to trust, not to speak and not to feel!" The words plunge like a blade through my core. How deeply I recognize the truth of that. The woman is offering a six-week workshop on the twelve ACA steps. I immediately decide to participate.

I learned that their essential method to heal childhood trauma is to become your own loving parent. This sentence in their "Red Book" struck me as remarkable: "By reparenting ourselves with gentleness, humor, love, and respect, we find our child within and a true connection to a Higher Power. This is the God who does not abandon."

Some two weeks into the workshop, I wake up from a devastating dream. I am cuddled up close to the man I loved with all my heart and am in seventh heaven, when he suddenly sits up and says, "I don't really want this!" I feel destroyed. I take myself to the next ACA meeting for the support I know will be available. The quality of presence and compassionate attention is remarkable. I decide to keep going to their meetings where I find such surprising emotional safety for my child-self.

One of the meetings is held in a cottage called "The Barn." It is set in a garden across from Arana Gulch, a beautiful park of tree-lined rolling meadows in the heart of Santa Cruz. I love the room. It has a Chinese rug on the floor, pillows all around and light filtering in through stained-glass windows. Chickens cackle next door. We sit around in silence, do some reading and then introduce ourselves. Just as in all Twelve Step recovery programs, there is no cross-talk. In ACA great attention is given to the emotional safety of all participants.

Here, I begin to perceive the almost physical presence of little Angela with me. One morning, I feel her small body lean into me as she gazes around the room at all those sincere people, sitting there so quietly. Then, inside myself, I hear her say, "I am home!" I weep. "Home" was exactly what I had missed for ten years of my early childhood.

Another morning, I wake up from a dream of being lost. I write in my journal: *My lost child-self. I see and feel little Angela just two years old walking hand in hand with her five-year-old brother in the village near Berlin. It is dangerous and we are not wanted. My father is gone, my mother nowhere in sight... We are in a strange land, our home lost forever. We'll never find our way back there. Poor little Almuth is lying in her baby carriage next to the compost pile, her little mouth broken out in eczema.* I grieve for her and for my lost child, so sad.

One of the techniques suggested in ACA is to give your inner child a means of expression by writing or drawing with your non-dominant hand. Since I had lost all natural communication with my parents as early as age two, my little Angela does not have many words. And, she expresses herself only in Dutch, of course. "Ik ben bang," she writes (I am afraid). One time I ask her where she is. "Ik ben alleen, achter de muur. Niemand kan me vinden." (I am alone, behind the wall. Nobody can find me.)

We meet once a week in this cozy, beautiful room. There, my psyche opens and allows Angela to come forth. I continue to experience her little being with me as a separate entity. I see her and feel her as an almost physical presence. After she had leaned quietly into me during several meetings, one day she climbs on my lap. It feels so very sweet. I am aware that her trust in me is growing. A week later, on my lap, she turns toward me and puts her sweet little arms around my neck. Our love and trust feel complete.

Over time, I begin to experience her in ever-progressing ages. One beautiful sunny morning that spring, after the meeting, I take a walk in Arana Gulch. The meadow is blooming with small purple, white and yellow flowers, the sun gleaming on the grass, meadows sloping down to the creek, surrounded with trees and shrubs. Suddenly, I am aware of my nine-year-old Angela walking quietly by my side. We enjoy being together and are so very happy. "Look at where we are and how joyous and at peace we feel now," I exclaim to her. I praise her, "You did good! And so did I." Everything sparkles all around us and inside of me.

I continue to go to AA. During one of my favorite Sunday morning AA meetings, the topic is again, judgment. Suddenly, I find myself spiraling down into my unconscious inner realms. I see a tall female figure standing behind me, sword raised. She is frightening. She watches for my slightest transgressions and mistakes and comes down hard, mercilessly. My Avenging Angel, a nun in black. My heart bounces in my throat. After a few minutes, I have the courage to speak out loud of my experience. In doing so, this internal figure is getting exposed for the cruel executioner she is. When I finish speaking, I see the nun lose control and crumple into nothingness.

And, here is my journal entry from a few months later: *I do not remember what it was in our reading this morning that made me acutely aware of my mother's muteness and how my father invaded and overwhelmed my psyche with his "sexual education" of me to make sure I would understand my future man and happily satisfy his every need, however twisted or quirky. I realized simultaneously that I had not known how to speak to my daughters in their early adolescence. I was afraid to be inappropriate and damage them. I became mute, as if I instinctively knew that I did not have the right words to speak with them of intimate matters. So, time passed and I did nothing...*

When I share about it in the meeting, my anger flares up, raging like a fire, at my father for having twisted me so. I become acutely aware, that only now, at age seventy-five, am I able to rage about my father's violation of my boundaries, about his lack of respect for my young innocent self. He tore the fabric of my innocence apart. And my poor mother did nothing.

After the meeting, tears of dismay keep flowing for my loss, but even more for the realization that my need for my father's love had been so great that I had not been able to see what he really did to me, or even realize the truth of his vastly inappropriate and harmful behavior. It twisted all my relations. He set me up to be an all-accepting do-gooder/helper/healer, without the slightest awareness of my own feelings or the ability to stand up for my own needs, let alone even know my needs.

A woman says in another one of my ACA meetings, "Violence was visited upon me." I look at my long seven years in boarding school and see the violence that was visited upon me by those backward nuns. No emotional safety was ever offered. Instead, we lived under the constant threat of their wrath. It was not the pinching of my arm, or the pulling of my ears, or rapping my fingers with a ruler or even locking me up in a closet—it was the constant threat of their disapproval and their rage. I see my young self walking in complete isolation through time and space, in the midst of others, as if enclosed in my own private cell, the walls tight around me. I realize that even now, I walk with a shield of protection around me, parting the crowds so I will not be... what? Invaded, overwhelmed, annihilated?

I share what I was seeing with the group. Then, as usual, I sit quietly while others speak, and grief starts washing over me. I weep for my child's absolute loneliness, her need to be so strong, her inability to have her feelings, her utter isolation.

Walking away from the meeting towards my car, I see and feel her, the upright, strong young girl of around ten, merge into me. I feel deep relief. We are now together. She is alone no longer.

Back home, I draw one of my soul collage cards and see a young girl's lovely, innocent and serious face. "I am the one whose innocence and beauty are forever unstained, trusting deeply in my own harmless self, observing all, free to question, and unafraid." I love this holy child within me and cherish her unabashed. She lives in the center of my being and there she is free from the past, restored to her original kindness, her true nature of love.

Doorstep Delivery

Inspired by a poem of the same title by Greg Hall

What was left on my doorstep
Like an abandoned orphan?
Will someone please take care of her,
Claim her and take her home?
But no, years later she was still there
Shivering in the cold
Silent and beyond hunger,
Her big eyes looking at me darkly.
Would I ever pick her up
and take her in?
When, finally it became clear
That no one else would claim her –
Now in a state of near despair myself –
I picked her up and brought her in.
I had to make up for decades of neglect.
I washed and dressed her,
Combed her hair. I nursed and
Rocked and soothed her to sleep.
I cooed over her and named her.
Slowly she softened and began to trust.
Over time she told me everything.
She learned to cry and rage.
I held her while she sobbed and screamed.
Together we shook our fists
and stomped our feet
at the injustice of it all.
Now she is my sweet and sparkling,
Happy and funny little girl.

Hand in hand we walk through life
Sometimes skipping, sometimes stalling,
Finding our way into Love.

Forgive Me for Loving My Father

As I near the completion of my story, I find myself stalling. I know the next step is to move towards publication and I am terrified. I imagine being "out" in public with the long shadow of my father's past. I am fearful of becoming the target of reproach from people who carry the unspeakable grief of entire families lost in the Holocaust. My apprehension makes me unable to write for many months. I have no idea how to move through this impasse.

I have participated in a women's writing group for years. On a Sunday, we gather for a retreat at one of our homes bordering the wilderness of the Santa Cruz Mountains. One woman is adept at reading the Tarot. She offers each one of us the opportunity to draw a card which she reads. Her offer gives us the inspiration for a few hours of soul-searching and writing.

I draw the Page of Swords. I have pulled the card upside down. She looks at me in surprise, not expecting such an innocuous card for me. The image is of a light-footed young hero, his sword effortlessly raised into the blue sky, with little white clouds and birds flying overhead. She says, "There is not a problem in sight. He made a decision and it is effortless." The fact that the card was upside down, she says, indicates that I have unnecessary fears. These can simply be discarded. I am completely safe to proceed, she says.

I feel a great relief come over me; a lightness of being returns. I find a quiet spot and start writing. Suddenly, these words appear on my page, *Forgive me for loving my father*. It feels like a crucial and central question and I wonder if it should be the title of my book.

Hearing from My Father

On March 8, 2010, I received an email from Lowie, a very good friend whom Ludar had mentored during his student years. With the email was a photograph of my father. Lowie mentioned that my father never wanted to be photographed, which I remember as part of his post-war paranoia, but that he had allowed Lowie to take his picture on that special occasion.

I had never been able to have a picture of my father on display in my home because of the shadow he still cast in my psyche and the darkness I saw in his. So, it had been years since I had seen his image. I took a deep breath before looking at the picture. My heart was pounding. Then, I clicked on the attachment, and there he was, life-sized on my screen. His great love and kindness were right there, beaming at me. I printed and framed this picture and placed it on my altar to be able to gaze into his loving eyes again. It felt like my father's love was being restored to me. I began to trust him again.

Two days before this email, his beloved, a remarkably psychic woman named Neeltje had suddenly received a strong feeling of Ludar's presence. It was March 6, Ludar's one-hundredth birthday!

I asked Lowie if there might be any possibility for Neeltje to receive a message from Ludar for me. I did not hear from them for a while. On May 5th I heard from Lowie that Neeltje had received a message from my father for me.

And so it was on May 5, 2010, Liberation Day in the Netherlands, after Lowie and Neeltje placed flowers in his name at a WWII Memorial in the Netherlands, twenty-nine years after my father's death, that I received this letter from him:

Deeply beloved daughter,

With profound sentiments and emotions, I am using this day symbolically to free and liberate myself and all those whose souls are linked to mine from feelings of guilt and shame connected with me, in order that each one can enter a new phase in their life on earth as well as in the spheres of my transitioned loved ones.

I am deeply moved that you are writing the book and I am glad to be given the opportunity to encourage you to complete and publish it. Not only as my confession of guilt but hopefully also as a stimulus to create understanding in others to penetrate or at least gain some insight in both the victims of misdeeds as well as the victims of indoctrination and erroneous ideals. Not to excuse myself and others nor even for us to be understood, but to be freed of the burden that continues to ravage my soul. I do not ask for forgiveness, but for factual openness and for the full expression of the emotions suffered by my loved ones whom I have caused a life of grief and pain and of greatly conflicted feelings. I have caused them irreconcilably conflicted, deeply felt emotions regarding my person.

I hope for the healing of our souls by making the various angles to all these emotions and problems public. A cleansing of my soul will be accomplished, as I continue to feel bound to my past from the war. I have become aware that I have dragged many with me through my ignorance and the idealism of my thinking at the time. As if brainwashed, I was blinded and believed firmly in the ideals I thought I had to pursue. I want to declare my sincere regret for my misdeeds that followed these beliefs and for the pain I have caused my loved ones. I am most grateful to them that they kept knowing and loving the human being behind these deeds and I am equally aware that they did not know how to reconcile these and that they suffered many painful and degrading consequences.

From the deep bonds of our love, which miraculously and to my great consolation continued to exist, this book will ring in a new phase for you and for the souls connected with me who have been harmed or who are bound to me and my past in feelings of ambivalence.

In the Love of our Souls,
Ludar

His words struck deep in my core. I cried so hard I felt torn asunder as if all the darkness and suffering of the past were being ripped out of me. For days, I was psychically and even physically upheaved. My very ground was shaken. Ludar and his great love had returned to me.

A couple of days later, I received another message from Lowie. Neeltje had turned again to Ludar, asking if he might speak to Lowie. This is the message she received from Ludar for Lowie:

My soul rejoices to tell you, my dear friend, that I was relieved yesterday, by communicating with Angela, of a great burden of karma which I have been carrying as a result of the thoughtless choices I made during my life. I would protect people from this. I wish to be an example, as a warning against impressive and indoctrinating forces which still populate the earth and influence people and youths. Even though the choice is often made consciously, people cannot foresee the consequences of their choices on the rest of their lives and thereafter.

The thought-patterns humans adhere to at any particular moment may be temporary and change many times during a lifetime but determine in that moment certain pathways one will take from that point of choice. In many cases, this does not need to create problems, but in certain situations, others are involved who become endangered by your "truth."

Negative karma results from a choice made, consciously or unconsciously, which later turns out to harm others. Dealing with the consequences can protect them and others by preventing further harm. When my eyes opened, I myself have tried to 'help' the people in the situation I found myself in, with danger to my own life. But what was the value of my life, after I had worked hard to awaken and found that my ideals did not fit with what was actually happening in front of my eyes—profoundly degrading situations which I realized could not possibly be in harmony with the good road I had envisioned myself to be on. My only choice was to expect instant death if my conversion became known to my comrades.

Again, I have absolutely no desire to justify my deeds and certainly do not wish to ask for forgiveness or understanding. For me, the proof is in God's help and power of forgiveness, the only One who can and may pass judgment and grant forgiveness. My soul has taught me that forgiveness by humans is not possible, and I know that only my own penance chosen entirely by myself has sufficed to surrender myself to this.

Now I wish that especially those who are closely related to me feel the energy of this liberation, the completion of which was facilitated by a symbolic laying of flowers on the day of my choice: Holland's Liberation Day, so that those who still live on earth and are still connected to me can fortify themselves by this force and release the suffering of the past. Not in order to forget but to give themselves the chance to move on in the growth of their soul and to progress into a new phase of their life on the earth.

One more thing about the choices people make. Believe me, Lowie, these choices happen every day, that is why we still don't have peace. The danger in people's thought processes is when they believe they have 'the truth' and that they know how things are and judge people from their personally colored subjective truth. There is no one truth. There is only a field of unity which is disturbed or which falls apart by the little human beings functioning on their own in the totality that is meant to connect everyone together. By learning and growing, this unity could be restored, which is exactly what it means to grow into the Light, to become whole again and become One. From lessons learned and understood through many lifetimes and the choices made by free will, earth could finally be restored to peace. The great error of people is that they focus on their differences rather than on their unity. One and all are equal. You begin to understand that later in your life and certainly after you traverse into the other spheres. Humanity still has a long road to travel.

I am grateful to you, dear Lowie, for what you have been for me during my life and I embrace our friendship in eternity.

Ludarji

I was profoundly moved and grateful for this communication from my father. Over time, friends have asked me if he ever regretted his actions. I didn't know how to answer that question, as I had never heard him speak of regret. This message from beyond the grave made it abundantly clear to me that my father experienced profound regret. In his letter to Lowie, he hopes to pass along the insights he acquired after his death to those of us immediately affected by his actions, but also to humanity as a whole, which is the very motive for offering my memoirs, especially to the American public, now that large sections of our population are being misled by the lies of powerful figures.

❀

Landing in My Father's Heart Presence

I recently came across a photograph of my parents in their early marriage. My mother is basking in the sun, leaning back in sweet abandon against my handsome smiling young father.

I travel down in inner space and
land in my father's heart-presence.
How deeply I am rooted in his love.
I came to his call
when he shared his passion with her.
She did not know much, but
he had chosen a kind, smart and beautiful girl
who for better or worse
chose to give him her trust
and followed him,
first into heaven,
then into hell.
I feel their energetic streams
converging in my blood.
These two and their ancestors
is what I am made of.
I am the result of a moment in time
where an amalgam of forces

rushing through the generations
converged and intersected
in one cellular explosion
creating this one breathing life,
this heart beat in which I dwell.

A maelstrom of colors glows in the dark.
My mother's music and my father's hum,
blending Chopin and
Rabindranath Tagore
in my blood.

Willem and Ellen in their early marriage

Love in the Time of Covid

For quite some years, I felt at peace within myself, enjoying my retirement and especially the delight of Aurelia and her darling sons close to me. Both Theo and Ezra would jump for joy when they spotted me arriving at their home and shout a happy, "Omi, Omi!" while flinging themselves into my arms. I had never been so happy. I sometimes wondered what else might still be in store for me.

A few months into the Covid-19 pandemic, just as I was beginning to feel the loss of my regular contact with Aurelia and my sweet grandsons, I met Andrew in a small online reading group for *Savitri*, Sri Aurobindo's epic sacred poem. Andrew was a research scientist and a writer, living in Montreal, Canada. I was delighted by the penetrating questions he would pose, which elicited my inner knowing—a rare satisfaction. After a few months, I noticed that when I gazed at his kind face and ample chest on my screen, my body would relax. It piqued my curiosity to get to know him. One day after our reading, I suggested we meet one on one, and he agreed.

We talked for hours and shared stories of our lives. We found out that we had both lost our loved one many years earlier and had not been in any significant relationships since nor were we looking for one. We resonated beautifully with one another and quite to our surprise, within weeks, we realized what a special connection we had. I loved looking at his kind face and was falling head over heels in love with him. Having found one another while reading *Savitri*, we both felt that our relationship was a gift, brought to us under the auspices of the great sage.

Online with Andrew

Andrew turned out to be a prolific writer. When I told him about my WWII trauma with my father, he exclaimed that he had written a trilogy about that war and had traveled to Poland and France for research. He was quite relieved by my honesty and said, "If you were not aware of your darkness, I wouldn't want to open up to you."

I printed a few pictures of him that I found on his Facebook page and placed them around my house for the delight of tuning into his presence. I frequently erupted into tears of joy when I looked at his dear face. Sometimes my body would burst into multiple kriyas—little shocks of joy in my belly—signaling that my erotic body was still alive. I was over the moon with happiness and delighted to find such a beautiful connection in my late seventies.

However, before too long, I began experiencing my old fears of abandonment. Andrew would often not respond to my emails, and he never picked up the phone. I got triggered pretty regularly. After all, when my father disappeared, he vanished for what seemed forever. Yet Andrew didn't seem to have any difficulty with our relationship himself. At times, I wondered why he was not reciprocating verbally on an emotional level, but since he always looked so happy to see me and was consistently very kind, I put my worries aside.

He did at times express his discomfort with my exuberant appreciation of him. I didn't think too much of it. I figured, "Well, that's my natural enthusiasm, deal with it." Then, one day, he started our video conversation with, "I have to talk with you." He had my immediate full attention. "When you 'gush' all over me, I feel not seen," he said. He added that he actually did not think so highly of himself. I respected his feelings and I was able to tone myself down some, which he noticed and appreciated.

We would have conversations about difficulties that can arise in relationships. If both have different understanding of the difficulty or on how to proceed, he said that in his experience, one then has to wait until a third path opens, which is usually a spiritual one. It would be intriguing for us to discover how that would unfold in our relationship.

At some point, the two of us began to study and chant the hymns from Sri Aurobindo's *The Secret of the Veda*. According to this ancient spirituality, the Absolute's true name is *Satchidananda: Sat* is Being, *Chit* refers to Consciousness and *Ananda* is Bliss, the Delight of Being. The Vedic hymns are dedicated to a variety of gods, all representing various forces within us. All these gods are aspects of the One. Their tireless work is to awaken and make us conscious of the ultimate bliss of creation.

In my understanding, the Vedic hymns originated some four thousand years ago before the awakening of humanity's rational mind. The images described in them are all quite earthy. Cows are the bringers of Light and horses represent Power. The dawn is the divine Mother shining her light on everything. Agni is the fire of our aspiration and Indra represents the Higher Mind. All the gods work to "bring the cows out of the cave," to bring our light out of the unconscious. The pressing stones symbolize the forces that press on us, to guide us over and over again on the path of purification of our energies and our unconscious formations. The stones press our obscurities through the sieve, the cosmic strainer, into the purity of wine or honey, the sweetness of delight.

The physical resonance from chanting the hymns was a remarkable experience and deepened with every chant as if my cells were opening to the Divine. Chanting these, one of us at a time, created a wonderful energy between us, too.

A year passed in the amazing joy of our connection. Andrew sent me flowers for our anniversary and gifted me with a lovely pair of earrings for my birthday. We happily celebrated.

Of course, we had imagined meeting in person some day. As the pandemic waned and travel became feasible again, I began to feel the desire to visit him in Montreal. I did not expect for us to be sexual, since he was quite overweight, and my nearly eighty-year-old body didn't feel up for that anymore. But I certainly longed for closeness and affection. He also believed that we needed to be together in person to see what the nature of our relationship would actually be. We should start with friendship, he proposed, which sounded sensible to me.

We both decided I would come for three weeks. It took me a while to renew my passport and get my ticket. Nothing was simple with the ongoing Covid travel restrictions. Then, Andrew was diagnosed with cancer. He was likely going to have surgery during or shortly after my planned visit. Right away, I knew that if the surgery would be scheduled not too long after my return date, I would postpone my ticket to be with him.

While pursuing all of these formalities, Andrew began to express some fear about our meeting in person. When I asked him what he was afraid of, he would say that he was worried about intimacy. Since I felt all along that we were emotionally quite intimate, I assumed that he meant sexual intimacy. I reassured him that I was actually not very interested in having sex with him. Not to worry.

Even as I did my best not to have expectations, I certainly imagined that when we would first see each other at the airport, we might have a quiet intimate embrace. With all my heart, I was looking forward to finally feel close to him.

The Pressing Stones

After a long day of flights and stressful situations, I finally arrived in Montreal. As I entered the baggage area, I looked through the glass doors and saw Andrew standing outside. I waved at him. He did not move. Strange. I turned to retrieve my luggage, then walked outside. He hesitated. We had a brief, somewhat obligatory hug, then off to his car. Wanting to make some contact, I touched him lightly on his back. "Oh, that feels good," he said.

After the drive from the airport, he parked on a narrow street in front of a three-story townhouse. We climbed up a flight of stairs to his living room. The couch had been pulled out into a bed, which he had made up for me with obvious care. We had a cup of tea. He told me that he'd gotten a call from his surgeon's office. He was to have his first appointment with her early the following morning. He then disappeared upstairs to his room. I explained his distance to me by considering how much he had on his plate with the cancer and surgery looming.

Early the following morning, we entered a dark, old-fashioned many-storied hospital building with tiled corridors and an old elevator. After the surgeon examined him, she said that he could expect a call to schedule surgery in about a month. I immediately canceled my return flight and left the date of my return open.

During our first few days together, we went from one medical appointment to another. Then we would get some groceries, go to a coffee shop and share meals. It was all comfortable enough, but I began to wonder what happened to the affection I had felt—and thought he had felt, too—when we were online. In an attempt to reassure myself, I wrote in my diary:

Finding balance.
After eighteen months of deep connection,
three-thousand miles and three hours distance between us, here
we are.
Time and space colliding,
having to start from scratch
finding the dance in the realm of the physical.
Suddenly, all is new.
All that eager waiting and longing coming to a sudden halt,
tentatively to find the flow between us that is true and thoughtful.

Each so habituated in rhythms of our own.
We do have time... and love.

Or so I thought. Several more days passed. Then, one day, after we had enjoyed a nice breakfast together, I felt compelled to ask, "I am curious what happened to the affection between us. You seem to have no inclination for any kind of closeness." He recoiled, then stammered something about us being friends. My breath halted. I stared at him in disbelief. "You think we are just friends?" The shock traveled to my core and I burst into tears. He stayed quiet. After a while, I said, "I wouldn't have come if I had known that!" He didn't make a single move or offer any kind of reassurance.

I thought of going back home, but that seemed like too dramatic a reaction. I left the house and walked around the neighborhood, bawling my eyes out. How could I have been so mistaken? All this time, I had grown to think of him as my significant other and had imagined we would cherish this relationship into our final days.

That afternoon I called my friend Stefanie back home in Santa Cruz. I needed support. After blubbering to her for a bit, she said, "He must be terrified!"

When we were about to retire for bed, I called out to Andrew with a desperate, "Can we talk for a bit?" He came and sat next to me. "I am so confused," I continued. "Last May, we celebrated our anniversary. You don't do that with a friendship. That's what you do when you have a relationship. When you told our friend Mateo about our connection, you told him 'Andrea and I have become an item.' How is it possible that you now talk about us being merely friends?" I couldn't help but burst out with a hearty "What the fuck?!"

After a pause, he quietly explained that he had tried to warn me about his concerns before my trip. Fortunately, he also said that he had known from the beginning that there was something very special about our relationship, so he hadn't wanted to do the usual—jump into bed with me and then have to clean up the emotional mess that might ensue. That is what he had always done, he said. He wanted to start with friendship, then wait and see how things would unfold between us when we were in physical proximity with one another. It helped me understand and, after calming down, I could even begin to appreciate his attitude.

I assured him, again, that I had no desire to be sexual with him, but that I did long for closeness. After all, I was exceedingly fond of him. I talked to him about intimacy without sex. The idea seemed foreign to him, and I watched him trying to wrestle with it. He then offered me a hug. From that day on, I got two hugs, one first thing in the morning and one before retiring at night. They felt wonderfully warm and comforting. I got to nestle my face into the side of his neck and would feel deeply nurtured.

We settled into an easy rhythm of daily activities. We planned, shopped and fixed meals together. He took me on his favorite walks in various parks along the river. The fall colors were spectacular. We always created space for him to withdraw into his writing. I amused myself with reading, writing in my journal, playing games on my iPad or taking a stroll around the block. In the evening, we would sometimes watch a movie or a Canadian comedy series that made him laugh a lot. Our best times were after breakfast when we would dive back into the

Vedas. It would invoke a peaceful and joyful energy between us. I began to trust our process.

As always, we did have interesting conversations. After we talked about how many people are still affected by the trauma of WWII, he found a book he thought I might be interested in from among the countless stacks of books around his house. It was a treatise on epigenetics, called *Kriegskinder* (*Children of War*), about the trauma, guilt and shame passed on down the generations. It was written from the perspective of children whose grandparents participated in WWII. Their children grew up with severe disturbances. The grandchildren, too, absorbed unresolved issues of shame, guilt, abandonment, misplaced responsibilities for the suffering parents.

It made me reflect on my own situation. I believe that Aurelia has felt responsible for me, especially after she heard some of the unhappy stories from my childhood, and I can only guess how Tara was affected. I do believe she carries some of my own and my father's shadow. Even though we love each other, she has chosen vast distances between us.

I loved meeting Andrew's friends. They had been aware of how happy Andrew had been during the past year and a half of our online relationship. They were fine people and were all very happy to see me. We shared lovely visits and were treated to delicious meals. I began to notice how happy he and I were when visiting with his friends. That's when he would sometimes briefly reach out to me with a bit of spontaneous affection. I figured that he must have felt safer in the company of his friends.

Andrew had a tradition with a small group of opera buffs, to see the Met live on the big screen. We went to see *Eurydice*.

One recurring line struck me, "But in his head there is always something more beautiful. This is what it is to love an artist." We both identified. Him being the artist in the relationship, we both realized how true that was between us. Where he had become my all, his real focus was on his various writing projects.

Andrew's surgery got scheduled for October 18, sooner than we expected. I asked him what he thought of setting my return date for a week after his surgery so I could still be present for his recovery time. He agreed. That's when he mentioned that, earlier, he had been upset when I had simply canceled my return flight without checking in with him first. "But, we found out about your surgery when I was still in Santa Cruz," I protested. "Already then, I knew that I would change my return flight if your surgery would be within a reasonable time frame." How strange that it was not self-evident to him that I would want to stay with him for the duration of his ordeal.

The surgery went well. They kept him in the hospital overnight. When I came to visit him, he was in good spirits. He had spent his time learning some of the Vedic hymns by heart. After bringing him home, the easy rhythm of our days continued. We were both aware that we were waiting for some kind of shift between us. When we only had a few days left until my departure, we chanted the Vedic hymns together after breakfast. When we arose, we simultaneously experienced a tangible ecstasy running through our bodies. We looked at one another and acknowledged the extraordinary unity we were experiencing. I said, "This is tantra." He agreed.

From that moment on, we felt a great harmony between us. When he took me to the airport and dropped me off, he came in for a big embrace.

Upon my return home, I still fully trusted in our relationship, even though it had been an emotional roller coaster for me at times. But, getting back in touch with him via email proved bumpy. I now had to wait again for him to respond. We did have some satisfying conversations during our first weeks apart. However, at one point, he starkly confronted me with his need for distance. I felt both hurt and angry. Later, during a Zoom conversation, I asked him if we were still "an item." He hesitated, then said, "I don't know." I didn't trust him anymore to be able to say "No."

That evening, I wrote to him, "How bitter it is that you cannot or will not receive my love, and do not open to the sweetness in my heart, my deep affection for you." I received a long email in reply. It started with, "I had a sudden realization of why I have labored so long and hard to keep my inner places free of your ministrations." I felt kicked in the gut and reeled with the insulting visceral rejection. I descended into an old pit of suffering and despair, losing the man I loved. At night, I sobbed so hard, my heart literally felt like it was breaking. I sobbed and heaved for breath until I was utterly exhausted.

I went to see Karen, my shamanic healer, and brought her my despair. We did a Gestalt session where the various parts of me got to sit on different chairs to see if these parts could communicate with one another. I sunk into her dark couch. I completely identified with my lost and miserable child self, sitting in my dark pit of despair. She put a white pillow in a chair and said, "That is the lap of God." Since God was all I had during the seven years of my isolated time in boarding schools, I took one look at it and said, "Oh, that one. I've been there. That's not what I need." She pointed to another chair and said, "That seat is for your adult self." I knew I needed to go sit in that one but felt stuck on the couch.

Reluctantly, after quite some time, I got up and moved into the adult chair. However, I couldn't become my adult. So, Karen began to tell me who I really was, a kind and wise woman with lots of love to give to the world. I came to the full realization that my relationship with Andrew needed to end. He had no place with my true self.

When Andrew and I came together on Zoom again, and I was all prepared to tell him that we did not have a relationship, he burst in with, "I don't know how else to say this, so I will just barge in. We don't have a relationship." I tried to chime in happily that I had come to the same conclusion. He had no space to hear me. He blurted out, "I do want to keep the friendship. I also don't want to read Vedas and I need space. Bye!" That was it. Where we could have had a harmonious ending of our relationship by our mutual discovery, it felt that I got the door slammed in my face instead.

The next morning, in need of consolation, I drew a tile from my little pouch of runes. I drew Radical Severance. When I looked it up in *The Book of Runes* by Ralph Blum, it indicated to sever my attachment to my innocence (my child self) and pointed to a radical departure from the past, a past of loving too much, to my detriment. The rune described how my heart was driven by the need for closeness and the need to belong at any cost. "Prudence falls by the wayside," it said, suggesting my need to grow up and be responsible for my heart's well-being. I realized that the man always becomes my saving grace. Then, when he refuses the job, my sweet heart gets clobbered again.

The Gift

When Andrew and I first got together, we knew that our relationship was a gift to both of us, especially since we felt that we had come together under the auspices of Sri Aurobindo. Little did I know what the actual gift was going to be. Even as the relationship had been a marvelous gift of happiness during the long Covid isolation, the real gift came after it was all over.

While I was still reeling from the harshness of Andrew's goodbye, Tara came to Santa Cruz to celebrate my grandson Ezra's eleventh birthday and be with the family for Christmas. She had to be in quarantine before coming to Aurelia's home. For many years I would only see her in the midst of Aurelia's family. She and I had not had any private visiting time since that fatal Christmas in 2006 when I was deep in my addiction. I invited her over for dinner.

We had an enjoyable time together. Suddenly, she asked if I knew about a book that had been published in Holland a few years ago about the Dutch collaborators during WWII, *In Dienst van de Nazis* (*At the Service of Nazis*) by Paul van de Water. I had indeed heard about it and had understood that the last chapter was about my father. From what I had been told, he was depicted as being purely evil.

Tara had purchased the book and, with the help of Google Translate, had been able to read it. Afterwards, she had gotten in contact with the author. She liked him. He had told her that he knew nothing about what happened to my father after his release. He had tried to connect with family members to get updated, but they all refused to talk with him. I burst out, "I will talk with him!" She looked surprised. "I want the truth to be out. That's why I am writing my book!" I could feel her perception of me shifting before my eyes.

Our conversation marked the first time that Tara and I ever really talked about my father and his past. I had always sensed that his past was particularly difficult for her. She asked me if I was aware of the psychological concept of cognitive dissonance. I was, of course. In the letter from my father that had been channeled for me some years ago, my father had expressed his understanding of the impossibility of me integrating my love for him with the crimes he committed.

Then, Tara said, "I'm happy I never met your father. This way I can see him for who he was, a terrible war criminal." And, "I do not suffer from cognitive dissonance." That hit me hard. I did not say it, but I thought, "How easy it must be to just see evil and not have to grapple with the reality of his big heart and his multi-dimensional being."

After she returned to her lodgings, she immediately emailed the author and let him know that I was willing to speak with him. The next morning, I received Paul's email. He was delighted. He wrote, "I would love to jump on a plane to visit you, but with Covid, it is not desirable." He hoped we could communicate by email. He suggested we talk after the Christmas holidays were over.

When Tara and I saw each other again, there was a clear sense that the chasm between us had been bridged. There was a sweet clarity between us and our hugs felt like we connected on a whole new level. Since we were in the middle of Aurelia's family, it was all non-verbal, but it was an unmistakable shift.

It turned out that Paul became ill over Christmas and when we finally reconnected, he said he had been diagnosed with pancreatic cancer and only had a short time left to live. I mentioned to him how special it is to face the end of life consciously. I hoped he could look back on his life with satisfaction; that we can experience great clarity towards the end which can contribute to a peaceful transition. He appreciated our conversation. He said it gave him strength. I offered to send him some of my chapters about my father's life after his release from prison. He enjoyed reading them. He was able to read all of the chapters about Ludar and about my coming to terms with his dark legacy. After having sent him this chapter as far as I had it at the time, I did not hear from him anymore. He left his body on December 8, 2022. I was glad I had been able to support him in his transition.

Back to mid-December 2021. I had already scheduled a follow-up appointment with Karen for the day after my conversation with Tara, to continue to deal with my painful experience with Andrew. However, when I walked into her office that morning, I was still quite shaken by the intensity of my conversation with my daughter. When I mentioned this to Karen, after a moment, she asked my permission to, as she said, get my father out of me. "Sure," I said, a bit surprised. I don't know what she did after that, but massive energy began streaming down and shaking out through my whole body, my legs and feet, until even my neck and head moved with a high-speed vibration completely beyond my control. When I got off the table, I felt a lightness of being that I did not remember ever having before, as if I had lived with the heavy weight of my father inside of me all my life. I had no idea, how much of him I had absorbed into my body. That feeling of lightness continues to this day.

We celebrated a delightful Christmas. I was happy to have Tara and Aurelia with her darling family over at my home for Christmas Eve dinner. On Christmas morning I went to Aurelia's for breakfast and to share in the excitement of unwrapping our many gifts. Being with her boys, Theo and Ezra, is always such a joy for me.

A few weeks later, I returned to see Karen for another session. I was still deeply hurting from the rudeness and the abrupt loss of my relationship. I did not know what to do with myself. She tuned in and, suddenly, she said, "You need help." After a pause, she added, "Your father is available." Immediately, I saw my father reaching out his hand to me. I realized that he was offering to pull me out of the dark pit of my childhood suffering. As I took his hand and he pulled me up, I saw pale, ethereal hands reaching behind my low back trying to keep me from leaving the dark abyss. She invoked the fierce goddess to help cut me free.

Afterwards, it dawned on me that maybe my father had been sticking around in the earth's atmosphere for *me*, to help me free myself from my painful past of which he was the originator.

That night, I felt myself shift back into my own center. I realized how completely I had made someone else the center of my being, just as I had many times before—starting with my father. Being immersed in the love of my father had given me my sense of self and I saw clearly how I had similarly immersed myself in my love of Andrew. The illusion of the ideal I had projected onto this man was peeling like shells off my eyes. I began to feel a profound sense of freedom, not just from him, but also from my ongoing need to belong to a man. I felt that I was coming home to myself at last. I was free.

However, I was somewhat puzzled to still feel the delight I had experienced with Andrew in my cellular body. I was particularly aware of an unusual joy-vibration all the way down my legs. I wondered how and when I would be truly free of this man. I talked about it with my long-time friend Stefanie. When I explained my confusion to her, she said, "The joy you experience is yours! Own it!" Clearly, I had identified my joy with him, too. "Oh, it's mine!" I laughed and I felt another radical shift inside of me.

Fortunately, a year or so after our break-up, Andrew and I were able to have a conversation about it. He explained to me that he had felt assaulted by the intensity of my emotional reactions to him and he was not up for more of the same. It was a significant relief to hear that. Understanding why things are done or said helps me process difficulties. I do know that when I get emotional, I tend to get rather intense. Anger easily arises. If he had expressed his feelings at the time rather than just blurt out his decision, I would have been fine with it. But, apparently, I had more healing to do. So, the trigger turned out to be quite significant to accelerate my healing process.

I Am the One I Have Been Looking for

Out of the bustle of the town
I enter the narrow passageway
leading to a stairwell.
Going down, the city noises disappear.
All becomes quiet.
I descend
until I stand before a tall wooden door
with many panels, but no handle.

A word appears on the door: Ave.
My soul bursts into the Ave Maria.
But it is I who is being greeted
I am welcomed and expected,
I am holy.
With a slight push, the door opens.
I enter a small circular room
with a tall domed ceiling.
On a table in the center
a book lies open.
There I leave my past behind
along with the suffering ones.

Effortlessly, I rise above the city
and up towards the stars
spreading large white wings
luminous.

I am only a slight silhouette
in the totality of being
the same and yet distinct.
I dissolve for a while
as in a silent dream.

Then, I find myself
walking back up the stairs.
I stand at the portal to the city.
I have my form but
my heart is a wide open cosmos
like a window to the infinite.

I am silent.
I know myself.
I will re-enter the world
But not be of it.
I am open and free.

Grace can flow
and Love unfettered.

My 80th Birthday

My eightieth birthday was coming up in May 2022. Aurelia helped me put together a simple celebration with family and friends. I wanted it to be outdoors. We rented a set of picnic tables in Santa Cruz's Harvey West Park, under the tall trees I had come to love. Aurelia decorated the tables and made the area look very festive.

Tara came from Vermont, so my whole family and almost all of my friends, including most of the women in my writing group, were gathered to celebrate with me.

Quite a number of friends spoke about the essence of their experience with me. I felt very loved and appreciated. We shared delicious food. Then came sweet hilarity with my grandsons, Ezra and Theo, performing a little skit that made fun of their "Omi."

Ezra, wearing a wide-brimmed red hat, carrying a purse over his shoulder, portrayed me sitting at a restaurant table. Theo was the waiter. When my coffee was served and Theo walked away, Ezzie turned around with a singsong, "Ooh ooh... Do you have raw sugar?" This little scenario was played out many times, with several more "Ooh ooh... could I have..." phrases, each with one of my little peculiarities they had observed whenever we would go out to breakfast together.

Aurelia spoke beautifully, reflecting on the many ups and downs in my life. She said, "With you everything is possible, nothing is set in stone and just like the sun dawns anew each day, you embrace each new situation with openness, curiosity and flexibility." Then, she quoted one of my favorite Rilke poems that made her think of me. Afterwards Tara mentioned she had searched for a poem to read for me and had come up with that very same one.

> I live my life in growing rings
> which encompass the things of the world.
> I may not reach the ultimate one
> but I will certainly try.
>
> I'm circling around God, around the ageless tower—
> I've been circling for numberless years;
> and I still wonder: whether I'm a falcon,
> a storm, or a boundless song.

I see how beautifully this poem describes my journey. I *have* lived my life in widening circles. I started in Holland, then India and now California, and have been through countless changes and relationships, always learning, healing and growing. No matter where I was on my journey, I kept my focus on my spiritual path. As Rilke says, I "circled around God." I never forgot the divine, and I never lost faith in the love and oneness to be found in That. It has given everything in my life meaning—from my wonderful successes to my awful failures. I see each and every part of my path as being essential to my learning and growth.

So, to my utter delight, after eight decades of suffering and happiness, through the many vicissitudes of my life, always working hard to clear myself of my entanglement with my father and his past, I end up in harmony with Ludar, my complicated father, and more importantly, with myself. Even my childhood trauma and attachment disorders feel resolved. Free at last!

🌸
Going Within

Going within I found
A soft, peaceful, golden radiance
Permeating everything—
Each molecule a particle of sunlight—
Everywhere the same density,
The same softness.

God's Comforter, I smile. But no,
It is not something I am in.
Nothing which is not That.

Inside of That, nevertheless,
Our little individual entities
Thrash about, seeking, forever seeking,
Sometimes finding, mostly losing.
Truly we are like fish
In the great Ocean of Life
Gasping for water.

After all these confusing millennia
Of our consciousness groping for light
And slowly waking,
I see the Sun shimmering on the horizon
We start to walk—together—
Eyes open,
Hands empty,
Hearts singing.

Afterword

Aurelia's Speech on My 80th Birthday

In honor of you and in celebration of the completion of your eightieth journey around the sun, I wanted to say a few words. When I think about the arc of your life so far, I am astounded at how far you have traveled: your physical journey around the globe and your inner pilgrimage from a childhood marked by deep suffering, through a profound transformation in your twenties and thirties, and since then around and up and down through what seems like many small lifetimes of self-discovery and opening and flowing effortlessly into this new phase of your life. It feels as if the many struggles and efforts to go deeper, to heal and to find meaning have softened and melded into a place of acceptance, appreciation and easy joy. If everyone could be so lucky to grow into a happy, relaxed and loving grandmother, still serving her community, still beating her grandkids in solitaire, never sweating the small stuff, and enjoying life for all its mystery and beauty. I hope to reach that place someday. For now I'll continue to do my best to try to take in your often yet softly given advice, just like the song says: "Don't worry about a thing, cuz every little thing is going to be alright."

In addition to helping me to learn to let go and trust life, I believe I've inherited from you a bit of your chutzpah, your "anything is possible" attitude. You're kind of a cowgirl at heart, really. Albeit in your Dutch, tea-drinking, rose-gardening kind of way. Though you have just turned eighty, there's an innocence and youthfulness in your attitude that endures.

It cracks me up every time to tell people the story of how, after you and my father separated, along with cutting off your long hair, changing your name, moving out, deciding to be with a woman and getting a television for the first time, you also decided to start eating meat after years of being a vegetarian. You can imagine it was a while before I recognized my mom again. Anyway, I still remember how you picked us up from school one day. It was our night to spend at your house. You told us excitedly that you had discovered a new hamburger restaurant that served really delicious burgers. That they had this really special sauce that was just so tasty and that you planned to take us there for dinner. When we pulled into the parking lot of Burger King to dine in, my sister and I looked at each other, confused and incredulous. I don't think we had ever eaten fast food in our lives. What I love about this memory is not just the hilarity of your non-native perspective on burgers but the fresh, un-jaded perspective you bring to all of life. With you everything is possible, nothing is set in stone and just like the sun dawns anew each day, you embrace each new situation with openness, curiosity and flexibility.

Speaking of embracing new situations, one of your most remarkable qualities is that, whatever you do, you go all in. I had to giggle when I told people that my almost eighty-year-old mom had met a younger man on the internet during the pandemic and was flying on a one-way ticket to Canada to meet him. I admire that with you, the adventure never stops! I hope this next decade is your best yet. I know that you will keep opening to and learning from life. You will keep offering your love and energy to others. And you will keep trusting yourself to follow the path that is right for you. I wish you the happiest of birthdays.

Acknowledgements

When I got motivated to write my autobiography, I knew I needed support. I took a memoirs class at Cabrillo College here in Aptos, near Santa Cruz. Kathy Cowan was the teacher. She offered enthusiastic support for my courage and for the quality of my writing. She also became my first editor. Then I participated for several years in writing groups led by Carolyn Brigit Flynn, a fine writer herself. To give us a prompt, she would guide us into a meditation, then ask a question. It worked like a charm. Eventually, the last group in which I participated became independent. There are seven of us. We call ourselves the Seven Sisters, referring to the Pleiades. We have come together twice a month for over a decade. We meet in each others' living rooms (on Zoom during Covid). I have read every chapter to them and gratefully received their emotional support when parts of my story were painful and I might find myself in tears. My memoirs would not be the same without their sensitive, intelligent and creative comments, each one offering their unique sensibilities. Bridget A. Lyons tirelessly helped edit and streamline my book throughout the years. Her edits tightened the text, dropped any excessive language, and her suggestions to elaborate here and there contributed significantly to the manuscript.

When my book was nearing completion, I became a member of the Cosmos Co-op, located in Longmont, Colorado. I had been participating in small online reading groups of Sri Aurobindo's works hosted by Infinite Conversations. Then, when the co-op initiated the Untimely Books publishing house, their first motivation was to publish their members, most of whom were writers. Marco V Morelli is the creative force behind all these endeavors. When he offered to publish my memoirs, I could hardly believe my good fortune. I have felt infinitely blessed and grateful to have him as my final editor and publisher. His kindness, his patience with me, his meticulous attention to detail and his literary sensibilities have made the publishing process an enjoyable experience. Marco's wife, Kayla Morelli is the fabulous designer behind the beauty of the copy you now have in your hands, or see online. I am also grateful for the thorough editing work done by the fresh-out-of-college Emily Byrne. When, to my delight, Marco invited me to come to Colorado to record the audio version of my book, we were grateful to have access to a professional recording studio at Longmont Public Media. Roger Dinardi, with his fine musician's ear, did a high-precision job editing the recordings. My generous friend, Cheryl Stone stepped up as a patron to help birth my book.

Without all of the above people and without the invaluable and loving support of friends, healers, astrologers, authors and teachers, I could not have accomplished *The Pressing Stones*.

Books on The Way

Allione, Tsultrim. *Feeding Your Demons: Ancient Wisdom for Resolving Inner Conflict.* Hay House, Inc, 2009.

Arroyo, Stephen. *Astrology, Karma and Transformation: The Inner Dimensions of the Birth Chart.* SCB Distributors, 2011.

Aurobindo, Sri. *Savitri: A Legend and a Symbol.* 1993.

—. *The Four Aids to Yoga-Siddhi.* Sri Aurobindo Ashram, Pondicherry, 2010.

—. *The Life Divine.* Sri Aurobindo Ashram, 2009.

—. *The Mother.* Lotus Press, 1995.

—. *The Secret of the Veda.* Sri Aurobindo Ashram, Publication Dept, 2003.

—. *The Synthesis of Yoga.* 2000.

Bass, Ellen, and Laura Davis. *The Courage to Heal: A Guide for Women Survivors of Child Sexual Abuse.* Random House, 2002.

Blum, Ralph. *The Book of Runes, 25th Anniversary Edition.* Macmillan, 2008.

Darr, Dominique. *Matrimandir - Hymn to the Builders of the Future.* Archana Press, 2008.

Dawes, James. *Evil Men*. Harvard UP, 2013.

Erickson, Milton H. *Life Reframing in Hypnosis*. 1985.

Fox, Emmet. *The Sermon on the Mount: The Key to Success in Life*: 2022.

Grof, Stanislav. *LSD Psychotherapy*. 2008.

Inc, Alcoholics Anonymous World Services. *Twelve Steps and Twelve Traditions: The "Twelve and Twelve" — Essential Alcoholics Anonymous Reading*. A. A. World Services, Inc., 2013.

Ish-Shalom, Zvi. *The Path of Primordial Light: Ancient Wisdom for the Here and Now*. 2022.

Kramer, Kenneth. *Martin Buber's I and Thou: Practicing Living Dialogue*. Paulist Press, 2003.

Lewis, Thomas, et al. *A General Theory of Love*. Random House of Canada, 2007.

Lidchi-Grassi, Maggi. *The Light That Shone Into the Dark Abyss*. 1994.

Maté, Gabor. *In the Realm of Hungry Ghosts: Close Encounters With Addiction*. Random House, 2018.

Merton, Thomas. *The Seven-Storey Mountain*. Signet Book, 1952.

Miller, Alice. *For Your Own Good: Hidden Cruelty in Child-Rearing and the Roots of Violence*. Farrar, Straus and Giroux, 2002.

—. *Thou Shalt Not Be Aware: Society's Betrayal of the Child.* Farrar, Straus and Giroux, 1998.

Mindell, Arnold. *The Dreambody in Relationships.* Gatekeeper Press, 2019.

Mother. *Flowers and Their Messages.* 1992.

—. *Mother's Agenda.* 1980.

—. *Prayers and Meditations of the Mother.* 1962.

Rilke, Rainer Maria. *In Praise of Mortality: Selections From Rainer Maria Rilke's Duino Elegies and Sonnets to Orpheus.* Echo Point Books and Media, 2019.

—. *Letters to a Young Poet.* Random House, 2020.

—. *Sonnets to Orpheus.* W. W. Norton and Company, 2006.

—. *The Book of Hours: Prayers to a Lowly God.* Northwestern UP, 2001.

Rinpoche, Sogyal. *The Tibetan Book of Living and Dying: A Spiritual Classic From One of the Foremost Interpreters of Tibetan Buddhism to the West.* Random House, 2012.

Satprem. *Mother: Or, the Divine Materialism.* Madras : Macmillan of India Press, 1977.

—. *The Mind of the Cells.* 2010.

Satprem, and Institut De Recherches Évolutives. *Sri Aurobindo or the Adventure of Consciousness.* 1996.

Shlain, Leonard. *The Alphabet Versus the Goddess: The Conflict Between Word and Image*. Penguin, 1999.

Shulgin, Alexander, and Ann Shulgin. *Tihkal: The Continuation*. Synergetic Press, 1997.

—. *Pihkal: A Chemical Love Story*. 1991.

Shunya, Acharya. *Roar Like a Goddess: Every Woman's Guide to Becoming Unapologetically Powerful, Prosperous, and Peaceful*. 2022.

Stolaroff, Myron J. *The Secret Chief Revealed*. 2020.

Stone, Randolph. *Polarity Therapy: The Complete Collected Works of This Revolutionary Healing Art by the Originator of the System: Volume One*. Polarity Therapy, 1999.

Teeguarden, Iona, and Jin Shin Do Foundation for Bodymind Acupressure. *The Joy of Feeling: Bodymind Acupressure*. 2006.

Van Der Kolk, Bessel, MD. *The Body Keeps the Score: Brain, Mind, and Body in the Healing of Trauma*. National Geographic Books, 2015.

Van Vrekhem, Georges. *Beyond Man: Life and Work of Sri Aurobindo and the Mother*. HarperCollins Publishers, 1997.

—. *Hitler and His God: The Background of the Hitler* Phenomenon. books catalog, 2006.

—. *The Mother: The Story of Her Life*. books catalog, 2004.

W, Bill. *The Big Book of Alcoholics Anonymous (Including 12 Steps, Guides and Prayers)*. 2015.

Walker, Pete. *Complex PTSD : From Surviving to Thriving: A Guide and Map for Recovering From Childhood Trauma*. Createspace Independent Publishing Platform, 2013.

Wilhelm, Richard, and Cary F. Baynes. *I Ching, or, Book of Changes*. Penguin Books, Limited (UK), 1989.

Yogananda, and Walter Yeeling Evans-Wentz. *Autobiography of a Yogi*. Self Realization Fellowship, 1971.

About the Author

Andrea was born as Angela van de Loo in the Netherlands in 1942 during WWII. She studied psychology at the University of Amsterdam. In 1971 she hitchhiked to India where she met the Mother at the Sri Aurobindo Ashram in Pondicherry. She lived in Auroville, South India, Mother's experimental city in the making, dedicated to the evolution of human unity, till 1978. Her two daughters were born there.

Andrea has been living in Santa Cruz, CA, since 1979, where she had a healing practice. After retiring in 2007, she continues to open and learn from life, devotes her energy and presence in service of family and friends, and dedicates herself to offer her memoir as her small contribution to a peaceful world.

About Untimely Books

Untimely Books is an independent publisher of literary works that illumine the mind, question the contemporary, and reimagine horizons of thought, feeling, and action for a planetary age. As an imprint of Cosmos Cooperative (a member-owned publishing platform and creative community) and Metapsychosis (a journal of consciousness, literature, and art), Untimely Books serves as a conduit for diverse forms of writing by Cosmos members, including original works of fiction, poetry, philosophy, essays, and memoir.

untimelybooks.com